Neurocomputational Poetics: How the Brain Processes Verbal Art

Neurocomputational Poetics: How the Brain Processes Verbal Art

Arthur M. Jacobs

ANTHEM PRESS

Anthem Press
An imprint of Wimbledon Publishing Company
www.anthempress.com

This edition first published in UK and USA 2023
by ANTHEM PRESS
75–76 Blackfriars Road, London SE1 8HA, UK
or PO Box 9779, London SW19 7ZG, UK
and
244 Madison Ave #116, New York, NY 10016, USA

British Library Cataloguing-in-Publication Data
A catalogue record for this book is available from the British Library.

Library of Congress Control Number: 2023941394
A catalog record for this book has been requested.

ISBN-13: 978-1-83998-770-0 (Hbk)
ISBN-10: 1-83998-770-7 (Hbk)

Cover Credit: Art generated using stablediffusionweb.com

This title is also available as an e-book.

CONTENTS

ACKNOWLEDGEMENTS

The research for this book was supported by a number of grants from the Deutsche Forschungsgemeinschaft (DFG, German Research Foundation) and from the EU.[1] I thank those who read parts of the book manuscript and associated materials, for their invaluable advice, especially Phil Davis and Annette Kinder. Early versions of some of the sections of this book have been presented as invited talks at many conferences and institutions, and I thank those who invited me. I thank Phil Davis for convincing me to submit this book to his series at Anthem, and I welcome the support from Megan Greiving and Jebaslin Hephzibah at Anthem, and the comments of Nigel Fabb and Gerhard Lauer encouraging the project. Finally, I thank the many members of my various research teams at several universities in France and Germany, as well as the many scientific collaborators from lots of countries, for their precious support, especially those who accompanied me during the last decade at FU Berlin. Special thanks go to my colleague Jana Lüdtke, who watched my back while I struggled with this book.

For Annette, Simon and Marius

PREFACE

The start of every act of reading a story, poem or book is a decision: the decision to go someplace else. This place can be a world we have not been to before and it can lead to forgotten memories or dreams, suppressed desires or emotions or to novel ideas that change one's life. There may be many hidden motivations or explicit reasons leading to this decision. The consequence is always the same: one abandons control of one's mind and lends it – for some time – to a writer. This is a risky business, for one is now loaned out to another who thinks, feels, suffers and acts within one. It is like a blend of two minds or consciousnesses. To a certain extent, reading removes the subject–object division that constitutes all perception. If the conditions are right, readers of verbal art will immerse into that other place, that other reality and forget the world around them. This *immersive experience* is one of two primary reasons why we buy and read stories and novels; the other being the *aesthetic experience* often reported when reading lyrics and poetry. A psychiatrist friend of mine once compared immersion with a psychopathological state. And indeed, reading can become an addiction. But even if engaged reading was a mild form of psychosomatic disease, the disease seems often better than the cure: being immune to the immersive and aesthetic effects of reading fiction, being indifferent to or unmoved by the actions or feelings of a protagonist would mean that one misses out on one of the greatest pleasures of the mind; but also, that one lacks empathy, which is fundamental for our social life. Indeed, moving your mind through the text worlds of fiction is good training for both cognitive and social-emotional skills. Both your IQ and EQ can only benefit – if you read the right stuff.

What makes literary reading such a captivating experience despite its rapidity is based on the fact that associative *semantic networks* are activated in the brain. These put in train thoughts and feelings as well as unconscious motion sequences. Semantic networks is a handy metaphor to describe how our brains organize information about the world in the form of a net of concept nodes linked by connections. The distance between the nodes and the weights of the connections are assumed to reflect the strength of association between two or more ideas. The brain is an association machine, and this machine is the main mechanism underlying the reading experience. It stores those bodily experiences of our life we connect with words as conditioned associations thematically in semantic memory. Mental echoes of these experiences and imagination of those of others, such as the protagonist's or antihero's, is what primarily moves us during reading.

From Simple to Complex

Ever since I was trained in *connectionism* and *machine learning* at Sorbonne and MIT during the 1980s, I have been convinced that semantic networks simulated on a computer can help understand this perhaps most complex achievement of the mind, which is reading. But isn't it too complex for scientific analysis? At least, this is what one of my Ph.D. grant tutors thought when I discussed my project about eye movement control during reading with him. Being a pioneer of neurogenetics specialized in the investigation of fly brains, he advised me to choose a simpler topic for my research. 'I have been investigating fly brains for decades and still I am fishing in the dark, so how can you think you will be able to understand how the human brain works during reading', or so he told me. 'Leave reading to literary scholars and study neuroscience' was his final counsel. I would not obey completely, though, and ended up doing both.

My thinking was that if reading is perhaps the most complex process the human brain is capable of, then there were basically two ways for a scientist to tackle it. Either one gives up the idea of any natural science approach altogether and chooses the 'humanities way', that is, *close reading* from a holistic first-person perspective. Such a hermeneutic approach can do without empirical studies, statistics or computer models. Or, one takes the rocky road of analytical (over-)simplification, wagering that starting simple will eventually open the gates of complexity that characterize reading.[2] Luckily, my Ph.D. advisers at Sorbonne, Kevin O'Regan – a trained physicist-turned psycholinguist – and Ariane Lévy-Schoen – a cognitive psychologist – supported this 'from simple to complex' approach. In this book, I'd like to demonstrate to readers, especially those critical of a reductionist neurocomputational perspective, the usefulness of computer simulations of what our brains do during reading and experiments testing their quantitative predictions.

Neurocomputational Poetics

This book is about one of the greatest pleasures the human mind can produce: verbal art reception. The perspective I have chosen to take on this unique achievement of evolution and civilization, producing meaning and pleasure out of ink blobs on paper, or pixels on screens, results from the cross-fertilization between several scientific disciplines. In 2015, I called it Neurocognitive Poetics, but given the pivotal impact of novel computational methods into my research, like that of my text-analysis tool *SentiArt*, I find *Neurocomputational Poetics* a better name. It has its roots in at least three flowerbeds: reading psychology, cognitive and computational poetics, as well as cognitive and computational neuroscience. I will deal with each now, in sequence. Neurocomputational Poetics is not only about poetry, but all forms of verbal art, starting with infantile word plays and children's literature. Most important is its goal to develop or find methods to best assess and predict measurable aspects of the reading act at all levels of scientific enquiry, that is, neuronal, experiential and behavioural.

Reading Psychology

The psychology of reading originated in Wilhelm Wundt's first experimental psychology laboratory in Leipzig around 1880. Right from the beginning of this then new science of psychology, researchers were interested in reading and soon made their first prodigious discovery: when presented in a word context, letters are perceived better than in isolation or in so-called pseudowords – pronounceable letter strings without meaning like 'shlunk'. This *word superiority effect* carries on to higher levels of meaning integration. Thus, words in a sentence context can be better remembered than in isolation or in a meaningless list of words, especially when the sentence is embedded in verse: this is the sentence or line superiority effect. In sum, context changes the way our brain processes the very same stimulus – words – and poets ever since Sappho knew how to transform this fact into art. Side by side with research on word recognition, the other main influence of reading psychology on my work was eye movement research. In 1879 the physiologist Ewald Hering attached a rubber tube to a cigar holder and listened to the sounds produced when it was placed on the eyelids. He heard a surprisingly strong and whirring roar and claimed that the sounds were a consequence of eye muscle contractions. In the same year, Emile Javal called these jerky movements *saccades*. When, back in 1981, I planned to spend a year in Ariane's and Kevin's eye movement lab in Paris, encouraged by my friend and mentor Dieter Heller, I had to look up the word 'saccade' in a dictionary. I was fascinated by the fact that during these ultra-fast movements we are functionally blind, the brain playing a trick on us to create the illusion of continuous vision. Otherwise, we would perceive the world in sequential snapshots. The counterpart of saccades, called *fixations*, were as fascinating: only during these short intervals of about one-fourth of a second our brain can process the information necessary for reading. But how could this feeling of understanding during reading result from three sequential snapshots per second? How does our brain manage to integrate these short samples of visual information and magically transform them into meaning and immersive and aesthetic experiences? Such questions drove me then and they still do now.

Poetics

The traditional triad of poetics, rhetoric and aesthetics form the second part of the cross-fertilization spiral leading to the Neurocomputational Poetics perspective. They offer to the neuroscientist interested in verbal art a treasure of information about the materials and their rules of construction that our brains process to (re-)create meaning and emotions out of words. I use the spiral as an image for the curvy road from simple to ever more complex models of the reading process. Indeed, we continually update and revise the 'under-complex' neuro-reductionist models and methods via feedback and cross-validation from studies in the humanities and other related research fields. Until very recently, reading psychology had a big blind spot: the affective and aesthetic aspects of texts and the emotions they evoke in readers. Scientists in this field investigated each and every cognitive process underlying reading performance, but they totally neglected the fact known to the ancient triad: that spoken and written words produce emotions, create pleasure and pain and can change persons or move masses.

Paraphrasing Plato's analogy, the Austrian poet Raoul Schrott with whom I worked for many years and co-published the book *Gehirn und Gedicht* (Brain and Poetry) in 2011,[3] says that 'Poetry is music and painting created with words'. My part in our collaboration was to find out what the brain does to achieve this miraculous transformation. Indeed, poetry is often 'read through the ear' and the painting with words makes the peeling off of each layer of meaning from the words on the page such a pleasurable experience. The sound of E. E. Cummings' 'On a proud round cloud in white high night' or the imagined solitude of a cloud in the sky in Wordsworth's 'I wander'd lonely as a cloud' are cases in point. In their recent book on psychopoetics, Willie van Peer and Anna Chesnokova[4] give a historical example for peeling off several meanings from the image of a rose painted in Goethe's poem 'Sah ein Knab' ein Röslein stehn' ('Once a boy a briar saw'): the flower, a young girl and the young woman's virginity.

Poems by verbal artists like Poe, Coleridge, Verlaine or Goethe also exemplify that musicality can powerfully attract readers' attention away from the meaning of the words, some readers even becoming spellbound or hypnotized by their sound. Either in concert with or in contrast to imagery, sound-gestalts created by rhythm and rhyme can stimulate memories in a way foregrounding the music at the expense of meaning. Taking example (A) of Goethe's 'Buch Suleika' (book Suleika), Schrott and Jacobs intuited that the more full-bodied a poem, the rounder its metre, the more female (bisyllabic) and richer (tri- or polysyllabic) its rhymes, the less likely the poem's meaning will be grasped: the overorchestrated sound reduces the words to a 'tinkle'. Thus, the onomatopoeia of the verses in German conceals the fact that the hard splashing and fanning out of a fountain ('Wenn steigend sich der Wasserstrahl entfaltet') has little to do with a nebulously wafting clouding ('Wenn Wolke sich gestaltend umgestaltet').

A)
'Wenn steigend sich der Wasserstrahl entfaltet,
Allspielende, wie froh erkenn ich dich;
Wenn Wolke sich gestaltend umgestaltet,
Allmannigfaltige, dort erkenn ich dich.'

('When rising the water jet unfolds,
All-playing, how gladly I recognize you;
When the cloud shapes and reshapes itself,
All-manifold, there I recognize you')

Further popular examples of interactive sound-meaning constructions are the first stanzas of Poe's 'The Raven' or Verlaine's 'Il pleure dans mon coeur':

B)
'Once upon a midnight dreary, while I pondered weak and weary,
Over many a quaint and curious volume of forgotten lore,
While I nodded, nearly napping, suddenly there came a tapping,
As of some one gently rapping, rapping at my chamber door.'
`'Tis some visitor,' I muttered, `tapping at my chamber door –
Only this, and nothing more.

C)
'Il pleure dans mon coeur
Comme il pleut sur la ville;
Quelle est cette langueur
Qui pénètre dans mon coeur?'

(It's crying in my heart
As it is raining in the city;
What is this languor
That pervades my heart?)

Thus, although language is used to convey meanings rather than merely sounds, prioritizing semantic over phonetic coding, in poetry, there is no simple one-dimensional function which links aesthetic liking to the ubiquitous human *effort after meaning* or the pleasure derived from a successful interpretation of an artwork. Poems can transport two (or more) sets of interweaved meanings by playing with lexical structure and formal organization. The final meaning, gestalt, emerges from the integration of both. Depending on the poem's composition as much as on the readers' personality variables like trait absorption, form and content can work against or with each other and exert separate or combined hedonic effects.[5] Hence, perceptual sound-gestalts and conceptual meaning-gestalts can either converge or diverge, inducing, for example, a contrastive dark mood (via dark sonorous vowels) at one level and a light humorous closure at another – via rhythm, rhyme and/or content. They can thus create new meaning layers through sound metaphors which provide additional sources for affective and aesthetic responses. The perceived similarity between the semantic content of a poem and iconic associations based on the phonological salience at the level of the whole poem as assumed by foregrounding theory[6] is a key determinant of its affective and aesthetic impact.

This can nicely be demonstrated with example (D) showing Goethe's classic poem 'Ein Gleiches' ('The Same'). In this poem, a secondary meaning layer is created by a *sound metaphor* stating the central thought of the poem (Your life, too, is like a breeze of wind and will pass away just as easily) not being expressed at the lexical level: the juxtaposition of an onomatopoeic sound-gestalt (*h* and *ch* in *Hauch*/breeze or breath) and the final words *du auch* (you, too), which form a rhyme pair.[7]

D)

Über allen Gipfeln ist Ruh.
In allen Wipfeln
Spürest du
Kaum einen Hauch;
Die Vögelein schweigen im Walde.
Warte nur, balde
Ruhest du auch.

(‚Over all the hilltops
is peace,
in all the treetops
you notice

hardly a breeze;
the forest birds cease singing their song,
wait a while - ere long
you'll rest like these!)[i]

Example (D) is a case of *metaphoric iconicity* in Charles Sanders Peirce's semiotic theory.[8] In metaphoric iconicity, the link between the icon and the referent is indirect and associative, that is, a sensation, a feeling (joy, sadness) or a property (sound, colour). In such or similar cases of iconicity, the psychological aspect of the process of language comprehension can be conceived of as the vicarious experiencing of events in the real world.

Most influential to the adventure of Neurocomputational Poetics that we started together with our book on brain and poetry was the work of Roman Jakobson on verbal art and his *poetic function* of language.[9] This laid the ground for later works on linguistic and cognitive poetics. The formalist and structuralist movements around Jakobson dissected complex literary texts into simpler cognitive and aesthetic units relating the attunement of verbal art to specifiable rhetorical devices such as rhyme or metaphor. It also showed how familiar elements can create artful effects by *defamiliarization* or *estrangement.* In one of Jakobson's early books on children's language,[10] one can find a simple example for defamiliarization: by exchanging the first letter of words, their meaning becomes blurred as in a '*t*airy *f*ale': a phonetic mode of estrangement also used by adult poets. This *foregrounding* technique of using unfamiliar expressions in ordinary surroundings or the reverse is generally constitutive of language and systematically and artfully enhanced in literature. An example at the level of morphemes are *portmanteaus,* word blends or contractions like 'brexit', 'edutainment', 'frenemy', or 'republicrat'. Portmanteaus are part and parcel of the daily newspapers – due to their conciseness often in headlines – , but also do appear in poetry from Lewis Carroll's 'frumious' to James Joyce's 'ethiquetical' as stylistic devices of foregrounding. Much like Carroll, Dr Seuss created many such neologisms, often adding humour, to help children with limited vocabularies enjoy reading.

Authors generally like to attract the attention of readers' minds by pushing linguistic elements into the foreground using devices such as rhyme or *functional shift* as in William Shakespeare's *Othello*: 'O, tis the spite of hell [...] to *lip* a *wanton* in a secure couch, and to suppose her chaste!'. This relates to the basic law of *figure-ground perception* discovered by the *Gestaltist* movement

i C) and D) were translated by: https://lyricstranslate.com

of the 1930s.[11] The many similarities between laws of visual perception or visual illusions and poetic language suggest that our brain at least partly uses the same neural networks when processing visual and linguistic objects. This bears the promise that the methods of cognitive neuroscience can be used to uncover processes underlying literature reception. As an example for literary figure-ground perception, in Ezra Pound's poem below, the title provides the background allowing the reader to identify the actual figure:

IN A STATION OF THE METRO
The apparition of these faces in the crowd;
Petals on a wet, black bough.

Through projection of 'faces' onto 'petals' our brain associates adjectives like pale or white; through projection of 'crowd' onto 'bough' it deduces that – in accordance with the Gestalt *law of good continuation* – people actually are not sitting but standing in a row. The metre of the first line emphasizes this by its musical gestalt: the *paeon* with its three short syllables and one long implies that this is no closed crowd, but that everyone keeps his or her distance. And the simple *ictus* or stress at the end of the verse marks the fact that the focus of the analogy is on the wet, black bough. The gestalt laws bestow the image with detail. A reader puts the crowd at the platform and not in the main hall, projecting the figure back on the ground. The *law of similarity* allows him or her to infer the focal point of the image: it can only be the opposite platform – elsewise the threading of the faces in the crowd could not be perceived. Finally, the laws of the good gestalt, proximity and similarity allow the reader to infer to what the wet black bough actually refers: not to a row of people, but rather the dirty black damp wall strips of the platform over the rails. People there stand in the same way in front of us as twigs and petals (bodies and heads) stick out from a branch.

No doubt, such qualitative analyses of which you can find plenty in our book from 2011 may well describe a subjective reading experience and suffer from all close readings in that it depends on the reader being sympathetic to the interpretation produced – in this case that of my co-author Raoul Schrott. For the purposes of experimentation in Neurocomputational Poetics, however, quantitative rather than qualitative text analysis methods are required. This is because most of the many measurements at the neuronal, behavioural and experiential levels of response are best predicted parametrically. Thus, one needs methods for turning text into numbers, for example, by transforming their discrete units (words) into vectors, that is, a matrix with only one row of numbers. Computational poetics is a field pioneered by linguists, mathematicians and psychologists in which researchers use state-of-the-art computer techniques from an interdisciplinary quest now termed 'Natural Language Processing' (NLP), a particularly prolific subfield of the new 'big data science' revolution. It combines the efforts of (psycho-)linguists, data scientists, machine learning engineers and many others in an attempt to analyze the world's texts for purposes of better understanding how they work and can be engineered with a focus on practical examination of texts. In Chapters 5 and 6, I will show examples for how this is possible and why it is useful, such as predicting the most likeable song lyrics from a selection of Bob Dylan's unreachable corpus or the most striking lines of the 154 Shakespeare sonnets.

Cognitive Neuroscience

The third and final force behind the Neurocomputational Poetics perspective are the fast-progressing methodological toolboxes of cognitive neuroscience. Observing changes in hemodynamic brain activity via *neuroimaging* and in concurrent heart rate variability or eye movement behaviour during the reading of a Shakespeare sonnet has only become possible since the 1990s. Without the neurocognitive laboratories of the Dahlem Institute for Neuroimaging of Emotion (D.I.N.E.) – for which I had the honour of becoming the founding director – and of its successor, the Center for Cognitive Neuroscience Berlin (CCNB), of the Freie Universität Berlin (FU Berlin), this perspective would remain purely theoretical. These labs produced the bulk of empirical data against which the ideas of Aristotle, Shakespeare, Jakobson or Schrott, as well as the central hypotheses of reading psychology, psycholinguistics and Neurocomputational Poetics could be gauged in this book.

To summarize, bringing together ideas, materials and methods from traditional humanities disciplines, psychology, neurosciences as well as computer and data science is at the heart of the perspective this book tries to popularize. Most of the studies discussed in it stem from my own team or collaborations with others. This was a deliberate choice mainly due to the fact that only very few teams work on Neurocomputational Poetics in the stricter sense, that is, combining state-of-the-art computational and psychological with neuroscientific methods as applied to (printed) verbal art reception. I'd like to end with a quotation from Arthur Koestler[12]:

> 'I have no illusions about the prospects of the theory I am proposing: it will suffer the inevitable fate of being proven wrong in many, or most, details, by new advances in psychology and neurology. What I am hoping for is that it will be found to contain a shadowy pattern of truth, and that it may stimulate those who search for unity in the diverse manifestations of human thought and emotion'

Chapter 1

INTRODUCTION

The Two Boons of an Unnatural Daily Activity

Can you put into words your experiences while you sit on a couch and move your eyes smoothly across a piece of paper or a screen, which – as the only sensory input your brain has to process – provides some ink blobs or pixels you have learned to identify as letters after years of training? The following two quotes nicely summarize what I think is essential about this, in terms of evolution, most unnatural daily activity of the mind. They reveal two different aspects or functions that you perhaps are also familiar with. One evokes experiences of immersing oneself in a textual world; the other stirs up emotions and feelings of beauty. Both, the immersive and the aesthetic experiences, so well described in these citations, emerge from an interaction between the contents of the texts they read and the associative semantic networks in their brains.

> A) 'It starts spontaneously, and it keeps on as long as I keep reading. [...] I have to concentrate and get involved. [...] I immediately immerse myself in the reading, and the problems I usually worry about disappear. [...] It starts as soon as something attracts my attention particularly, something that interests me. [...] It can start wherever there is a chance to read undisturbed. [...] One feels well, quiet, peaceful. [...] I feel as if I belonged completely in the situation described in the book. [...] I identify with the characters, and take part in what I am reading. [...] I feel like I have the book stored in my mind.'

> B) 'It is emotion put into measure. The emotion must come by nature, but the measure can be acquired by art. It should surprise by a fine excess and not by singularity – it should strike the reader as a wording of his own highest thoughts, and appear almost a remembrance. It lifts the veil from the hidden beauty of the world, and makes familiar objects be as if they were not familiar'. I would define it as the rhythmical creation of beauty.'

Throughout this book, I will treat these two aspects apart: *immersion*, mainly associated with the reading of prose, and *aesthetic feelings*, most often associated with the reading of poetry. This does not mean, however, that people *cannot* have aesthetic feelings when reading a novel or immersive experiences during the reception of poetry. But, on the one hand, this conceptual separation facilitates theoretical and methodological analysis. On the other hand, the empirical evidence discussed in this book strongly suggests that, in general, our brains process prose and poetry differently.

Immersion – A Multifaceted Phenomenon

The above quote (A) about prose bears witness to experiences of immersing oneself in a text world, and that is what people often tell you when asked about how reading fiction affects them. The quote also suggests that concentrated attention and emotional involvement play just as important a part in this process as the desire to forget oneself, escapism, identification, empathy or happiness. But they also raise the question of the *how* of the underlying mental processes, a central issue for this book. Phenomenologists like Wolfgang Iser describe the act of reading as a state of being 'in the midst of things'. In the normal process of perception, we relate to an object by standing in front of it. During reading, we occupy a vantage point as we move through the realm of word-objects presented to us. Thus, a text, in contrast to many other objects of visual perception, can never be grasped as a whole but always only as a series of distinct moments of reading – as a wandering point of view. This is what is specific to understanding the nature of aesthetic objects in fictional texts and that has consequences for how we process, understand and appreciate them.

Thus, reading requires the gaze to focus on a small section of the visual environment, a tiny window called *visual span*. To our visual system, it looks a bit like this:

xxxxx focus on small section+of the visual environment xxxxx

The + sign represents the position of the gaze where the retina's centre is located during a single fixation, a momentary stop of the wandering or, more precisely, jumping gaze. The x's represent letters a reader cannot see sharply or at all because of the low visual acuity in peripheral vision. This decrease of visual acuity towards the periphery of the visual field is the main reason why we move our eyes about three times per second; not only during reading, but all the time: the most frequent movement of our life, deftly programmed by the brain and executed by 2 x 6 muscles attached to the eyes.

I already mentioned that during these 'saccadic' moments of blindness our brains play a trick to keep up the illusion of a continuous world. But this limited and feigned continuous perceptual input is only half the story. The other half is memory. What has already been read quickly fades from our limited working memory –with a capacity of about five items – to make place for what comes. Only what has just been read is really present to the mind, while what has not yet been read is anticipated in terms of what is remembered and currently being experienced. Every moment of reading thus can be seen as a dialectic of expectations aiming at what will come and of remembering what happened, conveying a future horizon yet to be occupied, along with a past (and continually fading) horizon already filled. The three universals of narrative originate from this overall intersequencing: *suspense* at what happens next, *curiosity* about why something happened ('whodunit') and *surprise* about something unexpectedly happening.[13] Each of these encodes a distinct functional mental operation, the dynamics of *prospection*, *retrospection* and *recognition*.[14] Indeed, psychological research confirms the idea that a reader is caught in a temporal series of events, with events that are nearer to him in the story world also being easier to remember than those that happened further back in the past. I am no phenomenologist, but I can see what phenomenologists mean when suggesting that the medium of reading (book, tablet, kindle etc.) may not be so important after all, because it disappears when one is immersed in the work itself. The act of reading can indeed make the physical objects around us disappear, including the text itself. It can also replace those external objects with mental objects. An immersed reader whose visual field is limited to the above visual span filters out all extraneous environmental stimuli and often also all mental constructions not specifically induced by the text.

'One can only imagine what is absent' said Marcel Proust. And indeed, whether prose or poetry, texts always confront us with an impoverished world from which countless aspects are absent or unclear. One reason is that 'wording the world' is basically a process of extreme oversimplification, abstraction or categorization that makes communication easier. It consists of creating associations between a single sound and a mental image of more or less complex high-dimensional objects, such as a table or a book, that always have numerous and diverse features. What our sensory cortex can very accurately measure in terms of an object's size, shape, colour, pitch or loudness is magically turned into a single coarse *sound bite* supposed to capture the object's sensory richness. That is how ontogenetically the sensory world is first put into phonemes and then into graphemes or letters. The magic of the letters lies in the fact that despite being only ink blobs on a page they can re-ignite the sensory fire of the original objects in readers' minds. When we read the words ‘Venice is beautiful’ printed in black on a white page, they do not show us the colours, smells or emotions we may remember from our last visit to the city or our last readings about it in travel guides and novels. But they can transport us into the imaginary: this wonderful capacity to make manifest the latent structures of meaning available in a text via an active process of mentally filling out what is absent or purposefully left out by means of weak implicature (something not explicitly said). When we read Emily Dickinson’s line ‘Hope is the thing with feathers’ weakly implicating that the feeling of hope has something of a bird, we may mentally simulate how it beats with its wings or flies away. Much as computers can simulate the reality of climate change, earthquakes or brain activations, the brain itself simulates reality. Such mental simulations are central to reading and language processing in general. When heard or read, words evoke more or less conscious embodied memories of the thoughts, feelings or actions associated with the events they describe by partially activating the same neural networks as the corresponding natural events. This is why, when reading a story, you can (re-)experience the colour and scent of a rose, a warm breeze blowing on your skin or a kiss on your lips.

Immersion Potential

Among the factors that increase the *immersion potential* of texts, or in other words, make it easier for readers to forget the outside world, are:

- familiar events and characters with sufficient realistic detail
- consistency of time, place or causality
- perspectivity, that is, the imitation of the perspectivity of everyday experience with its limitation of perception according to the point of view and horizon of the perceiver
- relatively inconspicuous discourse
- a suspenseful dynamic plot generating an emotional interest and affective responses in readers
- the ‘celare artem’ principle, that is generally avoiding all rhetorical devices that foreground textuality or fictionality.

All these factors also facilitate the construction of *situation models* – mental representations of the situations described in a text. *Who* does *What* to *Whom Where*, *When* and *Why*? During reading of fiction, our brains are constantly in search of answers to these six ‘Wh-‘questions as much as to the fundamental ‘What happens next’ question that keeps us reading on. Thus, space and time, goals and causation, as well as people and objects (agents, patients) form the basic dimensions of the situation model our brains recurrently construct during reading. Whenever one or more of these dimensions change in a text, such as when the protagonist leaves one locale for another, that produces measurable traces in brain activity.[15] This suggests that readers use perceptual and motor representations in the process of comprehending narratives and that these representations are dynamically updated at points when relevant aspects of the situation are changing, the so-called *event boundaries.*

Immersion is a multifaceted phenomenon that broadly comes in two forms. The minimal or weak one merely involves representing an object located concretely in space and time. For example, if you read the word 'Paris', perhaps you cannot help but be mentally transported to the French capital and see the Eiffel Tower with your mind's eye. The rich and strong form involves not only thoughts about a concrete object or event, but also about its environment and the world that surrounds it. That includes the idea of being inside that world itself, in the presence of the object. This strong form that has been called the *Narnia Effect*[16] allows readers even to forget that they are absorbed in language, without forgetting that the textual world is not reality. Readerly perception of the passing of time is distorted by a kind of self-effacement and neglect of readers' physical reality, measurable as a non-responsiveness to distractions. In between those two and at a finer grain size, different degrees in immersion intensity can be distinguished, ranging from concentration to addiction, also called *Don Quixote Syndrome.*

To summarize, there is no shortage of definitions and theoretical approaches to immersive phenomena in literature or other media. Nevertheless, for an experimental scientist, this still begs the *how* question. How does immersive reading function, not only on the verbally communicable level of subjective experience, but also on the levels of cognitive and affective processes and their neuronal bases, which cannot be directly observed? The processes underlying reading that can be consciously communicated are those that most literary critics and psychologists refer to, and which are generally measured using questionnaires and psychometric scales. But they only represent the tip of the iceberg. The iceberg itself consists of a myriad of unconscious processes which Neurocomputational Poetics researchers aim to illuminate using methods such as eye movement and brain activity recordings. In our book, Raoul Schrott and I postulated two neuronal mechanisms for the phenomenon of immersion: *symbol grounding* and *neuronal recycling.* At the time, this was still pretty speculative, but thanks to the results of studies published after 2011 – some of which are reported in Chapters 7 and 8 – we now can be confident that these mechanisms really contribute to immersion in literature.

The Neuronal Bases of Immersion

What is the secret behind reading's flabbergasting capacity to hold our attention and make us forget the world around us? How can supposedly abstract symbols as words – extremely recent cultural objects in evolutionary terms – induce sensory delusions and quasi-real feelings in us, captivating us in the cinema of the mind? Early research already hinted at a possible solution anticipating modern theories of embodiment and symbol grounding. Thus, Sigmund Freud claimed that words have a substance and that the brain processed them in much the same way as any other kind of object, that is, it codes them in terms of their sensorimotor features including their vocalized form and articulatory operations. The language theoretician Karl Bühler suggested that words have a *spheric fragrance*.[17] If, for example, the word 'garden radish' appears in a text, a reader is immediately transported to the dining table or the garden, that is, to an entirely different sphere than the one associated with a word such as 'ocean'. According to both Freud and Bühler, words therefore evoke embodied cognitions, and the activities they are used for – speaking, reading, thinking, feeling – are themselves substance-controlled. This is why 'garden radish' can evoke red and white colour impressions, crackling sounds or earthy smells and spicy tastes in the minds of the readers and transport them either into a garden or to a dinner table.

Symbol Grounding

Imagine a child hearing the sentence: 'Simon sat on a chair and teetered'. Could the child comprehend this sentence if it could not imagine teetering itself or had not seen someone else do it? As a cognitive neuroscientist, I can even surmise that the meaning of the word 'chair' consists of nothing other than a neuronal pattern of actions relating to this object: feeling it against the body, hearing it scratch on the floor, bumping against it, falling down after teetering and so on. The embodied meaning – the sensorimotor concept 'chair' – is composed of the summed experiences of a chair a person has already had and the judgements she has been able to form as a result. As well as being distinguishable by standard linguistic and affective features such as number of syllables or *valence* – the fact of being emotionally positive or negative – words can also be differentiated by many other features such as concreteness or imageability. Thus, words such as 'sea' or 'house' exhibit a high imageability, while 'purpose' or 'philosophy' have a lower one. From time immemorial, poetry has used this knowledge of the sensorimotor and affective associative potential of words, skilfully linking these with their phonetic qualities. Our hypothesis for solving the *symbol grounding* problem[18] claims that the memory images evoked by words and sentences we hear or read are similar to those evoked by the objects they refer to. This phenomenon, sometimes called the *Madeleine Effect* in reference to Proust and the memory triggered by the eating of a cake, points to the fact that, when reading or when listening to language, the processes involved are based on the same or similar neuronal mechanisms as those used in direct experience. This mental simulation of situations described verbally or in writing is therefore, under certain circumstances, capable of holding our attention with an intensity comparable to real perception, and sometimes even greater.

The symbol grounding hypothesis contradicts the traditional understanding of these matters in cognitive psychology, which postulates a strict division between language on the one hand and perception or action on the other, considering language to be based on the manipulation of abstract symbols. This view does overlook the fact that the visual appearance of words and sentences constitutes the same kind of sensory stimuli as objects or faces. They are also automatically associated with their auditory form. Light and sound waves, transformed into neurochemical signals, affect our brains in a way that transforms these waves through complex intermediary stages into multi-modal symbols: letters and graphemes on the one hand, and their corresponding sounds and phonemes on the other. A word is therefore symbolically grounded by those learnt sensorimotor activities connecting its reception (seeing, hearing) with its production (speaking, writing). What at first sight appears as an abstract, amodal object composed of letters of the alphabet acquires its familiar, almost obvious meaning only after many laborious years of learning. And anyone who has watched children or adult patients with brain lesions learning to read and write will know how hard this process is. Today, neuroscience is able to actually prove the existence of Bühler's spheric fragrance hypothesis. Reading the sequence of letters that makes up the word 'radish' causes various sensory response areas of the brain to become active, while 'ball' also causes motor regions to 'light up', and 'kiss' activates networks that deal in emotions. The mind actually (re-)experiences events it is really only reading about, and this power of simulation (mimesis, reliving) is one neuronal substratum of immersion.

Already at the beginning of the nineteenth century, neurologists like Carl Wernicke[19] thought that the concept of a rose is composed of a tactile memory image – an image of touch – in the central projection field of the somaesthetic cortex. It is also composed of a visual memory image located in the visual projection field of the cortex. The continuous repetition of similar sensory impressions results in such a firm association between those different memory images that the mere stimulation of one sensory avenue by means of the object is adequate to call up the concept of the object. In some cases, many memory images of different sensory areas and in others only a few correspond to a single concept. This sum total of closely associated memory images must 'be aroused into consciousness' for the perception not merely of sounds of the corresponding words but also for comprehension of their meaning. Wernicke also postulated the existence of 'association tracts' between the sensory speech centre of word-sound-comprehension and those projection fields which participate in the formation of the concept. In sum, the meaning of a word results from the fusion of a mental sound and a multidimensional and multimodal image schema.

Neuronal Recycling

The second hypothesis, *neuronal recycling,*[20] postulates that structures in the brain eventually adapt so well to their environment that culturally determined processes such as reading end up operating through them, even though they had not evolved for this purpose. This means that cultural inventions such as writing have occupied brain networks that are older in evolutionary terms by taking over, at least in part, their general structural framework, and forming a kind of neuronal niche. In the roughly 6,000 years since the development of writing, evolution hardly had time to develop completely new, reading-specific structures, capable of specializing in the construction of such amodal symbols. Since neuronal networks in all four lobes of the brain, as well as the cerebellum and other subcortical structures, play a part in recognizing just a single word, we may assume that structures are being used here that performed comparable functions among our ancestors; for example, recognizing patterns, objects and faces.

In a way, this is a kind of creative evolutionary misappropriation sometimes called *exaptation*: the utilization of a characteristic for a function it wasn't originally intended for. The theory of neuronal recycling claims exactly this: that a particular part of the left cerebral hemisphere's *fusiform gyrus* – a structure in the lower temporal lobe – represents just such an exapted region of the brain. The process of learning to read, which often takes years, recycles the circuits of this region, reshaping structures that had initially served to recognize objects and faces: a classic example of how the actual form of the brain can react to new cultural inventions. This so-called *visual word form area* includes a series of neuronal circuits, that on the one hand are reasonably close to the original function of recognizing patterns, objects and faces which the other parts of the fusiform gyrus specialize in. But on the other hand, they are also malleable enough to be able to muster considerable resources for tasks that are culturally determined, such as recognizing letters and words. One can therefore claim that the brain's design made reading possible, and reading's design changed the brain in multiple, critical, still evolving ways.[21]

Aesthetic Feelings

The quote about prose at the beginning of this chapter is only about half of the story of verbal art reception. Unlike it, the quote about poetry in (B) spotlights key words such as rhythm and emotion, or, most prominently, beauty. Curiously, although the interest in empirical studies on feelings of beauty dates back to the origin of psychological science, such studies almost exclusively dealt with *non-verbal art*, mainly paintings and music. Having been something like a bibliophile all my life, this really nagged at my scientist's soul for many years. But until rather late in my career, I did not dare tackle such overcomplex things as verbal art or aesthetic feelings, which many scientists view as impossible to study anyhow.

Languages of Emotion and the (Neuro-)Aesthetics of Verbal Art

Luckily, in 2003 I moved to Free University (FU) of Berlin, where my friend and colleague Helmut Leder was developing his theory of aesthetics[22] and we decided to change this disturbing state of affairs together. Unluckily, our grant proposal within a large Collaborative Research Centre of the German Research Foundation (DFG) was rejected by the reviewers. It was somewhat clumsily termed 'On the beauty of words and paintings: affective processing as a basis of aesthetic experience and evaluation of verbal and pictorial stimuli'. The reviewers either argued that words can have no beauty, only texts, or that beauty cannot be measured, only experienced. Barely two years (and a lot of preparatory work) later, I became an integral part of the largest grant FU Berlin had acquired so far and its biggest high-risk scientific adventure. It should be discontinued by an international review panel some seven years – and ~50 million € spent – later. The buzz arguments hit: 'interdisciplinarity only leads to alignment on a lower level', or, 'the humanities and sciences will never become compatible because they have different epistemological aims', or, most devastatingly, 'such scientific adventures are too risky to produce palpable results within the financed time interval'. Still, when we started this 'cluster of excellence' of the DFG called *Languages of Emotion*, we were convinced that only such a giant conglomerate of over 20 different disciplines, forcing together scholars from literature, theatre or film science with researchers from neuroscience, psychiatry or psychology could achieve their common scientific goal: the so far badly neglected investigation of the role of emotions in theories of language and the role of language in theories of emotion. Without this high-risk adventure, there would be no book about Neurocomputational Poetics.

Encouraged by this success together with some fearless colleagues, I thus took up the previously rejected idea of the (Neuro-)Aesthetics of verbal art. Because this time I had access to unseen amounts of research money, lab technology – a new building for harbouring the newly acquired fMRI scanner was constructed within a year – and scientific workforce (e.g. overall ~100 Ph.D. students). At the time of Languages of Emotion, aesthetic feelings associated with verbal art were a kind of virgin soil both in reading psychology and cognitive neuroscience, which both generally focused on cognitive aspects of reading. On the other hand, theoretical studies in modern poetics investigated the aesthetic potential of metre, rhyme or metaphor starting with Jakobson's work in the 1940s–1960s without bothering to test whether their elaborate assumptions had anything to do with the realities of readers. Ultra-rare empirical reports like I. A. Richards' often-cited qualitative study on poetry reception produced misleading conclusions – due to a lack of statistical analyses – to the effect that further empirical investigations of literature were discouraged by the misinformed view that people do not agree in their readings and judgements of texts: 'a hundred verdicts from a hundred readers'.[23]

Fortunately for my own later research interests, empirical studies of literature were jolted by the creation of the journal *Poetics* in 1971 and of the 'Internationale Gesellschaft für Empirische Literaturforschung' (IGEL; International Society for the Empirical Study of Literature) in 1987. These represent important steps towards grounding literary theory in the work of psychology and linguistics. Applying the theoretical and quantitative methodological tools of these sciences to the study of questions on literature reception led to a wealth of data which still await theoretical integration and unification, while comprehensive models of aesthetics for non-verbal art have guided empirical studies for some time. The advent of neuroaesthetics with the introduction of the methods of cognitive neuroscience – primarily neuroimaging – to investigate the evolutionary and biological underpinnings of aesthetic experiences then primed the development of Neurocomputational Poetics that led to this book. Basic assumptions of the latter approaches are (i) the *aesthetic triad*, that is, the notion that aesthetic experiences like pleasure or repulsion emerge from an interaction between sensory-motor, emotional valuation and meaning–knowledge systems in the brain, and (ii) the *aesthetic trajectory*, that is, the idea that aesthetic experiences include at least three temporal stages: an initial stage of (partial) familiarity, recognition or stability; a second stage of surprise, ambiguity or tension; and a third stage of integration, resolution or synthesis.[24]

Ontogeny of Literary Aesthetic Experiences – Euphony and Eusemy

Aesthetic experiences with verbal materials appear to have their origin in the one-word poetry described by Jakobson and others. A prominent example is the word 'mama', in which the phonotactically optimal combination of phoneme contrasts already triggers a positive response at the phonological level (*euphony*). When associated with an object promising warmth, care, intimacy and nourishment (*eusemy*) the word becomes the first and perhaps most beautiful one-word poem of all.

Human beings do not learn to read as they learn to talk or walk. Learning to read means to expect something unnatural, artificial of oneself (or others), and, occasionally, in the case of poetry, something superficially pointless. Nevertheless, most humans usually manage to acquire reading skills through structural and dynamic reorganization, adaptation and specialization of ancient brain circuits originally designed for pattern recognition and speech and thus to develop a new kind of thinking and feeling and of influencing the mental life of others. In this often long-lasting process of learning to read, poetic and lyrical texts play a significant role and are ubiquitously used in daily life to teach children to speak, read, write or count, e.g. in ABC- or counting-out rhymes. Thus, playing, playful learning and lyrical texts go together even before and during reading acquisition. Miall and Dissanayake[25] describe it as follows:

> The poetic texture of the mother's speech – specifically its use of metrics, phonetics, and foregrounding – helps to shape and direct the baby's attention, as it also coordinates the partners' emotional communication [...] To us, this is evidence of design in neural organization, and it supports our view that a capacity for mutuality or intersubjectivity – the coordinating of behavioural-emotional states with another's in temporally organized sequences – is a primary human psychobiological endowment that has not been sufficiently incorporated into adaptationist thinking.

Neurocognitive Bases of Literary Aesthetic Experiences – The Panksepp–Jakobson Hypothesis

If evolution did not have enough time to develop emotional circuits and 'pleasure centres' for the specific enjoyment of non-verbal art, it was even less so for literature. Rather, as the neuroscientist Jaak Panksepp hypothesized the feelings experienced during reading are based on the ancient circuits of affect that we share with all other mammals, mainly in the so-called *limbic system*.[26] Whether (vicarious) fear for a protagonist or the aesthetic enjoyment of a beautiful metaphor, i.e. Jakobson's famous poetic function of language, these circuits are in play. In honour of the two scientists representing the opposite poles that span my research interests, I called this the Panksepp–Jakobson hypothesis. It follows from this hypothesis that whenever readers report subjective feelings of beauty or disgust during reading, parts of the ancient pleasure networks in the brain such as the *ventral striatum* must be active. The empirical evidence discussed in Chapters 7 and 8 confirms this.

Liking vs. Wanting

According to Immanuel Kant's foundational definitions, aesthetic emotions are associated with subjectively felt pleasure or displeasure and are an important predictor of resultant liking or disliking. Moreover, in spite of frequent misinterpretations, Kant's notion of 'disinterested pleasure' – often cited as an argument for the autonomy of art – only was meant to point out that pure aesthetic judgements should be independent of any pragmatic interests, and not that they are wholly devoid of personal relevance or cannot be self-rewarding. Still, humans often report aesthetic feelings of engaging with an art object without accompanying desires to acquire, control or manipulate it. Such mental states of 'disinterest' could have their neuronal correlates in two separable brain systems for pleasure, one more strongly associated with liking, the other dominantly involved in wanting. Both systems typically work in concert and have overlapping neural circuitry, especially within the ventral striatum, that is the brain's 'lust centre' or liking system. However, mental states of liking seem more mediated by neurochemical opiate and cannabinoid systems, while activity of the dopamine neurotransmitter systems typically correlates with wanting.[27] It is thus tempting to assume that the subjectively felt 'disinterested interest' reflects activity in the liking system without activity in the wanting system, with the corresponding experience of pleasurable aesthetic emotions.

This so far unconfirmed assumption could explain how pleasurable aesthetic responses are a subset of rewarding experiences distinct from desires for objects that drive consumer behaviour with poetry being a case in point. On the other hand, many reader reports indicate the utility of Jakobson's poetic function, for instance when wanting to reread appreciated poems or finding solace in reading sad texts, both suggesting a wanting component. Thus, a simple dichotomy based on two discernible neural systems may not be a full account of the subtleties of diverse forms of liking with or without wanting poetic literature or art in general.

Prose and Poetry – Background and Foreground

To sum up the two preceding sections, there is enough intuitive and empirical evidence – experiential, behavioural and neurocognitive – for the idea that the two boons of reading rely at least partially on distinct neuronal networks with occasional movement or blending between them. Although without doubt prose texts *can* elicit aesthetic feelings and readers *can* immerse in poetry, stories and novels nevertheless generally are the chief realm of suspense and immersion, while poems are the prevalent source for feelings of beauty.

In any case, empirical studies of literature have shown that texts with a high immersion potential typically are those full of 'what happens next?' or 'whodunit?' moments as in crime stories and suspenseful novels. On the other hand, texts with a high aesthetic potential typically are those full of stylistic devices like metre or metaphor in upscale fiction and, particularly, poetry. Thus, when readers are asked 'Please write down terms that could be used to describe the aesthetics of literature', their most frequent response is 'suspenseful' for novels and 'beautiful' for poetry.[28] Texts mainly renouncing on stylistic devices but offering many familiar and realistic details to draw readers into the story world can be characterized as primarily *backgrounded.* In contrast, texts that offer only a minimum of common ground – just enough to put forward their stylistic elements – are primarily *foregrounded.* This is a simplified version of *foregrounding theory* which distinguishes between several types of background in literary texts: (i) ordinary language, (ii) the literary tradition relevant for the text to be read, and (iii) the linguistic norms established by the text itself. Any deviation from this triple background then has foregrounding potential.

Figure 1.1 illustrates this dichotomy in a simplified way along two dimensions when, in reality, the textual and mental spaces associated with literary reading are high-dimensional. The point of this diagram is to visualize

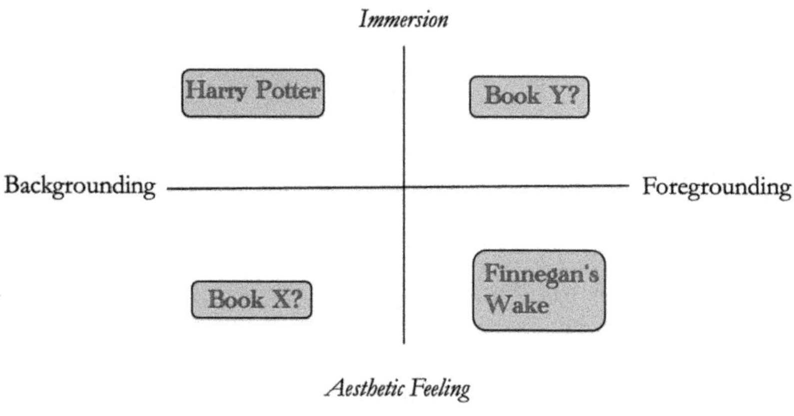

Figure 1.1 Four books are located in a hypothetical 2d space with the poles Backgrounding vs. Foregrounding (X-axis) and Immersion vs. Aesthetic Feeling (Y-axis).

the idea that, although both phenomena, immersion and aesthetic feelings, can be construed as lying on the same continuum, they also appear to happen in special locations of the 2d (or higher-dimensional) plane. Dimension 1 (X-axis) represents the degree of foregrounding as determined by the number (and type) of stylistic devices in a text that activate Jakobson's poetic function and inhibit the automatic, fluent, non-reflective reading process. Dimension 2 (Y-axis) represents the immersion potential of texts. A good example of a highly immersive text with a lot of backgrounding elements is the Harry Potter book series[29] that provided the stimulus materials for a series of neurocognitive experiments on immersion I report in Chapter 7. James Joyce's 'Finnegan's Wake', on the other hand, is full of foregrounding elements and – to believe reports of many readers and experts – has a high aesthetic potential. As a puzzle and challenge for anyone who wishes to falsify this simplified notion, which serves as the central architectural hypothesis of the Neurocomputational Poetics Model (NCPM) introduced in the next chapter, I put two other hypothetical books into the diagram. Indeed, if there exist books full of foreground elements that induce strong immersive processes (book Y), or books that are practically bare of them but evoke strong aesthetic feelings (book X), then my model is falsified.

Psychologically, what is sketched in the diagram can be interpreted as processes that typically inhibit each other, since the subprocesses driving them do not normally take place at the same time or in the same neural networks. In reality, background and foreground elements of texts often overlap at different levels – as discussed in the following chapters – as do the associated neuronal processes. But again, my approach here is from simple to complex, and I hope you can follow me in this. While some scholars jump to complexities too soon, as stated in the preface, I prefer starting simple and developing complexity out of simple elements, a bit like DNA which creates life out of a myriad of combinations of just four letters.

The Grisham and Amis Effects

Similar assumptions about two separable processes underlying literary reading have been proposed before. Thus, Keith Oatley distinguished between a *Grisham effect* (what will happen next?) and an *Amis effect* (making things strange) in literature. He associated the former with assimilative and the latter with accommodative processes, that is, integrating a piece of experience into existing mental schemata vs. changing or extending these in response to new experiences. Others distinguished a *reactive* from a *reflective* reading mode: the former being typical for reading plot- and suspense-oriented novels or novels full of profound exploration of the viewpoint and experiences of characters; the latter being associated with meaning and emotion blends typical for poetic texts.[30] Thus, although there might be exceptions to the rule, for instance aspects of immersion that facilitate aesthetic responses, I would generally agree with the conclusion of my colleague Frank Hakemulder to whom I gratefully owe the recruitment as a member of the IGEL society: '[…] but for now, based on the spontaneous reactions of the respondents, we must conclude that beauty is not associated with absorption'.[31] Of course, this conclusion depends very much on how we operationalize, induce and assess immersive or aesthetic experiences and the underlying processes, an issue addressed in the remaining chapters of this book.

Summary

In this introductory chapter, I focused on the contrast between two modes of verbal art reception, an immersive and an aesthetic one. These are typically associated with different types of literature, prose vs. poetry, and with separable neural, affective-cognitive and experiential processes, for which I presented theoretical arguments to be followed by computational and empirical ones in the impending chapters. I also discussed the likely neuronal bases of these two modes of literary reading, as well as a number of related effects and hypotheses: the *Narnia*, *Madeleine* and *Grisham* effects, or the Panksepp–Jakobson hypothesis. In the next chapter, I introduce a theoretical model of verbal-art reception that centres around these two modes. The model serves to organize empirical knowledge about reading literature into a unified framework that offers a set of related hypotheses and allows me to make qualitative and quantitative predictions about reading prose and poetry. These are put to test in the computational and empirical studies discussed in Chapters 5 to 8.

Chapter 2

MODELS AND METHODS

If asking the right questions is part of the art of science – those that, if answered, will make a difference and ideally can be answered during an academic career – and if you are engaged in a long-term scientific adventure like reading research, it is generally favourable to work with models in search of answers. They provide theoretical guidance and prevent you from straying in the dark. They put a spotlight on parts of the a priori infinite search space that hypercomplex research objects like language or reading confront you with. This limits your search to a few corners you can shed light on with a few shrewd, testable hypotheses. As a fallibilist, I believe that having to reject a hypothesis is more informative than confirming it, but I know that learning from errors requires more courage and frustration tolerance than enjoying the rewards of having been right again. Of course, in reality, both sides of the game – learning from erroneous predictions and being motivated by (partially) confirmed ones – complement each other just as is the case in life. What drives us always is a mixture of fear of failure and hope of success; with the right balance, you can go far in reaching your goals.

The Neurocomputational Poetics Model (NCPM) of Verbal Art Reception

How would we look for a new law? [...]

First, we guess it. [

Then, we compute the consequences of the guess. [. . .]

And then we compare these computation results to [. . .] an experiment [. . .]

If it disagrees with experiment, it's wrong.

And that simple statement is the key to science.

—Lecture by Richard Feynman[i]

i http://amiquote.tumblr.com/post/4463599197/richard-feynman-on-how-we-would-look-for-a-new-law

Although the first publication of my main theoretical torch, the NCPM, happened in 2011, my love story with cognitive and computational modelling started much earlier: during my undergraduate studies at the University of Würzburg in Bavaria when I first learned about Egon Brunswick's *lens model.*

The World Seen through a Lens or What Bananas and Books Have in Common

The lens model was an early attempt at modelling human perception as a process of correlating sensory cues like the colour of a banana with judgements (and resulting actions) regarding an object's useful properties, for example its degree of ripeness. In the 1930s Brunswick already understood that the brain is a correlation machine, long before the neural network models I use in my research were invented. Using advanced statistics for his time, he also proposed that the *multiple regression* weight[ii] of a cue estimates its informativeness or *ecological validity.* Thus, like other objects, a banana has many cues or features (colour, shape, size etc.), but when judging its ripeness for eating purposes not all of them are equally valid. The weight of the feature colour primes, while to what extent size or shape matter might depend on your state of hunger and personal aesthetic preferences. Ultimately, the decision to eat the banana or not is based on observing it through the lens of these cues and weighing their relative importance for the task at hand. When, later in this book, I analyze the importance of text features like word order or semantic complexity using computational models, the idea is basically the same. Although conceptually, the step from Brunswick's lens model to the neural network models of today is not a big one, acquiring the programming skills – and keeping up-to-date with the ultra-fast developments – to efficiently use these is another matter. A short visit at MIT was crucial for this in my career.

ii Multiple regression is a statistical technique for analysing the relationship between a single response variable and several predictor variables. Its goal is to use the predictor variables whose values are known to estimate the value of the single response value. Each predictor value is weighed, the weights denoting their relative contribution to the overall prediction: $Y = a + x_1 * b_1 + x_2 * b_2 + ... + x_n * b_n$. Here Y is the response variable, and $x_1,\dots,x_n$ are the n predictors. In calculating the weights b_1 to b_n, regression analysis ensures maximal prediction of the response variable from the set of predictors. This is usually done by least squares estimation, i.e. minimizing the sum of the squares of the differences between the observed and fitted values (provided by the regression).

A Goofed Grant and David Marr's Three Levels of Explanation

The reason I visited MIT in 1986 was that someone close to the late David Marr had offered me a post-doc position in a grant of hers that continued his pioneering work on computer models of human cognition. I never got the grant funding, though, which shortened my stay at MIT considerably. Still, I was fascinated by Marr's tripartite view of scientific explanation[32] and stuck to the idea of working on his proposals. At the highest level of explanation, he placed the *computational theory* which must clearly state the What and Why of a computation: what is it for, why is it appropriate and by which logic can it be carried out. At the level below it, the *algorithmic model* must specify the input, throughput and output representations in a way allowing to implement the theory as a computer model. Finally, at the lowest level, the *hardware implementation* must specify how the algorithmic model can be realized physically or neurally. While at the time Noam Chomsky's theory of syntax served as an example for a *computational theory,* to me the computational neural network models developed by connectionism[33] were the most promising ones for the algorithmic level. Since sophisticated neuroimaging methods were not yet around in 1986, I did not worry much about the lowest level.

Lacking a general theory of literary reading, which back then I considered to be beyond my possibilities, I thus focused on the algorithmic level, starting to work with computational models of the two basic processes underlying reading: word recognition and eye movement control. Indeed, fluent reading is only possible if single words can be effortlessly recognized and the gaze can be moved efficiently across a series of words in a sentence or line. If one and/or the other process is impaired – like in certain types of dyslexia – reading becomes a drag: children and adults deprived of the pleasures and socio-economic advantages of fluent reading can tell you about it. Studying the possible causes, from genetic to cognitive, and the multiple effects of dyslexia to find possible cures also became a central research topic of mine.[34]

Methods Must Fit the Questions

The most important lesson I learned from scientists like Marr, Brunswick or Chomsky is this: If you have a good theory or model, then the *right questions* will fall from the tree of that theory. Otherwise, you might fish in the dark for your entire career. Once a question reckoned to be right has been formulated and turned into a hypothesis or quantitative prediction by help of computational models, the right method must be selected: the one that best fits for answering the question and testing the prediction. The key concept here is that of *validity* or whether a method, test, study or experiment really measures what it claims to measure. Thus, one can ask whether a self-report like the Literary Response Questionnaire (LRQ)[35] is as valid a measure of literary experiences as say the IQ test is for human intelligence, or the so-called *big5* for human personality. Similarly, to what extent an increased heart rate, a dilated pupil, a prolonged gaze duration or a locally increased activity in some brain region validly reflect an effect of the emotion potential of words in a text is often difficult to tell. If a theoretical model, however, predicts exactly such an effect for such a measure on grounds of a set of coherent hypotheses, confidence in the validity of the test increases. Regrettably, the art of finding the right method for the right question is much underestimated in my field of research. The main reason is that most people interested in Neurocomputational Poetics simply lack the means to use costly methods like eye tracking for testing predictions about gaze durations in reading Shakespeare sonnets, or a brain scanner to test whether beautiful proverbs activate parts of the brain's reward system (see Chapter 8). In the worst case, you can find studies that 'employ a stethoscope to measure blood pressure' or 'an IQ test to measure neuroticism', that is plainly invalid methods (cf. Chapter 4).

To sum up, good models usually generate good questions, and then one must find the best-fitting methods to answer them. In my case, developing good working models for word recognition, eye movement control and reading became an obsession during my time at MIT and Sorbonne. Finding the grant money to acquire advanced, expensive apparatus like high-speed eye tracking, electroencephalography (EEG) or functional Magnetic Resonance Imaging (fMRI) was the other obsession. In later chapters, I show a selection of relevant results obtained with such apparatus, from simple response-time measures and ratings to peripheral-physiological markers such as heart rate, pupil size or skin conductance, to complex pictures of brain-electrical and hemodynamic activity.

Ideally, a neurocomputational model of literary reading should link hypotheses about neuronal, cognitive, affective and behavioural processes with assumptions from linguistics and poetics in a way allowing predictions about which (con-)text elements evoke which processes. And it should describe these processes in sufficient detail to make them measurable and testable. In contrast to mainstream neurocomputational models, it should go beyond *cold information processing* aspects by including emotional, immersive and aesthetic processes, as well as experiential aspects of concern or self-reflective states of mind which are characteristic of verbal art reception. In the following, I present a revised extended model that is based on the original NCPM published in 2011 in our book in light of recent empirical findings. Strongly simplifying, the original model focused on 'on-line' aspects of literary reading, restricting itself to the microstructure of texts: short moments of reading sentences or passages which last from seconds to minutes and lie within the capacity of verbal working memory. Other meso- or macroscopic aspects like the narrative structure of a text or the link between different episodes of a novel, which concern reading activities of several hours or days, were left aside. The revised, more general NCPM goes beyond that by including pre- and post-reading episodes and general tenets connecting it to other theories and models of literature and reading.

Tenets

The revised NCPM provides both an extension and a refinement of the original NCPM by embedding it in broader theoretical contexts of literary text processing, and by providing greater specification of hypotheses about the neuronal, affective-cognitive and behavioural correlates of prose and poetry reception. The NCPM is not a theory about literary texts, but a model of the reception of verbal art. It offers predictions about how readers respond to quantifiable features of literary texts and hypotheses about the processes likely underlying these responses. In short, it tries to explain how we come to understand and like literature.

Tenet 1. Adaptive Value

> *As art reception in general, verbal art experiences have adaptive value by promoting self-rewarding integrative mental skills that sharpen individuals' sensibility for language and prepare them for empathy, creativity, social interactions or self-reflecting and –altering processes.*

Tenet 1 adopts an evolutionary perspective proposing that literary experience in the broad sense has adaptive value, stimulating, among others, the adaptation and fine tuning of a person's cognitive and emotional schemata and resetting his or her readiness for appropriate social action.[36] Engaging in the simulative experiences of fiction literature facilitates the understanding of others who are different from ourselves and can thus augment our capacity for empathy and social inference. As a form of consciousness of selves and others passed from an author to a reader, fiction in general, and poetry in particular, can be internalized to augment everyday cognition. Recent behavioural and neurocomputational studies summarized in Chapters 7 and 8 support this view. For example, a neuroimaging experiment run in our lab on children aged 4–8 years[37] found evidence that empathizing with a character not only entails understanding why the other person is happy or sad, but also the ability to experience these emotions with her/him. The observed brain activation in parts of the brain's *orbitofrontal cortex* suggested a possible neural correlate of the positive effect of fiction reading on performance in mentalizing tests. Another more recent neuroimaging experiment from our lab used excerpts of fiction to study individual differences in mental perspective-taking and sensorimotor simulation during language comprehension in adults. The results suggested a neuronal correlate of the individual tendency to put oneself into fictional characters in parts of the right *medial prefrontal* and *frontopolar cortex*.[38] Although this tendency may have various origins including genetic components, Tenet 1 holds that it is promoted by reading fiction and experiencing poetic episodes.

Literary language in general and poetic language in particular work with a catalogue of stylistic devices and figures of thought such as polysemy, irony, hyperbole or oxymoron. These reflect partially innate perceptual, affective and cognitive schemata. And they allow to process the linguistic input in analogy to stimuli that produce visual illusions or basic emotions, thus presenting us an experience perfectly designed for the human brain. Among the multiple beneficial effects of metred poetry, the stimulation and sensitization of the endogenous reward system of the brain, enabling enhancement of the integrative powers of our minds is of special relevance here, because it can, at least in part, be tested experimentally using neuroimaging techniques. Indeed, the data of a recent neuroimaging study using short poetic and prose texts suggest that the encouragement to consider alternative and nuanced meanings through active reading of texts may generalize to encourage more adaptive, less rigid and biased meaning derivation in everyday life, thus facilitating mental health and well-being.[39] Reading fiction and poetry in particular has been shown to lead to self-transformations, and generations of educators all over the world seem to believe in the positive powers of learning and reciting poetry by heart in the service of memory training and personality development.

In sum, Tenet 1 submits that reading literature and poetry is perhaps risky – in that things may not be the same as before after a reading act – but promises various short- and long-term rewards. Tenet 1 also puts emphasis on the interactive nature of poetic episodes: Poetic effects cannot be understood independently of reader and context. Whether a reader affectively responds to and/or aesthetically appreciates Paul Celan's famous initial oxymoron 'black milk' from the *Death Fugue* as a felicitous image, idle babble or a disgust-arousing trope depends as much on his/her semantic memory and many other context factors as on the theoretical poeticity of the trope or line.

Tenet 2. Poeticity

> *Literary experiences or poetic episodes are not unique to encounters with the writings of specialized authors such as poets and there are no absolute features allowing the identification of literary or poetic language.*

Tenet 2 submits that poeticity in the broad sense as the deviation of a text from ordinary language and its capacity to evoke Jakobson's poetic function can be found wherever language is used; in early life encounters with micropoetic materials such as lullabies, nursery rhymes or *found poems,* as well as in fairy tales, narrated stories or spontaneous utterances in daily life. Thus, how poetic the same type of style figure – Dylan Thomas's 'A grief ago' and a German pop song's adaptation 'Three men ago' – appears to readers/listeners depends as much on the lexical choice as on the context situation and the 'eye of the beholder'.

People have subliminal poetic competences and previous work has clearly shown that single utterances or words – even outside lyrical contexts – can fulfil the *poetic function* and cause aesthetic reactions, such as experienced interest, liking or beauty. Poetic effects, thus, are not considered to be exclusive to poetry, or literature in general, and, on the other hand, also are not guaranteed by the reading of what is accepted to be literature. In line with relevance and commonality theory[40], the NCPM views them as special effects of an utterance which achieves most of its relevance through a wide array of *weak implicatures* – something the author implies without literally expressing it – and salient, innovative features. The NCPM further assumes that, depending on context factors, poetic effects can arise from both interference between linguistic constructions and cognitive principles and conformity with cognitive principles. That is, poetic figurative expressions conform to general cognitive principles or constraints just as everyday language does.[41] An example is the preference for mapping more accessible, that is, concrete, salient, domains onto less accessible ones in metaphorical expressions. The general principle is that the A term or *tenor* represents a more abstract concept than the B term or *vehicle* which is used to explain the A term. Thus, in a paper titled 'The Brain Is the Prisoner of Thought: A Machine-Learning Assisted Quantitative Narrative Analysis of Literary Metaphors for Use in Neurocomputational Poetics', Annette Kinder and I analyzed a corpus of over 400 literary and non-literary metaphors from dozens of authors including Shakespeare or Dylan Thomas using computational modelling.[42] Among others, we could confirm the above principle: in the over 200 poetic metaphors, five nouns were used five times or more as tenors: 'man', 'love', 'death', 'time' and 'life'. Five nouns were used four times or more as vehicles: 'winter', 'bird', 'tree', 'fire' and 'beauty'. In line with the principle, the vehicles were notably more concrete than the tenors: they had a mean concreteness value of 5.5 (on a scale from 1 to 7), tenors one of 3.5.

Tenet 2 allows me to extend standard models of language and text comprehension or literary reading to poetry processing without having to make a *category leap.* I can thus refer to basically the same processes used to simulate the reading of other fiction, while introducing some auxiliary assumptions necessary to deal with particularities of poetry reception. Such superadded constraints concern physical aspects like the typical graphic isolation and organization of poems on a page, as much as psycholinguistic aspects like rhythm, rhyme or metaphor, as well as sociocultural aspects of interpretive strategies derived from conventions. The NCPM considers the formal structures typically accompanying poetry (verse) to be neither a necessary nor a sufficient condition for poetic effects to emerge in readers' mindbrains. Rather, following up on reader response theories, it assumes a continuous multidimensional compound *poeticity scale* that goes from totally 'unliterary' (a phone book) to extremely literary (*Finnegan's Wake*) and takes reader features into account. Thus, even though it might seem trivial, it is worth mentioning that an a priori poetic text read by novices who exhibit all kinds of difficulties in approaching poetry could have no measurable poetic effects at all, while a certain Shakespeare sonnet, judged of minor quality by some expert, can have subtle poetic effects on another reader.

Tenet 3. Phonological Iconicity

> *A strictly arbitrary relation between the (implicit) sound and meaning of words is a myth. In both everyday language and verbal art motivated sound-meaning mappings involving structural resemblance, or natural association between signifier and signified, frequently occur.*

Tenet 3 submits that *iconicity* is not a negligible peripheral phenomenon, as assumed by de Saussure and many modern (psycho)linguistic theories which regard it as irrelevant to the understanding of language evolution, development or processing. Rather, as illustrated by the example poems in the *Poetics* section of my *Preface*, it is a powerful means for bridging the gap between language and human sensorimotor experience and is essential to jump-start the phylo- and ontogenetic development: it facilitates both *displacement* (the capability of language to communicate about things that are not immediately present) and *referentiality* (the mapping of linguistic labels to objects or events in the world during vocabulary development). Iconicity thus provides an additional mechanism to *Hebbian (correlational) learning* and, regarding language processing in later stages, consequently embodies language in experience by grounding it in our sensorimotor systems.[43]

In particular, the NCPM assumes that the sound of words is implicitly processed, even during silent reading, via a mechanism of *phonological recoding*. This refers to an automatic and generally subconscious activation of a printed word's sound in the brain prior to its identification. In many behavioural and Neurocomputational studies, my team has produced evidence for this mechanism, considered to be fundamental for the (affective) meaning of words, which operates as early as 150 ms after a word appears on a screen.[44] The 'iconicity' studies on the interplay between sound and meaning I report in Chapter 8 will show that, in general de Saussure's axiom of a totally arbitrary sound–meaning relationship is falsified.

Nested Structures

Following standards of cognitive and computational modelling introduced in previous work, I propose a nested, multilevel approach. Thus, the NCPM is embedded in *meta- and macromodels* and can itself embed several *micromodels*. The nested structure gives the model both *horizontal and vertical scope*. Horizontal scope refers to a model's ability to generalize across different stimulus sets (stimulus generality), different tasks (task generality) or response types or measures (response generality). Thus, the NCPM can predict the ratings or eye movements related to the comprehensibility or likeability of simple or complex texts in multiple tasks, from single word recognition to line marking or poem reading. Vertical scope refers to a model's ability to generalize across different scales of the modelled process: for example, the macrostructural static asymptotic behaviour – the directly observable end product of a process such as a response time vs. microstructural dynamics – the only indirectly measurable time-course of a process; or across different types or sizes of a processing structure, such as the size and density of the model's artificial semantic memory.

Metamodel: Situating NCPM in a Global Significative Network

The metamodel sketched in Figure 2.1 describes the system within which a *reading act* takes place and which determines its general conditions. Drawing on classic communication and semiotic models and applying them to written texts, the metamodel deals with the *significative network*. This describes the multiple relations and functions determining the meaning potential of a text and the reading act in the object–author–text–reader nexus. The quadruple relationship between the basic relational nodes of object, author, text and reader is complemented by the codes – the linguistic and other codes like readers' native language or culture – that determine their interpretation of a text as much as their world knowledge and personal experience.

Each major node in the network comes with a multitude of specifiable basic features and superfeatures. Thus, the object(s) of a text can be real or imaginary, more or less complex or have different degrees of novelty. The narrative or fiction potential of an object is regarded as a superfeature representing the

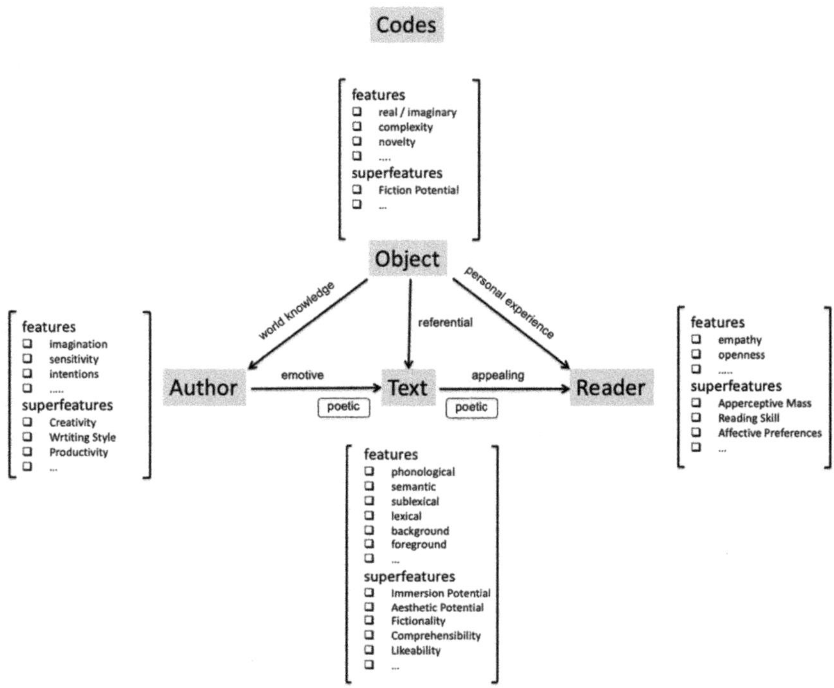

Figure 2.1 Metamodel: Significative Network describing the multiple relations and functions that determine the meaning potential of a text and the reading act in the object–author–text–reader nexus.

summed theoretical influence of many or all subordinate features. It specifies how well an object is suited to become the motif of a fictional narrative. Authors also have all kinds of features such as their degree of imagination, sensitivity, vocabulary and so on, adding up to superfeatures like creativity, writing style or productivity. The same holds for readers who can be more or less empathic or open to experience and whose superfeatures like *apperceptive mass* (this term highlights the integration of *world knowledge,* as for example acquired *via* reading books, into semantic memory[45]) or reading skill will co-determine how well they understand and like texts. The texts have quantifiable features of different types such as phonological or semantic, and, at different levels, such as the sublexical or lexical levels. Some serve as background, others as foreground, and all influence superfeatures like immersion potential, comprehensibility or likeability. A comprehensive list of these features is discussed in Chapter 3. Finally, the codes also have innumerable features not specified in Figure 2.1, such as cultural conventions. In principle, all features of each node in the network can dynamically and nonlinearly interact with each other and those of other nodes in shaping a reading act.

This makes predicting their effects on readers' brain activity, experience and behaviour so challenging.

At a higher level of abstraction than the feature interactions, the relations between these nodes are governed by several functions, four of which are specified in the metamodel. The referential or *representational function* concerns the relation between a text (sign) and the object(s) it refers to, providing information about the world. This information is used to construct a mental situation model of the text world with its main dimensions mentioned earlier: space, time, cause, object, character and goal. As exemplified in Chapter 3 with various texts, an author can make situation model building easy or difficult by creatively playing with background and foreground features, thus shaping the immersion and aesthetic potential of the text.

The referential function is complemented by three others. The expressive or *emotive function* concerns the relation between author and reader. It adds information about the author's internal state, as presumably in Wordsworth's famous 'I wander'd lonely as a cloud'. More generally, this function can be considered to emphasize author's – or their character's – attitude towards the content of a text as signalled by emphatic speech, interjections or emotion-laden text passages of free indirect speech, inner life or dialogue. The *appealing function* (sometimes called conative) adds a prompting, requesting aspect to the text. More generally, it can be considered to refer to those aspects of texts which aim to create a certain response in the reader. Finally, Jakobson's celebrated *poetic function* draws a reader's attention to the form(ing) of the text, the basis for foregrounding by stylistic devices. The metamodel views the global meaning of a text as resulting from the interplay of all elements and relationships of this interpretive network.

The *cognitive* aspect of the metamodel considers reading literary texts in general as an act of problem-solving which requires all kinds of reasoning (inductive, abductive, deductive, analogical, blending). Since no text can ever make explicit all presuppositions necessary to understand it, readers' interpretation of literature must be based on inference (and imagination) from what is not stated but supposed to be implied in the text. Readers who engage with a text (re-)construct not only a literal representation of the story, but also enriched situation models that include multi-layered, interpretive inferences. In doing so, they attempt to *re-enact* the text states designed by the author and to implicitly or explicitly reconstruct the author's stylistic modifications of normal language use. In a sense, readers translate the text or parts of it into their critical idiom. The double indeterminacy (i) between text and reader; and (ii) text and reality characteristic for fiction, the polyfunctionality of the text in interaction with the polyvalence of the recipient, the polysemantic possibilities and open meaning–gestalts of a literary text, the ubiquitous many-to-many correspondence between form and function (or word and object), dubbed the *proteus principle*, the connotative density and wealth of associations, they all require additional information to solve interpretative challenges or difficulties.[46] Apart from translation, readers need to use all kinds of contextualization, mainly based on the world knowledge condensed in their apperceptive mass, to overcome and enjoy interpretive difficulties with literary texts.

The *affective* aspect of the metamodel puts the emphasis on a process of *ludic reading*, on learning and enjoyment through discovering new meanings that offer the promise of novel insights: enjoying word plays, sounds and rhythms, self-rewarding feelings of curiosity or surprise and (vicarious) joy or sadness (cf. Tenet 1). Such joyful or enlightening encounters with literature are likely to be rooted in early life experiences with micropoetry. Regarding these cognitive and affective aspects, a text's corresponding superfeatures *comprehensibility* and *likeability* emerge from a dynamical interaction between basic text features and the reading skills, apperceptive masses and affective preferences of its readers. Both aspects, cognitive and affective, are not fully independent of each other, though. Just as problem-solving in general has a ludic component with potentially rewarding outcomes, liking a text which cannot be understood at all is rather improbable. Although the proper function relating text likeability to comprehensibility is still unknown, in Chapter 4 I will present data suggesting that it surely is a nonlinear one.

Neurocomputational methods do not easily lend themselves to testing the metamodel, but linking the better testable parts of the NCPM, that is, the *mesomodel*, to the phenomenological, semiotic and linguistic literature reflected in the metamodel aims at protecting them from the often-advanced criticism of undercomplexity or irrelevance. Specificity and generality are both important criteria for evaluating psychological models and theories in general. Here, I attempt to find a compromise, being faithful to the maxim of cross-fertilization or creative blending between neuroscience and (empirical) studies of literature. The next nested level, the *macromodel*, continues this integrative effort.

Macromodel: Situating NCPM in the Reading Cycle

The macromodel describes processes that go beyond the proper reading act of a text, including pre- and post-reading phases. Michael Burke's theoretical framework of literary reading, cognition and emotion provides an adequate basis for the macromodel.[47] The theory assumes that literary reading does not begin when the gaze scans the words on a page or end when it stops; rather, the mind, brain and body are actively 'reading' both before and after the physical act of literary text processing starts and finishes. It posits a sequence of stages that precede, include and follow a literary reading act organized in a 'literary reading loop' that is captured in the four interconnected stages of pre-reading, actual reading, post-reading and non-reading. Most interestingly, the theory compares reading a book with making oneself part of an oceanic wave: 'readers mingle, like the waters of a growing wave, with the text they read and, as the story progresses, the wave rises with a gathering tension until at last it break', and, at the moment of closure, the tension is released in an epiphany, sometimes accompanied by 'a felt motionless movement through space' termed *disportation*. Even though the apparent object of this framework is the reading of prose consisting of entire books, one can adapt it to the reading of smaller units like chapters or poems.

The seven stages, two preceding, two following and three accompanying the reading act, can be generalized to poetry reading without any significant revision. Since only stages three to five lend themselves naturally to neurocomputational investigations, the focus here will be on them. Of course, the other stages can also be examined by empirical research using direct online or offline methods, such as verbal protocols, interviews or questionnaires discussed in detail in Chapter 4.

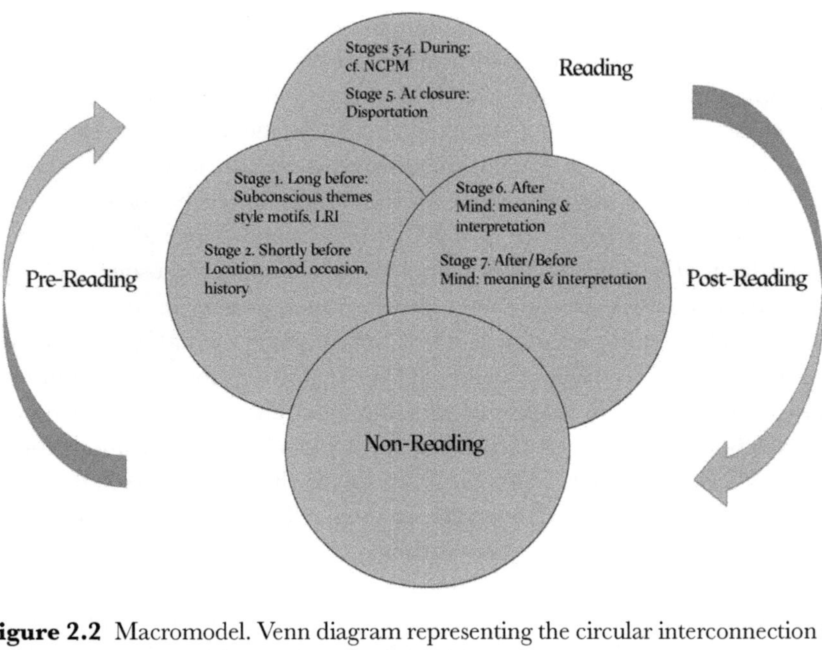

Figure 2.2 Macromodel. Venn diagram representing the circular interconnection of seven reading stages. Adapted from Burke, 2011.

Stage 1. Previous reading episodes leave their traces in readers' semantic memory. This stores themes as well as style motifs and what Burke calls LRI, *Literary Reading-induced mental Imagery*. The idea of longing for style figures like metaphors, amazing rhymes or functional shifts being a hallmark of some author or genre is a matter of desire, and for some readers even can become addictive. Repeated literary reading generates a sensitivity for such textual patterns and those, when recognized, can induce increased enjoyment, much like children enjoy recognizing a known rhyme pattern. Regarding LRIs, ask yourself how you mentally pictured Harry Potter or Juliet before seeing any movie or theatre play. How do you imagine the Eiffel Tower or the Sphinx when reading about them? How do you mentally visualize a kiss[48] mentioned in a poem or the marvellous image 'wandering lonely as a cloud'? Burke, like others before him, maintains that mental imagery is a central component of literary reading. Furthermore, literary scholars have long recognized the optical poverty of images during literary reading, being indistinct and fragmented rather than clear and vivid. Indeed, if humans experienced picture-like images during reading, this would be cognitively too costly to be an effective reading strategy. Explicit imagery takes a lot of time for the cognitive system, and is generally much slower than the speed at which we read. In a direct comparison, it was shown that responses in cortical motor areas during explicit motor imagery, and during reading of action verbs, could be dissociated, suggesting different neural and cognitive computations.[49] Thus, we should conceptually distinguish between implicit mental simulation or LRI and explicit, deliberate mental imagery. Anyway, the nature of the images evoked during literary reading is still unclear, as are questions of how exactly they influence our reading experience, and how they impact appreciation and memory for narratives.[50]

An important avenue for future research is to add to our understanding of the impact of our propensity for simulation on our fiction experience, for example, the dependence of LRI simulation on personal experiences. In his classic *The Poetics of Space* from 1958, the French philosopher Gaston Bachelard contends that childhood locations such as interior locations from the home play an important role when building our mental models of new situations encountered during reading. One hypothesis the author submits is that this has to do with readers comforting themselves by reliving memories of protection, a basic need in psychological models of human motivations. One prediction naturally following from this is that, since personal experiences differ, readers will differ greatly in their reliance on and preference for mental simulation during literary reading.

Stages 2–4. see *mesomodel* below.

Stage 5. Disportation is Burke's term – connotating movement and affect – for an embodied affective-cognitive shift from one state (tension) to another heightened emotive state (release). It is his example for literary *epiphany* or, in his words: 'When endorphins flood the synapses, a reader is overwhelmed by intense emotion, and experiences a sense of rapid rising and forward movement followed by a gentle felt sense of slowing and descending'. As an example, Burke offers an extensive cognitive stylistic analysis of the last paragraph of F. Scott Fitzgerald's *The Great Gatsby* that fills an entire chapter and that I cannot reiterate here. Suffice it to say that, as regards the NCPM, I consider Burke's stage 5 as a special extreme case of tension building towards a sense of release; a general phenomenon often reported by readers during or at the end of the reading act. In the NCPM, it is part of the aesthetic trajectory characteristic for feelings of beauty described later in the mesomodel section.

Stages 6–7. As mentioned in Burke's book, F. Scott Fitzgerald once wrote to Ernest Hemingway that 'the purpose of a work of fiction is to appeal to the lingering after-effects in the reader's mind'. According to Burke, the after-effects are often a blend between five affective inputs that have emoted readers during past literary episodes and linger in their minds recurrently, being interpreted and scrutinized for meaning and, by doing so, influencing the meaning-making of present and future events. These are themes, location, style, LRI and mood, the last and most important of all. As a justification of these inputs as being 'affective', Burke lists the following arguments:

- personal fragmentary remembrances of LRI
- preparatory excitement and projection of mood
- somatic pleasures of location like memories of colours, smells and so on.
- sentimental, cultural universals of themes, such as love and hate, good against evil or life and death
- the pleasurable balance and rhythm and the breaking thereof in style.

To what extent each of these inputs also has a cognitive component is a question whose answer depends on the psychological emotion theory one adheres to. In one of my favourite simpler theories – more than 100 emotion theories make emotion psychology an awkward business – the *belief–desire theory* of emotion,[51] each emotion is the product of cognitions (beliefs) and motives (desires). Thus, there can be no emotion without cognition. Whether an event induces an emotional response, and if so which one, depends on what a person desires and believes. For example, a reader may desire that Harry Potter's team wins the quidditch game but believe that this is uncertain. The corresponding emotion, according to this theory, would be hope. Or, if a reader desired that Voldemort does not kill Harry in the end and believed this to be certain (perhaps because 'happy ends' dominate children and youth literature), the resulting emotion would be vicarious or real joy. Applying this theory to the second of the above five 'affective' inputs, one could assume that a reader desires to experience the same or a similar mood when reading 'Emma' as during the reading of *Pride and Prejudice*. And being certain of that, the reader will likely be in a positive mood or feel anticipatory joy or happiness. Thus, in terms of the belief–desire theory, the after-effects of a literary reading act involve both cognitive and affective components. The same holds for the pre-reading stage when readers desire, for instance, to enjoy another love theme or some particular style figures such as Joyce's chiasm (*'faintly falling, [...] falling faintly'*) or functional shift ('he was *wived* to a kind and beautiful woman') when reading the next poem by their preferred author.

In summary, Burke's oceanic wave theory provides a macroanalytic framework for the following mesomodel that helps to describe effects of literature happening before and after the reading act. Empirically, very little is known about the pre- and post-reading stages, and Burke's study on 20 Dutch readers of *The Great Gatsby* using his novel reading questionnaire is a praiseworthy, valiant exception. The next section introduces the *mesomodel* corresponding to stages 2–4 in the *macromodel.*

Mesomodel

'There is nothing more practical than a good theory

—Kurt Lewin

The mesomodel sketched in Figure 2.3 describes key elements and processes that occur during the reading of a literary text at the neuronal, affective-cognitive, and behavioural levels; only the latter is directly observable. The model belongs to the family of 'boxological', prequantitative dual-route models, which is popular in cognitive psychology. Its hypothetical boxes such as 'implicit' and 'explicit processing' are neither to be understood as mutually exclusive, nor as static. Rather, they stand for partially overlapping, non-linear dynamic subsystems which ultimately have to be simulated in the form of neural network models, such as those my friend and colleague from University Aix-Marseille, Jonathan Grainger, and I have developed for single word recognition[52] (see later micromodels section). However, such systems cannot easily be represented graphically, hence this simplified flow chart here as a broad orientation help. The mesomodel focusses on online aspects of literary reading.

In a nutshell, the model hypothesizes a dual-route processing of literary texts. The first, depicted in the upper half of Figure 2.3 (upper panel: blue background and blue boxes), is a fast, automatic route for implicit text processing dominantly – but not exclusively – operative during the reading of prose or any text in which background elements are much more likely than

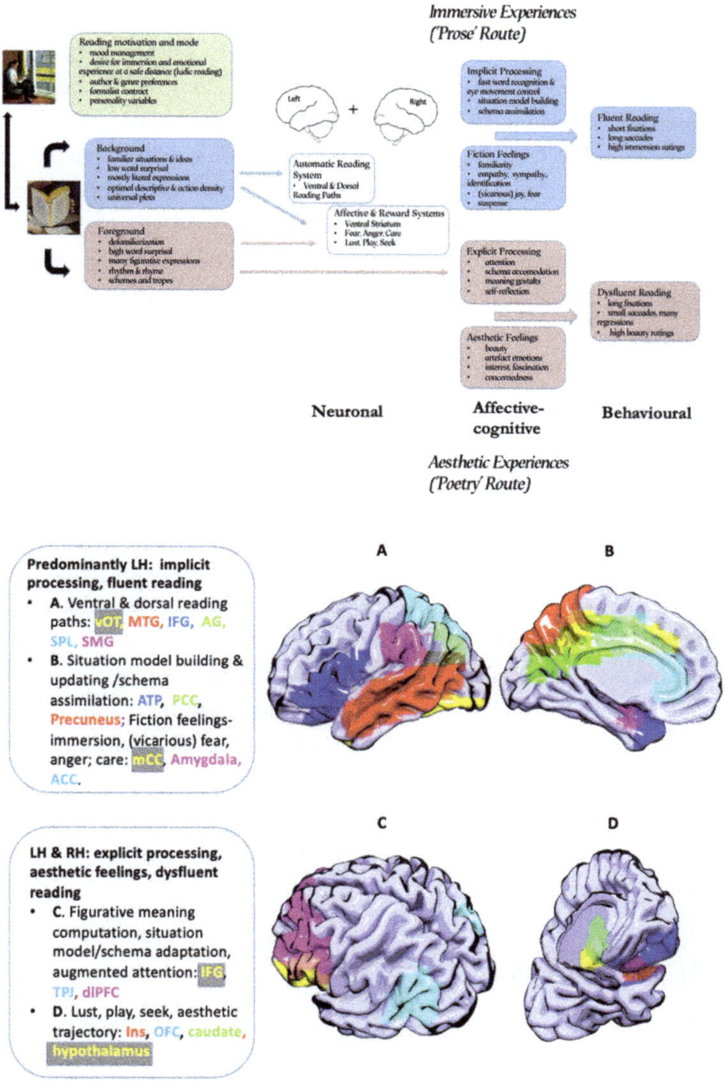

Figure 2.3 Upper panel. Mesomodel, detailed version. **Lower panel**. 'Neuronal model'. A–D. Main neural correlates of subprocesses involved in implicit and explicit fiction processing, for example, situation model building, immersion or aesthetic appreciation. Some of these structures are included in networks, in particular: the *default mode network* sometimes also called 'empathy network' (PCC, *dmPFC*, ATP) nodes, the *working memory network* (dlPFC, superior and posterior parietal nodes) and the *salience network* (putamen, left dorsal caudate nucleus). **Abbreviations**: LH = Left hemisphere; RH = right hemisphere; vOT = ventral occipito-temporal cortex; MTG = medial temporal gyrus; IFG = inferior frontal gyrus; AG = angular gyrus; SPL = superior parietal lobules; SMG = supramarginal gyrus; ATP = anterior temporal pole; A/PmCC = anterior/posterior/medial cingulate cortex; TPJ = temporo-parietal junction; dl/mPFC = dorsolateral/dorsomedial prefrontal cortex; Ins = Insula; OFC = orbitofrontal cortex.

foreground elements. Those elements, like familiar words with low surprisal values, or familiar locations known from experience of other media (pictures, movies) inform readers about the facts of a story. They allow them to easily build up and update situation models and thus make meaning out of the series of events described in the sentences. When embedded in appropriate plots or narrative structures such as the universal suspense or curiosity schemes supported by an optimal ratio of descriptive and action density, as well as 'what happens next' or 'whodunit' moments, those elements facilitate immersion, the experiencing of narrative or fiction feelings, for example, sympathy, suspense or vicarious fear and hope, and finally easy meaning making.

The second, slow route depicted in the lower half of Figure 2.3 (upper panel: red background and red boxes) is dominantly activated during the reading of poetic texts characterized by a low ratio of background to foreground elements. As hypothesized in Jakobson's 'poetic function', foreground elements such as rhyme or metaphor attract readers' attention to formal text aspects and evoke a braking or even momentary stopping of the fluent reading process. This is often reflected by gaze refixations (regressions), due to difficult meaning-making with open-meaning gestalts which can start processes of self-reflection or the three-phase aesthetic trajectory characteristic for feelings of beauty mentioned earlier: (i) familiar (partial) recognition, (ii) surprise, ambiguity and tension, (iii) closure of meaning gestalts and tension. The third phase results from processes of integration and synthesis, occasionally supplemented by an 'aha' experience or feeling of good fit, rightness or harmony motivating one to continue to read even texts hard to comprehend.

I will now discuss the contents of the boxes of the mesomodel in the upper panel of Figure 2.3.

Reading Motivation and Mode

Any reading act can be understood as goal-directed behaviour, for the most variable reasons. Information seeking and instruction, curiosity, distraction and escapism or ludic reading and mood management, are only some of them. People indeed very often choose novels and poems to spend pleasurable moments or find solace, sometimes driven by the desire to forget the world around them or to change their mood by experiencing emotions at a safe distance. There are extreme examples for the power of literature. Thus, I will never forget how a former prisoner of a Nazi concentration camp told me at a reception in Paris that only the silent recitation of poetry saved her life. There are also numerous testimonies of soldiers who found consolation in the trenches of Verdun reading Baudelaire or Goethe. Still, mostly people do their ludic reading at home in a comfortable environment facilitating immersion and aesthetic pleasure. Ludic reading of literature also has desirable side effects: it offers countless learning opportunities for mentally simulating the social world and thus fosters the understanding of social information and the development of intellectual and emotional competencies.

Furthermore, people have reading habits. More often than not, their choice of a text is guided by personal preferences for authors, genres or time periods. Literary genres and text types such as fairy tales, short stories, novellas, novels or poetry, act on what David Miall and Don Kuiken have termed the *formalist contract*: 'A reader taking up a literary text thus makes several related commitments that guide the act of reading'.[53] The four components of this contract are:

- The bounded text. Readers treat the text as a whole thing, bounded and complexly interconnected.
- Communicative intent. Readers know that some new understanding can be acquired from the text – not necessarily in perfect concord with a reader's opinions. They know that the act of reading can in itself be made creative by the encounter with the text. I guess they usually see this (risky) business as a chance.
- The openness of reading. Foregrounding in the text arouses memories, feelings, a sense of self, a sense of empathy and so on, which the reader places at the disposal of the reshaping functions of the text. Thus, readings will vary, often in major ways, between individuals from the same community. Literary reading is fundamentally personal and private.
- The adaptive function of literature (cf. Tenet 1). The primary function of literary reading is to equip readers to better understand and respond to the environment. Literature can do this by invoking and reshaping people's feelings 'offline', that is, in isolation from behaviours and actions in the everyday world that have real consequences.

The last three of these components depend on personality variables such as extraversion, openness to experience or conscientiousness that can be assessed by personality inventories like the 'big5', which I will discuss in more detail in Chapter 4. As an example, empirical studies have shown that readers with high openness scores prefer reading philosophical novels, science fiction or plays, while highly conscientious readers seem to like religious and mystery books. To summarize, in the mesomodel I assume that competent readers use their experience, knowledge and motivations to make text choices and accordingly take a reading perspective which co-determines their reading mode and behaviour. This introduces a bias in favour of one of the two routes. If the hierarchical, nested effects of para- and metatextual factors bias a reader to choose a poem, selecting a subgenre of poetry, such as narrative, lyric or mood poetry also can significantly alter his or her responses with regard to other subgenres. Thus, responses to a narrative ballad like Coleridge's 'The Rime of the Ancient Mariner' will resemble those elicited by a novel more than responses to highly abstract modernist poetry such as Quasimodo's 'And suddenly it's evening'.

Background and Foreground

Once a genre and author choice has been made and the reader starts to move his or her eyes across the pages, the main goal of the reading act is meaning construction; just as in general language use where the standard expectation is one of meaning constancy (same meanings in same contexts). Like people in a communicative act, readers have a need for meaning and they strive for meaning-making. A text offers *meaning gestalts* – often in the form of ambiguous figures – that a reader can resolve or close more or less well on the basis of the text's potential and individual capabilities. By definition, literary meaning gestalts are open to many different closures or interpretations. Much as perceptual gestalts, ambiguous figures or visual illusions, they can trigger feelings of tension or even suspense which ask for a solution according to the principle of a good gestalt mentioned earlier.

A central question of the Neurocomputational Poetics perspective is: What are the text features that shape this self-rewarding activity of meaning making? A vast literature on this issue exists, produced by formalists and structuralists, reception-aesthetic and linguistic works on poetics and hermeneutics and, of course, essays and empirical reports on cognitive poetics.[54] Whereas most of this literature deals with the notion of foregrounding, that is, defamiliarization or alienation effects evoked by stylistic devices such as metaphor, ellipse or oxymoron, relatively little has been said about backgrounding: the elements of a text that create a feeling of familiarity in the reader. Without these elements, there can be no foregrounding. Any literary text thus contains both back- and foreground elements and a sometimes-tense relation between them, inspired by the gestalt-psychological notion of figure-ground. According to Iser, this tension is created by the fact that the background of a text, includes the repertoire of familiar literary patterns and recurrent literary themes and allusions to familiar social and historical contexts which, however, inevitably conflict with certain textual elements that defamiliarize what the reader thought he recognized, leading to a distrust of the expectations aroused and a reconsideration of seemingly straightforward discrepancies that are unwilling to accommodate themselves to these patterns.[55]

Thus, background elements include those conventions that are necessary for situation model building like common schemata or scripts, and perhaps all that structuralists have termed 'extratextual reality'. Iser calls it the *primary code* of a text which provides the necessary ground for the creation of a *secondary code*, the deciphering of which brings about the aesthetic pleasure assumed to be mainly associated with the lower route of the NCPM. Without this background, the foregrounding features aiming at 'making the familiar strange' would not work. Naturally, the concoction of back- and foreground elements differs across texts, genres or authors. It is also safe to say that not every accumulation of foregrounding devices such as rhyme, metaphor or ellipse necessarily produces foregrounding effects. What produces back- or foregrounding effects is, after all, an empirical question. The NCPM presents a conceptual help in that it sets a framework within which to predict and interpret such effects. An example is the model of processing rhetorical figures discussed later in this chapter.

To specify in greater detail what I described in a nutshell above, the NCPM's central hypothesis distinguishes background effects from foreground effects at all three levels of description. In its simplest (categorical) version, the model postulates that texts full of background elements

- are implicitly processed mainly by the brain's left-hemispheric reading network along the dorsal and ventral paths;
- evoke non-aesthetic fiction feelings such as (vicarious) joy or fear; and
- are characterized by fluent reading, that is high words per minute (*wpm*) rates like, say, 250 *wpm* and more or higher immersion ratings.

In turn, texts full of foreground elements

- are explicitly processed, involving more right-hemispheric networks;
- likely produces aesthetic feelings; and
- a slower reading rate with many backward saccades (regressions), and more or higher beauty ratings.

Reading texts with mainly background elements is hypothesized to facilitate immersive processes, while reading those with lots of foregrounding devices likely produces aesthetic feelings. As a starting point, this 'black and white' version has the merit of being easily falsified by the hopefully increasing number of neurocomputational studies on verbal art reception.

Effects of Background Elements

At the neuronal level, the effortless functioning of the strongly lateralized left-hemispheric reading system described in numerous neuroscientific studies[56] provides the conditions for more complex processes of inference, interpretation and comprehension which involve right-hemispheric networks. This usually highly automatized system – exceptions are certain neurodiverse readers (formerly called 'dyslexic') – includes the dorsal and ventral paths with the ventral occipito-temporal cortex (vOT, yellow in Figure 2.3A, lower panel), the medial temporal gyrus (MTG, bright red in Figure 2.3A), the left inferior frontal gyrus (LIFG, dark blue in Figure 2.3A), the angular gyrus (AG, light green in Figure 2.3A), the superior parietal lobules (SPL, light blue in Figure 2.3A) and the supramarginal gyrus (SMG, magenta in Figure 2.3A).

Another key brain area for reading texts full of background and for the creation of a coherent representation of a story is the anterior temporal pole (aTP, bright blue in Figure 2.3B) associated with situation model building and updating, as well as schema assimilation when readers relate new information in the text to old cognitive structures (schemas). Furthermore, the posterior cingulate cortex (PCC, light green in Figure 2.3B), the ventral precuneus (bright red in Figure 2.3B), the dorso-medial prefrontal cortex (dmPFC, not highlighted in Figure 2.3), and the aTP serve the 'theory of mind/*ToM*' network operating when readers take the *protagonist perspective* and, more generally, try to empathize with characters. While the dmPFC seems to serve as a monitor, an executive processor activating throughout the processing of a narrative, the aTP serves as a simulator, a processor whose role may be to actively generate expectations of events based on an understanding of the intentions of the protagonist. The anterior and medial cingulate cortex (ACC, light blue, and mCC yellow in Figure 2.5B), as well as the amygdala (AMY, magenta in Figure 2.5B) play a role in fiction feelings when readers experience vicarious joy or fear. Of particular interest is the mCC because at least one study, described in Chapter 7, has obtained evidence that it might be the neuronal correlate of feelings of immersion.[57] Of course, cognitive neuroscience is only beginning to understand the complex connectivities between brain regions and networks involved in literary reading and the NCPM's neuronal hypotheses therefore still are somewhat speculative.

When we zoom into the experiential, affective-cognitive level, the model's upper route describes mainly implicit word and text processing, as specified by numerous cognitive models of word recognition, eye movement control or situation model building and text comprehension. Some of them exist in a computational form and might be implemented in a future computational version of this model, in particular the Associative *Multiple Read-Out Model* (AROM) of word recognition[58] discussed in the micromodels section below. Apart from the assumption of multidimensional situation model building, the NCPM also hypothesizes that readers create 'event gestalts' by segmenting a story into discrete events. This process is a spontaneous part of reading which depends on neuronal responses to changes in narrative situations associated with the PCC and precuneus regions.

At the affective level, background elements go together with a feeling of familiarity accompanying the recognition of known items. This is assumed to be of positive valence and low to middle arousal. The NCPM hypothesizes that background elements are processed in a configurational mode evoking non-aesthetic, bodily feelings of stability and autobiographical emotions related to memories about events similar to those read about, like fear or joy. Some authors speak of narrative emotions or *fiction feelings*, like sympathy or empathy for narrative figures, and resonance with the mood of a scene.[59]

Immersion and Suspense

As discussed in Chapter 1, the phenomenon that people become emotionally involved, or carried away imaginatively, in fiction is multifaceted, conceptually far from being unified, and difficult to measure empirically – be it with behavioural or neurocognitive methods. In accordance with media-psychological studies, the model assumes that immersion is strongly related to suspense. A suspense discourse organization involves an initiating event or situation which could lead to significant consequences, either good or bad, for one of the characters in the narrative. Ultimately, the event structure must also contain the outcome of the initiating event to allow for the resolution of the reader's suspense.[60] I tentatively assume that the ancient core affect systems FEAR, ANGER or CARE common to all mammals, as described in Jaak Panksepp's aforementioned emotion theory, are involved in this suspense-building process; when a reader, for instance, experiences suspense through vicarious fear, because a protagonist she cares for is in danger, especially if this danger is only known to the reader. In any case, several empirical studies discussed in Chapter 7 show a strong correlation between immersion and suspense ratings ($r = .96$).[61] Not surprisingly, immersion was also highly correlated with the rated amount of action in the story ($r = .95$). Interestingly, several authors claim that there is an optimum of descriptive and/or action density for eliciting immersion: descriptive over-specification or too many, not evenly distributed references to transitive bodily movements can be detrimental to immersive experience.[62]

Immersion, Empathy and Identification

Besides feelings of familiarity, tension or suspense, the identification of the reader with the protagonist or other characters of a novel through empathy is assumed to facilitate immersive processes. There is a vast literature on various kinds of identification processes in media reception,[63] but here I focus on the role of empathy when reading short stories, because there is an abundant neuroscientifc literature on it including some work of my team (see

Chapter 7). The term actually is sort of a misnomer. In 1900, Theodor Lipps made the German word *Einfühlung* the key notion of his aesthetic theory and 10 years later, the American psychologist Edward Titchener translated this as *empathy*, meaning to preserve the idea of the self-projected into the perceived object. With respect to reading, the hypothesis that reader and text qualitatively coalesce through empathy, that is, the impression that the text is alive, full of energy and force, is derived from Lipps' theory. This feeling is considered a sort of 'depletion of the self into fiction' through embodied, that is, kinaesthetic mimetic, affective immersion. Like many others in psychology, empathy is a somewhat fuzzy multidimensional construct, as evidenced by the view that the two questions empathy is supposed to answer are related 'to eight distinct phenomena that all have been called empathy' including projection, or perspective taking.[64] Empathy has been described as a 'way of knowing' to contrast it with sympathy as 'a way of relating'[65] and one can further make a distinction between cognitive and affective empathy on grounds of their association with distinct brain areas. Whereas cognitive empathy can be equated with affective ToM, that is, with mentalizing the emotions of others, affective empathy is about *sharing* emotions with others. Cognitive empathy involves the ventro-medial prefrontal cortex (vmPFC), and affective empathy the anterior insula (aI, red in Figure 2.3D), mCC (yellow in Figure 2.3B), AMY (magenta in Figure 2.3B), secondary somatosensory cortex (SII, not highlighted in Figure 2.3 lower panel), and inferior frontal gyrus (IFG, yellow in Figure 2.3C).

According to my colleague from Humboldt University Berlin, Henrik Walter, a rich concept of affective empathy is characterized by the following features.[66] It is

- an affective state that is
- elicited by the perceived, imagined or inferred state of the affective state of another,
- is similar (isomorphic) to the other's affective state,
- is oriented towards the other,
- includes at least some cognitive appreciation of the other's affective state comprising perspective taking, self–other distinction and knowledge of the causal relation between the self and the other's affective state.

This feature-based characterization allows us to tentatively distinguish between sympathetic and cognitive vs. affective empathic responses to a story's characters. Thus, affective empathy is supposed to share more features with sympathy than with cognitive empathy, for example, affective experience. In Chapter 6, I will discuss the issue of personality traits of characters:

perceived similarity between a character and a reader, for example, when both supposedly share a trait like conscientiousness or extraversion, increases empathy and identification – the process when readers psychologically merge with the character, adopt the character's position within the story and vicariously experience the fictional world through that particular character.

Just like empathy, identification is a complex multifaceted construct for which many authors have proposed many different definitions and I will not reiterate them here. Suffice it to say that in the NCPM I assume that identification requires affective empathy: 'experience taking' rather than just 'perspective taking'. Some key factors shaping identification are perceived character-reader similarity (similar traits, locations, experiences, preferences etc.), character virtue (usually virtuous and morally sound characters with sympathetic features evoke stronger identification), narrator perspective (first-person perspective is supposed to increase identification likelihood) and richness of the mental event description (more detailed descriptions facilitate mentalizing and identification). However, research suggests that even minor and stereotypical and also controversial characters (hybrid heroes) can elicit identification. And who can tell whether there are no readers who identify at least partially with Voldemort? While the last word on exactly which text features most efficiently evoke affective empathy and identification has not been said yet, what matters for the NCPM is the assumption that both facilitate immersive experiences, although they are neither necessary nor sufficient.

A study from my lab examined the potential of a set of quantifiable text features to induce immersion during the reading of a suspenseful text (E. T. A. Hoffmann's *The Sandman*). Among them were simple word-based (*lexical*) features like valence, arousal or imageability, more complex *interlexical* features concerning the relation between two or more words like the arousal span (the difference between the words with the lowest and highest arousal value in a text part), but also *supralexical* features concerning the narrative structure like the proportion of text parts describing the inner life vs. those with a high action density. The overall best predictors of higher immersion ratings were word imageability, arousal span and action density. Generalizing this result would suggest that, all other things being equal, texts with (i) a lot of verbs describing actions, (ii) many concrete, easy-to-imagine nouns, and (iii) adjectives that cover a wide range of arousal values from very calming to very exciting, have a high immersion potential. Depending on the text's homogeneity, the frequency, duration or intensity of such effects can be countered by foreground elements.

An interesting 'empathy scale' for fiction processing based on cognitive grammar has been proposed by Peter Stockwell.[67] It includes not only persons but also objects and predicts the following rank order of 'empathic attraction': abstractions < landscape objects < immovable objects < human-scale objects < machines < plants < animals < groups < ill-defined individuals < specific persons. Earlier elements in the scale can take on attractive and person-like qualities by stylistic devices like personification and anthropomorphization. Thus, as can be expected, maximum empathy of readers will concern specific persons, but in principle they can also empathize with animals or landscapes, just as in Lipp's original conception. Testing the psychological reality and empirical validity of such a scale would be an interesting task for future studies.

Effects of Foreground Elements

Regarding the neuronal level, pioneering studies in the 1980s[68] provided first evidence for brain-electrical effects of semantic deviations in simple isolated non-literary sentences like 'He shaved off his moustache and city' – which are one simple possibility of foregrounding by defamiliarization. A few more recent neuroimaging studies from my lab discussed in detail in Chapter 8 demonstrated that the degree of affective involvement elicited by foregrounding depends on the type of defamiliarization: enhanced activation in affect-related regions (orbito-frontal cortex/OFC, light blue in Figure 2.3D lower panel; and mPFC) was found only if the defamiliarization altered the content of the expressions (in our case German proverbs).[69] In contrast, when the original proverb's wording was changed but not its meaning (original proverb: 'Who dares, wins' vs. defamiliarized; altered content: Who asks, wins' vs. defamiliarized, same content: Who risks, wins') the brain's 'pleasure centre' did not light up. Another neuroimaging study using sentences featuring functional shifts mentioned earlier, showed that those produced significant brain activation beyond regions activated by typical language tasks.[70] These included the left caudate nucleus (green in Figure 2.3D) which is part of the brain's reward system, as well as the inferior frontal and temporal gyri (IFG, ITG) of the right hemisphere.

The involvement of the theoretically 'mute' right hemisphere in this study supports the NCPM's assumption that figurative language processing in the lower route more likely recruits right-hemispheric networks than the mainly literal language processing in the upper route. Apart from the IFG (yellow in Figure 2.3C), the model also assumes involvement of the temporo-parietal junction (TPJ, light blue in Figure 2.3C), as well as the dlPFC (magenta in Figure 2.3C) in figurative meaning computation and schema accommodation – when new schemas are created, the old ones not being able to assimilate the text's creative elements. When foregrounding evokes aesthetic feelings, the NCPM assumes activation in the ancient LUST, PLAY and SEEK circuits described in Panksepp's theory including the insula (INS, red in Figure 2.3D), OFC (blue in Figure 2.3D), caudate nucleus (green in Figure 2.3D) and hypothalamus (yellow in Figure 2.3D).

At the affective-cognitive level, the model integrates standard assumptions on foregrounding effects such as schema accommodation or feelings of concernedness. It also highlights the aesthetic trajectory hypothesis mentioned earlier. Note, however, that there can be a constant oscillation, integral to the aesthetic experience in reading, between illusion-formation and revision, frustration and surprise. For some authors, the *sine qua non* of the aesthetic experience is the non-achievement of a 'final reading'. Thus, in the model I assume the third phase of the aesthetic trajectory (closure of meaning gestalts and tension) is never really completed, but always open to new interpretations and reflections during re-reading. Indeed, poetry, being the perhaps most challenging kind of fiction, can reveal new layers of meaning at each and every backward eye movement or rereading act.

Graphic Form

At the surface level, the distinctive graphic form of many poems on a page of print or screen will produce a special *perception-attention space for* and *in* the reader. Compared to prose, this space is smaller, well-structured and offers linguistic information ideally packaged for readers' working memory. The metred 10–12 syllables per line distributed across 6–10 words take 2–3 seconds to be pronounced (around 30–50 seconds of reading time for the roughly 110 words of an entire sonnet). They make a sonnet line a cultural quasi-universal.

Les Chats

Les amoureux fervents et les savants austères
Aiment également, dans leur mûre saison,
Les chats puissants et doux, orgueil de la maison,
Qui comme eux sont frileux et comme eux sédentaires.
Amis de la science et de la volupté,
Ils cherchent le silence et l'horreur des ténèbres;
L'Erèbe les eût pris pour ses coursiers funèbres,
S'ils pouvaient au servage incliner leur fierté.
Ils prennent en songeant les nobles attitudes
Des grands sphinx allongés au fond des solitudes
Qui semblent s'endormir dans un rêve sans fin;
Leurs reins féconds sont pleins d'étincelles magiques
Et des parcelles d'or, ainsi qu'un sable fin,
Étoilent vaguement leurs prunelles mystiques.

The Cats (Translation of the French original 'Les Chats' by Charles Baudelairee[iii])

'They are alike, prim scholar and perfervid lover:
When comes the season of decay, they both decide
Upon sweet, husky cats to be the household pride;
Cats choose, like them, to sit, and like them, shudder.
Like partisans of carnal dalliance and science,
They search for silence and the shadowings of dread;
Hell well might harness them as horses for the dead,
If it could bend their native proudness in compliance.
In reverie they emulate the noble mood
Of giant sphinxes stretched in depths of solitude
Who seem to slumber in a never-ending dream;
Within their fertile loins a sparkling magic lies;
Finer than any sand are dusts of gold that gleam,
Vague starpoints, in the mystic iris of their eyes.'

'They are alike, prim scholar and perfervid lover: When comes the season of decay, they both decide. Upon sweet, husky cats to be the household pride; Cats choose, like them, to sit, and like them, shudder. Like partisans of carnal dalliance and science, they search for silence and the shadowings of dread; hell well might harness them as horses for the dead, if it could bend their native proudness in compliance. In reverie they emulate the noble mood off giant sphinxes stretched in depths of solitude who seem to slumber in a never-ending dream; within their fertile loins a sparkling magic lies; finer than any sand are dusts of gold that gleam, vague starpoints, in the mystic iris of their eyes'.

If the poem were presented in the prose format above instead of in its canonical 4+4+4+2 line format, it would be processed very differently both at the behavioural level of eye movement patterns and the internal levels of situation model building and meaning making. A prose format very likely leads to a less efficient cognitive processing, a different *attention resonance* and an overall diminished affective and aesthetic response. Poems presented this way receive lower poeticity judgements. Moreover, a recent study from my lab[71] examining the eye movements during the reading of Baudelaire's 'Les Chats' – famously analyzed by Jakobson and Lévi-Strauss[72] – showed that total reading time is notably longer for the poetic line format than the prose format, suggesting different processing modes: as predicted by the NCPM,

iii https://www.poemhunter.com/poem/cats/

the poetic format induces a strong bias towards the lower route and more explicit and affective-aesthetic processes that take more time, as expressed in shorter saccades, more regressions and longer fixation durations. Another prediction of the NCPM is that – being strongly foregrounded elements – end rhymes in the poetic format should attract longer fixation durations than other words in a line, and also longer than the final words of sentences that are known to produce longer fixation durations due to semantic integration efforts. The data of this study also confirmed this prediction. Finally, regarding the visual features of poetry, capitalization, spacing, punctuation and the use of non-alphabetic symbols like '!' or '…' and so on, can change the attentional and affective-cognitive processing.

The Line

The line is the fundamental unit of metred poetry. Its canonical duration of 2–3 seconds – at least in about 70 per cent of German poems[73] – is important for neurocognitive models of verbal art reception, since brain processing can be viewed as basically rhythmic. The line is ideal for entraining other recurring processing units, such as sentences, clauses or phrases to the basic acoustic rhythm. This can produce a 'pleasing sensation of fit and inevitability which is part of the delight of verse', and is so helpful to the memory. The line is what most marks off poetry, and lines can be perceived as a single perceptual gestalt, if they can be contained in working memory, which functions in the acoustic mode like an echo box. Moreover, the iambic pentameter line can be seen as optimal for neuronal processing: due to working memory limitations, five stressed syllables are the maximum people can comfortably handle within a single rhythm or tone-unit.[74] Hence, in the NCPM's lower route, the line is treated as a central unit for cognitive, affective and aesthetic processes. It is where all the other influencing factors at the metric-sublexical (stress), lexico-semantic (valence), phonological-interlexical (rhyme) or morphosyntactic-supralexical (syntactic complexity) levels come together to act upon the subconscious brain and the bodily, as well as the verbally reportable processes that make up the experience of poetry.

Style Motifs

The NCPM assumes that the words of a line are processed as simulated by extant computational models of word recognition like the associative multiple read-out (AROM) discussed below. However, lines also sometimes can be processed like a sentence gestalt – with some notable differences. Thus, for example, a sonnet's graphical, and rhythm and rhyme structure – known and expected by typical poetry readers – may affect not only the perceptual-attentional processing, but also the phonological-prosodic recoding, as well as the affective-semantic processing. In metrical verse, the predominance of pattern-affirming parts over occasional pattern-contradicting parts within a line generates expectations: establishing, frustrating and reaffirming such expectations of a recurring pattern is considered to be a fundamental aesthetic process of poetry reception. More generally, depending on the individual author, features called *style motifs* (or also *signposts* or *poetic links*) influence a poetic reading act.[75] These are specific elements within the text considered to be meaningful by the reader, because of the pattern formation rules of a specific interpretive community. Examples are repeating, rhyming or alliterating words, or, more generally, pieces of surface information such as phonetic, graphic or syntactic patterns that may be assigned hierarchical significance within a poetic genre. Style motifs are an integral part of stage 1 of the above *macromodel*: as textual cues defined by a literary system, they can trigger internal representations of such motifs, often making readers want more of them. Experienced readers intuitively know or guess what comes next in a poetic text, for instance, based on rhythmic, metrical, grammatical or conceptual symmetry. These expectations, based on style motif representations, might at least partially be rooted in the micropoetry of early life, such as word games or nursery-rhymes. Part of the magic of literature and poetry is challenging and disappointing such expectations. This refers to the dynamics of schema assimilation and accommodation as described in the mesomodel.

Motif and Title

Other relevant supralexical features shaping the way poems are read at subordinate levels of processing are motif and title. Behavioural studies have established effects of poetic subgenre and motif at several levels of observation (ratings, reading times, heart rate), showing, for example, that poems belonging to the motif category 'stillness' induce higher mood empathy than other categories such as 'city' poems.[76] Titles not only may be suggestive of the author's intentions when creating an artwork. Empirically well-supported general text processing theories also predict that knowledge of a title or keyword can completely change the meaning-making of a text segment through the interaction between semantic macro- and microstructures in both working and episodic memory. According to those theories, titles affect the coherence of text representations by activating schematic information stored in semantic memory. These schemata increase comprehension by disambiguating references and events during encoding, making the representations coherent.[77]

Thus, prior knowledge of, or inference about, the overall motif of a poem might well account for top-down effects in reader responses to subordinate levels of text features. If the title does not support such effects, as is arguably the case in Shakespeare's 154 sonnets, which are numerated rather than titled, readers' efforts after meaning and aesthetic feelings will likely exhibit a different dynamic than when this is the case. This is supported not only by the aforementioned literature on text processing, but also by studies on visual art reception. Titles can increase both the comprehension and aesthetic experience of art, the latter only when they contribute to rich and coherent mental representations. Most interestingly, metaphoric titles such as 'One day at a time' seem more effective for aesthetic ratings than descriptive titles like 'Woman planting flowers', because they suggest an alternative explanation to what can be readily inferred from the explicit artwork.[78]

Together with the 'sound' foregrounding effects produced by rhythm and rhyme, and the effects of graphic form, the line, style motifs, as well as motif and title, the semantic foregrounding effects evoked by schemes and tropes are central to verbal art and the NCPM. Therefore, in the next section, I discuss them in greater detail.

Processing Rhetorical Figures

In *Brain and Poetry* we compared rhetorical figures to figures of perception and cognition; the bio-ecologically predetermined way we perceive, act and think. We also argued that there is basically only a dozen such figures. Through these figures as basic rules of word combinations, we make the world 'thinkable'. As an example, a proto-logic of thought starts with opposition and negation, or, as Albert Camus said, 'The first discovery of the mind is the contradiction'. A negation always draws a richer picture than a positive statement; it allows to

- imagine events that did not happen;
- describe people who aren't present; and
- ponder possibilities no one expects, or oppose them to the real present.

Thus, negation as a fundamental figure of thought becomes one of the basic style figures when used in literature. A brilliant example of *antithesis*, *negation* or *oxymoron* is Shakespeare's expression 'sightless view' from sonnet 27, which we will bump into repeatedly in this book. There appear to be around 200 cases of antithesis in the 154 Shakespeare sonnets. They create a contrast: by emphasizing the background, the figure will emerge stronger. This is assumed to evoke a disjunctive thought process, etching the main ideas into relief via inverse notions. Thus, Shakespeare can artfully make readers imagine the negative of words: waking to sleeping, day to night, old to new or mind to body. By arranging the opposite pairs jewel-night/night-beauteous in a mirror-inverted way (a-b/b-a) the author even stresses the antithesis into a special form of cross-line *chiasm.*

Sonnet 27

Weary with toil, I haste me to my bed,
The dear repose for limbs with travel tired,
But then begins a journey in my head
To work my mind, when body's works expired.
For then my thoughts (from far where I abide)
Intend a zealous pilgrimage to thee,
And keep my drooping eyelids open wide,
Looking on darkness which the blind do see.
Save that my soul's imaginary sight
Presents thy shadow to my **sightless view**,
Which like a jewel (hung in ghastly night)
Makes black night beauteous, and her old face new.
Lo thus by day my limbs, by night my mind,
For thee, and for my self, no quiet find.

Other fundamental figures resemble visual illusions that can be grouped into four categories named after errors of language: ambiguity, distortion, paradox and fiction. We can apply these to a simple analysis of style figures in Dylan Thomas's 'Do not go gentle into that good night':

Do not go gentle into that good night,
Old age should burn and rave at close of day;
Rage, rage against the dying of the light.

Though wise men at their end know dark is right,
Because their words had forked no lightning they –*Distortion*
Do not go gentle into that good night.

Good men, the last wave by, crying how bright
Their frail deeds might have danced in a green bay,
Rage, rage against the dying of the light.

Wild men who caught and sang the sun in flight,
And learn, too late, they grieved it on its way, – *Fiction*
Do not go gentle into that good night.

Grave men, near death, who see with blinding sight – *Paradox*
Blind eyes could blaze like meteors and be gay, – *Ambiguity*
Rage, rage against the dying of the light.

And you, my father, there on the sad height,
Curse, bless, me now with your fierce tears, I pray.
Do not go gentle into that good night.
Rage, rage against the dying of the light.

- Ambiguity. 'Blind eyes could blaze like meteors and be gay' oscillates between the aspect of the blind and the glowing of meteors.
- Distortion. They can be found in the *hyperboles* of the poem, from 'words that fork lightning', to the 'men that catch and sing the sun'.
- Paradox. The 'blinding sight of blind men' opposes contrasting features.
- Fiction. The 'grieved sun' implicates the fiction of a personified sun.

The simplicity of this proposal, reducing rhetorical devices to universal perceptual illusions, had its charm when we published our book in 2011. But it reached only so far and did not really allow useful predictions for our neurocognitive experiments. A more general model that does so is presented next.

According to this model, the processing of schemes, typically considered as stylistic devices based on syntax, and tropes considered as semantic devices, can be compared along three dimensions: X-axis = *deviation*, Y-axis = *complexity* and Z-axis = *irregularity*, that characterize all rhetorical figures. In line with

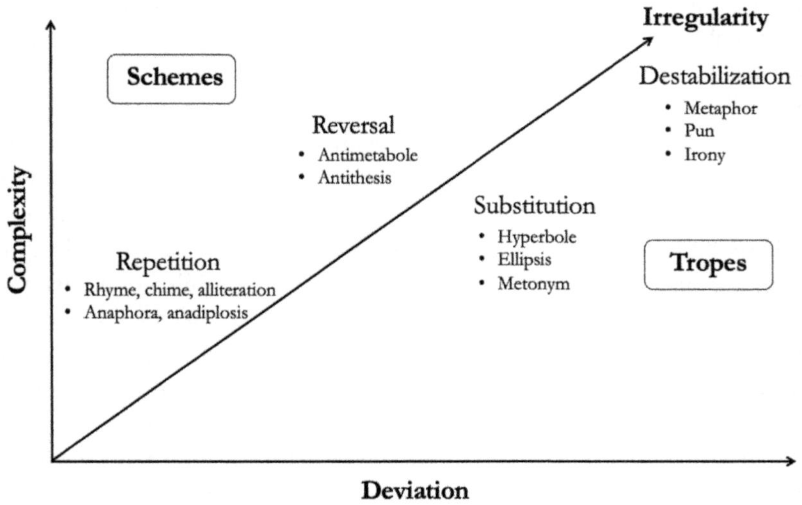

Figure 2.4 3d model of the processing of rhetorical figures. Adapted from McQuarrie and Mick, 1996.[79]

Tenet 1, we can define deviation in terms of speech act and relevance theories. Since every communication encounter sets up expectations, more general expectations holding across many encounters function as conventions. These are stored as probabilistic language patterns in readers' brains. Note that this principle also applies to *internal deviations*, regular patterns in a text that are violated, such as the iambic pentameter in quite a few lines of Shakespeare sonnets. Looking at the X-axis, deviation relates to these conventions yielding a hypothetical rank order: repetition < reversal < substitution < destabilization. If you recall the examples of phonological iconicity discussed earlier, they all violate the convention that sounds are generally irrelevant to the sense of an utterance. They thus go against a reader's expectation that the distribution of sounds across a word sequence is essentially unordered except by the grammatical and semantic constraints imposed by a language system. Complexity on the Y-axis refers to the rhetorical operation and cognitive processing of schemes and tropes with the following slightly different hypothetical rank order: repetition < substitution < reversal < destabilization. Thus, deviation and complexity have additive effects: whether scheme or trope, the more complex a figure, the more difficult it is to process: although less deviant, reversal schemes are theoretically more difficult to process (or complex) than substitution tropes. Finally, irregularity on the Z-axis describes schemes and tropes in terms of an additional *depth of processing* perspective: excess regularity can be processed at the perceptual level since it operates with surface features such as sound repetition in rhyme. But detecting irregularity can also require deeper semantic processing to see, for example, that *metaphors* are generally less regular than *hyperboles*.

In this model, schemes are semiotically *overcoded* verbal stimuli that offer more possible organizations of information than necessary for understanding. They are less deviant and therefore easier to process than tropes, which are *undercoded* stimuli. Both prompt readers to search for *implicatures* – something the author implies without literally expressing it – because they do not add to a texts' explicature – what is explicitly said. However, they require different processing efforts. Repetition (rhyme, anaphora) and reversal (antimetabole, antithesis, chiasm) provide excess regularity and are less deviant than irregular expressions like substitution (ellipsis, hyperbole) or destabilization (metaphor, paradox). Reversal is more complex than repetition because recognizing 'mirror images' of expressions such as the chiasm or antimetabole: 'I wasted time, and now doth time waste me' in Shakespeare's *Richard II* indeed requires more mental effort than recognizing repeated syllables or words. Moreover, destabilization is more difficult and potentially rewarding than substitution: although both operations involve a semantic turn such that an expression takes on an unexpected or unconventional meaning, substitutions usually have a tightly constrained resolution, while tropes produced by destabilization only have loosely constrained resolutions, or in terms of relevance theory: weaker implicatures. As an example, metonyms like 'the crown' as a substitute for the monarchy are among the most frequently occurring tropes in everyday language, because they correspond with our principles of perception. We usually perceive details of objects before recognizing them as a whole, and according to the gestalt law of good continuation, we interpolate what is missing. Mentally relating a crown to monarchy is more direct and cognitively less demanding than recognizing the relation between a tongue and a bayonet, as in Dylan Thomas's aforementioned metaphor.

In *Brain and Poetry* Raoul Schrott and I proposed the following scale of processing difficulty for tropes (from 1 to 5), which suggests fuzzy borders between the categories of substitution and destabilization.

1. Properties of A also belong to B. This defines *synecdoches* in which a 'pars pro toto' is a concrete, real part of a whole.
2. Properties of A depend on B. This characterizes *metonyms* in which the relation between part and whole is somewhat looser and more abstract.
3. Properties of A relate to each other as do properties of B. This corresponds to *analogies* which project structural relations and entire concepts from A to B.
4. Single properties of A look or act like B. This is typical for *similes* as in Shakespeare's 'Is love a tender thing? It is too rough, too rude, too boisterous, and *it pricks like thorn*'. (*Romeo and Juliet*)
5. A is not B, but there is something in A that reminds of B. This defines metaphors. In processing similes like in Sting's famous song 'Fragile' ('Like tears from a star')', we become onlookers who notice similarities within a unified and objective area from outside. The reference points for metaphor processing, however, are subjective, depending on our semantic memory, a look from inside. A simile compares two things with each other, a metaphor correlates them indirectly via a 'tertium comparationis'. This third thing gives a metaphor more depth, a third dimension compared to the two-dimensional simile.

An apparent lacuna in the above model is emotion. Every student of historical or modern rhetoric is familiar with the claim that style figures can induce (strong) emotions. As an example, according to Longinus, word order reversal devices such as *hyperbaton* ('Some rise by sin, and some by virtue fall') are supposed to throw hearers into a panic. Demetrius, another classic of rhetoric, claims that *aposiopesis,* which drops a final word from a clause or sentence ('No, Percy, thou art dust, And food for – '), produces elevation. Despite numerous theoretical claims about the emotive forces of the over 400 rhetorical devices listed in standard works,[80] I do not know of any empirical studies that actually demonstrate these effects for at least a decent number of devices, allowing us to rank order them with regard to their impact on some neural, experiential or behavioural response. This is a distressing state of affairs, which I would like to change if I had the time and means.

There is one exception though concerning the perhaps dominant poetic device, metaphor. At least for conventional metaphors like 'She looked at him sweetly', as compared to literal paraphrases like 'She looked at him kindly', there is neuroimaging evidence that the metaphorical expressions are more emotionally evocative than the literal ones: parts of the brain's limbic system responsible for a lot of emotional processing like the amygdala only 'lighted up' for the metaphors.[81] Other neuroimaging work discussed in Chapter 8 indicated that idiomatic expressions like 'He kicked the bucket'[82] trigger a higher affective resonance than literal expressions, as seen, again, in amygdala activity. Together, these studies suggest that the ancient rhetoricians may have been right, but without more empirical research constraining my hypotheses, I dare not include emotion as a fourth dimension in the already intricate model sketched in Figure 2.4.

In sum, according to this model, when readers encounter a deviating verbal stimulus, they will implicitly search their semantic memory for a context that makes meaning out of the convention breach. For example, they could use the *semantic similarity* and *bigram probability heuristics* I shall explain in detail in Chapter 3: word pairs that occur very rarely together – or were never seen before – and that seem semantically distant, such as the above 'sightless view', likely require a figurative interpretation. When this mental process is successful in discovering an additional (figurative) layer of meaning, readers tend to respond with an aesthetic feeling. Some simple predictions follow from this model. For example, that more complex figures attract longer fixation durations than simpler ones in an eye-tracking experiment (see Chapter 8). Or, that in a neuroimaging study, more irregular figures evoke stronger hemodynamic activity in the LIFG, a brain region that indeed is activated more strongly by novel metaphorical expressions than by conventional ones, and that generally is associated with semantic integration.[83] I hope such predictions may trigger future work. Let me note that the original variant of the model sketched in Figure 2.4 was empirically verified in two studies in which participants rated the 'artfulness' of a set of rhetorical figures selected from consumer ads, such as the metaphor 'Science you can touch'. Both confirmed the model's rank-order predictions.

Computational Micromodels – The AROM

To give you an idea about how the processes specified in the boxes of the mesomodel can be transformed into computational ones – at Marr's algorithmic level mentioned in Chapter 1 – I will briefly present one example, the associative multiple read-out model (AROM) of word recognition published in 2011.[84] It was actually the first computational model of this kind that really implemented a working 'semantic layer'. Three years later – meanwhile we had our own neuroimaging machine thanks to the aforementioned 'Languages of Emotion' super-grant – we used that model to successfully predict brain activity: on a computer the AROM could simulate associative activation spreading across semantic memory. More specifically, we used the AROM to examine whether *semantic neighbourhood density*, as estimated via the number of semantic associates for a given word, can account for effects previously ascribed to affective word features (emotional valence). This finding was most helpful for the development of my computational models of word valence and beauty presented in Chapter 3.

As shown in Figure 2.5A, the AROM has a four-layer architecture. Each of these layers contains one type of representation and consists of units – sometimes called *neurodes* – that receive input from the other units at the same level

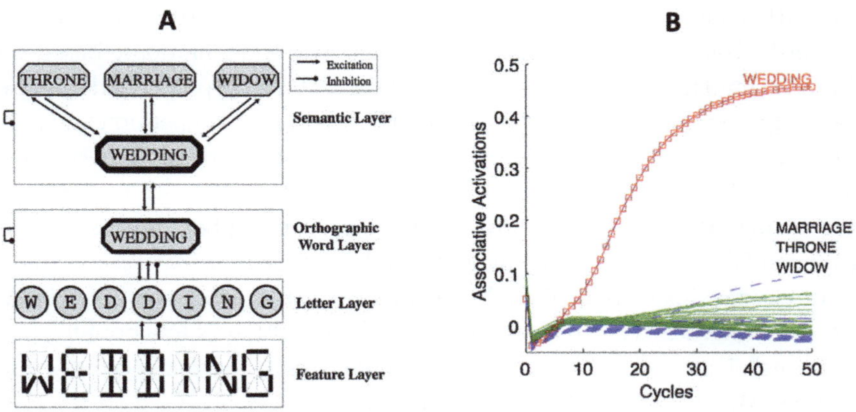

Figure 2.5 A. Small excerpt of the AROM architecture. The semantic layer receives input from the orthographic word layer. The semantic unit of the presented word WEDDING activates associated units in all layers which feed activation back. Therefore, semantic associates in the context increase activation of the target word unit. **B**. An example simulation of a stimulus with a high number of associates. The X-axis shows simulation cycles (computer time), and the Y-axis displays the relative activation of semantic word units. When WEDDING (red boxes) is presented to the model, the most strongly co-activated items in the stimulus set are 'marriage', 'throne' and 'widow' (solid green). Adapted fromHofmann & Jacobs, 2014.[85]

and those from lower and/or upper levels (e.g. via feedback), transform them according to some *throughput function*, typically a sigmoid function resembling the letter 'S', and finally send output to the other units. The first layer represents visual features like '|' as a straight line at a particular position, for example, in the left part of the first letter. The second layer contains letter units, which are activated by the visual features of the subordinate layer. For instance, 'I' is composed of two vertical features. When the corresponding units become activated by the input, the unit for 'I' will become more active than its competitor units like 'J' or 'L'. The third layer represents orthographic word forms, such as 'WEDDING', which receive activation from certain letters at particular positions. As shown in Figure 2.5B, the activation of the WEDDING unit and competing units like MARRIAGE builds up gradually over time – represented by computing cycles – in all layers; only a little excerpt of the highest semantic layer is shown here. Similar to the behaviour of real neurons in the brain, when this activation reaches a threshold, the word WEDDING is fully identified and, in the model, becomes 'conscious'. This book has no space for explaining in detail how such computer models that often take many years to develop function, but interested readers will find this information in the original articles.

Micromodels like the AROM allow us to quantitatively predict human behaviour or brain activity. Thus, we could successfully predict how activation in the LIFG varies with the semantic neighbourhood density of words. The LIFG supports the selection of an appropriate semantic representation of words from multiple, pre-activated long-term representations. Based on AROM simulations such as the one in Figure 2.5B, we hypothesized that the more representations are active, the larger the semantic competition and thus LIFG activation. In the AROM, weaker association strength between two words produces greater semantic competition. To test this, we re-analyzed neuroimaging data from a study of my team on metaphor processing presented in Chapter 8 and confirmed the model's prediction.

In closing this section, should I mention that, like other computer models, the AROM is not a realistic model of the mindbrain's functioning? Just as meteorological computer models are not realistic representations of the weather. What they are, though, are currently the best tools we have to simulate the functioning of complex nonlinear dynamic systems like the brain or the climate. And in this respect, they fulfil a very useful function that 'boxological' models like those sketched in Figures 2.3 and 2.4 cannot.

The Methods

The NCPM generates a set of hypotheses and quantitative predictions that can be tested in Neurocomputational Poetics studies that use specific methods of three types:

- Methods for analyzing the *reading materials*, such as the *SentiArt* text analysis tool introduced in the next chapter
- Methods for analyzing the *reader*, such as measuring readers' personality, preferences or reading proficiency
- Methods for analyzing the *reading act*, such as self-reports or eye tracking

Text analysis methods help specify and quantify the input part of the complex nonlinear dynamic system representing a reading act. They provide information about the features and super-features that co-determine how readers come to understand and like texts or the opposite. Reader analysis methods provide useful information about variables that interact with those specified in the text analysis, such as reading age, skill, habits, preferences and interests (e.g. for specific authors or genres) or interindividual differences in personality (e.g. empathy, openness to experience). Finally, reading act analysis methods provide measures of

- reading experience, such as the *Literary Response Questionnaire* mentioned earlier;
- reading behaviour, such as eye movements; and
- the neural correlates of the former two, such as brain activity in selected regions or networks.

These methods will be discussed in the next chapters about the toolbox one needs when doing Neurocomputational Poetics research.

Summary

Setting the ground for the NCPM, I started this chapter by discussing the value of theoretical models for explaining empirical results at different levels. The NCPM is based on three tenets about the (i) adaptive value of literary experiences, (ii) the relativity of poeticity and (iii) the reality of phonological iconicity, and it is nested in a meta- and macromodel which situate it in a global significative network and a typical reading cycle. The core of the NCPM, the mesomodel, was discussed in detail, including the likely neural correlates of its main (sub)processes, focusing on effects of both back- and foreground elements of texts. The special role of schemes and tropes was highlighted by presenting a submodel of processing rhetorical figures. Finally, I presented the AROM as an example of how processes specified in a prequantitative manner in the boxes of the mesomodel can be implemented computationally in a micromodel. In closing, I outlined three kinds of methods necessary for Neurocomputational Poetics research.

Chapter 3

TEXT ANALYSIS

To go one stage further, 'consistency' and 'tendency' are most naturally reduced to 'frequency', and so, it appears, the stylistician becomes a statistician

—Leech & Short[86] (2007, p. 34).

What gets readers to be 'on loan' to an author, thinking, feeling, suffering and acting within them? Why did Sappho and Homer know so well how to move, surprise and please their readers so that they want to read on? The first step when trying to predict how readers' thoughts and feelings are controlled by what they read is to analyze the tools of the trade. Since Aristotle's days, uncountable books and articles from numerous scientific disciplines have been devoted to the issue of revealing the secrets of the power of verbal art. My approach is a 'from simple to complex' one. In the previous chapter, I talked about textual back- and foreground features that co-determine reading acts. Here, I will show examples of such features, and in Chapters 5 and 6, I will explain how these features can be quantified via current methods of *distant reading* and computational stylistics. These include novel techniques of machine learning and attempt to answer questions that are of interest to literary scholars and critics, reading psychologists or people working in education or the book industry. Combining quantitative text and reader analyses with my NCPM will allow me to predict effects of these features on reader responses at all levels of psychological enquiry: neuronal, behavioural and experiential.

Simple Text Features, Tropologies, Close, Distant and Middle Reading

My Ph.D. advisor Kevin O'Regan always told me that reading is just visual perception and thus obeys basic laws of pattern recognition. With one crucial difference: unlike most other visual stimuli, such as visual scenes, texts have a clear advantage for quantitative analyses, because they represent highly structured material, just as with the rule-determined languages they are written in. In general, their elements – letters, words, sentences – are compositional: simple units are combined to form larger, more complex ones, thus allowing an 'infinite use with finite means' as Wilhelm von Humboldt put it. And many of these units can be quantitatively described and analyzed into even simpler basic features via statistical and computational methods.

In tackling the central question of how writers can act on my sweat glands, limbic system or feelings through stringing together syllables and words, it is useful to have a close look at their verbal toolbox. Vocabulary, plot, the personality profile, attractiveness or believability of protagonists and antagonists, word order or stylistic devices like schemes and tropes all are features of a text which co-determine a reader's literary experience. In the humanities, the identification of stylistic elements of texts is typically done either in an idiosyncratic way – intuitive *close reading* and interpretation like in Helen Vendler's book about the Shakespeare sonnets[87] – or by help of qualitative tools that often list and categorize hundreds of rhetorical devices. Such 'tropologies' usually are too vague or coarse-grained for our purposes. They also often are assembled in a rather ad hoc fashion, and not meaningfully linked to reader responses. That is, they lack a theoretical background, unlike the process model of rhetorical figures presented in Chapter 2, which provides testable predictions about why, for example, figures of destabilization are more complex and difficult to process than figures of substitution.

In general, a Neurocomputational Poetics perspective seeks generalizable and testable predictions based on quantitative feature analysis (distant reading[88]). In digital literary studies and Neurocomputational Poetics, it is no bad thing to replace intuition by prediction, where necessary, or complement it, where possible – as demonstrated in the final empirical study presented in this book (see Chapter 8). It can only help in correcting and advancing ideas and hypotheses. Technological progress in NLP has produced 'culturomics', that is, computational analyses of huge text corpora (~6 million digitized books containing ~4 per cent of all books ever published) enabling researchers to observe cultural trends and subject them to quantitative investigation. The aims of these computer techniques are, for example, (i) to replicate and predict readers' sentiments towards products like books or movie scripts, (ii) to foresee the success of advertisement campaigns, or, as is the case in this book, (iii) to explain affective-aesthetic reader responses to (pieces of) novels or poems. Using powerful computers and algorithms to try to automatize, approximate and complement 'from a distance' what a literary scholar or critic with hermeneutic skills can do by close reading appears justified in the face of the myriad of possibly relevant text features appearing in the wealth of the world's books and poetry collections. Combining close and distant reading approaches into a *middle reading* one can be useful as we will see in

Chapter 8 when investigating the effects of style figures in Shakespeare sonnets on reader responses.

Propp's and Jakobson's Through Passes

How both close and distant reading approaches to text analysis can be fruitfully combined was already shown in the 1930s by Vladimir Propp or in the 1960s by Roman Jakobson – still without the help of computers. In his morphology of Russian folk tales, Propp already 'thought in algorithms' much like today's computational linguists. Jakobson's linguistic approach to poetry was rather based on principles that aimed at revealing the structurally determinable elements of poetic language. His work presents plenty of prototypical examples of the application of these principles, such as accurately describing these elements in terms of four linguistics aspects: metric, phonological, morphosyntactic and semantic. I was struck, for instance, by the ground-breaking case analysis of Charles Baudelaire's 'Les Chats' ('The Cats'; with Claude Lévi-Strauss) introduced in Chapter 2 where they analyzed the phonological texture by quantifying the number of nasals in the poem's first quartet ('two to three per line'), or the interaction between phonological and semantic features in the last trio (nasal vowels and the idea of light). They also identified and interpreted metaphors like 'loins' (arguably evoking sexual potency) or uncovered archetypal symbolisms such as 'a vision of gold'. Other features analyzed by Jakobson in his book on poetry by Hölderlin, Klee and Brecht which are now part of any text-analytical computer tool were verse, word types or word repetitions. Contemporary cognitive poetics approaches follow in Jakobson's steps by combining qualitative text analyses like metaphor identification and interpretation with quantitative ones (e.g. computing the semantic distance between the two terms of a metaphor). However, just like Jakobson's, most of these approaches either fail to derive testable predictions from their analyses or provide no empirical support for their hypotheses. But, what is needed to extend Jakobson's approach so that quantitative predictions of the reading act testable with neurocomputational methods become possible in general? Basically, we need the following ingredients for a Neurocomputational Poetics toolbox for text analyses: *feature engineering*, *semantic models* and methods to predict the comprehensibility and likeability of literary texts. Let us see what these are and can do.

Feature Engineering

Say we describe a person X by a simplified 3d vector of features (height, weight and age) and then plot the values as a point in a coordinate system together with the values of hundreds of other persons. As a result, X would hardly be identifiable in the cloud of dots, because too many other 3d-reduced persons would share these values and X's location would not be unique. To improve things, we can add features that can either be categorical (coded as a, b, c, etc.) or continuous (coded as real numbers). A facial feature like eye colour could be added as 'b' for blue, personality features like IQ or extraversion score could be mixed in (e.g. numbers like 135 and 10) or more complicated features of speech and semantics, such as the probability 'p' that X utters the expression 'damned' (e.g. $p = .05$), and so on. The vector thus becomes longer and the likelihood of X's discriminability and identifiability increases. Eventually, every person can be described by a vector of feature values that maximizes identifying that person. The same holds true for things or words.

Now imagine you meet that person during a date. Which of the dozens of features you perceive during that date, subconsciously or consciously, will contribute to your first impression and likelihood of finding the person sympathetic? You will be able to explicitly name a few, but others will exert their effects on you more silently. Also, you will probably not be able to exactly specify the weight each feature had in, say, your decision to meet the person again. One reason is that features interact often quite subtly: for example, it's likely not the eye colour by itself that really matters but in concert with the form of the nose, mouth, speech content, facial emotion expression and so on. *Feature engineering* could help here: it is about finding the weight of interacting features to determine those that make a difference (cf. lens model in Chapter 2).

Analogously, when you read a poem, it is not easy to tell exactly which of its features – words or units smaller or bigger than words – influenced your decision to read on, or how much you understood or liked it. But for purposes of Neurocomputational Poetics, we need to learn this by inventing progressively better methods of feature engineering. Poetic language in prose, lyrics or poetry develops its cognitive and emotional effects in a wonderfully entangled way via emergent interactions between all feature types at all text levels, creating multiple layers of meaning potential across word groups, lines or stanzas. In NLP research, feature engineering is the process of using expert domain knowledge, like that of Jakobson, to select, create and compute textual features that make machine-learning algorithms work better. For instance, the lexical (word-based) feature *word valence* is most often selected in sentiment analyses to help computer algorithms learn whether a text such as a book review is positive or negative.

The 4x4 Matrix

For purposes of computational text analyses allowing quantitative predictions, Jakobson's linguistic approach distinguishing between four linguistic aspects (metrical, phonological, syntactic, semantic) is too coarse. I therefore complemented it by four feature levels: sublexical, lexical, interlexical and supralexical. *Sublexical* features, that is, at a level below or smaller than entire words, concern aspects of syllables, such as syllable stress. *Lexical* features concern those at the level of single words, like word beauty. Sometimes, two or more words can exert an affective or aesthetic effect over longer distances than a simple two-word sequence. To better analyze this kind of long(er) distance interaction, I proposed the term *interlexical* feature: a feature not proper to a single word, but most often emerging from the interaction between two (or more) words separated by some textual distance. Perhaps the best-known case is situated at the phonological level, *rhyme*: it ties together two words by their sound, across lines or sentences, that can be more or less semantically related. Finally, *supralexical* features concern all aspects that can be integrated over larger amounts of text, like sentences, chapters or entire poems and books, such as syntactic complexity or plot.

Combining Jakobson's four linguistic aspects with my four feature levels yields a systematic 4x4 matrix useful for the identification and quantification of both back- and foreground features assumed to influence readers' literary experience. Much like previous feature lists (e.g. that of Leech and Short), the matrix discussed in this section is heuristic, but with a focus on features that can easily be computed while occasionally referring to features that require semi-automatic or qualitative assessment. Thus, the 4x4 matrix is a practical tool for feature engineering, not a theory about linguistic units.

Among reading researchers, it is generally agreed that during reading, a text is processed by the brain at three levels:

- The *surface form*: a verbatim memory of the exact word form, sound and order.
- The *textbase*: a memory for the abstract propositions and ideas that were contained in the text itself.
- The *situation model*: a referential representation of the events described by the text.

Each level appears to have its own forgetting curve. Thus, different mechanisms seem to be at work when short and long texts are processed, and research on literary reading must integrate micro-, meso- and macroscopic aspects in a comprehensive theoretical framework like the NCPM. The *4x4 matrix* definitely helped to develop this by motivating and facilitating testable predictions based on relevant text features which can be meaningfully linked to reader responses.

Each cell in the matrix contains only one example feature, and many more can be hidden behind them, making the task of feature engineering a

Table 3.1 4×4 matrix with example features.

Linguistic Aspect / Feature Level	*Metrical*	*Phonological*	*Morphosyntactic*	*Semantic*
Sublexical	stress	number of syllables	functional shift	morpheme type
Lexical	stress pattern	sonority score	word type	word beauty
Interlexical	rhythm	rhyme	word order	metaphoricity
Supralexical	global swing	global affective meaning	syntactic complexity	semantic complexity

challenging one. I will briefly comment on these features next, going into the details of their computation in later chapters.

Metrical Features

At the sublexical metrical level, syllables vary in terms of whether they are stressed or unstressed, using a qualitative metree[i] like English, or long vs. short, using a quantitative metre like classical Greek. Similar to music, *stress patterns* create *rhythm* at the lexical and interlexical levels: a regular periodic beat or rhythm is something deeply physical; our heart, breath and brain work with rhythms. In rhetoric, stressing a syllable is called *ictus* (Latin for to beat). The etymology reflects an instinctive behaviour: when a voice offsets from its base tone, this is interpreted as an alarm signal in the entire animal kingdom. Humans also perceive a voice that suddenly grows louder and stronger as an aggressive stimulus, which automatically prepares or evokes a fright-and-flight response, only stopped by a subsequent lowering of the voice signalling 'all-clear'. Such alternations of intonation, a metre of stressed and unstressed syllables, already appear in baby-talk and it characterizes poetic language. At the highest supralexical metrical level, the subordinate features stress pattern and rhythm finally combine to shape a language's *global swing.* The effects of stress or rhythm are not exclusive to poetry, though, since languages differ considerably as to their typical stress pattern and global rhythm or swing. In English, the most frequent word pattern consists of disyllabic words with a stressed initial syllable, that is, a kind of *trochaic swing*, as in COMmon PATterns OFTen HAPpen. About 85 per cent of English polysyllabic nouns have a stressed first syllable. About 80 per cent of German or Spanish disyllabic words have initial stress, too. Thus, in contrast to the

i I note that metre and rhythm are constructs still waiting to find a definitive theory.

French *iambic rhythm* (taTA, taTA; also notated as 'x /'), these languages all can be viewed as having a trochaic swing: FAther, MOther, CHILdren. Some experiments suggest that baby talk already swings in the rhythm of the mother tongue, since German six-month-old babies pay more attention to (interesting) non-native patterns, such as the iambic gaGA, gaGA (typical for French), than the native trochaic GAga, GAga (also notated as '/ x').[89]. How this early learned swing affects later reception of Shakespeare's iambic pentameter sonnets read by a native English or French speaker, I can't tell. What I can tell is that French swings better in my ears than both German or English.

Phonological Features

The sublexical feature *number of syllables* per word not only co-determines its pronounceability and sound pattern, but also becomes relevant when a poet must fit words into the metre of a line, such as the iambic pentameter. Sometimes, the trick of shortening a syllable helps, such as in line seven of Shakespeare's sonnet 60 ('Crooked eclipses 'gainst his glory fight') and many other poems. At the lexical level, the *sonority score* is a quantifiable feature that determines how well a word sounds depending on how sonorous its syllables are. It is explained in detail in Chapter 5, where I demonstrate why 'piss' sounds ruder than 'pee'. Regarding the interlexical phonological level, everyone can *rhyme*, but not all rhymes sound like poetry or appear hackneyed like 'love-dove' or 'Herz-Schmerz' (heart-pain) in German. Making rhymes 'poetic' is a craft and in Chapter 5 I demonstrate how to compute the saliency of rhymes as an index of their foreground potential in Shakespeare sonnets. The final supralexical phonological feature mentioned in the above matrix, the *global affective meaning*, concerns the overall emotional mood of how a poem is received. Along with metre, rhyme and rhythm, poets also make use of onomatopoeia, which plays with the sound structure of words, and influences their basic affective tone. A poem full of words sounding nicely thus can induce a happy mood. In Chapter 5 I show how to compute the sound beauty of single words (their *euphony*) and in Chapter 8 an empirical study on the global affective meaning of entire poems demonstrates that, in concert with the words' meanings, their sound structure can make poems sad, joyful or spiteful. These empirical results justify putting the feature in the 'phonological' column.

Morphosyntactic Features

The example feature in the sublexical morphosyntactic cell of the matrix, *functional shift*, is not often mentioned in psycholinguistics. I chose it because it was the object of one of the most innovative empirical Neurocomputational

Poetics studies.[90] When morphemes are used to form novel words (neologisms), they can become an interesting feature having poetic potential as in these functional shifts. The sentences 'How Shakespeare *tempests* the brain' or 'He was no longer alone in the world; he was *wived* to a kind and beautiful woman' confront the reader with a morphosyntactic deviation, an artistic *defamiliarization*, which has this potential. Turning one-word type into another, like nouns into verbs, is a stylistic device dear to professional authors but also frequently found in everyday language ('googling'). At the lexical and interlexical levels, *word type* that is, part of speech/POS (noun, verb, etc.) and *word order*, such as Subject Verb Object/SVO, both co-determine the supralexical feature *syntactic complexity* (of a sentence or paragraph). Thus, deviations from the standard 'noun phrase + verb phrase' predication pattern, or the prototypical SVO order of English, are abundant in poetry and they make texts harder to understand. In Chapter 6, we will see whether a measure that represents variation of word type and order called *Shannon entropy* can help explain why readers prefer one line of a Shakespeare sonnet over others.

Semantic Features

Depending on the specific language, morphemes – typically considered the smallest linguistic units that carry meaning – can signal grammatical case (nominative), tense (past tense), number (singular, plural), gender (female), aspect (I am eating, I have eaten) or mood (e.g. the imperative mood in 'let's go'). At the sublexical level, morpheme types such as the prefix '*un–*' or the suffix '*–able*' play a role in changing the meaning of the base morpheme, as in 'un-EAT-able'. Adding prefixes and suffixes to existing words was a favourite foregrounding device of Shakespeare, who thus created many new English words as in "What, quite UNmanned in folly?" from his play *Macbeth*, line 4 from sonnet 3 ('Thou dost beguile the world UNbless some mother'), or line 8 from sonnet 2 ('Were an all-eating shame and thriftLESS praise'). At the lexical level, the sound beauty (euphony) of a word can more or less match its *meaning beauty* (*eusemy*). Thus, in 'piss' there seems to be a match emphasizing a negative affective meaning, while in 'pee' there is a mismatch, as the quantitative analyses I present in Chapter 5 and the empirical data presented in Chapter 8 will demonstrate. At the interlexical level, *metaphoricity* is listed as a semantic feature in this matrix, as in Sting's 'tears of a star' which conveys a nonliteral meaning for 'rain'. However, there also is evidence that word order and type, such as in the *adjectival* metaphor 'golden heart' vs. Neil Young's *genitival* version '*Heart of gold*' vs. the *nominal* 'Her heart was pure gold', can influence metaphor processing. The final example feature of this matrix at the supralexical semantic level, called *semantic complexity*, presents a special challenge to feature engineering, because many features at lower levels and of different types may contribute to it. Generally, the higher the feature level (supralexical > interlexical > lexical > sublexical) the more difficult it is to find computational methods for quantifying it in a valid and reliable way. Thus, determining the lexical feature *word length* (in number of letters or syllables) is relatively easy compared to finding appropriate measures of semantic complexity (e.g. of a poem). Before I discuss the most promising measures of semantic complexity, a little excursion on semantics in general and semantic similarity in particular seems in order.

Semantics, Oh Dear!

The semantic level of texts is the most important one, since we read for meaning. It is also the most complex level of all. Especially when we read poetry, the meaning-making process can be influenced by a myriad of features at other levels, such as rhythm and sound, as exemplified in the poems discussed in the *Preface*. That makes quantifying the contribution of semantic features to reader responses a whopping challenge, as rightly recognized by a former French minister. Indeed, when I was a post-doc in psycholinguistics at the French National Centre for Scientific Research (CNRS) in Paris back in the 1980s, there was a minister for education and science who had just declared that no more national grant money was to be spent for grants on semantics. The reason apparently was that one could not empirically investigate meaning via experimental research, because the issue was simply too complex (that is, to promise ground-breaking results during his term of office). My whole lab was very much impressed by this most curious ban and for years we focused on non-semantic psycholinguistic topics like orthography and phonology for which grant money was still coming in. Another reason why I was not working on semantics for many years was that even for the best computer modellers of the time, some of which I had met and worked with at MIT in 1986, semantics was a white spot on the map. Their models of reading had functional computational layers for visual, orthographic and phonological processing, and also a top layer for semantics, but unlike the AROM of the preceding chapter, this was purely hypothetical, or, as we said at the time, 'not implemented'. The problem was that back then neither psychologists nor computer scientists really knew what the appropriate semantic units or nodes in their models should look like. They called the hypothetical units *sememes* – in analogy to graphemes, phonemes and morphemes – but what information exactly these sememes were supposed to encode and how they should interact with the other units remained unclear. The turning point came in the 1990s with the publication of the semantic models explained next.

Distributional Semantics and Meaning Arithmetic

Words do not have meaning; they are cues to meaning. —Jeffrey Elman (2004)[91]

Which word pairs resemble each other more, table-book, table-peace or book-peace? No need to muse too long on that, because the degree of semantic similarity[ii] between two words (or other linguistic units) can be modelled as a function of the degree of overlap among their linguistic contexts. Based on the distributional semantics axiom 'Linguistic items with similar distributions have similar meanings', or in John Rupert Firth's words 'You shall know a word by the company it keeps', freely available NLP tools like *word2vec*[92] or BERT[93] ('Bidirectional Encoding Representations from Transformers') use this distributional information to quantify meaning by transforming each word of a corpus into a vector from the semantic space provided by a language model. Formally, a language model is just a probability distribution over sequences of words computed via machine learning. For computing such a probability, the language model needs to be trained on a reference corpus of literature, the *training corpus*. Training a model refers to an NLP procedure during which *neural nets* or other machine-learning tools such as *decision trees* or *support vector machines* acquire knowledge about statistical properties of a language. The 'language' typically consists of a collection of books serving as the reference corpus. My standard corpus for training the language models used in this book is the publicly available *Gutenberg Literary English Corpus* (GLEC) specialized in literature from the nineteenth century.[94] It contains ~900 novels, 500 short stories, 300 tales and stories for children, 200 poetry collections, poems and ballads, 100 plays, as well as 500 pieces of non-fiction, for example, articles, essays, lectures, letters, speeches or (auto-)biographies, with *~12 million* sentences and *250 million* words from a wide range of ~150 different authors such as Austen, Byron, Coleridge, Darwin, Dickens, Einstein, Eliot, Poe, Shakespeare, Twain, Wordsworth, Wilde or Yeats.

---

ii I use the term 'semantic similarity' in a loose sense here. More generally, two words are *semantically related* to the degree that they share attributes such as *synonyms* (poem and verse), *meronyms* (face and human), *antonyms* (ugly and beautiful) or words that are frequently associated or functionally related (book and author). The *attributional similarity* between two words, a and b, $sim_{att}(a, b) \in R$, depends on the degree of correspondence between the attributes of a and b. The more they share, the greater sim_{att}. The *relational similarity* between two pairs of words a:b and c:d, $sim_{rel}(a : b, c : d) \in R$, depends on the degree of correspondence between the relations of a:b and c:d. The higher it is, the greater sim_{rel}. For example, man and woman have a relatively high degree of sim_{att}, whereas dog:bark and cat:meow have a relatively high degree of sim_{rel}.

In contrast to *word2vec* models, which compute a single, static vector for each word – neglecting semantic ambiguity and multiple meanings – the substantially more complex and recent family of *BERT* models computes vectors for entire sentences and thus can represent context-dependent multiple meanings for a given word. But what does it mean for a word to have meaning or multiple meanings? If you know what the word 'table' *means*, then – in contrast to a special type of patients with brain lesions suffering from *semantic aphasia* – you are able to recognize objects that are tables, you can tell whether a table is more similar to a chair than to a book, and you can use the word in the proper speech or written context. If you read the word instead of seeing the object, its meaning is re-constructed in our brain from the fusion of a mental sound and a multidimensional, multimodal image schema. This is standard knowledge, and all fine, but from the perspective of Neurocomputational Poetics, the problem with letters and words, or image schemas, is that you cannot really calculate with them. That makes it hard to compare the meaning of two words and impossible to say how similar they are semantically or how big their associative strength is. Are 'table' and 'chair' semantically more similar than 'man' and 'woman', 'book' and 'text', or 'atom' and 'peace'? Without a quantitative metric of meaning, Neurocomputational Poetics is hopeless: reading is meaning-making and predicting what happens during the reading act requires methods to numerically express meaning. This is what freely available tools for computing semantic models like *latent semantic analysis*, *word2vec* or *BERT* can do.

Similar to our earlier example of the 3d-reduced person X, let us choose some simplified 4d vectors of arbitrary values here, to represent some words: say 'table' would become [0.1, 0.2, 0.3, 0.4], 'book' would become [0.9, 0.2, 0.5, 0.8] and peace [0.2, 0.2, 0.4, 0.3]. These numbers could represent the values of four features describing each word. Just as for person X, these features can be qualitative – for instance, 0 for concrete and 1 for abstract. Or they can be quantitative as calculated by a computer programme, such as the sonority score or word valence, both hard or impossible to calculate 'manually'. Even a combination of both is possible. What matters is that the key advantage of such a transformation into vectors is that we can quantify how distant or similar two words are by simple trigonometric operations like the Euclidean distance or the cosine between vectors. Semantic distance is analogous to physical distance, except that your movement from point A to B is a mental one and the space is not 3d but a high-dimensional semantic one.

Semantic similarity is often computed as 1 minus semantic distance or as the angle (cosine) between two vectors (here represented as arrows): If it is zero, they are identical, and the cosine is 1. Two vectors oriented at 90° relative to each other have a similarity of 0, and two vectors diametrically

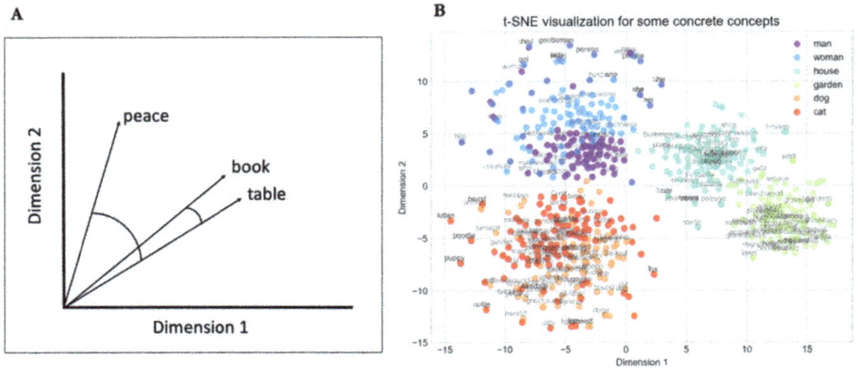

Figure 3.1 A. Simplified 2d representation of vectors for three words in a high-dimensional semantic space provided by a language model (here: word2vec). B. 2d diagram based on the 't-SNE' algorithm[95] showing the closest semantic neighbours of some concrete concepts in a small part of the artificial semantic memory of a hypothetical reader.

opposed have a similarity of −1. Figure 3.1A illustrates this. Since it is hard to visualize spaces with N>2 dimensions, typically only two are used for the X and Y-axes after some mathematical transformations. Analogous to a photograph, which reduces the real 3d space to a 2d map, these transformations reduce an N-dimensional space to a 2d one (or generally to an Md one, with M<N). The data in Figure 3.1B show the location of the 50 concepts most strongly associated with six exemplary concrete concepts in another section of the semantic space than that sketched in Figure 3.1A. It represents a part of a computer model of human semantic memory at the general level of an *average* or *ideal reader*. The semantic model underlying this was trained on the *GLEC corpus* and splits living from non-living objects (right half) very well, showing some overlap between related concepts that share features (e.g., man–woman). Thus, the training apparently was successful, and the model has face validity. Later in this book, we will see whether it also has empirical validity when using it to predict reader responses to texts.

So now I have everything I need to find out how similar 'table' is to 'book' and 'peace' (or 'puppy' to 'poodle' in the lower left corner of Figure 3.1B): I just do the cosine calculations and the results are *s*(table, book) = 0.17 and *s*(table, peace) = 0.05 (*s* standing for similarity). This tells you that (i) 'table' and 'book' have a positive semantic relatedness (>0) and that (ii) 'table' is more similar to 'book' than to 'peace' (on a scale from −1 to 1), 'book' being closer to 'peace' than 'table' (cosine = 0.13). The magic power of this 'words to vectors' trick lies in the fact that I can apply it not only to word pairs but also to metaphors or entire poems, that will come in handy to solve countless problems in NLP and Neurocomputational Poetics research like analogy problem-solving,[96] classifying books into genres or predicting the sentiment of readers' book reviews.

Analogies and Metaphors

As a simple example, consider the analogy-problem solving task: 'man' is to 'king' as 'woman' is to X. By doing a little semantic arithmetic, the problem can be solved by: queen = king + woman – man. We just apply the *parallelogram rule* by adding the difference vector between woman and man to that of king in the underlying semantic space provided by the language model. The same can be done with the task: *king is to queen like man is to X.* A more sophisticated application of meaning arithmetic concerns metaphors. Since neurocomputational research has established that metaphors are processed by readers in much the same way as literal sentences, metaphorical predication can be considered a special case of predication in general. One can think of metaphor comprehension as performing a *semantic leap,* hopping from the first term of a metaphor (the tenor or target) to the second (the vehicle or source) – and vice versa. The farther both terms are apart in semantic space, the more difficult comprehension is. In other words, and all other things being equal, the less semantically similar the tenor and vehicle are, the harder the metaphor will be to understand. Theoretically, for instance, the semantic distance to cover in this mental leap would be smaller for Lord Byron's 'Time is a bird' than for Dylan Thomas's 'The sky is a parliament'. The neuroscientific experiments in my lab discussed in Chapter 8 have indeed shown that a region in the left hemisphere we already have encountered several times in the preceding sections, the LIFG (cf. Figure 2.3A lower panel), is the more active, the greater the semantic distance between the two terms.

Let us consider metaphors of the nominal or attributional type (A is P), where A is the *tenor* of the metaphor (that is the *argument* of the underlying proposition) and P is the *vehicle* (that is the *predicate* of the proposition). Lord Byron's 'Time is a bird' is a case in point. Computing the similarity between A and P gives us a cue that this proposition is likely meant figuratively, not literally, since it is very low (cosine = .06) and literally makes no sense (the latter can be revealed by checking whether both words are synonyms using the *wordnet* tool[97] or some dictionary). To compute the vector representing the meaning of the metaphor, we simply select those neighbours of P that are also relatively close to A in the semantic space provided by the language model. The predication vector then is the mean of the vectors for A, P, and the set of terms similar to both. The term 'flies', for example, would be part of this set.

Psychological studies have indeed provided evidence for the validity of this simple vector model of metaphor comprehension.[98]

To summarize, I have introduced the necessary tools for a promising quantitative text analysis or distant reading approach: the *4x4 matrix* and the semantic models allowing sophisticated feature engineering. I know from many discussions with colleagues and experience with peer reviewers that some people have their problems with accepting the very idea that one can transform a metaphor by Dylan Thomas or a line from a Shakespeare sonnet into a vector of numbers – as if it were an object whose dimensions we measure with a metre. But if this allows us to quantify which sonnets are more semantically similar to each other, or which sonnet is the most creative or has the most beautiful line, then even these people could compare what our models say with their own intuitions and perhaps they'd be amazed or even shocked about the outcome. In this regard, this book is just another attempt at changing things towards an open-minded, truly cooperative cross-disciplinary science of verbal art. In the final paragraphs of this chapter, I discuss the ultimate goal of feature engineering and quantitative text analyses: computing two superfeatures that can predict the two crucial aspects of a reading act.

Comprehensibility and Likeability

No matter what you read, expository texts or fiction, prose or poetry, two factors influence your decision to read on: whether you understand and whether you like what you read. Although reading psychology has long known this fact, when it comes to methods and models for measuring and explaining which features of a text are most important for its comprehensibility (often used synonymously with readability) and likeability (based on a text's *emotion potential*), current research provides a controversial picture. Regarding measures of readability, the development of sophisticated computational methods has opened up a way to overcome the deficits of the low-dimensional, under-complex measures of the past, such as the still widely used *Flesch-Kincaide Index*.[99] This measure reduces readability to the number of syllables, words and sentences in a text, thus neglecting many other important features such as word frequency and concreteness, text cohesion or emotion potential.

Syntactic Complexity

Just as word length, whether counted in number of letters, syllables or morphemes, is an often-used proxy for *word complexity*, sentence length (in number of words) is a proxy for *syntactic complexity* in the psychology of reading or educational research. In both prose and poetry processing, it affects how well readers understand and/or appreciate a text. A line or sentence difficult to understand on grounds of its complex syntax can nevertheless be appreciated or liked just because it presents a puzzle to the mind, eventually promising resolution and reward.

In linguistics, a simple sentence typically consists of only one clause ('I like Ike'), a compound sentence has two or more independent clauses ('I like Ike, but I don't like Putine'), and a complex sentence has at least one independent plus one dependent clause beginning with a subordinate conjunction ('I enjoyed the book that you bought for me'). Naturally, using passive instead of active constructions will also change the complexity of sentences, as will other lexical or supralexical features categorized as belonging to 'syntax'. *Coh-Metrix*, a semi-commercial online toolkit for assessing text *cohesion* which only works for English, includes the following indices of syntactic complexity of a text (there are many more, though, not all being useful for analyses of texts shorter than 1,000 words)[100]:

- sentence and word length;
- content word overlap (all sentences, proportional, mean), a feature estimating text cohesion;
- left-embeddedness, that is, the number of words appearing before the main verb of the main clause in the sentences of a text; and
- overall readability (*CM-RL2*; i.e. English for second language learners).

Other, more recent tools include a dozen or more morphosyntactic features – ignoring the many other features (e.g. semantic) that also modify sentence complexity – and we will come to this level of complexity later in this book. But, for now, just consider the following two examples:

A) 'Pippi had not forgotten her father. He was a sea captain who sailed on the great ocean, and Pippi had sailed with him in his ship until one day her father was blown overboard in a storm and disappeared. But Pippi was absolutely certain that he would come back'.

B) 'But then, despite the importance he attached to navigation on the Elbe, he at once abandoned the topic and demanded that Joachim tell him more about life "up here" and about the guests; which Joachim proved ready and willing to do, happy to open his heart and unburden himself. He had to repeat the part about the bodies being sent down by bobsled and once again asserted unequivocally that he knew it to be true. And when Hans Castorp was taken by another fit of laughter, Joachim joined in, seeming heartily to enjoy the opportunity, and then told more comic stories, just to add fuel to the general merriment'._

Simply counting the number of words or the number of commas per text can already tell us something about their syntactic complexity and potential comprehensibility without recurring to complex constituency (phrase structure) or dependency grammar analyses as applied in linguistics and NLP. Astrid Lindgren's text (A) features three sentences with 49 words and 1 comma, that is, ~16 words per sentence. In contrast, Thomas Mann's text in (B) has 110 words, that is, ~36 per sentence, and eight commas/semicolons. It is thus not difficult to tell which of the two is syntactically more complex. Confirming intuition more formally, Coh-metrix computes:

- An overall text readability (*CM-RL2 score*) value of 20.8 for Lindgren's three sentences in (A) vs. 12.0 for Mann's in (B), a clear advantage for Lindgren
- In Lindgren's text, sentences are considerably shorter (16.3 words) than in Mann's (36.3), and the words are shorter too (1.36 syllables vs. 1.54).
- Moreover, the content word-overlap which helps cohesion and comprehension by repeating words across sentences, is .21 for Lindgren vs. .09 for Mann, while the difference in left-embeddedness is remarkable: Lindgren: 1.3 vs. Mann: 8.7.

That means that the brains of readers of Mann's text have to process a lot of text before the main action, marked by the verb, happens, while readers of Lindgren's text very quickly know what happens thanks to an easily built-up situation model. When it comes to poetry, things get more complicated, though, if only because poetry is characterized by its 'crazy syntax,' to borrow a term dear to my colleague Nigel Fabb. Indeed, poets can violate any syntactic rule for the sake of defamiliarization and foregrounding, even at the sublexical morphosyntactic level (see the above functional shifts).

In summary, the comprehensibility of texts depends to a large extent on syntactic complexity. This can be estimated by low-dimensional readability metrics or higher-dimensional NLP tools like Coh-Metrix. However, a more complete account of text comprehensibility requires including affective-aesthetic features, too, especially when analyzing poetry. In Chapter 4, I will demonstrate this by showing that likeability features can predict comprehensibility and vice versa. Furthermore, a full account of text comprehensibility must additionally include reader features, such as those discussed in Chapter 4.

Quantifying features shaping the *likeability* of texts has proven to be even more complicated than estimating their *comprehensibility*. In what follows, I will introduce several tools to compute likeability indices:

- sentiment analysis;
- topic analysis; and
- semantic complexity measures.

Sentiment Analysis

A standard procedure for sentiment analysis of texts goes like this. In step 1, one chooses an appropriate word list or dictionary which provides quantitative values for relevant semantic or emotional lexical features like *valence* for a limited set of words. The concept of valence stems from one of the oldest emotion theories of psychology by Wundt and refers to the extent to which an object, or word, is positive or negative. Publicly available word lists providing valence values for thousands of words can be found for many languages, such as the *Berlin Affective Word List* (BAWL) for German.[101] They are based on human ratings – collected in often costly empirical studies – of the valence of single words like 'fear' or 'sex', typically on a 7-point scale from −3 (very negative) to +3 (very positive). To give an illustrative example from research with children (8–12 years old), the five most positive words in our German *kidBAWL* database, a word list based on children's valence ratings assembled and tested by my former Ph.D. student Teresa Sylvester,[102] are: nature, mama, gift, smile and friend; those least liked are: violence, murder, cadaver, deception and steal. In step 2, one uses a computer programme to compare each word in a test text with the word list and, if a word gets a hit, then the computer stores the corresponding valence value; but you could also do it manually, if you prefer. These values can then be summed and averaged across larger units like sentences, paragraphs or chunks of 100–10,000 words. Consider the following sentence from J. K. Rowling's *Harry Potter and the Deathly Hallows*:

> Then he heard a terrible cry that pulled at his insides, that expressed agony of a kind neither flame nor curse could cause, and he stood up, swaying, more frightened than he had been that day, more frightened, perhaps, than he had been in his life

Here, a lot of negative words like 'terrible' or 'agony' would result in an overall negative sentiment quantified by the average valence of these words as looked up in a word list like the BAWL. If we plot the aggregated valence values against 'book time', that is, the serial number of sentences, word blocks or chapters, this can result in a diagram like that of Figure 3.2. It visualizes the theoretical emotional roller coaster of a story or book.

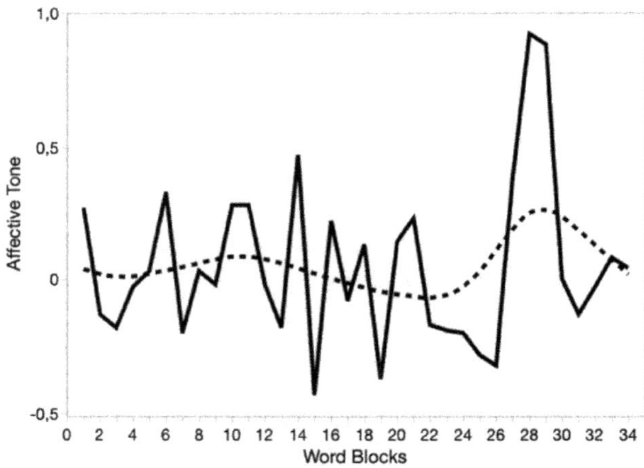

Figure 3.2 Theoretical affective tone plotted against book time (in blocks of approximately 100 words. Source: Adapted from Anderson and McMaster, 1982.[103] Dotted line = moving/smoothed average.

The diagram in Figure 3.2 stems from an early paper published in 1982 by C. W. Anderson and G. E. McMaster in the pioneering journal *Computers and the Humanities*. These authors, who probably invented the method, called it 'computer-assisted modeling of affective tone'. It was based on the idea that engaging narrative is an ebb and flow of *emotional tension*, traditionally expected to build towards a gratifying release near the end of well-crafted stories. Figure 3.2 illustrates the results of their method when applied to the second chapter of *Wonderland* by Joyce Carol Oates. It was chosen because it contains a subjectively convincing example of a catastrophic emotional event. The authors chopped the chapter into 34 blocks of around 100 words, looked to see whether each word in the block appeared in an emotion word dictionary, and if it did, assigned it the corresponding valence value. They then computed the average over all words in the block and plotted this in a diagram. Although due to the limited dictionary of only 1,000 words the hit rate was far from great (it covered only ~25 per cent of the story's words), the results were convincing, as evidenced by comparison with a precis of the story plot summarizing the major events and actions. This 'hit rate problem' and other issues associated with this early approach (e.g. costly collection of human ratings, availability in English only) can be avoided, though, by applying computational sentiment analysis tools based on semantic models like *SentiArt* rather than emotion dictionaries, as discussed in Chapter 5.

About 15 years ago, at the time of *Languages of Emotion*, diagrams like the one shown in Figure 3.2 made me feel that our projects in this 'supergrant' could lead somewhere I hadn't been before in my career: a place in which computational text analysis methods allow us to make innovative empirically testable predictions about the most fascinating achievement of the human mind, reading verbal art. And that meant that I was less worried about failing to fructify and justify the enormous investments in people and equipment, such as the ~2 million € for the big neuroimaging machine (our fMRI scanner) in the Dahlem Institute for Neuroimaging of Emotion (D.I.N.E.) that I was then directing. Because here was a simple means to bring together (printed) language and emotion in a way useful for cognitive neuroscientists and, so I hoped, literary scholars alike. If stable patterns of the emotion potential of texts can be detected by analysis of connotative meaning scores of words, just as the mean scores on the Y-axis of the diagram, and if they can predict human behaviour (ratings, eye movements) well enough, then perhaps we could also find signals of the brain's affective responses that reliably corresponded with these patterns. Moreover, with a bit of luck similar brain signals could also be predictable from quantifying at least some of the other higher-order features of literary texts which typically are of greater interest to literary scholars than lexical features, such as para- and *hypotaxis*, metaphoricity, the type and quality of schemes and tropes, the event structure of a narrative, the personality traits and mental conflicts of the protagonists or character interaction networks.

Topic Analysis

Imagine you have three lists of words either closely related to sports, or to culture, or to politics, such as ['football', 'goal', 'trainer', [...]] vs. ['art', 'theatre', 'literature', [...]] vs. ['president', 'election', 'government', [...]]. You go through a text with them and each time you encounter a word from one of the lists you check. The list with the biggest tally then estimates the text's topic. Basically, this is how topic models work. Technically, in NLP research, a *topic model* is a probabilistic model: a statistical model based on probability distributions for discovering the abstract 'topics' which occur in a collection of documents, typically the sentences of a text. A *topic* is a more or less hidden pattern discovered by specific algorithms such as *Latent Dirichlet Allocation* (LDA) based on the grouping of both documents, which use semantically related words, as well as words which occur in a similar set of documents. Thus, if semantically related words often occur together across documents, they likely form a topic. Together with sentiment analysis, topic analysis was used in 2016 by Jodie Archer and Matthew L. Jockers to crack the 'bestseller code' and predicted the likelihood of a book being a bestseller with accuracies of up to 80 per cent.[104]

A standard way of displaying topics is *word clouds* in which the size of key words representing a topic is proportional to their frequency of occurrence, displaying more frequent words bigger. The following practical word clouds illustrate the words most highly associated with a topic and thus nicely bring out their internal structure (in this case only nouns were selected, without proper names too revealing for the guessing task). Figure 3.3 shows a selection of two of the 10 most probable topics for each of four novels from GLEC. Can you guess which novels hide behind these topics?

(A) is relatively easy, also because I included names in this analysis, but can you guess the others too? Well, the first two clouds in (A) are from Edgar Rice Burrough's *Tarzan of the Apes*, those in (B) from Herman Melville's *Moby-Dick*, the next ones in (C) are from Robert Louis Stevenson's *The Strange Case of Dr. Jekyll and Mr. Hyde*, and the final ones in (D) are from George Eliot's *Middlemarch*. All topics were extracted using a standard computational tool called *LDAMallet,* which is freely available

Figure 3.3 Word clouds representing key words most highly associated with two selected topics for four novels from GLEC.

on the internet.[105] For simplicity, only nouns and verbs were taken into account, and I used no filtering such as for proper names or abbreviations like 'Mr.'. Current topic analysis tools are pretty good at getting the right topics for sports vs. political or cultural news, for example; when it comes to sophisticated literary texts like Jane Austen's novels, there is still space for improvement though. Anyhow, topic analysis and topic probability distributions play a major role when, in the next section, I compare different text categories and authors in GLEC and propose a method for computing perceived *book beauty*. Moreover, sentiment and topic analysis can be combined, thus allowing one to estimate the emotion potential of a novel's main topics and to improve likeability prediction. However, knowing the general sentiment and topics of literary texts and poetry does not suffice for predicting their likeability. Just as syntax can be more or less complex, semantics can be too, and this semantic complexity should influence how well we like (and understand) a text.

Semantic Complexity, Literariness and Foregrounding Potential

Psycholinguistic research has produced quite a few heuristic and formal measures of syntactic complexity, but its sister semantic complexity has been somewhat in the shadows, perhaps due to the fact that semantics is a more tacit or hidden layer of texts. Recent NLP research, however, has supplied several highly interesting and easy-to-compute measures of semantic complexity and creativity, all based on the above-mentioned distributional semantic models. The basic idea – introduced earlier in the context of metaphor comprehension – is that the greater the semantic distance between words or larger text units in a sequence, the more difficult meaning integration is – and the higher the semantic complexity.

Consider the following simple sentences:

A) The poet read a book.
B) The student reads a papyrus.
C) The dolphin reads the Bible.

Semantic anomalies as deviations from norms and expectations based on world and language knowledge can easily be quantified by semantic models. Thus, the semantic distance between 'poet' and 'book' in (A) would be smaller than that between 'student' and 'papyrus' in (B) or 'dolphin' and 'Bible' in (C). Hence, the corresponding theoretical order of semantic complexity would be: A < B < C. Next, I introduce three recent measures that allow us to quantify semantic complexity.

Forward Flow and Creativity

The sequential semantic distance between the words of a line or sentence can be used as an index of verbal creativity, called *forward flow* (FF). Recent empirical studies have indeed shown that it is a good predictor of creativity (as assessed by independent psychological tests like divergent thinking tasks) in:

- college students;
- a representative sample of Americans;
- membership in real-world creative groups like performance majors, professional actors or entrepreneurs; and
- the creative achievement of celebrities' social media posts like Twitter.

You can easily try out the measure yourself[106] with the crucial word pairs from the above sentences or your own creative texts. Thus, the sequence (A) 'read-book' gets an FF of 0.31 vs. (B) 'read-papyrus': FF = 0.78, identifying the latter one as more creative. Now let's see how this method fares with real poetry like the first lines of Shakespeare's sonnets 1 and 18: 'From fairest creatures we desire increase' (FF = 0.8) vs. 'Shall I compare thee to a summer's day?' (FF = 0.7). I leave it to you to judge the poeticity of these two lines and the validity of the FF measure. If you are not happy with it, there are two others that may match your feelings of poeticity better.

Stepwise Semantic Distance and Intra-textual Variance

Applying the above ideas to chunks of text of a given size (typically 1,000 words, roughly corresponding to 75 sentences), one can compute the mean and variability of the semantic distances for an entire poem or book as another index of their semantic complexity: the degree of difficulty of meaning integration across larger text units. All other things being equal, text chunks that are semantically very similar by sharing a lot of concepts are considered to be simpler than those which confront readers with lots of less related, varying and potentially more interesting or surprising concepts.

One method to do this is to compute the sequential or *stepwise semantic distances* between all the sentences or text chunks in a book, sum them up and divide by their number to obtain the mean and variance. This method can uncover the difference between small, gradual topic changes on the one hand, and large, sudden changes on the other, with respect to the linear progression of the text. It thus uncovers semantic leaps – sudden big alterations in semantic distance between two text chunks. This may function as a foregrounding device that captures readers' attention and sparks their associative imagination to fill in such unforeseen gaps in semantic space.

Another method is to compute the *intra-textual variance* of the sentence or chunk vectors of a book. If a book is represented as a cloud of points corresponding to sentences or chunks in a reduced 2d vector space, this cloud can be either dense (a set of chunks highly similar to each other) or expansive (a set of chunks highly dissimilar to each other). The semantic variance of a book can then be measured by the *Euclidean distance* of its chunks to the *centroid* of the novel (i.e. its mean value). This method reveals how semantically homogeneous or coherent a text is. It can also be used to locate text pieces with a higher foregrounding potential, based on their distance to the centroid or deviation from the 'text norm': the greater the distance, the higher the foregrounding potential.

Figure 3.4 shows examples. In Figure 3.4A, the sequential or stepwise semantic distances for the initial 10 text chunks of two books from GLEC are plotted in the same semantic space (reduced from 300d to a handy 2d

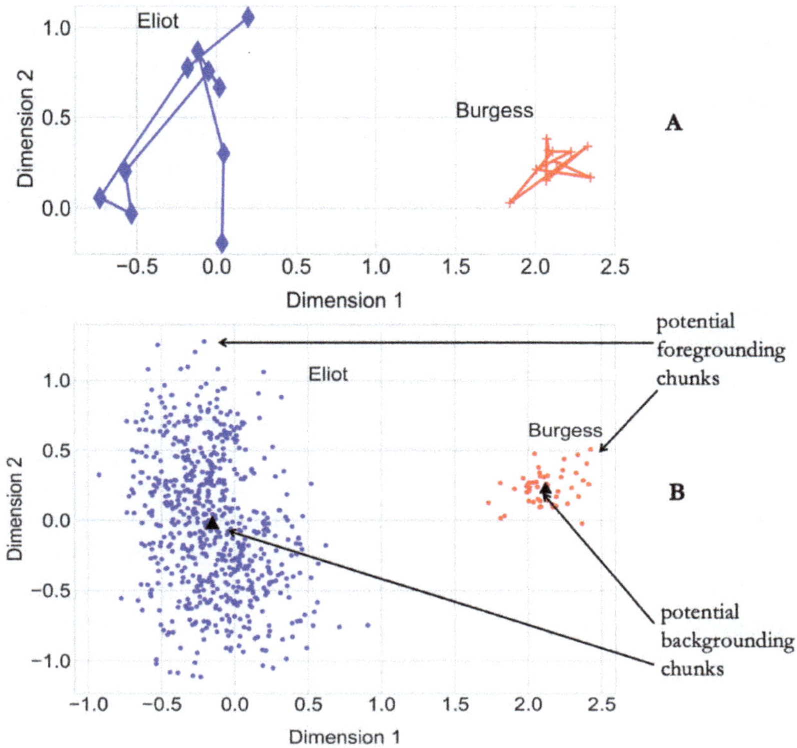

Figure 3.4 A. *Stepwise Distance* measure reflecting the semantic distances between consecutive text chunks starting at the beginning of a text. B. *Intra-textual Variance* measure representing the average semantic distance between chunks of text and the centroid, that is, the mean of all dots.

representation by a statistical method called principal component analysis/PCA[iii]). It becomes immediately obvious that George Eliot's *Middlemarch* (blue diamonds) offers greater semantic leaps to its readers than Thornton Waldo Burgess' children's book *Blacky the Crow* (red crosses). The overall index of semantic complexity according to this method is 5.1 for Eliot vs. 2.1 for Burgess. In Figure 3.4B, both books are plotted as clouds by the *intra-textual variance* method, the big black triangles marking the centroids. Again, it becomes immediately obvious that George Eliot's *Middlemarch* (blue dots) offers greater semantic variety than Thornton Waldo Burgess' *Blacky the Crow* (red dots). The overall index of semantic complexity according to this second method is 3.4 for Eliot vs. 1.4 for Burgess. Of course, Eliot's book is much longer (672 chunks) than Burgess' (49 chunks), but I checked that in GLEC there is no correlation between the number of chunks per book and the two measures of semantic complexity. Note that chunks farther away from the centroid represent candidates for foregrounded pieces of text, those closer to the centroid represent candidates for backgrounded text. Both methods have their pros, but from a Neurocomputational Poetics perspective, we must ask which of these two methods is best for estimating the foregrounding potential of texts and predicting reader responses. This can only be decided empirically, and fortunately, a recent study on around 400 novels in Dutch provides evidence that both measures are promising predictors of human literariness ratings with a slight advantage for one (stepwise distance: $r = .43$, intra-textual variance: $r = .34$).[107] Note that in this study, readers were not provided with any definition of what literariness or literature is supposed to be, to encourage them to provide their own intuitions of what literariness is and not one provided by the authors.

In summary, current NLP research offers at least three measures that can quantify and help estimate the semantic creativity and complexity of texts. All three have been empirically tested and qualify as promising. In another practical example, in the next section I apply the last two measures to help answer the question which author of plays is theoretically more 'literary', the latter term being operationalized via measures of semantic complexity rather than being defined in any qualitative way. After all, why should the semantics of plays behave differently from those of the novels from the Dutch study?

iii https://en.wikipedia.org/wiki/Principal_component_analysis

Author of Most Literary Plays in GLEC

If the two measures, stepwise semantic distance and intra-textual variance, provide a plausible quantitative answer to the above question, this might stir up debate and motivate empirical research. Would William Shakespeare (36 plays in GLEC) win the competition, or would he be surpassed by George Bernard Shaw (30 plays)? What about Oscar Wilde (8 plays) or William Butler Yeats (6 plays)?

The diagram in Figure 3.5 gives a tentative answer to the question: the theoretically most literary author in this set is, as many may think, William Shakespeare. Although both Shaw and Dryden have slightly higher intra-textual variance scores, Shakespeare has the highest stepwise distance score by lengths, and taking both measures together his plays win. James Matthew Barrie's plays, on the other hand, appear to be less literary, if these measures have any face validity. Of course, this is all purely theoretical and may not match personal tastes or stand empirical validation. Moreover, I do not believe that a construct as complex as *literariness* –which has been under heavy debate among stylisticians for centuries[108] – can fully be explained once for all by a mix of two complex semantic features only. Rather, I believe that such computational measures will ultimately help solve the issue by providing empirically testable predictions which provide a benchmark of what is possible with the help of NLP technology and what needs to be added via middle reading or alternative close reading approaches. Indeed, in the only large-scale empirical study on human literariness ratings, the above-mentioned

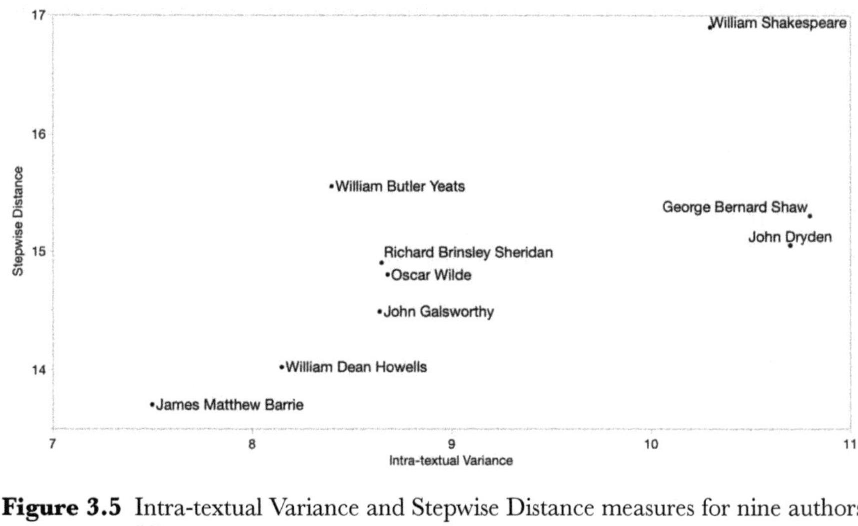

Figure 3.5 Intra-textual Variance and Stepwise Distance measures for nine authors of plays in GLEC as an estimate of their relative literariness.

Dutch study, these two measures left about 50 per cent of the variance in ratings unaccounted for, that is, they explain at best half of the construct. But I also know of no other approach or method which could do as much. My remark also applies to the examples of the next study: they provide benchmarks or lower limits of what is possible thanks to computational methods – regularly improved in ever shorter time intervals – and thus challenge any alternative approach to do better. This is the main rule of the science game I was trained to play by my Ph.D. advisors and I'll stick to it.

Predicting Perceived Book Beauty

This final application example is my favourite in this chapter. When I met Walter Kintsch, the author of the crazy idea of *text beauty*, to talk about my book *Brain and Poetry*, I asked him why he and other great pioneers of Cognitive Science had never published anything about affective or aesthetic reader responses. This intrigued me especially because, together with the literary scholar Teun van Dijk, he had pioneered the interdisciplinary research on text processing and semantic models in the 1980s, both central to my perspective. His answer was as stunning as it was simple: at the time, we had enough to do with the 'cognitive turn'; emotions could wait. In his admittedly complicated 2012 paper 'Musings about Beauty' which as he told me took several years to be accepted by the very critical peer reviewers of the journal *Cognitive Science* he caught up on this.

Since the days of Gustav Theodor Fechner, empirical aesthetics has strived for quantification and produced several more or less successful equations for perceived beauty, the holy grail of that research field. Birkhoff's equation is an example. In 1942, George David Birkhoff claimed that our pleasure in any work of art depends on only two variables: the amount of Order (O) and of Complexity (C) in the object. These are measured in various ways for different classes of objects, but all classes obey the general formula: *P* (the amount of pleasure) = O/C. Other more or less convincing aesthetic equations were proposed in psychological research, but as far as I can tell, until 2012, apparently no one ever thought of coming up with a formula for the perceived beauty of verbal art.[109] As one of the leading cognitive scientists of the last 50 years, in his paper Kintsch wanted to challenge the widely accepted assumption that 'beauty is hopelessly complex' and 'a theory of aesthetics is impossible'. Very few papers I have read influenced my work in the last decade as much.

In his work on low-complexity art, the computer scientist Jürgen Schmidhuber had advanced and formalized the idea that objects that are complex and unfamiliar enough afford complexity reduction.[110] Kintsch drew upon his work and put forward the simple idea that perceived beauty of an object relies on its balance between *harmony* and *variety*.[iv] If the parts fit well with the whole, the object has harmony; if they vary sufficiently among them, it has variety. When both conditions hold and the theoretical variety value is bigger than that for harmony, the object is likely to be perceived as beautiful. Fechner's principle of 'absence of contradiction' already claimed that harmony is aesthetically preferable to disagreement or contradiction. Moreover, he assumed that we prefer objects which are both unified and complex over objects which are homogeneous or excessively diverse. When both conditions are combined, they produce a total satisfaction greater than the sum of these conditions taken separately, for example, melody and harmony in music, or meaning and rhythm in poetry.

Kintsch proposed that a story is encoded as a mental model, and that harmony requires that it is indeed possible to encode the whole as well as the parts with the same model. This is because according to Fechner's principle of economy, the cost of transforming its aspects must be small. Variety, on the other hand, requires that the parts are all different, that is, that the cost of transforming one aspect into another is large. Thanks to his expertise with semantic models and statistics, Kintsch could operationalize these ideas and came up with equations for computing harmony and variety for entire books on the basis of topic analyses. Harmony thus is the distance – as measured by some standard statistical metric like the Hellinger distance I used here[111] – between the topic probability distributions of the whole book and those for its chapters, both computed with the method outlined above. Variety is the average distance between the topic probability distributions of the chapters. This resembles the stepwise distance and intra-textual variance measures from above, but Kintsch meaningfully relates both measures within a cognitive model of perceived beauty that goes beyond simple descriptions, and he also introduces the requirement that variety > harmony. Otherwise, the object risks being boring. For some reason, Kintsch never implemented or tested his model, noting: 'A serious test of such a model would be a major undertaking, requiring a careful selection of representative texts'. During the last years, I dared this 'major undertaking' using my *SentiArt* tool with the integrated aforementioned *LDAMallet* topic analysis algorithm and this is what I present in this section (for technical details, see our recent paper in *arXiv*[112]), taking

iv Actually, he added a third component, the dynamics of complexity reduction called *compression*. I must neglect this here for the sake of simplicity and because it concerns changes in perceived beauty over repeated acts of contact with an object, which are hard to measure and simulate on a computer.

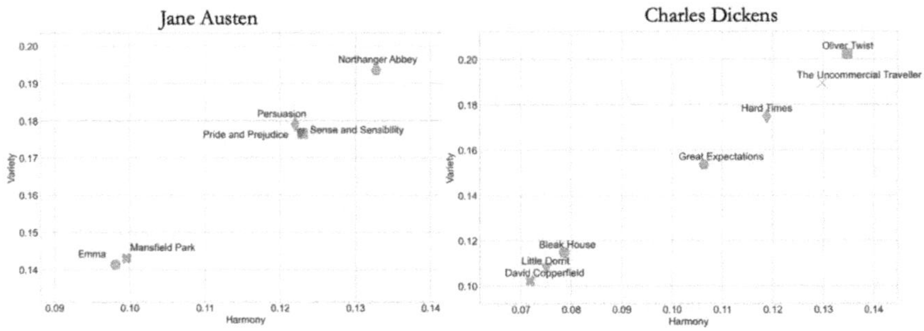

Figure 3.6 Harmony and Variety values as estimates of book beauty for a selection of novels from GLEC by Jane Austen and Charles Dickens. Note that on the X-axis, smaller (distance) values represent greater harmony or similarity between the books' and chapters' main topics.

the examples of books by two of the most popular authors on *Project Gutenberg*, Jane Austen and Charles Dickens.

Jane Austen

As one can imagine, when googling 'best novel by author = X', one finds more answers than one was looking for. But there are some serious sources of information such as the homepage of the *The Reader*,[113] a marvellous extremely successful charity bringing literature to people who may otherwise have little opportunity to get in touch with it. *The Reader*'s homepage came up first on my query 'Best novel by Jane Austen' and it said: '[…] But that's not to say that each of Austen's six major novels do not have their own individual charms and merits. In fact, we've taken each of the six books in turn and have ranked them in order of utter brilliance'. But do you agree? Their ranking goes like this: Pride and Prejudice > Persuasion > Emma > Sense and Sensibility > Northanger Abbey > Mansfield Park. Corroborative evidence comes from *goodreads* ranking[v] which is identical, and from the *Gutenberg* top 100 downloads list in which *Pride and Prejudice* was the leading rank for the month of July 2022, followed by *Persuasion* (rank 34), *Emma* (53) and *Sense and Sensibility* (75).

So, now that we have some converging clues for the popularity of Austen's novels, what does the tentative model of book beauty say? The data in Figure 3.6 (left panel) first show that all six books fulfil the criterion that variety be greater than harmony. Second, there is a linear trend: the greater

v https://www.goodreads.com/list/show/1986.Best_Jane_Austen_Novels

the harmony is (i.e., smaller values), the smaller the variety is. This could be expected, since when chapter topics are more similar to each other, then they likely also are more similar to the book's main topics. Third, *Emma* is the most harmonious book, the one with the smallest value of all. However, it also produced the smallest value for variety, which is greatest for *Northanger Abbey*. Being short of any precedence case and prior empirical values, it looks like the group formed by *Pride and Prejudice*, *Sense and Sensibility* and *Persuasion* strikes a good balance between harmony and variety. These three would thus be the likely most beautiful books in the set. So let us see next what the model says about Dickens.

Charles Dickens

In the 'greatest books of all times' hit parade, Charles Dickens' *Great Expectations* is ranked 27th, followed by *David Copperfield* on rank 45, and *Bleak House* on 116.[114] In the above Gutenberg top 100 downloads list, *Great Expectations* was ranked 18, followed by *David Copperfield* (62) and *Oliver Twist* (64). In Figure 3.6 (right panel), the most harmonious book appears to be *David Copperfield*, the most varied *Oliver Twist*, but the combination of harmony and variety of *Great Expectations* makes it the best candidate for Dickens' most beautiful novel.

The present *null model* of perceived book beauty allows to discuss such ranking results based on download statistics or expert opinions in light of quantifiable features that answer two questions of interest which, as far as I can tell, have not yet been answered by a computational method before:

- How well do the main topics of a book fit with those of its chapters?
- How much do the latter differ from one another?

The model's metrics being applicable to any book with a clear chapter structure also permits comparative statements like: *David Copperfield* is more harmonious than *Emma*, and *Northanger Abbey* more varied than *Great Expectations*. To what extent such quantifications make more sense than subjective interpretation and speculation must be decided by future fundamental and applied research, why not sponsored by the book industry. This being said, the limits of the model which only considers statistics derived from topic-based content are obvious. It ignores any kind of form beauty like style figures, and it certainly does not capture 'unique selling points' like the one highlighted on *The Reader*'s homepage cited above in regard to *Pride and Prejudice*'s superior popularity: 'The family relationships of the Bennetts are as key to the narrative as the love story between Elizabeth and Darcy, although it is the latter which produces the most memorable scenes and quotes in the novel'. Still, in principle, its predictions can be tested empirically, just as those concerning the literariness of novels, and it has potential for updated versions. Thus, I could include sentiment and plot analyses – which was the basis of Archer and Jockers' bestseller code success – or character analysis (see Chapter 6) to augment the model. In any case, in my eyes, a model of verbal art reception like the NCPM gains enormously when being able to propose a computational sub-model of perceived book beauty.

To summarize, these two exploratory studies in GLEC pave the way for many more of the kind. Quantifying the literariness of plays and authors or the perceived beauty of books replaces or complements speculation by measurement, and this is what Neurocomputational Poetics is all about. In Chapters 5 and 6, I will put such measurements to test and see what they can or cannot achieve when confronted with human data.

Summary

In this chapter, I have argued that, following in the steps of Propp and Jakobson, middle and distant reading techniques for literature analysis offer useful complements or alternatives to the close reading practise common in the humanities. To make these prolific and successful, I proposed a feature engineering approach guided by the *4x4 matrix* and discussed examples of metric, phonological, morphosyntactic and semantic features relevant to Neurocomputational Poetics research. I then showed how distributional semantic models can be used to do meaning arithmetic and solve analogy and metaphor comprehension problems. Starting from the premise that the successful prediction of the comprehensibility and likeability of literature is the ultimate goal of the Neurocomputational Poetics approach, I discussed various methods for computing syntactic and semantic complexity and applied some of them to the prediction of the literariness of plays and the perceived beauty of books from Jane Austen and Charles Dickens.

Chapter 4

READER AND READING ACT ANALYSIS

As sketched in the metamodel of Chapter 2, literary experiences result from the dynamic interaction between author, (con-)text and reader. Neurocomputational Poetics focusses on text and reader because these can best be characterized by quantifiable features. In the previous chapter on text analysis, I presented methods for computing text features that, according to the NCPM, can bias a reader's mind more towards the upper or the lower route of processing. This bias can be induced globally by the choice of a novel instead of a poetry collection, for example, or locally when re-reading a section of a text to reflect upon its form or content. In this chapter, I deal with both the reader and the act of reading. The 'reading motivation and mode' box of the mesomodel in Chapter 2 brings a number of reader-related factors into play that also influence this bias towards one of the two routes. Among those are stable personality variables called 'traits' or more transient, local aspects like spontaneous mood management called 'states' in personality psychology. Here, I discuss methods for analyzing these in Neurocomputational Poetics studies.

Reader Analysis

Most empirical studies of literature and reading psychology focus on the 'average reader': a purely statistical creature typically represented by mean values averaged across the data from some rather small (N~20) and generally non-representative sample. Indeed, the large majority of empirical studies on reading so far have used undergraduate psychology students. When examining the processing of non-literary, short expository texts – so-called *textoids* – typical for these studies, the distortion in the data produced by this overselective sampling method may not be as detrimental as when studying the reception of verbal art. But even if the error introduced by this sampling method were negligible, reading ultimately remains a solitary, subjective and private act. It goes without saying that readers have different cultural and social backgrounds, education, habits, skills, personalities and preferences.

And all these produce variables that contribute to the reading act and can be more or less well assessed. Luckily, psychology also offers methods to study readers' reading skills, personalities or interests, and these provide useful data when trying to predict the outcome of a reading act via models like the NCPM. Indeed, empirical studies have shown that reading can change both personality states and traits, and these, in turn, can change the way texts are read and appreciated. Thus, we have a bidirectional, two-way relationship between personality and literature. In the following, I discuss exemplary tools for reader analysis. I start with several methods for reader personality assessment, the *big5*, empathy and trait-absorption scales, continue with computational reader-specific language models (RLMs) that usefully complement the general semantic models introduced in the previous chapter, and end with a test of reading proficiency developed in my lab.

Words, Scales and Tests

> *I tried to gain an idea of the number of the more conspicuous aspects of the character by counting in an appropriate dictionary the words used to express them [...]I examined many pages of its index here and there as samples of the whole, and estimated that it contained fully one thousand words expressive of character, each of which has a separate shade of meaning, while each shares a large part of its meaning with some of the rest.*
>
> —Francis Galton, *Measurement of Character* (1884)

Big5 and Reading Habits

Since the days of Francis Galton, psychologists have measured personality and individual differences with words – in the form of single items, statements or questions – combined with scales. The *Likert scale*, usually going from 1 = 'strongly disagree' to 7 = 'strongly agree', is a typical example. A very popular specimen of a personality test containing a set of items grouped into factors (typically 2–5 items) is the *big5* personality inventory. Depending on the version, it can use between 10 and 400 items altogether, such as 'I see myself as someone who [...]':

- is reserved;
- is generally trusting;
- tends to be lazy.

The aim of the personality test is to find out the score of a person on each of five dimensions: Openness to experience, Conscientiousness, Extraversion, Agreeableness and Neuroticism. Due to the initial letters of these five personality dimensions, the model underlying the scales is also called the *OCEAN model*. The five factors (dimensions) of this model are thought to capture enduring personality characteristics that are most important in people's lives (traits). These are hypothesized to eventually become part of their language and more likely to be encoded into language as a single word or phrase than others. The empirically well-validated 10-item version, called *BFI10* (Big Five Inventory 10), is advertised by claiming 'test your personality in a minute' and can easily be administered. It is interesting for reading research because a recent large-scale study has shown significant correlations between the *BFI10* dimensions and book preferences. Thus, for example, readers with high Openness scores like to read philosophical novels, science fiction or plays, while more conscientious readers prefer religious and mystery books, as is illustrated in Figure 4.1. Openness is associated with intellectual endeavours, imaginative tendencies, curiosity or creativity. As discussed earlier, imagination is essential for narrative comprehension, allowing to mentally simulate the surroundings and situations being presented to us in literary fiction. This capacity may also facilitate perspective-taking, that is, placing ourselves in the shoes of story protagonists and better understanding other people. Neurotic individuals seem to like narratives reflecting their own emotional states, such as sad endings and mental issues, and books on alternative realities. This fits with the hypothesis that these genres provide a special means of escape. Extroverts indulge in books with social themes, like

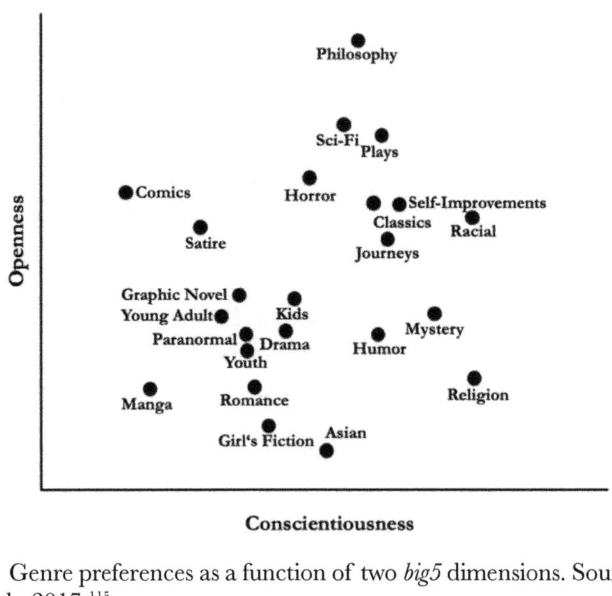

Figure 4.1 Genre preferences as a function of two *big5* dimensions. Source: Adapted from Ng et al., 2017.[115]

relationships, and are interested in reading about the lives of others, from memoirs to celebrity romance. Introverts, who are said to be more sensitive to environmental stimuli, causing them to live more inside themselves, have a preference for books with themes such as fantasy, science fiction and supernatural forces, exhibiting a tendency to indulge in imagination. Finally, agreeable personalities prefer books with family and religious themes, both of which promote positive social relationships.

In my lab, we regularly collect *big5* data from our readers and correlate the obtained scores with experiential or behavioural response data such as the answers to a reading experience questionnaire or eye movement parameters. In several studies, we found significant correlations. For example, extrovert readers tend to evaluate fictive texts as more positive than introvert readers. Or, more neurotic readers tend to rate negative text parts more negatively than less neurotic ones, confirming the above finding that they prefer narratives reflecting their own emotional states.

Empathy and Immersion

Another personality trait relevant for reading but not explicitly included in the *big5* scales is empathy, discussed in detail in Chapter 2. Still, intellectually open and agreeable individuals – as assessed by the *big5* test – likely show a tendency towards empathic and prosocial responses and to manifest the empathy required to understand fictional characters. This makes narrative engagement more real and perhaps more pleasurable or interesting for them. However, personality traits not only co-determine how verbal art is received. Verbal art also can shape personality. We thus have a kind of feedback system between verbal art and reader personality. In the first direction (reader -> text), neuroimaging experiments in my lab – discussed in detail in Chapter 7 – revealed, for example, that individuals showing a co-activation in two brain regions associated with attention and control, and, more importantly, with mentalizing and empathy, reported a stronger tendency to put themselves into characters of novels and movies. This tendency was assessed via the fantasy subscale of the Interpersonal Reactivity Index (IRI) a personality test assumed to measure four aspects of empathy. The fantasy subscale is assumed to operationalize *affective empathy* as discussed in Chapter 2 and presents items like 'I really get involved with the characters of a novel', or 'When I am reading an interesting story or novel, I imagine how I would feel if the events in the story were happening to me'.[116] The interplay between the neural networks of both brain regions activated in readers with higher IRI scores appears to be crucial for internally driven thought such as goal-directed simulations. Meaning-making requires a balance between inferences upon the text that readers generate via abstraction and association to prior knowledge on the one hand and attentional control to prevent *mind wandering* away from the text on the other. It has been shown that frequent mind wandering compromises situation model building and reading comprehension and leads to longer, uncharacteristic eye fixations.

In the other direction (text -> reader), several empirical studies have shown that reading fiction can improve scores on psychological empathy scales and change those of other personality tests.[117] For example, the self-reported tendency to become highly engaged in stories was positively correlated with fiction print exposure. Print exposure can be indirectly measured by the *Author Recognition Test*, which assesses people's lifetime exposure to print by asking them to identify more or less famous authors they know.[118] In other words, the more you read fiction, the easier it becomes to immerse yourself in promising pleasurable literary experiences. If you are an avid reader and a person scoring high on the scale introduced next, then your own personal immersion potential may be optimal.

Trait Absorption

A final relevant scale I want to familiarize you with is the 'Openness to absorbing and self-altering experiences' scale.[119] Using items like 'The sound of a voice can be so fascinating to me that I can just go on listening to it' or 'I am sometimes able to forget about my present self and get absorbed in a fantasy that I am someone else'. it is assumed to measure readers' *trait absorption*, that is, their tendency to be transported into a narrative. That is, high scorers on that scale likely immerse faster or deeper into text worlds. Indeed, trait absorption is correlated with the intensity of experiencing presence in a virtual reality world, with the big5 factor 'openness to experience', visual imagery and motivation to read for insight. All these seem to facilitate the ability to identify with characters. In a recent large-scale internet study,[120] the authors could show that the effects of personality traits on absorbed reading are generally mediated by reading habits, and that sustained concentration and attentional flexibility are generic aspects of several absorption-like states predicted by openness to experience scores. Basically, this confirms what I said in the last sentence of the preceding paragraph: If you are a character open to (new) experiences and intellectually curious, you probably read more than others and train your immersion potential. If you read more, that facilitates becoming even more open, as well as absorbed or immersed. In turn, being frequently immersed should increase the likelihood of scoring high in the absorption scale. It's a bit like the chicken and egg dilemma. What causes what is unclear, because we face a complex feedback system.

Whatever, your partly innate personality traits – including phenomena of neurodiversity (such as 'dyslexia') – interact dynamically with your environment and the reading habits it stimulates or inhibits, such as when your parents or granny read aloud a lot to you during your childhood, or you find a lot of books in your home and read a lot. There is nothing better to make you a proficient reader, that is one with a high word per minute (wpm) index or reading test score, as introduced in the next section, than to read a lot. Practice, practice, practice! No secret here. And, much like in music, the more you rehearse, the higher the likelihood of reward. In playing an instrument, the reward you feel is not only related to error-free performance, but also much to immersing in the sweet sound world you produce yourself. In ludic reading of prose, it is mainly related to immersing in the text world produced by your imagination; in poetry, the (implicit) sound world created by prosody and sonority is an extra reward, as can be the discovery of ever new layers of meaning peeled off via slow reflective reading on an aesthetic trajectory.

To summarize, psychology offers a whole lot more scales than those discussed in this chapter, which are potentially relevant for empirical studies on verbal art reception; but these three are the ones we have used most often in our own research. Given that a full-blown empirical study will also include other scales for measuring aspects of the reading act as well as the collection of biographical data such as reading habits, the typical duration of a reading experiment of one hour prohibits the use of too great a number of scales. Thus, adequate care should go into the selection of the right scales for testing the hypotheses proper to an empirical study.

Psychologists also distinguish between *self-report questionnaires* and scales on the one hand and *performance tests* on the other. The data produced by the former can always suffer from the two big subterfuges of personality tests: deceit of oneself – not being honest to oneself about, say, how lazy one is – and deceit of others – responding to a questionnaire with a social desirability bias or bluntly lying. Performance tests probing memory or reading skill provide more objective data. Thus, a combination of both in a study is a good idea. The next but one section presents my team's favourite performance test, but before that, I would like to introduce the perhaps most promising virtual diagnostic instrument based on semantic models.

You Are What You Read – Reader-specific Language Models

Normative corpora like GLEC and the semantic models derived from them represent samples of the learning experience of average 'ideal', that is, non-existent readers. They cannot answer the question which texts are most representative for which *real* person such as those participating in a neurocomputational reading study. A Neurocomputational Poetics perspective using complex literary materials including poetry must fail, however, if ultimately it cannot explain individual reader preferences, experiences or behaviour. After all, ample empirical evidence shows that especially poetry has strong differential impacts on individual readers, due to personal resonances, reading skills or their empathy aptitude. The reading of prose, too, can have differential impacts depending, for example, on how readers' personality profiles match those of the characters they most identify with in a novel. Thus, standard corpora and ideal reader models need to be complemented by *individual corpora* and RLMs that reflect parts of the learning experience of individual readers.

But how can we obtain RLMs? As sketched in Figure 4.2A, the first step is to collect individual corpora/IC. For this, we invite fully anonymized participants to record a part of their everyday reading activity, either during daily internet surfing ('googling') or during regular reading sessions on tablets. The latter can also be equipped with an eye-tracking device. A costly longitudinal design is necessary for such studies with typical sample periods of 12–24 months and sample sizes of $N \geq 100$ readers. In step 2, these IC*s* are then used to create RLMs using *word2vec* or *BERT* models. Trait-descriptive adjectives from personality scales like the *big5* such as 'academic' or 'reliable' are then collected (in our case more than 200 labels were used to gain statistical power) and in step 4 the average similarity of the 2,500 most frequent words of each RLM with each of these *big5* labels is computed. This provides *virtual big5 scores* for each reader. For example, the similarity between the RLM of reader X and the adjective 'reliable' may be small (say 0.05) but large for reader Y (say 0.5). According to this computational '*you are what you read*' approach, reader Y thus may score higher on the 'conscientiousness' dimension of the *big5* scale for which 'reliable' is one item (among others). In step 5, a neural net model is trained to predict the real diagnostic data collected from each reader (*big5* scores obtained via testing with the original questionnaire) on the basis of these virtual scores. This involves computing the probability that the RLM value for a given label like 'academic' is diagnostic of a trait like openness. In other words, readers whose RLM-to-label similarity is high are likely to score higher on the openness dimension.

Pilot studies in the lab of my colleague Markus Hofmann, who invented the technique sketched in Figure 4.2, show that one can use it to plausibly predict personality features of readers relevant to verbal art reception, like extraversion, openness to experience or emotional stability. Additionally, they can predict a set of both affective-cognitive psychological indices, like EQ and IQ, empathy or reading test score. Finally, as schematically illustrated in

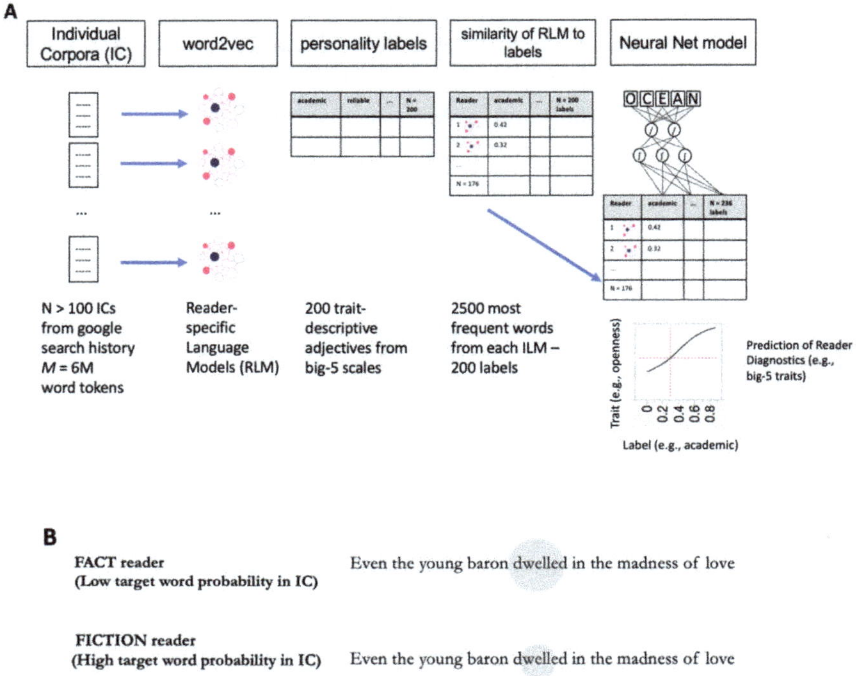

Figure 4.2 A. Individual corpora (IC, each colour = 1 reader) are collected over longer periods of internet surfing or tablet reading and transformed into RLMs via machine-learning tools like word2vec or BERT. Using labels from *SentiArt* and personality tests like *Big5*, the semantic similarities between the IC words and the labels are computed and averaged. Using individual diagnostic data from reading or personality tests fed into deep neural nets together with the language model data, we then can compute how well the latter predict reader skills or traits like openness to experience. **B.** Fixation durations of two readers on the target word ('dwelled') of a test sentence as predicted on the basis of their IC. The radius of the circles on the target word corresponds with the duration of the fixation: bigger = longer. High word probability in IC = the target word occurred relatively often in the reader's IC; Low word probability in IC = the target word occurred rarely in the reader's IC. Source: Adapted from Hofmann et al., 2023.[121]

Figure 4.2B, IC-based word probabilities can even predict how fast readers who differ in their reading preferences process a target word in a metaphorical sentence. The data of the upper sentence example stem from a reader characterized by a preference for reading expository texts and practically no fiction, labelled 'FACT reader' for simplicity. In contrast, the lower example comes from a reader preferring fiction. The prolonged fixation duration on the target word 'dwelled' for the 'fact reader' indicates a greater processing difficulty. This is likely caused by the lower probability of the target word in his IC and the figurative meaning of the sentence. In contrast, the relatively short fixation duration of the 'fiction reader' suggests that his IC is better equipped – and his semantic memory better trained – for processing figurative meaning than that of the 'fact reader'.

To summarize, by collecting reading data over longer time periods from a large sample of readers and using them to construct RLMs one can reliably predict personality traits or reader responses. The approach is time-consuming and laborious, though, and requires larger teams of experts to produce promising results. Still, I think it represents the future of Neurocomputational Poetics and will ultimately provide better explanations of personal reading acts and verbal art reception in general than the ideal reader models of the past.

Reading Proficiency – The SLS-Berlin ('Salzburger Lese-Screening'; Salzburg reading screening)

Reading habits and skills are important reader features shaping reading acts and co-determining the comprehensibility and likeability of texts, as well as the likelihood of immersion or aesthetic feelings. *Reading proficiency* means that a reader is able to successfully integrate early word-based information, as measured on a neural time scale of milliseconds via brain-electrical methods, and utilize this information in later processes of sentence and text comprehension. It has been subject to extensive international research, but screening tests for German-speaking adults across the life span were basically non-existent until my team, together with cooperating partners from the University of Salzburg in Austria, the University of Aix-Marseille in France and the Max-Planck Institute for Human Development in Berlin, tackled the issue about five years ago.

Based on the original SLS invented by the Salzburg group of our colleagues Heinz Wimmer and Florian Hutzler – both pioneers in applied reading and dyslexia research – we developed a standardized computerized sentence-based screening measure for German adult readers. Our goal was to assess reading proficiency, including norm data from over 2,000 participants covering an age range from 16 to 88 years. In empirical studies, the novel *SLS-Berlin* test distinguished very well *between* proficient and less-skilled readers and also *within* less-skilled readers. The construction principle of the test is an increasing sentence complexity both at the syntactic and semantic level. To minimize shallow processing and skim reading, all sentences included at least one long word with more than six letters. The short sentence #1 (five words) in Table 4.1 follows a simple A = B pattern. Sentence #4 is already is longer (10 words) and semantically more challenging, while the last of the

Table 4.1 Easy and complex examples for correct and incorrect sentences used in the *SLS-Berlin*.

Sentence ID	*Condition*	*Sentences (English Translation)*
1	Incorrect	Ein Nashorn ist ein Blechblasinstrument. (A rhinoceros is a brass instrument)
4	Correct	Ein Mobiltelefon ist sehr praktisch, wenn man unterwegs telefonieren will. (A mobile phone is very useful if you want to make a phone call on the road)
76	Incorrect	Bei einem Symposium folgt dem Vortrag eines Referenten über kontroverse Inhalte gewöhnlich ein Wettrennen. (At a symposium, a speaker's presentation about controversial contents is usually followed by a race)
77	Correct	Bei sportlichen Aktivitäten empfehlen sich Kleidungsstücke aus funktionellen Materialien, die schnell trocknen und besonders reißfest sind. (For sportive activities, it is sensible to wear clothes of functional materials, which easily dry and are extremely tear-resistant)

overall 77 sentences has 16 words and is the most difficult in this test. The test uses a so-called *sentence verification task* assumed to tap into readers' semantic memory. The sentences contained either confirmations or violations of basic world knowledge and require readers to decide as fast as possible whether a sentence is semantically correct or not. Thus, 'A rhinoceros is a brass instrument' requires a 'no' response, while 'A mobile phone is very useful to make a phone call on the road' requires a 'yes'. Response time (RT) and accuracy (% of correct responses) are measured for each reader and compared with the norm data of the large sample to establish the individual SLS reading proficiency score.

Figure 4.3 (left panel) shows relationships between several sentence features and RT. Thus, Figures 4.3A and B clearly establish that with increasing sentence number (ID) and rated complexity, RTs are prolonged. The same holds for the number of words (sentence length) in Figure 4.3C. Figure 4.3D shows that the SLS score is a good predictor of first fixation duration/FFD, as assessed in an eye tracking study: for both texts, FFD decreases almost monotonically with an increase in readers' proficiency (i.e. higher *SLS-Berlin* scores). In this study, 34 native German speakers read two expository texts with different levels of complexity while their eye movements were recorded with a high-speed eye tracker. The less complex text was about the planet Venus and consisted of a heading and 10 sentences (150 words in total). The second, more scientific text covered the topic of using plants as energy storage. It also had a heading but was only seven sentences long (34 words in total).

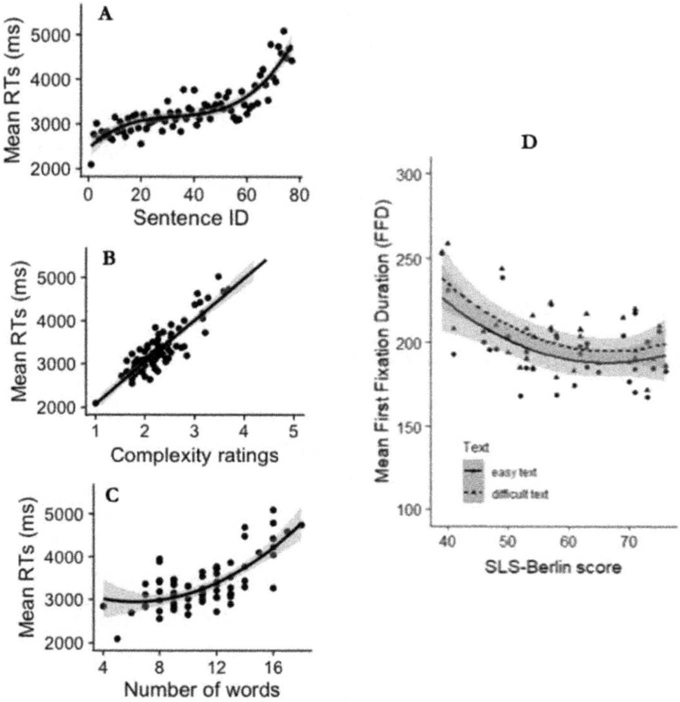

Figure 4.3 Left panel (A–C): Relationships between several sentence features and response times. **Right panel (D)**: SLS-Berlin scores predicting First Fixation Duration/FFD for an easy (continuous line) and a difficult text (dashed line). Source: Adapted from Lüdtke et al., 2019.[122]

It should be noted that we do not use the *SLS-Berlin* for measuring the *reading act,* but to quantify a *reader feature* – reading proficiency – and thus be better able to predict aspects of their reading acts in later empirical studies that measure eye movements, for example, and produce data like those shown in Figure 4.3D.

To summarize, personality *scales,* ICs and RLMs, as well as reading *performance tests,* are useful tools for providing data about readers that complement those from text analyses and help to make predictions about the outcome of reading acts more personal and accurate. Knowing whether a reader scores high on the *BFI10* openness scale or the IRI fantasy scale makes as much difference when it comes to predicting how well she comprehends or likes a text depending on the wealth of its features, as knowing her *RLM* and *SLS-Berlin* score. Admittedly, this kind of knowledge comes at a cost and, at present is beyond the scope of standard empirical studies of literature. But *the future is wide open*!

Supposing that we have done an appropriate text and reader analysis using the tools discussed in Chapter 2 (or similar ones) and the sections above, we would now be 'ready for the kill': the analysis of the reading act. This analysis reveals how our qualitative hypotheses or quantitative predictions fare when confronted with the data produced in experiments that use more or less sophisticated methods for measuring reader responses. The next section tells you more about the traps and tricks of that job.

Reading Act Analysis

My Gaze Strolling on a Love Poem

Figure 4.4, taken from our book 'Gehirn und Gedicht' (Brain and Poetry), shows my eye movements and gaze fixations while I read the first part of the love poem 'Wo hast du all die Schönheit hergenommen' ('Where Did You Get All This Beauty') by the German poet Ricarda Huch. The text has 8 lines, 61 words and 84 syllables alternating between 11 and 10 per line, and I read it on a computer screen in one of our eye-tracking labs in about 20 seconds. The circles indicate the places where my gaze rested to allow

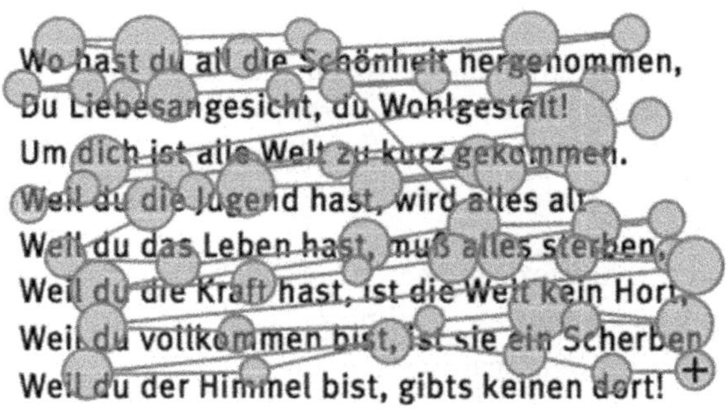

'Where did you get all this beauty?
You face of love, you shapely one!
For thee all the world has come short.
Because you have youth, everything grows old,
Because you have life, everything must die,
Because you have strength, the world is no refuge,
Because you are perfect, it is a shambles,
Because you are heaven, there is no one there!

Figure 4.4 Eye movement pattern (of this author) while reading the first part of the love poem 'Wo hast du all die Schönheit hergenommen' ('Where did you gather all this beauty') by the German poet Ricarda Huch. For details see text.

the brain to take in the visual information required for achieving the ultimate goal of reading, making meaning. Their size codes the duration of these fixations, and the lines indicate the saccades that propel the gaze forward or backward to the next stop. During these saccades, I was virtually blind, while during the roughly 50 stops, lasting about one-fourth of a second on average, my brain went through the highly automated routines of word recognition, sentence comprehension and situation model building. It also computed the next landing point on the line, anticipated the next word and/or sentence, reactivated and partly re-enacted memories generating only partially conscious emotions and reflective thoughts and did a myriad of things I was not aware of and will never be.

As soon as my gaze stopped, for example, on the sixth word on line 1, 'Schönheit' (beauty), millions of neurons and synapses in a fraction of a second generated the neural activity producing the visual word form and word sound. In addition, they also produced images and feelings, memories associated with beauty, as well as the experience of the words preceding and those likely following it – that is, words already read and fading in working memory while the fixated one is processed and others are concurrently anticipated. All four brain lobes then worked together to compute what 'beauty' in this particular – and probably unique – context might mean. First, the occipital lobe generated lines and angles from the pixel patterns on the screen, which were re-assembled to 'mental letters' via the synchronization of about 40–60 nerve impulses/second. Approximately after one-tenth of a second, the so-called visual word form area in the fusiform gyrus had created the preconscious orthographic word form. For it to become conscious and verbally available, it had to be coupled with the corresponding phonological form in parts of the temporal lobe dedicated to hearing and speech processing. After another tenth of a second, all of a sudden practically the entire information I had about the word 'beauty' became consciously available: what it means, that it is a noun, has two syllables and so on.

This magical moment of 'lexical access' coincides with activity in neural networks in the left temporal and frontal lobes and the computation of semantic, syntactic and pragmatic information associated with the orthographic and phonological word form. The semantic computations are widely spread over the left hemisphere and also include parts of the right hemisphere. For example, for concrete action verbs, notable activity can be observed in frontal parts of the brain near the motor cortex. But subcortical brain parts, ancient emotional circuits including the ventral striatum, hippocampus, or amygdala, also likely took part in the meaning making and 'one-word poetry' for the word 'beauty'. To do all this, my brain needed a lot of blood flow and chemo-electrical energy, the changes of which we can measure via neuroimaging methods. We then must meaningfully relate them to the oculomotor activity and the conscious parts of the meaning-making process we call reading or literary experience, as assessed via scales, for example. Other parts of my body also responded to this series of pixels on the screen and perhaps my blood volume pulse (heart rate) changed significantly, my 'sorrow muscle' between the eyes (the corrugator) slightly relaxed, my pupils zoomed *out* on some words and *in* on others, or some of my sweat glands became temporarily more productive at the end of a line that I found beautiful, as measured by skin conductance responses (via electrodes on some fingers).

Now let us start asking some questions – inspired by the boxes of the NCPM mesomodel – about what is shown in and hidden by Figure 4.4.

For example,

- Why did I choose to read this love poem and not something else?
- What did I know about Ricarda Huch, and what mood was I in when I selected this poem?
- What makes me believe the lines constitute part of a poem and not a piece of prose?
- What would change if I read the poem from a book in my favourite chair at home?
- How different would my thirteen-year-old son's gaze pattern look? (context and reader analysis).
- How does the poem's form with an alternating 11–10 syllables per line or ABAB rhyme structure affect my understanding and liking of the text? (text analysis).
- Why did I read this poem at a rate of approximately 250 wpm?
- Why did my gaze involuntarily, that is, without my conscious control, stop only twice on the word 'beauty' but four times on the word 'Liebesangesicht'? (face of love).
- Why do I like the poem, and exactly what about it, especially line three? (reading act analysis).

All these and countless other questions can be generated on the basis of Figure 4.4 or similar data collections, which only represent one aspect of a reading act requiring hi-tech equipment. But which ones are the right questions to ask for students of the scientific study of literature? Which theories can guide them in this game called 'the secret of science is to ask the right questions'? Which methods are best suited to address the right question once we are sure to have one? [123]

Literary Experience

Literary experience has been designated the object of the scientific study of literature, but there is no explicit operational (or other) definition for the construct. I propose that, in the broadest sense, it encompasses the responses accompanying the reading act, including

- the measurable bodily (peripheral-physiological) responses, such as heart rate or skin conductance changes;
- neurocomputational responses, such as brain activity modulations as measured via EEG or neuroimaging;
- experiential responses, as measured by verbal self-reports or ratings; and
- behavioural responses, such as eye movements.

This entails that Neurocomputational Poetics invents interesting questions about both the conscious aspects of, and the unconscious processes underlying, literary experience; and that it develops innovative models – potential, systematic answers to these questions – and methods to tackle and answer them, that is, procedures for testing and constraining these models. Together, these should lead to a valid general description of those aspects of the stimulus (i.e. literature) and context (i.e. reader personality, socio-historical environment) that systematically influence readers' (or listeners') directly observable or indirectly measurable responses.

I have now discussed the basics of text and reader analysis. When we plan a reading act analysis, however, we first need to

- select appropriate reading materials;
- a representative, sufficiently large sample of readers;
- methods for measuring their responses to the texts; and
- hypotheses about the likely effects the text has on readers in interaction with their own features, such as personality traits, reading habits, and so on.

How do we do that?

Stimulus Materials, P-Hacking and Predictive Modelling of Reader Responses

Empirical studies of literature and experiments in reading psychology always face the same problem of how to deal with the sheer complexity of the task and still produce statistically reliable, significant and generalizable effects. The dilemma for Neurocomputational Poetics is this: Do we use oversimplified *textoids*, that is mostly non-literary, expository, experimenter-designed materials in a laboratory context and an artificial reading-related task like single-word recognition or sentence processing? Or, do we opt for complex natural texts like a Shakespeare sonnet in an ecologically more valid multivariate design?

The first option – favoured by the bulk of reading research during the last decades including my own Ph.D. thesis – allows maximum control to focus on a few factors of interest, typically in uni- or bivariate designs. A typical design would examine the effects of the two factors word length and word frequency on mean fixation duration during the reading of well-controlled, single, isolated sentences – sometimes called '*textoids*'. Such simple designs maximize the chances to find statistically significant effects – effects believed to be reproducible and non-random. However, as the recent 'replication crisis' in medicine and psychology has shown, exclusively founding scientific progress on significance tests applied to usually rather small, non-representative samples of participants in uni- or bivariate experimental designs is perhaps not the optimal (or only) strategy. This procedure has been lampooned as *p-hacking* on grounds of the often-misleading probability or *p*-values used in such tests to minimize errors.

The ecologically more valid alternative allows us to look at the interactive effects of many different features, mimicking as far as possible a natural reading act. But it is faced with the challenge of sorting out which of those text features had which effect on what kind of reader response and how so. This represents a case of what statisticians call the 'small *N* large *P* problem', where the number of predictor variables (the features), *P*, is often greater than the number of participants, *N*. Luckily, with the help of machine learning methods, we can use *predictive modelling* to sort out which features were the most important ones in creating an observed effect such as the prolongation of gaze durations. A predictive model typically is a neural network or other machine learning tool, such as so-called *support vector machines* or *decision trees*[124] that is trained in a *supervised learning* procedure on some data (the training set, usually 70–90 per cent of all data) to predict some other data (the test or validation set, usually 30–10 per cent). What is needed for the supervised learning is an adequate training corpus that contains both the input data – for example, lines of text – and the output or response data – for example, a label classifying these lines as either 'literal' or 'figurative', or some human behavioural response to the lines, such as a liking rating, or even some neuroimaging measures, such as the brain activity elicited by a line of text.

To reuse the simpler banana example of the *lens model* discussed earlier, the training corpus could be a large set of photographs of bananas varying in colour, shape or size, each having a label annotated by some experts (*the supervision*) specifying whether it is ripe (or ready to eat) or not. The model then would learn – on the basis of this training set – to predict the ripeness of some new, structurally similar set of banana pictures. As a more relevant example, in Chapter 5 I will train a neural net to predict the likelihood that a sentence is a figurative expression on the basis of a corpus containing 800 sentences, of which 50 per cent were labelled as literal and 50 per cent as figurative expressions, like 'The invitation chimed in their ears' vs. 'The bells chimed in the wind'. The model takes as input the sentences transformed into vectors via automatic text analysis tools such as *SentiArt*. The vectors represent the values of features like number of words, word concreteness or valence computed for each sentence. During training, the model learns to connect these input vectors in such a way to the output data that the prediction error is a minimum. During the test phase, the model's capacity to predict whether a sentence it has not 'seen' before (in the training set) is correctly classified as literal or figurative. Detailed examples for predictive modelling are given in the following chapters.

Accurate prediction of relevant properties of complex stimuli such as images, or of complex human neural or behavioural responses is a high scientific goal and an achievement in itself. But this approach also allows us to explain *why* a prediction was successful, say with a 90 per cent accuracy. This is possible because of the analysis of *feature importance* (FI) values. Just as the weights in the *lens model* example favouring colour over other features, these FIs indicate the relative contribution of each feature to the model's overall predictive accuracy. By application of inference statistical procedures such as the *permutation* or *Granger causality* tests,[125] this in principle purely explorative approach can produce more than mere correlational results and show *predictive causality* by finding those features that had more impact on the response than others and really made a difference. These features can then be selected for further examination, for example, in a typical experiment using simpler designs to determine causal effects.

In summary, a decision to use natural literary texts as stimuli for an empirical study instead of textoids also confronts researchers with the sheer infinity of literature. Millions of texts in multiple languages are possible materials, but which one to choose? Lacking a standard publicly available database for empirical studies of literature, here I propose to use materials selected from standard corpora such as GLEC. A valuable advantage is that ideally the texts come with a number of features already quantified, such as the 154 Shakespeare sonnets,[126] and perhaps even with some publicly available reader response data.[127] This leads to a second advantage: the pre-analysed features facilitate hypothesis generation regarding the potential effects of the text on reader responses. Once the verbal stimulus material has been selected and the hypotheses formulated, the choice of the right method is already constrained by both. As a first example of a simple combined text and reading act analysis – the latter using only the rating method – the next section shows an application of the predictive modelling approach advocated here to the reading and rating of emotional short stories.

Predictive Modelling of Comprehensibility Ratings

Can you like what you don't (fully) understand? Surely, in most cases of verbal art reception, there is some kind of interaction between these two driving forces behind reading. Disappointingly, psychological reading research on the question of whether or how comprehensibility and likeability influence each other is more than meagre. However, the data of a recent multilingual study on reading and rating 250 emotional short stories in seven languages (English, Finnish, French, German, Portuguese, Spanish, Turkish) from the IDEST (International Database of Emotional Short Texts) database can shed some light on the issue.[128]

Thus, in a reanalysis of the publicly available data,[129] I trained a predictive model on a part of them to find out how well the collected comprehensibility ratings (for the remaining part) could be predicted by text features computed via *SentiArt.* The model used 10 features including three standard readability indices used in the authors' original analyses (Flesch Kincaid Grade Level, Automated Readability Index, the aforementioned Coh-Metrix RL2 index introduced earlier), four morphosyntactic predictors (number of content words, word length and frequency, phrase density) and also three affective-semantic features (valence and arousal ratings collected in the original study, and the mean of the *affective-aesthetic potential* [AAP] for each sentence as computed by *SentiArt*). The latter feature is explained in detail in the next chapter. Figure 4.5 illustrates the results of my reanalysis. As shown in Figure 4.5A, the model-generated data predicted the actual ratings quite well (R^2 = .76[i]) accounting for almost 80 per cent of their variance.

i R^2 is a standard statistical estimate of the goodness of fit (or predictive accuracy) of a predictive model corresponding to the squared correlation coefficient; it ranges from 0 – meaning no fit at all – to 1 – maximum fit. This coefficient of determination, pronounced 'R squared', indicates the proportion of the variation in the response variable that is accounted for by the predictor variable(s).

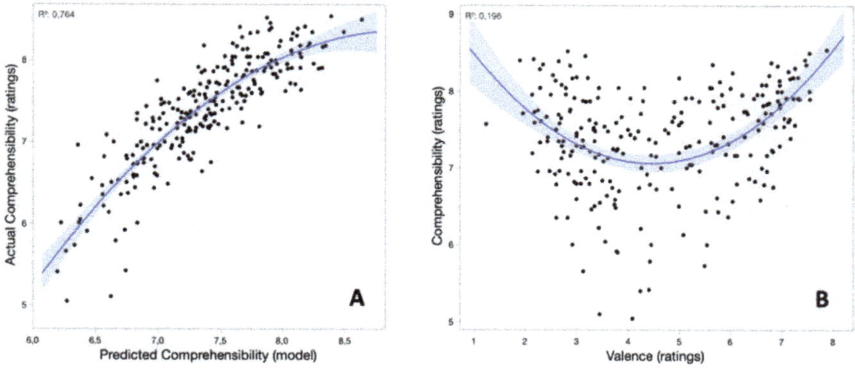

Figure 4.5 A. Actual vs. model-predicted (*SentiArt*) comprehensibility ratings. B. Comprehensibility as a function of valence. The blue shades represent confidence intervals.[130]

When I looked at main effects of features, that is the effect of a single feature ignoring its interaction with the other features, I found that among the 10 considered here the best predictor of comprehensibility ratings was the original valence ratings with an FI value of 0.2. The second and third strongest predictors were the number of content words (FI_{main} = 0.12) and the original arousal ratings (FI_{main} = 0.11). However, when taking into account all nonlinear interactive effects (called total effects) the most important feature was arousal (FI_{tot} = 0.33), followed by valence (FI_{tot} = 0.25), the Coh-Metrix RL2 index (FI_{tot} = 0.153), and *AAP* (FI_{tot} = 0.151). Thus, overall valence – a valid index of likeability – was the strongest predictor of comprehensibility, although on its own it only accounts for about 20 per cent of the variance (R^2 = .196). The data in Figure 4.5B suggest that the relation between comprehensibility and likeability is a curvilinear, U-shaped one: very negative and positive stories received higher comprehensibility ratings than 'neutral' ones.

To summarize, during the reading of short stories from the IDEST database, likeability notably influenced comprehensibility, as demonstrated by the effects of valence, arousal and AAP. The only readability measure that showed an effect – in concert with the other nine features – was the Coh-Metrix L2 index. In the original study, seven readability measures, among which the *Flesch-Kincaide* and Coh-Metrix L2 indices, none explained more than 3 per cent of the variance in comprehensibility ratings as indicated by simple correlational analyses. Since these measures do not include affective variables like valence, together with the present results, this flamboyant failure suggests that improved future multivariate measures of comprehensibility must include affective-semantic features (cf. Chapter 6).

Methodological Choices or How to Avoid 'Stethoscoping' Blood Pressure

The problems concerning the selection of the appropriate text materials as stimuli of an empirical study are matched by those regarding the choice of an adequate reader response measure. Research in Neurocomputational Poetics has led to the same ubiquitous debate as psychology in general about whether to use *explicit measures* that presumably reflect the conscious, verbally communicable experience or rather *implicit measures* that reflect subconscious cognitive or affective responses. The overarching issue is that of *validity*. Do the task, stimulus materials and the response measure really assess and reflect what the researcher says they do? You expect a valid intelligence test to really quantify the IQ of a person, and not, say, her degree of motivation or cultural background biases. Similarly, you expect an *absorption questionnaire*, for example, to measure felt absorption, and not what a reader *thinks absorption might or should be*. No one wants to have his or her blood pressure measured with a stethoscope; but in reading research and psychology as well as neuroscience in general I'm afraid to say that such cases happen more often than I like.

In principle, what is at issue here is simple. It concerns the decision to use either *direct* vs. *indirect* or *on-* vs. *offline* measures. As an example, if I want to know whether your working day was *stressful*, I can simply ask you about it. That's a direct, offline measure or way of finding out the truth, because it directly relates to the phenomenon of interest (stress) and the 'participant' (you) provides the interpretation of the mental state I want to learn about; there is no need for me to generate an interpretation based on external considerations or theory. It's offline because you answer after your work has been done, not during it. If I asked you during it, it would be a direct, online measure. Now, if say I measured your pulse during one of your theoretically stressing work tasks, that would be an indirect, online measure of the phenomenon. Indirect, because it requires an inferential process on my part to connect the measurement to your experience; my theory being, say, that higher-than-normal pulse rates reveal stress. Online, because the measurement is simultaneous to the presumably stressing event(s). Taking your pulse after work would be the indirect, offline measure variant. Applied to a reading act, this leaves us with the following choices:

- Should one use a *direct offline* measure such as self-report questionnaires readers usually fill out *after* the reading act? The advantages are clear: questionnaires or scales are easily available to many and of low cost, and, as mentioned above, the data collected with them pertain directly to one's experience, requiring only minimal interpretational inferences from the researcher. However, these must be gauged against possible concerns such as memory distortions or social desirability effects that lead to the two subterfuges discussed earlier, or even worse, simply untruthful or unengaged answers. At best, reader responses collected offline after the fact conflate what is remembered about the reading act with what was really going on.

- Or, alternatively, is an *indirect online* measure such as eye movement recordings or neuroimaging a better choice? Their advantage lies in the uncovering of unconscious processes impossible to see in the self-reports of the preceding methods. But that must be weighed against their being related in a rather unknown way to your experience. And, of course, they are not as easy and cheap to come by as questionnaires and scales. Complex statistical and other inferences can help here, as well as predictive modelling. But one needs to be trained in them, and that is mostly not the case for the typical bachelor or master programmes, be it in psychology or literary studies.
- Why then not use a *direct online* measure like text annotation or verbal protocols? Well, these often destroy the phenomenon they are supposed to measure. Thus, being asked to continuously rate the degree of immersion during the reading of a text will change the normal reading act and, at worst hinder any form of immersion.
- Finally, can an *indirect offline* measure like free recall do the job? Again, much as for direct offline measures, what is recalled may or may not reflect what was truly experienced during the reading act, thus leaving a lot of uncertainty about the validity and reliability of the measure. Free or cued recall, that is, using cue words to help remembering, can however be very useful to check whether readers truly read a text for meaning instead of only skimming it. Answering detailed questions about who did what when or where in a story therefore is an often-applied technique to ensure valid results.

Since there seems to be no methodological gold standard, a combination of at least two such methods is advisable whenever possible. It covers more aspects of the genuine reader experience and thus provides more constraints on theoretical models than only a single measure. As an example, one can monitor readers' eye movements while reading a Shakespeare sonnet (indirect online measure) and afterwards have them fill out a questionnaire (direct offline measure), as well as ask them memory questions regarding the text (indirect offline measure). Or one can measure readers' brain activity while they read, say, E. T. A. Hoffman's *The Sandman* and have them rate the felt suspense for different text segments in a scanner (cf. Chapter 7). In sum, buying two for the price of (almost) one method generally is the better option, if only because it reduces the risk of *stethoscoping* blood pressure.

Direct Offline and Online Measures

Regarding empirical tests of the NCPM's predictions, those direct offline and online methods are especially relevant that assess either immersive or aesthetic experiences. Among the direct offline measures, self-report scales that are popular for assessing remembered experiences related to immersion are the *transportation scale*, the *narrative engagement scale* or the *story world absorption scale/SWAS*. A more general *reading experience scale* that includes items for measuring immersion is only available in German.[131]

Absorption (Immersion)

As an example, the story world absorption scale (SWAS) has 18 items that are assumed to measure four aspects of narrative absorption (only one item per aspect is shown here):

- *Attention*: 'I felt absorbed in the story.'
- *Transportation*: 'The world of the story sometimes felt closer to me than the world around me.'
- *Emotional engagement*: 'I felt sympathy for the main character.'
- *Mental imagery*: 'I could imagine what the world in which the story took place looked like.'

The *SWAS* has been successfully used in several empirical studies on literary reading, like the study on personality traits and reading habits mentioned earlier.

Aesthetic Experience

Regarding remembered aesthetic experiences, two scales especially designed for poetry reception are the extensive 58-item *Experiencing Questionnaire*. It features items like 'This poem continued to influence my mood after I finished reading it' and can be applied to the analysis of both prose and poetry reading.[132] The shorter 12-item *Poetry Reception Questionnaire* (PRQ), with items like 'This poem describes a mood', was specifically designed to measure *mood empathy*, that is, the capacity of poems expressing moods of persons, situations or objects to engage readers in mentally simulating and affectively resonating with the depicted state of affairs.[133]

These direct offline measures can be complemented by online *verbal protocols*, such as when asking readers to comment on what they were reading by giving an interpretation of a line or stanza of a Shakespeare sonnet; or by freely describing what they felt as in: 'Have your feelings changed during reading? If your answer is "Yes", please write down how your feelings have changed'. For example, in the qualitative-quantitative study from my lab on affective-aesthetic responses to three Shakespeare sonnets discussed in Chapter 8, the qualitative analysis of the answers to such questions showed clearly distinct categories of aesthetic feelings for each sonnet.[134] An alternative direct online method which can be carried out either during the first reading of a text or during re-reading is *text annotation*: for instance, readers simply mark the most striking line(s) or key words of a poem. There are no real standards in the field for these techniques, which are only rarely applied and a bit challenging to analyze, but we will see an example in Chapter 6 where I test predictions based on *SentiArt* regarding the most striking line in each of the 154 Shakespeare sonnets.

Indirect Offline and Online Measures

Asking readers detailed memory questions about the contents of a sonnet, for example, can provide valuable complementary information about their degree of engagement and comprehension. Free-recall or multiple-choice formats have been used as indirect offline measures and, again, there are no standards so far in the field. An example from my lab is an extensive multimethod study – combining direct with indirect on- and offline measures – on mental imagery and eye movements during the reading of texts dominated by either an 'enactive' style or a 'descriptive' style. Enactive style texts render characters interacting with their environment, 'descriptive' style texts render environments dissociated from human action. Texts were selected from Georges Perec's 'Les Choses', Jean-Phillippe Toussaint's 'L'appareil-photo', and Lydia Davis' 'The End of the Story'. Enactive style texts were hypothesized to be more likely to induce mental imagery than the latter. This hypothesis was confirmed by results showing that readers experienced more difficulty conjuring up mental images during reading descriptive style texts (direct offline measure) and longer fixation durations on words (indirect online measure) of the enactive style text.[135]

Naturally, use of indirect online measures like eye tracking or neuroimaging requires the biggest funds and efforts of all four measurement methods, access to a well-equipped laboratory, and some fair amount of training. That explains the limited number of studies in the field that apply these. Which of the multiple indirect online methods is best suited for measuring immersive or aesthetic processes is still an open question. For example, bodily (peripheral physiological) measures such as heart rate variability have been shown to vary with both immersion-related processes during the reading of prose (e.g. suspense) *and* aesthetic processes during the reading of poetry; thus, clever control conditions are required to disambiguate interpretations here. An especially interesting measure that has been shown to correlate with feelings of thrill during *listening* to poetry is *piloerection* (goose bumps),[136] but I know of no applications to reading tasks so far. Regarding the many parameters measured by eye tracking, mean gaze duration, the sum total of fixation durations on single words, has been shown to be sensitive to features related to aesthetic processing during the reading of Shakespeare sonnets, such as the sonority score I will explain in the next chapter.[137] By far the most complex method, neuroimaging, has produced a wealth of results relevant for both immersive and aesthetic processes, a selection of which is also reported in Chapters 7 and 8.[138]

Virgin Texts or Chimera Stimuli?

The lion's share of empirical studies of literature uses one of four design types resulting from two major decisions: text manipulation (yes or no) vs. indirect vs. direct measures (yes or no). The first trench separates advocates of virgin texts – originals left unchanged – from those who like to tinker with the originals. This creates chimeras for the sake of experimental manipulation of selective text aspects, such as the defamiliarization of German proverbs or of the lines from poems by Wilhelm Busch in two of our studies discussed in Chapter 8.[139] A second trench opposes fans of indirect online measures like myself from those who think that only direct measures, whether on- or offline, truly reflect what characterizes a reading act. Again, there is no gold standard here and recommending combinations of these options comes naturally to scientists like myself who are lucky to have the necessary means. Regrettably, in reality such methodological choices are most often severely constrained by the limitations of the research environments available to the average reading researcher, such as a lack of an eye tracker or scanner. In a comprehensive review in my favourite journal *Scientific Study of Literature* (SSOL) you can find exemplary case studies for all of the above methodological options: (in)direct on- and offline measures with either original or manipulated stimuli.[140]

Summary

I started the reader analysis section of this chapter by introducing some exemplary personality scales relevant for verbal art reception and an innovative method of constructing RLMs that can predict both reading skills and behaviour, as well as reading habits or personality traits, ending with a discussion of a reading proficiency test. The section on reading act analysis began with a figure showing my gaze wandering along a love poem and the many questions that can be raised by inspecting the eye movement recording. This was followed by an attempt at delineating the term 'literary experience' and a discussion of the important methodological issue of choosing between significant tests and predictive modelling. An application of the predictive modelling approach to recent data from the *IDEST* databank indicated that standard readability measures are not adequate predictors of comprehensibility. Rather, affective-aesthetic features like valence, arousal or *AAP* must be included. In the final sections, I contrasted the pros and cons of direct vs. indirect and on- vs. offline measures, as well as those of using original texts vs. manipulated ones. Noting the absence of a methodological 'gold standard' in the field of scientific studies of literature, I recommended to always combine at least two of the four methods to cut the risk of 'stethoscoping blood pressure' and increase the pressure on theoretical models: generally, two response measures are harder to predict than only one.

Chapter 5

COMPUTATIONAL POETICS I: SIMPLE APPLICATIONS

In the preceding chapters, I have laid the ground for actual applications in Neurocomputational Poetics: we have the model and a set of methods for text, reader and reading act analyses. The next two chapters discuss concrete examples of how we can apply this toolbox.

My aim in the present chapter about simple applications is to

- make people who love literature aware of methods for computational poetics and their utility to further our understanding of how the pleasures of reading are constructed in the brain in response to a myriad of simple features that, in concert produce a complex symphony;
- show people who have no skills or interest in programming languages how to apply simple tools and ready-to-go apps so that they produce fascinating analyses of complex texts that not only offer new insights about verbal art but also testable predictions for scientific studies.[i]

Euphony and Eusemy: Sound and Meaning Beauty

In poetry speech sounds spontaneously and immediately display their proper semantic function.

—Jakobson and Waugh, (1979, p. 225).[141]

According to Tenet 2 in Chapter 2, *poetic effects* start at the micropoetic level of single words, and already young children are able to both perceive and produce them. There are a number of simple methods to compute the potential of single words to create such effects based on two fundamental aspects:

i The example studies in this section do not require any programming skills to be replicated. In general, the computations can be carried out with the help of a spreadsheet (or even by hand), or via ready-to-use apps and software freely available on the internet.

sound and meaning. No doubt, words can have a more or less pleasing sound such as in 'pee' vs. 'piss' and they can have more or less ugly meanings such as in 'murder' vs. 'beauty'. But how do these two potential sources of micropoetic effects interact at the lexical level? And what role do they play when acting in the context of a line or stanza?

From the very beginning of poetry on Sumerian plates in the twenty-fourth century BC, poets knew that sound and meaning must not be independent – as posited in de Saussure's famous first principle of general linguistics – but could very well influence each other. A book summarizing results of the annual elections of the most beautiful German word is full of examples for words in which 'euphony ~ eusemy', that is, they are beautiful in both sound and meaning.[142] On the other hand, there are words that mean something beautiful, a colourful butterfly for instance, but they do not sound nicely. The German word for butterfly, 'Schmetterling', is a notorious example. Its counterpart is 'Lindwurm' which sounds nicely in German, but designates an ugly dragon. Try to pronounce both words and you will see.

These examples demonstrate that features at the sublexical phonological level, which represent the sound of the letters (phonemes), can alter the affective meaning of words – a lexical feature – although, by standard definition, phonemes have no inherent semantic content. But even a naïve reader – without prior knowledge of such literary devices as cacophony or euphony – would experience how, for instance, in Edgar Allen Poe's verse '[...Hear the loud alarum bells – Brazen bells! – What tale of terror, now, their turbulency tells!', the explosive consonant /t/ and other harsh and discordant sounds (e.g. hissing sibilants /s/ and /z/) can evoke a feeling of 'terror' provoked by 'brazen' bells. And is it pure coincidence that in Paul McCartney's lyrics the single phoneme /l/ occurs more often than in John Lennon's[143]? Is there a reason why /r/ appears so often in the lyrics of Led Zeppelin or the thirteenth canto of Don Juan? Could it be true that – debunking de Saussure – the sound of words can affect their meaning?

As a matter of fact, single phonemes or syllables often do have affective meaning, a *basic affective tone*, which mainly subconsciously impacts a reader's literary experience. This is true even during silent reading, via the empirically well-studied process of *phonological and prosodic recoding:* the automatic and generally subconscious activation of a printed word's sound in the brain prior to its identification. This explains, for instance, why words with short vowels, voiceless consonants and hissing sibilants such as 'piss' feel more arousing and negative, and thus have an especially unpleasant eusemy beyond its denotation. Recent computer models developed in my team can indeed predict why the word 'piss' is judged ruder than 'pee': because even in silent reading, words' acoustic profiles provide quantifiable affective perceptual cues that language users implicitly use in the construction of words' overall meaning.[144]

Computing Euphony

If you don't have a sophisticated computer model at hand, you can use several heuristics to roughly estimate the sound beauty of a word. The heuristic is based on the idea that each speech stream can be specified for a certain number of natural class features that determine its *sonority*: [syllabic], [vocalic], [approximant][ii], and [sonorant]. Put simply, speech sounds have a high sonority value when they are positively specified for as many of these four features as possible. The only segments with positive specification for all four features are vowels, which in German and most other languages represent the syllable nucleus; all other sound classes are defined without the feature [+syllabic]. English glides, also called *semi-vowels*, like /w/ and /j/, are also positively specified for the three remaining features, [+vocalic, +approximant, +sonorant]. Liquids, like /l/ and /r/ are [+approximant, +sonorant], nasals are [+sonorant], and obstruents have no positive specifications, notated, for example, as [-approximant, -sonorant].

Sonority and Obstruent Quotients

Shakespeare's sonnets have been known since Jakobson's ground-laying works to offer sound meaning coherences lending credence to the reality of the iconic function of sonority. Let us therefore compare the theoretical euphony of two sonnets the sound of which is supposed to differ greatly using a simple method that computes *sonorant and obstruent quotients* (*SQ* and *OQ*)[145]. The class of sonorants includes all vowels and vowel-like sounds, that is, nasals, liquids and glides; the class of obstruents includes all other sounds, that is, the 'true' consonants. Shapiro's method for computing *SQ* and *OQ* ignores vowels and considers only sequences of two sonorants which are counted for each line of a poem and then averaged across the number of syllables per poem, that is 140 for Shakespeare sonnets (apart from a few exceptions). Applying this simple method to the 154 sonnets and using the *SQ* as the more significant measure for English poetry, Shapiro identified sonnet 4 (*Unthrifty loveliness, why dost thou spend*) as the least sonorous. Sonnet 55 (*Not marble nor the gilded monuments*) was the second most sonorous (#1 was sonnet 33 *Full many a glorious morning have I seen*), but since he used sonnet 55 as an example in his paper, I stick with it here.

---

ii Approximants are speech sounds that involve the articulators approaching each other but not narrowly enough nor with enough articulatory precision to create turbulent airflow. They fall between fricatives, which do produce a turbulent airstream, and vowels, which produce no turbulence. Sonorants are speech sounds produced without turbulent airflow, like vowels, approximants or nasal consonants.

The Sonority Score

While the above method only allows for differentiating between *SQ* and *OQ*, some recent methods offer more differentiated measures based on the sonority construct. Although the construct is still under debate, my favourite phonetics theory by G. N. Clements relates sonority not to loudness or audibility, but the relative resonance of speech sounds.[146] Indeed, this theory provides a better explanation of the form of the *sonsority scale* – a hierarchical ranking of speech sounds – than others. This scale offers a more differentiated measure of the sonority and potential euphony of words than Shapiro's method.

The widely accepted sonority scale for English ranks phonemes' sonority from highest to lowest:

[a] > [e o] > [i u j w] > [ɾ] > [l] > [m n ŋ] > [z v ð] > [f θ s] > [b d g] > [p t k]

At the top of the 10-point scale, open vowels like [a] need the biggest amount of air for vibrations in the vocal tract and, in this system get rank 1 and 10 points for the most sonorant sound. According to their rank, the vowels [e o] get 9, and high vowels [i u] and glides [j w] 8 points. The points for the remaining phones are: flaps [ɾ]: 7, laterals [l] 6, nasals [m n ŋ] 5, voiced fricatives [z v ð] 4, voiceless fricatives [f θ s] 3 and voiced plosives [b d g]: 2. The natural frequencies called *resonances* of the vibrating air in an acoustic system like the human vocal tract depend on parameters such as size, shape or elasticity. Sonorant speech sounds like vowels have a relatively slow decay of formant oscillation, while sounds perceived as having low sonority like consonants show a faster decay of formant oscillation. Thus, *relative resonance* forms the psychoacoustic basis of this very practical scale.

Computing the *sonority score* of syllables and words can be done manually or by help of *prosodic*, a freely available software which is a metrical-phonological parser written in *Python* currently restricted to English and Finnish texts.[147] *Prosodic* tokenizes text into words and then converts each word into its *stressed*, syllabified, phonetic transcription. For example, 'pee' is first converted into [p, iː] and then gets a mean sonority score of 4.5 [(1+8}/2], while [p, ɪ, s] gets 4 [(1+8+3)/3]. In contrast to Shapiro's heuristic, *prosodic* also allows to compute a number of other useful features such as the most likely metre, stress pattern or alliteration and assonance scores. Let us consider sonnets 4 and 55:

Sonnet 4 with sonority score values for each line:

'Unthrifty loveliness why dost thou spend, 6.46
Upon thy self thy beauty legacy? 6.18
Nature's bequest gives nothing but doth lend, 5.09

And being frank she lends to those are free: 5.81
Then beauteous niggard why dost thou abuse, 6.12
The bounteous largess given thee to give? 5.67
Profitless usurer why dost thou use 6.72
So great a sum of sums yet canst not live? 6.11
For having traffic with thy self alone, 6.19
Thou of thy self thy sweet self dost deceive, 5.83
Then how when nature calls thee to be gone, 5.77
What acceptable audit canst thou leave? 5.59
Thy unused beauty must be tomb'd with thee, 5.55
Which used lives the executor to be.' 5.45

Applying my sonority score heuristic to the two sonnets examined by Shapiro gives us the data in Table 5.1 .

Both methods sharply disagree on both the least and most sonorous lines of sonnet 4, and of sonnet 55: the reasons are that the *SQ* ignores vowels altogether while the sonority score offers differentiated values to all phonemes. Only empirical data can tell which measure suits best, but unfortunately, we still lack such data. However, in contrast to Shapiro's heuristic, the sonority score measure is empirically well validated in studies reported in Chapter 8.

Table 5.1 Least and most sonorous lines according to two scoring methods for two Shakespeare sonnets.

Sonnet	*SQ*	*Sonority Score*	*Least and Most Sonorous Lines, SQ*	*Least and Most Sonorous Lines, Sonority Score*
4	1	4.7	SQ = 0[iii]: Unthrifty loveliness, why dost thou spend SQ = 3: Nature's bequest gives nothing but doth lend	Score = 5.09: Nature's bequest gives nothing but doth lend Score = 6.72: Profitless usurer, why dost thou use
55	2.9	5.4	SQ = 0: Even in the eyes of all posterity SQ = 6: Not marble, nor the gilded monuments	Score = 5.77: Stealing unseen to the west with this disgrace: Score = 6.86: With all triumphant splendour on my brow;

iii Actually, several lines had an SQ of 0. I just took the first in the sonnet.

To sum up, with a simple heuristic based on sonority theory and the English sonsority scale, you can compute an estimate of the sound beauty of words or lines. You can use this, for instance in a little game on name sounds using the app called 'The-Name' I created with my brother Joachim Jacobs and my son Marius Jacobs, available freely in Apple's app store. It will tell you that 'Romeo' has a theoretically more lovely sound (10.8) than 'Juliet' (6.67; keep in mind that sound only counts here, not what you associate with these fictive persons). Still, compared with 'pee' or 'piss', both sound very nicely. My own (first) name also fares pretty well with a sonority score of 7.25. What about yours?

Computing Eusemy

The second aspect that makes words more or less pleasing, and which is not part of '*The-Name*' has to do with the semantic associations they evoke more or less consciously in our brains. Ultimately, Neurocomputational Poetics research should be able to come up with a theory of the most likely associations and connotations an ideal or individual reader (re)produces when reading a given text. In his theory of conscious experience that may have inspired William James' division of the stream of thought into a (conscious) 'nucleus' and a (pre-conscious) 'fringe', Marcel Proust submits the main idea that the function of art is to evoke the underlying associative network indirectly in the mind of the observer.[148] This is accomplished by using carefully chosen sensory surfaces to control the stream of thought, that is, letters, syllables and words. Cognitive neuroscience tells us that this process involves distinct neural mechanisms, including associations supported largely by the medial temporal lobes (e.g. the hippocampus – a structure that has been shown to be bigger than usual in London taxi drivers). These determine the relationship between the current *nucleus* and other potential thoughts and feelings forming the *fringe*. All we need is a method to compute the fringe for a given target word (nucleus) and an index of its potential to arouse feelings of ugliness or beauty.

Single words already have most of the basic features that characterize entire texts. They can be rare and surprising, sound lovely, be joyful and beautiful and fit more or less well into a sequence or context. Single words can be micropoetry, as evidenced in the aforementioned book about the most beautiful German words. There is good reason to believe that this micropoetic experience with single words is the beginning of later immersive and aesthetic experiences with larger pieces of text, and that understanding the underlying word recognition process(es) is a key element of any theory of prose or poetry reception. From the subjective report of the nine-year-old reader, two elementary lexical features co-determining the perceived beauty of words emerged besides the sublexical articulatory-phonological feature (the three gliding Ls). The first is a sensorimotor-perceptual feature, its *imageability:* the reader liked the wobbling and colour of the dragonfly ('Libelle' in German). The second is an *affective-semantic* feature: the reader said 'to have no fear of this beautiful animal'. A study involving adult readers confirmed the nine-year-old's intuitions empirically: 'Libelle' was indeed rated as the most beautiful word in a corpus containing 450 German words.[149] This supports the view that associations with both discrete emotions and embodied cognitions play a role in both the normal processing and the aesthetic appreciation of words, as hypothesized in Chapter 2.

*The Affective-Aesthetic Potential (*AAP*) Score*

In Chapter 1, I mentioned my failure to obtain a research grant on the beauty of words in 2006. Apparently, the resulting frustration turned into a main motivational drive, because ever since I have been thinking of developing a computational model that allows me to predict human ratings of word beauty. So now that we know some simple proxies for *euphony*, how can we compute *eusemy*? The answer is given by the construct of AAP, a lexico-semantic feature based on the association between a word and a set of special *labels*, sometimes called seed or anchor words. These represent core concepts associated with affectively and aesthetically positive or negative things. Examples are 'art', 'beautiful', 'bliss', 'joy' or 'romantic' (positive), as opposed to terms like 'apathy', 'gloomy', 'horror' or 'ugly'. One can think of this set of labels as a theoretical frame or template set for the preconscious associative network of readers – learned during lifetime experiences with art and other objects – from which William James' fringe is recruited whenever a particular nucleus appears in a text. This idea is supported by empirical studies mentioned earlier that have mapped the aesthetic space of literature by asking participants to list adjectives that they use to label aesthetic dimensions of literature in general and of individual literary forms and genres in particular (e.g. novels, short stories, poems, plays). For poetry and plays, the label 'beautiful' was the top term, for novels, stories and comedies it was 'suspenseful'. The broader theoretical concept underlying the AAP computation was introduced in Chapter 3: the theory of distributional semantics. We now have a simple heuristic for eusemy: the higher the semantic similarity of a given word with our template set of affectively and aesthetically positive labels, the higher its AAP score (and the higher the similarity of a given word with a set of negative labels, the lower its AAP score).

Based on an empirically well-validated label list that I have been developing over the last five years – consisting of 60 positive and 60 negative labels

– the *SentiArt* tool provides AAP scores for hundreds of thousands of words in Dutch, English and German (French, Italian and Spanish are forthcoming). These scores can simply be read out from Excel sheets you can download on my *github* page.[150] The top 10 words in English (in the GLEC corpus of ~270,000) are: 'beautiful, charming, delightful, beauty, freshness, lovely, graceful, harmonious, radiant, and loveliness'. The ugliest flop 10 are: 'insult, oppression, torture, cruel, murder, cowardly, curse, dishonour, shameful, and cowardice'. Whether these are among your own personal top and flop 10 or not is a matter of individual taste, but as a general result, this gave the AAP construct enough face validity to be tested in empirical studies, which so far have supported it very well.

So, if you want to know how beautiful the word 'beautiful' is, the first thing you have to do is compute its similarity with each of the 60 positive and 60 negative labels. Then you sum up and average both the first and second 60 values and subtract the latter from the first. If the result is a positive number, the word is in principle beautiful; if it's negative it is theoretically ugly. Using a large corpus of words like GLEC, you can normalize these values and thus obtain a better interpretable scale from -6.5 to +6.5, allowing you to tell which of two words is more beautiful or ugly. Formally, this comes down to solving two equations. First, the similarity between a word (a) and a label (b), s(a,b), is computed by the cosine between the 300d vectors for word and label, as given by a semantic model. This is expressed in equation (1), where A_i and B_i are the vectors corresponding to words a and b.

$$s(a,b) = \frac{\sum_{i=1}^{300} A_i \, B_i}{\sqrt{\sum_{i=1}^{300} A_i^2}\sqrt{\sum_{i=1}^{300} B_i^2}} \tag{1}$$

Second, to obtain the AAP value of a word, *v(w)*, simply subtract the average similarity (s) between a test word (w), and the m = 60 positive emotion labels (1_{pos}: e.g. 'art', 'beautiful', 'bliss', 'joy' or 'romantic') – as obtained by equation (2) – from the same for the n = 60 negative labels (1_{neg}: e.g. 'apathy', 'gloomy', 'horror' or 'ugly').

$$v(w) = \sum_{i=1}^{m} s(w,\, l_{pos_i})/m - \sum_{i=1}^{n} s(w,\, l_{neg_i})/n \tag{2}$$

For example, the average similarity between the word 'beautiful' and the 60 positive labels as computed by a 300d semantic model generated from the GLEC corpus is 0.2, while the one for the negative labels is 0.04. The difference is positive (0.16) and when normalized gives a maximum value of 6.5.

For 'murder' we obtain values of 0.01 and 0.15, the difference being negative (−0.14), resulting in a normalized *AAP* value of −5.1. This makes 'beautiful' a beautiful and 'murder' an ugly word, at least according to *SentiArt*.

We can visualize the associative network for individual words like 'beautiful' or 'murder' using a simplified 2d plot you are already familiar with from Chapter 2. In Figure 5.1, the magenta dots simulate the unconscious *fringe* for the *nucleus* 'beautiful', the orange ones for 'murder'. These stand for mental representations of concepts semantically close to the target (nucleus) which are neuronally activated to a certain degree – depending on their similarity or associative strength – when the target word is read. As one can see, there is no overlap between the top 50 semantic neighbours of the two rather unrelated target concepts: this indicates that the computer model has been well trained and has learned its concepts quite right.

We can also read out the semantic similarity values underlying Figure 5.1 from the *SentiArt* tool and determine the top 5 semantic neighbours for 'beautiful' (cosine similarity values in brackets): lovely (0.82), charming (0.69), wonderful (0.59), delightful (0.58) and splendid (0.57); and for murder: crime (0.69), committed (0.54), guilty (0.52), deed (0.44) and offence (0.37). These values allow the NCPM to make quantitative predictions with regard to the most probable key associations (pre-)activated in readers' minds that co-determine whether they like a word or sentence, or a line of poetry, or not.

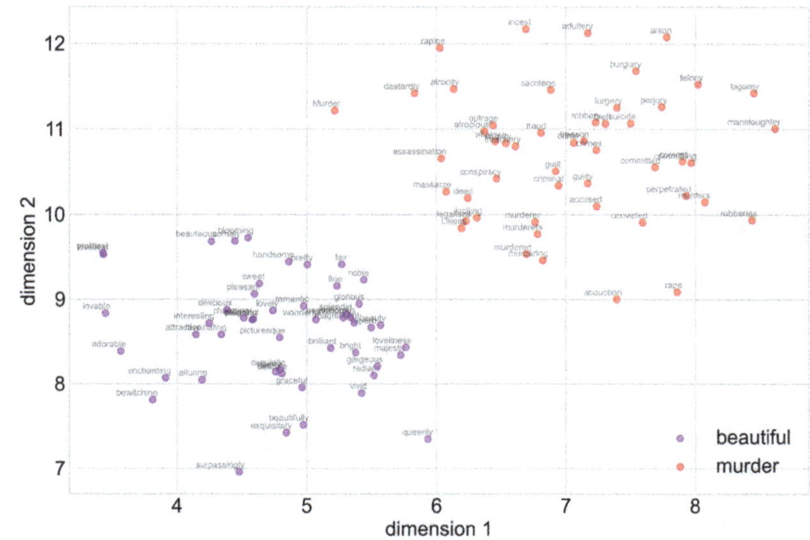

Figure 5.1 Nearest semantic neighbours (fringe) for two nuclei words ('beautiful' and 'murder') represented in a 2d space reduced via the t-SNE algorithm (cf. Figure 3.1 in Chapter 3)

Thus, for the first line of sonnet 27 'Weary with toil, I haste me to my bed' *SentiArt* computes an average AAP value of −0.81. For line #12 'Makes black night beauteous, and her old face new', the AAP is 0.52. Thus, all other things being equal, we would predict line #12 to have a higher likeability than line #1. Of course, a bunch of other features of that line, its context and its readers will ultimately determine readers' affective-aesthetic evaluation of it, but let me do a little spoiler here and reveal that we know from several empirical studies summarized in Chapters 6 and 7 that AAP is among them.

In sum, we now have simple computational methods to estimate the sound and meaning beauty of words separately and can use these to make quantitative predictions about how much readers like words or entire texts. Of course, both estimates concern the lexical level of single words and it remains to be seen how far such context-independent estimates reach into the mysteries of the likeability of entire poems, for instance. As argued in Chapter 3, the higher the feature level, the more difficult it usually is to find computational methods for quantifying it in a valid and reliable way: (supralexical > interlexical > lexical > sublexical). In the remaining sections, I discuss a set of higher-level compound features relevant for Neurocomputational Poetics studies that can be applied to text units of varying sizes. Some of them are still computationally 'experimental', others not yet quantifiable at all. These are

- metaphor aptness and literariness;
- word order;
- morphosyntactic patterns;
- stress pattern and rhythm;
- rhyme saliency; and
- schemes and tropes.

Multiword Expressions

Why is my verse so barren of new pride?
So far from variation or quick change?
Why with the time do I not glance aside
To new-found methods, and to compounds strange?

—William Shakespeare, sonnet 76

At both the inter- and supralexical levels of bi- and trigrams, phrases, lines or sentences, the increased linguistic combinatorics are used for creative multiword expressions like idioms, puns, wellerisms or proverbs. They all defy computational analyses because of their mostly hidden semantic relations.

The meaning of single words results from the fusion of a mental sound and a multidimensional and multimodal image schema and can often be inferred from its context. Presented in isolation, single words usually have just a literal meaning, although this can be more or less abstract. But what determines the meaning of word pairs (bigrams) and decides whether they should be read literally? And which features tip the scale as to whether readers like the 'change-strange' rhyme in the above quatrain from sonnet 76 more than the 'pride-aside' rhyme?

Metaphor Aptness and Literariness

In the canonical nominal type of metaphor (A is B), we have a central word pair formed by the *tenor* and the *vehicle.* A key question in psychological research on metaphor comprehension is how metaphor aptness is related to the interlexical semantic feature *tenor-vehicle similarity* or, formally, *s(t,v)*: is it a simple linear function, that is, the smaller the better, or some nonlinear one having a maximum, e.g. an inverse U-shaped curve? Empirical studies have indeed shown that *s(t,v)* is crucial in determining both a metaphor's comprehensibility and its perceived aptness. As a rule, and all other things being equal, metaphors are better comprehended and perceived as more apt when *s(t,v)* is neither too high nor too low: if the meanings of two words are very close, then the use of one for explaining the other is no longer metaphorical. On the other hand, if the words' meanings are oceans apart, a metaphor that links them is hard to comprehend. Hence, the curvilinear (inversely U-shaped) relation between perceived metaphor aptness (on the Y-axis) and *s(t,v)* on the X-axis has an optimum (or maximum) in the middle.

Consider these three examples from Dylan Thomas:

A) '*God* is a fiddling *devil*', *s(t,v)* = 0.87 (cosine scale from −1 to 1 based on *SentiArt* computation).
B) 'The *tongue* is a *bayonet*', *s(t,v)* = 0.22.
C) 'The *sky* is a *parliament*', *s(t,v)* = 0.13.

Which one do you like more and find more apt or poetic?

If we compute *s(t,v)* for each bigram (god–devil, tongue–bayonet, sky–parliament) using our standard semantic model based on *GLEC* and adopt the curvilinear hypothesis, the prediction for human ratings of metaphor aptness gives the following rank order: B > A ≥ C. Thus, the metaphor with a medium *s(t,v)* should be rated as more apt than the other two. A look at the biggest database for human ratings of poetic metaphors[151] with ~200 items indeed confirms this prediction: (B) gets the highest aptness rating (5.1, scale from 1–7), followed by (C) (2.8) and (A) (2.2). Interestingly, (B) also gets the highest comprehensibility score (5.8), followed by (C) (3.7) and (A) (3.6).

A bit more complex than predicting metaphor aptness is to quantify their literariness or poeticity. While the above examples can well be ranked by help of a single semantic feature such as *s(t,v)*, when more complex metaphoric expressions are considered, some *multivariate* measure based on an amalgam of several features may be required. Consider the following two expressions:

A) LONELINESS IS A DESERT.
B) DOUBT IS A SWORD.

Can you tell – and on what grounds – which of them, A or B, stems from a poet as opposed to a layman, or is substantially more poetic? Perhaps length helps, so let's take 9- and 10-word metaphors, respectively, rather than 4-word ones, giving the professional poets more space to unfold their creativity and readers more information to justify their decisions.

C) THE BLUSHES OF YOUTH ARE ROSES SPREAD BY JOY.
D) THE FLASH OF LIGHTNING IS THE CRACK OF GOD'S EYE.

A recent algorithm we developed is indeed able to correctly classify ~500 metaphors of the (A)–(D) kind, whose authors are known (i.e. poets vs. laymen), into non-literary and literary ones on the basis of about a dozen partially complex computational features.[152] These

- have around seven words;
- combine concrete words with relatively complex grammar and a high lexical diversity;
- have a higher surprisal value;
- share concepts with metaphors from other poets;
- express ideas in a rather familiar way;
- comprise rather dissimilar tenor and vehicle terms; and
- be rather difficult to comprehend.

According to this algorithm, metaphors (B) and (D) are the literary ones, and indeed they were created by poets. To summarize, our simple univariate word similarity measure derived from a semantic model not only helps to predict the perceived meaning beauty of words, but also helps explain the curvilinear relationship between metaphor understanding and liking. However, when dealing with metaphors created by either professional poets or laymen and trying to predict their literariness, a multivariate measure taking into account features like metaphor length, grammar or surprisal is the method of choice. It is a pity that only one database with poetic metaphor ratings has been published so far and also only in English. My Neurocomputational Poetics perspective definitely needs more of these in more languages.

Word Order and Poeticity

In a felicitous poem, each syllable and each word must be in the right spot. Any creator of song lyrics or lyrical poetry must be able to juggle with word type and order, as well as sound and meaning, to follow the call of the rhythm. We thus have an interaction between various features from Table 3.1 in Chapter 3 at several levels, which we need to disentangle by help of machine learning, combined with middle and close reading procedures where possible.

In line with this Table 3.1, I consider the order of words in a line or sentence as an *interlexical morphosyntactic* feature relevant for Neurocomputational Poetics research if it bears the promise to change the line's perceived poeticity. Of course, word order can also change the comprehensibility of a line, for example when using a passive instead of an active construction. And, as we have seen in the previous chapter, comprehensibility and likeability are not independent of each other. But for now, let's start simple with a little test in empirical poetics: please read the following two lines borrowed from Wainwright's[153] book on poetry and judge their *poeticity*:

A) 'I wander'd like a lonely cloud'.
B) 'I wander'd lonely as a cloud'.

Semantically, both lines express the same sentiment or idea and thus are quasi-identical. Phonologically and metrically, they have the same number of syllables and the same beat (i.e. placing of stressed and unstressed syllables). Apart from a single word (*as* instead of *like*) they most strikingly differ in their order. Despite identical beats, do you feel a difference in rhythm between the two?

For me, this morphosyntactic feature interacts with the phonological and semantic ones, changing the felt rhythm and making the second line (from Wordsworth's most famous poem) more poetic. Perhaps the *interlexical* semantic interaction between the bigrams 'wandered lonely' vs. 'wandered like' also contributes to this conspicuous poetic effect, only the first creating an immediate new emergent meaning, while the second delays the meaning-making process by two other words ('like a'). Also, the trigram 'I wandered lonely [...]' binds the crucial emotional term more directly to 'I' than 'I wandered like a [...]' reinforcing the 'I am (also) lonely' idea promoted by Wordsworth's metaphor. This fits with the so-called *locality constraint* in psycholinguistics, proposing a reader's preference for an interpretation associated with a local attachment as in (B) over an interpretation associated with a more distant one as in (A). Of course, within Neurocomputational Poetics, such a hypothesis requires some empirical validation.

Using the *BERT* language model, we can easily compute the likelihood of both lines in a large reference corpus that the neural net underlying *BERT* was trained on.[iv] This gives us an idea of which of two lines has a higher foregrounding potential because its higher novelty or salience captures readers' attention and increases chances of reflective aesthetic processing. Indeed, *BERT* computes a lower log-likelihood value of −33.3 for line (B) than for line (A) −29.1, complementing the intuition that it has a higher foregrounding potential or theoretical poeticity. The point here is that researchers interested in Neurocomputational Poetics but without special computational skills become aware and learn to handle internet tools like *BERT,* allowing them to generate quantitative predictions – as null models – testable in scientific studies of literature.

Shakespeare's Sonnets' Morphosyntactic Patterns

Shakespeare masterfully played with morphosyntactic features like word types and orders. For one, he liked to alter word types, thus creating the style figure of *functional shift,* which alone can alter the poeticity of a line. We already saw an example from line 3 of sonnet 4 in Chapter 3: '*Thy unused beauty must be* ***tomb'd*** *with thee*'. Other typical stylistic foregrounding features at the line level are violations of both surface and deep structure, such as non-standard word order, lack of main constituents, noun phrase juxtaposition or subordination, and multiple embeddings in relative or other clauses. The first three lines of the first sonnet that opens the group of 17 sonnets sometimes called *'the procreation'* sonnets (because they each beseech the young man to bear children as an act of defiance against time) are a case in point:

'From fairest creatures we desire increase',
'That thereby beauty's rose might never die',
'But as the riper should by time decease',

iv Downloaded from: https://huggingface.co/Geotrend/bert-base-en-cased on September 4th, 2021.

Breaking the regular English SVO pattern, the author translates the sentence "We desire increase from fairest creatures" by shifting the adverbial phrase from its conventional position after the verb, achieving a nice change of rhythm and at the same time drawing readers' attention to the star of this and many sonnets to follow: the 'young man'. He also opens the door for a feature we will look at in greater detail in a few minutes: *rhyme saliency*. What would be the most common two-syllable rhyming unit (one or two words) you'd expect for 'increase'? 'Greenpeace', 'earpiece' or 'hair grease' may come to mind in this day and age, but a word that resonates with death ('decease')? Perhaps; after all, the last word of the preceding line as well as the fourth of the same line may have primed an associative network in your brain that subconsciously 'proposed' it. In any case, these three opening lines already show the author's craftsmanship, combining word order magic with polysemous diction, facilitating rich imagery at contrasting levels (human and nature's beauty vs. old age and death) and forcing readers to do what they like best: read on to know what happens next and how it all ends.

Regarding word type order, I used the Python library *spacy* to look at the typicality of patterns in all 154 sonnets. Would it detect a predominant one? Well, not really. A pattern that occurs relatively often is that the line ends with a verb, which is often the 'root'. In *dependency grammar*, the root is the head of the entire tree structure, the one node that is not dominated by one of the other nodes. This pattern occurs in around 300 lines (i.e. ~14 per cent of the total 2155), such as in the tenth line of sonnet 4: 'Thou of thy self thy sweet self dost deceive' or the twelfth line of sonnet 39: 'Which time and thoughts so sweetly doth deceive'. This deviation from the standard SVO order in everyday language and prose is dear to the poet and by itself has poetic potential. In terms of dependency grammar, the order in line 10 of sonnet 4 is: subject (nsubj), preposition (prep), possession modifier (poss), noun phrase as adverbial modifier (npadvmod), possession modifier, adjectival modifier (amod), object of preposition (pobj), auxiliary (aux) and root. The computer programme output looks like what is shown in Table 5.2:

Together with the dependency grammar tags, the *POS tags* are very helpful for text analyses, too. For example, they allow computing the *adjective–verb quotient* which along with the so-called *type-token ratio,* is considered a major indicator of lexical diversity, linguistic complexity, poetic quality or aesthetic success. In his pioneering computational text analysis work, D. K. Simonton[154] argued that better Shakespeare sonnets are distinguished by a higher type-token ratio, more unique words called *hapaxes* (words that occur only once in the entire set: ~10 per cent of all ~17.5k words), and a higher adjective-verb quotient. According to *spacy*'s *POS tags*, the adjective-verb quotient for the tenth line of sonnet 4 would be: 1, the type-token ratio 7/9 = 0.77, since there

Table 5.2 Tokens with their corresponding dependency and POS tags for line 10 of sonnet 4.

token	*dependency tag*	*POS tag*
thou	nsubj	PRON
of	prep	ADP
thy	poss	PRON
self	npadvmod	NOUN
thy	poss	PRON
sweet	amod	ADJ
self	pobj	NOUN
dost	aux	AUX
deceive	ROOT	VERB

are nine tokens but only seven types of words: thy and self are duplicates. The average adjective-verb quotient for all 2155 lines is 0.27, the average type-token ratio 0.97; thus, by this simple two-feature metric, on its own, this line would not be considered remarkably poetic.

Both line ends and line beginnings are important in sonnets, and the parsing analyses tell us something about hidden patterns. In 211 cases, lines start with the subject, such as in line 10 above, but as concerns wording, Shakespeare's favourite line openers are conjunctions like 'and' (242 times), or 'but' (89). For line closures, he prefers 'thee' (48) and 'me' (33), which lend themselves to easy rhyming, but also the everlasting poetic buzzwords 'heart' (17 times), 'sight' and 'eyes' (16 and 14 times), or 'time' and 'love' (both 14 times).

Coming back to the question of a predominant syntactic pattern, what strikes most when analyzing Shakespeare's lines with the *spacy* parser is that when considering the full dependency-parsed structures as for the tenth line from sonnet 4 above, only 24/2155 (1 per cent) occur more than once (within some error margin due to occasional mistakes made by the computer parser). This reflects the poet's huge creativity regarding word order and type relations, especially within the tight confines of the sonnet mould. Mixing complex word types and order with a clearly focused motif, repeated polysemous vocabulary and rich imagery is another signature of Shakespeare sonnets.

To sum up, using freely available *NLP* tools like *BERT* or *spacy,* one can add interlexical morphosyntactic features like word (type) order to the lexico-semantic features eusemy and word similarity to improve predictions about the poeticity of multiword expressions. What still lacks so far is a method to compute the rhythm of poetry. Here it comes!

Stress Pattern and Rhythm – The Implicit Prosody Hypothesis

Rhythm must have a meaning

—Ezra Pound

The above examples show that word order should not be analyzed without a look at rhythm. But can you feel their rhythm also when you read Shakespeare's sonnets silently? There was a long-standing debate in cognitive psychology and psycholinguistics as to whether syllables are functional units not only for speech perception and production – which goes without saying – but also for the silent reading act. Today it is safe to answer this question with a 'yes'. Even in silent reading, our brains process written text in a rhythmic way guided by a kind of 'inner voice', as expressed in the *Implicit Prosody Hypothesis,*[155] a variant of the aforementioned phonological recoding hypothesis.[156] It states that during reading, readers generate representations of sentence intonation, stress and rhythm – by recoding the orthographic input into a phonological one – and that these representations can affect readers' interpretation of the text.

As a measure helping to estimate the interlexical metric feature rhythm, the stress pattern of written texts can be analyzed with freely available software such as *prosodic,* already applied earlier: it can indeed find the best available metrical parse for each line of text by attempting all logically possible parses and keeping those that least violate a set of user-defined constraints.

Here's an example of Shakespeare's sonnet 1 as parsed by *prosodic.*

from|FAI|rest|CREA|tures|WE|de|SIRE|in|CREASE
that|THERE|by|BEAU|ty's|ROSE|might|NEV|er|DIE
but|AS|the|RI|per|SHOULD|by|TIME|de|CEASE
his|TEN|der|HEIR|might|BEAR|his|MEM|o|RY
but|THOU|con|TRACT|ed|TO|thine|OWN|bright|EYES
FEED'ST|thy|LIGHT'S|flame.with|SELF|sub|STAN|tial|FU|el
MAK|ing.a|FA|mine|WHERE|ab|UN|dance|LIES
thy|SELF|thy|FOE|to.thy|SWEET.SELF|too|CRU|el
thou|THAT|art|NOW|the|WORLD'S|fresh|OR|na|MENT
and|ON|ly|HER|ald|TO|the|GAU|dy|SPRING
with|IN|thine|OWN|bud|BU|ri|EST|thy|CON|tent
and|TEN|der|CHURL|mak'st|WASTE|in|NIG|gard|ING
PI|ty.the|WORLD|or|ELSE|this|GLUT|ton|BE
to|EAT|the|WORLD'S|due|BY|the|GRAVE|and|THEE

The example shows that *prosodic* not only captures the sonnet's overall *iambic pentameter*, but also some of its variations. It accurately captures the rhythm break of the *trochaic inversions* in the lines '*MAK*ing a *FAM*ine *WHERE* ab*UN*-dance *LIES*' and '*PI*ty the *WORLD* or *ELSE* this *GLUT*ton *BE*'. Such violations of rhythmic patterns in poetry are a foregrounding device having aesthetic potential. Moreover, *prosodic* also captures the double-strong beat that can often follow a double-weak beat as in 'Thy *SELF* thy *FOE* to thy *SWEET SELF* too *CRUEL*'. However, like all text-analytical software, it is not wholly error-free. Thus, it seems to get some lines wrong: 'feed'st thy light's flame [...]' for example. Still, the overall performance of *prosodic* as gauged against the accuracy of two human experts appears to be very good (>90 per cent) and you can very well use it to predict reader responses to poetic metre and its violations. So now we have methods for estimating likely poetic effects of euphony, eusemy, metaphoricity, word (type) order and rhythm. But what is rhythm without rhyme?

Most Salient Rhymes in Shakespeare's Sonnets

In the preceding sections, we saw how to compute the poetic potential of single words and word sequences for some very simple examples. Let us now consider an entire poem in which textual features can exert poetic effects that function over longer distances than word pairs or single lines. Perhaps the best-known example is (end) rhymes, either of the perfect or slant type.

Rhyme and Bisociative Thought

As a poet being able to recite by heart the first 20 songs of the Iliad – translated by himself into modern German –my friend and book co-author Raoul Schrott has always argued that the syllable, not the word, is the basic unit underlying the organizing principle of our mental lexicon – the brain's vocabulary. His theory is that upon seeing a word, in this 'rhyme lexicon' first all word representations reminiscent of a certain sound gestalt are activated preconsciously – via a phonological similarity mechanism – until the one is selected that fits best. This then allows access to the concept and associative network linked with that word, as well as the motor programme needed for articulating it.

Rhyme variants frequently found in poetry but also in prose, such as:

- *Alliteration* ('***D***oubting, ***d***reaming ***d***reams no mortals ever ***d***ared to ***d***ream before'; Poe, *The Raven*).
- *Consonance* ('And the **s**ilken **s**ad un**c**ertain ru**s**tling of each purple curtain'; Poe, *The Raven*).

- *Assonance* ('H***i***s t***e***nder h***ei***r might b***ea***r h***i***s m***e***mory'; Shakespeare's sonnet 1, also rich in consonance; 'On a pr**ou**d r**ou**nd cl**ou**d in wh**i**te h**i**gh n**i**ght'; E.E. Cummings) or
- *end rhyme* ('bells – tells'; Poe, *The Bells*).

reflect the phonetic bandwidth of what our brain cognitively performs in order to retrieve words and their meanings. Rhyme necessarily involves a semantic relatedness between the rhyming units: by reminiscing the sound gestalt of the base word, a rhyme also activates its associative network in addition to its own. This mechanism is strongly responsible for the pleasure readers experience from the nursery rhymes of their childhood to the poetry of Shakespeare. Thus, much like *phonological iconicity* – the structural resemblance, or natural association between signifier and signified, as in *onomatopoeia* – rhyme is an example of a feature relevant to the phonological and semantic levels at the same time.

Word pairs or *ngrams* (sequences of *n* words) often feature rhyme, like 'double trouble', or alliterations and assonances, like 'I like Ike' or '*whisper words of wisdom*'. This provides them with increased memorability or pleasantness even when being separated across larger units of text, as in the first quatrain of Shakespeare's popular sonnet 12 below. The *sound gestalt* of words is what stabilizes their mental representation in verbal *working memory* (the brain's buffer for spoken and written language and main tool for thought processes), for purposes of reading and thinking when the eyes have moved to the next word in a text and the mental orthographic representation of the previously fixated ones has already decayed. This sound gestalt thus constitutes the basis for making meaning from word pairs, phrases or verses. But word sound echoes too have a limited mental life during reading, unless they are refreshed by stylistic tricks of assonance, alliteration or rhyme, like in sonnet 12.

Sonnet 12 (First quatrain)

'When I do count the clock that tells the time,
And see the brave day sunk in hideous night;
When I behold the violet past prime,
And sable curls, all silvered o'er with white [...]'

The assonance to the sound gestalt of the base word ('time') provides a rhyme with the creative power of evoking – by association – that other word's ('prime') semantic field and contrasting or fusing it with its own. This associative process likely constitutes the most basic skill underlying creativity and poetic experiences in (figurative) language reception and production, namely the ability to discover hidden similarities in word pairs, idioms, proverbs, puns, metaphors or verses. Arthur Koestler called it *bisociative thinking*, a process allowing the discovery of a relationship between one object or pattern and another object or pattern.

Rhyme Saliency and Foregrounding Potential

Everyone can rhyme, but not all rhymes sound like poetry or appear hackneyed like 'love-dove' or the worn 'Herz-Schmerz' (heart-pain) in German. Above, I asked what would be the most common two-syllable rhyming unit (one or two words) you'd expect for 'increase'? Basically, two features indicate how surprising a rhyme pair is: the frequency (probability) with which the pair appears as end rhymes in a reference corpus such as all Shakespeare sonnets or all poems in GLEC, and the semantic distance of the two rhyming words. A third feature can come into play when the rhyme is slant or impure according to current pronunciation rules, such as 'prove-love', 'moan-gone' or 'forth-worth'. Together with rhyme pair probability, the mixed phonological-semantic feature rhyme pair distance functions as a measure of the *saliency* of rhymes, which is an index of its *foregrounding potential.* If the semantic distance – as computed by *SentiArt* – is high like in 'sense-commence' (0.999; sonnet 35) and the probability (within all 154 sonnets) is low (1/1979, $p = 0.0005$), this becomes a salient rhyme. If both semantic distance and probability as an index of subjective familiarity are high as in 'thee-me': (0.53, 14/1979, $p = 0.007$), the rhyme's saliency is lower. Here are some potentially striking rhyme pairs on the semantic distance dimension: 'fault', 'halt' (sonnet 89), 'mine', 'define' (sonnet 62) or the slant rhyme 'moan', 'gone' (sonnet 44). In concert with others, this feature might well play a role when readers select the most striking or beautiful line of song lyrics or poems (see Chapter 6). Metaphor aptness, word (type) order, rhythm and rhyme saliency all play a role in the comprehension and appreciation of poetry. But, naturally, there is more.

Schemes and Tropes

The last group of the six higher-order features useful for computational analyses of multiword expressions discussed in this chapter is also by far the most complex one and the one defying computational analysis most strongly: *schemes* and *tropes*. In standard catalogues of rhetorical devices often listing more than 500 of them, schemes are typically considered as syntactical forms in contrast to the semantic tropes, although there is the occasional debate on which is which given the fuzzy borders between syntax and semantics. Arranging words artfully in schemes often defies computational text analyses, much like trope detection (metaphor, chiasm, oxymoron), but there is promising progress.

Schemes

In addition to the two simple types considered in the process model of Chapter 2 (repetition and reversal), current computational approaches offer a more differentiated analysis considering other schemes such as *omission* or *balance*. An example for the former is *asyndeton*, the omission of conjunctions between clauses, as in: *Veni, vidi, vici*. An example for balance is *isocolon*, a series of similarly structured elements having the same length as in: *What the hammer? what the chain?*. Repetition arguably is the most powerful of these four types of schemes – as Aristotle reckoned – but also the most frequent; and it is easy to detect by computational means. Shakespeare's famous line from *King Lear* 'Never, never, never, never, never' is a case in point, as is the 'and' *anaphora* in sonnet 66 ('Tired with all these, for restful death I cry'). Among repetition devices that can be detected computationally with accuracies of ~30 to 80 per cent are the following:

- **Epizeuxis.** repetition of words with no others between, as in the King Lear quote from above.
- **Epanalepsis**. repetition at the end of a clause of the word that occurred at the beginning of the clause, as in Shakespeare's *King John*: 'Blood hath bought blood, and blows have answer'd blows.'
- **Mesodiplosis**. repetition of the same word(s) in the middle of successive sentences, as in:

We are troubled on every side, yet ***not*** *distressed;*
we are perplexed, ***but not*** *in despair;*
Persecuted, ***but not*** *forsaken;*
cast down, ***but not*** *destroyed. —2 Corinthians 4:8–9*

Much like repetition, omission and balance devices are also relatively easy to detect automatically with accuracies between 25 and 100 per cent. In contrast, reversal devices such as *hyperbaton* ('Some rise by sin, and some by virtue fall') or *anastrophe* ('The City Beautiful') still appear too complex to be detected automatically – a real challenge for computational poetry analyses – but they are still worth a closer look. Such devices typically reverse the syntactically 'correct' or expected order of words in a sentence such as the standard SVO for English or German, the second most frequent order of known languages, after SOV (e.g. Japanese). Together with others, reversal devices help to keep readers' expectations – all that can be predicted from their experience with language and literature – in abeyance as long as possible, both contextually and syntactically or semantically. If reversal is used for the sake of maintaining a rhyme scheme, it is sometimes considered a literary defect, although one can also find it in the second quatrain of Shakespeare's perhaps most famous sonnet 18 ('Shall I compare thee to a summer's day?') where it does not seem to derange the poetic lilt at all:

'Sometime **too hot the eye of heaven shines**,
And often is his gold complexion dimmed,
And every fair from fair sometime **declines**,
By chance, or nature's changing course untrimmed:
So long as men can breathe, or eyes can see,
So long lives this, and this gives life to thee.'

According to classic rhetoric reversal devices can have emotional effects on readers/listeners (cf. model in Chapter 2). Thus, in his *Anthem Press* book from the same series as mine, *A Theory of Thrills, Sublime and Epiphany in Literature*', my colleague Nigel Fabb quotes that re-ordering words in hyperbaton 'throws the hearer into a panic lest the sentence collapse altogether, and forces him in his excitement to share the speaker's peril'. Transcripts of heated debates in politics, academia or families support this conjecture, because there people break the 'normal order' of words at will without the increasing incoherence necessarily perturbing mutual understanding. Despite what many linguists may think, normal human speech production does not follow a strict system of rules but rather only a norm based on a static dominance. Poetry but also political rhetoric plays with this dominance, as in Winston Churchill's famous 'This is the kind of nonsense *up with which* I shall not put', a figure adequately coined *cacosyntheton*. Whether drastic emotional effects of reversal as described by Longinus are generally true, I doubt, but future Neurocomputational Poetics studies should definitely examine the powers of this device. Given the amazing things an AI tool like *chatGPT*[157] can do, I can only speculate here that scheme detection will become a lot more accurate in the future, for instance, if a GPT-like computer programme was submitted to a supervised training on a large number of expert-annotated poetry texts. It seems only a question of time and money before a *poetGPT* will hit the stage. Actually, the latest version of chatGPT, chatGPT4, has been shown to produce song and other lyrics that can come close to those created by professional authors.

Tropes

Tropes generally represent an even bigger challenge than schemes for computational approaches: they are hard to detect and their potential effects are even harder to predict. Here I will focus on the most common and theoretically and empirically best studied trope – as evidenced by dozens of competing linguistic and psychological theories and experiments – which is also the prevailing one in literature: metaphor. In an early study on the occurrence of several forms of figurative language in literary texts,[158] metaphors were the most frequent (29 per cent), followed by hyperbole (27 per cent) and idioms (18 per cent), while similes (8 per cent) and irony (3 per cent) were relatively rare.

When is an expression a metaphor, when is it a literal statement and when is it just plain meaningless? Can this issue be solved by a simple algorithm based on semantic models? Basically, metaphor detection in NLP is performed by two approaches: semi-automatic middle reading approaches and supervised machine learning procedures. Semi-automatic methods like *MIP*[159] combine a formal algorithm with a manual procedure. Supervised machine learning techniques use annotated corpora to train a neural net or other algorithms to discriminate between literal and figurative verbal expressions.[160] So far, these training corpora usually contain only very limited examples of metaphors and their literal counterparts from non-literary texts, mostly adjective–noun or verb–noun bigrams like 'bald assertion' vs. 'bald eagle' or 'blurred distinction' vs. 'blurred vision' (they reach predictive accuracies of 70–80 per cent for these benchmark stimuli). Moreover, the machine-learning techniques used in current approaches are very sophisticated and too heavy for the present focus on simple applications. However, there is a remedy.

First, there is a more ecologically valid corpus of 800 extremely carefully constructed pairs of literal and metaphorical sentences (400 each) for use in neurocomputational experiments, matched on a number of crucial features like overall length, frequency or concreteness, henceforth called the *Cardillo database*.[161] Second, there is a much simpler approach based on the model introduced in Chapter 3. There I had argued that the meaning of Lord Byron's metaphor 'Time is a bird' crucially depends on discovering common semantic neighbours such as the concept 'to fly' – more or less deeply hidden somewhere in the subconscious fringe of the semantic memory of a reader. The first task then is to uncover these common semantic neighbours of both tenor and vehicle, that is to determine as precisely as possible the union set in Figure 5.2.

Hypothetically, this union set should generally be smaller in metaphorical expressions than in their literal counterparts. Consider four examples from the *Cardillo database*:

A) The bells chimed in the wind.
B) The invitation chimed in their ears.
C) The baby talk was babble.
D) The story was pretentious babble.

As with all other items in the database, sentences (A) and (B), for example, are carefully matched on a number of features, such as that they both have six words, refer to an auditory imagery domain and have a positive valence. Intuitively, the semantic relation between 'bells' and 'chimed' seems closer than between 'invitation' and 'chimed'. This is because both words appear more often together in everyday language, making it easy for the association machine – which is our brain to predict one from the other. If well trained, neural nets mimic this association mechanism, and this is why they are so good at predicting human performance in many cognitive tests.

So, in sentence (A) argument (tenor) and predicate (vehicle) are closely related; the predicate selects and highlights one or more of the potential features of the argument. In (B) the relation is less direct; the association between both words is much weaker because they do not appear so often together in everyday language or literature. The same holds for the nominal type metaphor examples of (C) and (D). The semantic glue between 'baby talk' and 'babble' also seems stronger than that between 'story' and 'babble'. The strength of that glue can be estimated by the number of semantic neighbours shared by tenor and vehicle, the union set in the above Figure 5.2.

In addition, the two difference sets also can play a role, since salient features of the tenor that the vehicle lacks may override common ones (or vice versa). Taking the example of Byron's metaphor, 'bird' has the feature 'animate' whereas 'time' hasn't. Being inanimate can mentally conflict with the concept 'to fly' and thus impede understanding of the metaphor. The second

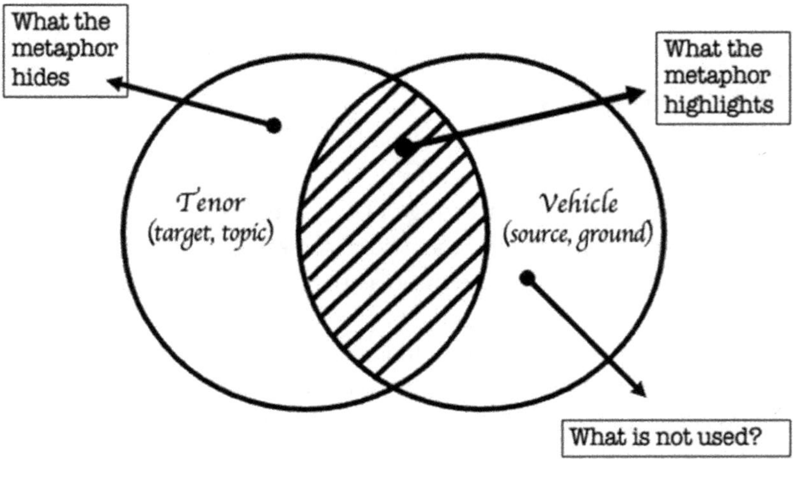

Figure 5.2 Venn diagram illustrating commonalities and differences between the tenor and vehicle of generic metaphors.

task therefore is to estimate the influence of both difference sets. To do so, I computed the average semantic similarity between the 100 nearest *non-common* semantic neighbours of tenor and vehicle. Again, hypothetically, this measure should generally be smaller for metaphorical expressions. Thus, the semantic neighbours that 'story' does not share with 'babble', as in (D) above, should be less similar to those that 'babble' does not share with 'story' than those that 'babble' does not share with 'baby talk', as in (C). For instance, in Byron's metaphor, 'day' or 'hour' are neighbours of 'time' but not of 'bird', whereas 'nest' or 'hawk' are neighbours of 'bird' but not of 'time'. Their average similarity is 0.1. What matters now is that the average similarity between these non-common neighbours is smaller than between those of a literal expression like, for example, 'Time is a measure'. This is indeed the case: 'degree' or 'extent' are both neighbours of 'measure' (but not of time), and their average similarity to 'day' and 'hour' (neighbours of time but not of measure) is 0.17.

We can now formulate a simple but general and testable hypothesis for discriminating literal from figurative expressions having the structure of those of the Cardillo database:

- If the number of common semantic neighbours between the tenor and vehicle terms of an expression and the semantic similarity between their non-common neighbours is relatively small, then it is likely to be metaphorical.

Fortunately, thanks to semantic models, it is easy to quantify our intuition and implement this hypothesis computationally. To do so, I first transformed each of the 800 sentences in the database into a vector. To create these vectors, I computed the following quantities:

- The set of the 1,000 most similar semantic neighbours for the tenor.
- The set of the 1,000 most similar semantic neighbours for the vehicle (N = 1000 is recommended in the literature).
- The number of shared semantic neighbours in both sets, henceforth coined CN for *common neighbours*, as an index of the union set.
- The average similarity between the 100 closest neighbours of the tenor and those of the vehicle as an index of the *difference sets* (DS).
- The average similarity between the 10 closest neighbours of the tenor, henceforth called semantic neighbourhood density or $SND_{ten.}$
- The average similarity between the 10 closest neighbours of the vehicle (SND_{veh}), as an index of semantic neighbourhood density, higher values indicating greater density.

The first three quantities estimate the union set. The fourth estimates the difference sets, and the last two were included for completeness because some interesting recent empirical work suggests that the density of the semantic neighbours of tenor and vehicle is important for metaphor comprehension: If density is low, metaphor comprehensibility and appreciation increases. Concepts from less dense regions in semantic space appear to be more easily retrieved from memory.[162] To what extent those last two features also predict the metaphoricity of expressions was an open question that I tackle in the next section.

Multivariate Nonlinear Predictive Modelling of Sentence Metaphoricity

As explained earlier, generally a predictive model is a computer model trained on some data to predict some other data. This something can be a human behavioural response, such as a liking rating for sentences, or, as in the present case, some property of texts such as the likelihood that a sentence like those in examples (A) to (D) is a figurative expression. Here, each sentence was represented by a 4d vector (CN, difference set/DS, SND tenor, SND vehicle) with the values of each of these quantities serving as features of the predictive model. Table 5.3 shows examples.

In the present computational approach, the input variables (features / line vector) from columns two to five of Table 5.3 and the binary response variable in column six of each of the sentences were fed to the computer model. A standard training procedure looks like this: in each learning epoch only a part of the data is used to train the model (usually 70 per cent drawn randomly), the rest is used for testing the model's predictions. This makes sure that the model is not 'overfitting'.[v] During training, the model predicts

Table 5.3 Four features as predictors for sentence metaphoricity.

Line/Features	*CN*	*DS*	SND_{ten}	SND_{veh}	*Literal/Metaphoric*
The bells chimed in the wind	[36	0.18	0.62	0.51]	L
The invitation chimed in their ears	[4	0.23	0.58	0.59]	M
The baby talk was babble	[5	0.39	0.6	0.64]	L
The story was pretentious babble	[4	0.22	0.67	0.64]	M

v Put simply, a machine learning model is said to 'overfit' the data when it learns the noise of the training data. For example, suppose our data set was a point cloud around a straight line representing the linear function Y = aX + b. If instead of learning the linear function underlying the data, the model would learn a nonlinear 'zig-zag' function oscillating around the best-fitting line, it would have overfitted.

the true value of the response variable – in this case the binary values L vs. M – as a function of the input vectors. This is much like computing a correlation between them. The *prediction error* (the difference between the actual and the predicted value) is fed back to the model – hence the term supervised learning – and the model's parameters, such as the weights between the nodes of a neural net, are dynamically adjusted. This procedure is repeated until the prediction error reaches a minimum and the model parameters are then frozen. In the final test phase, the frozen model is used to predict the remaining 30 per cent of the data.

In a simple *multiple regression* model, this prediction procedure could come down to an additive equation of the type:

- Metaphoricity = constant + feature 1 * weight 1 + feature 2 * weight 2 + [...] + feature N * weight N

Here, the weights indicate the contribution of each feature to the overall accuracy of prediction. During supervised learning, these weights are adjusted to minimize the prediction error. But you can also vary the type and number of features to improve the model's accuracy. Thus, each time you run a predictive model on the computer, it is a bit like *fishing with a net* say for 100 trials: if you catch the wrong fish, you adjust the grid – the weights representing the strength of the links between the nodes of the neural net – to increase the likelihood of catching your favoured fish.

However, the reality of reading literary texts seems more complex than what a simple additive model like the one above can simulate. Many empirical studies from our and other labs have indicated that numerous text and reader features nonlinearly interact in shaping reader responses. For instance, as shown earlier, features influencing the comprehensibility interact with those affecting the likeability. Thus, a major characteristic of our approach is that it uses many text features that can dynamically and *nonlinearly* interact, such as word frequency, the *AAP* value of words, sentence length, semantic complexity and so on – hence the term *multivariate nonlinear* models. Neural nets are among the most popular and successful types of such models.

In this study, I trained the neural net on a subset of the 800 sentences of the database – the training set – using a standard cross-validation procedure, and tested it on the remaining set of sentences. Note that, in line with Tenet 2 of Chapter 2 hypothesizing a continuum between literal and figurative language, the model predicts a likelihood for each expression for being metaphorical. However, since the database uses a binary classification (400 literal and 400 metaphorical expressions), the model also does so. The results yielded a decent predictive accuracy of 0.82, that is, a misclassification rate of 8 per cent (the odds being 50 per cent). The most important feature (main effect) was CN (FI = 0.61) with higher CN values signalling literal expressions, as hypothesized. The similarity between the non-common neighbours (difference set) was the second best predictor (FI = 0.25), again, as expected, with higher values predicting literal expressions. The remaining two features had no important impact (FIs < 0.1) on metaphoricity classification.

To summarize, the reliable and accurate detection of metaphorical expressions in literary texts remains a substantial challenge for computational approaches. Even semi-automatic middle reading approaches involving experts' judgements on a set of computationally preselected expressions that are metaphor candidates are not yet error-free, meaning that inter-rater agreement indices are well below 100 per cent. Even so, progress is inexorable as exemplified by the successful classification of well-controlled verbal expressions as either literal or figurative via a simple four-feature predictive computational model.

Summary

In this chapter, I first introduced simple computational methods for predicting how nicely a word sounds and how beautiful it appears to readers. Moving from single words to multiword expressions, I showed how the degree of metaphor aptness and literariness or the influence of word order can be computed using semantic models. I then showed the potential of dependency grammar parsing and *POS tagging* for computing measures relevant to Neurocomputational Poetics, such as *morphosyntactic pattern*, *adjective-verb quotient* or *type-token ratio*. I also showed the merits of the software *prosodic* for determining the stress patterns and rhythm of poems. A special section was dedicated to the computation of rhyme saliency in Shakespeare sonnets as an indicator of their foregrounding potential. Finally, considering schemes and tropes, I introduced a working hypothesis on how to discriminate between simple literal and figurative expressions implemented in a computational model. Applied to the Cardillo database, a *multivariate nonlinear predictive modelling* approach achieved a decent predictive accuracy of around 80 per cent.

Chapter 6

COMPUTATIONAL POETICS II: SOPHISTICATED APPLICATIONS

In the previous chapter, relatively simple computational analyses were discussed without any comparison to human response data. In this chapter, I compare the predictions of more sophisticated theoretical and computational models to human ratings collected during the reading of entire chapters, books and poem collections.

Story Analysis I: Plots

After having discussed the complexities of computational analyses of multi-word expressions in the last chapter, it is now time for considering the biggest text units readers can process: stories, novels and poems. Two superfeatures playing a major role at this macrostructural level of the reading act are *plots* and *characters*, discussed in the first two sections of this chapter. Narratologists and literary critics still continue to debate on the exact definition of the term plot.[163] For the present purposes, I adopt a structuralist position according to which plot is considered a pattern that yields coherence to the narrative by enchaining story events in a limited number of typical sequences. As we will see, such *prototypical plotlines* can well be identified via computational analyses.

Plot, Event Detection and Sentiment Analysis

Plot is about the causal and temporal patterns arranging the events in a story and how this arrangement in turn facilitates identification of their motivations and consequences. This 'plot as global structure view' facilitates the application of sentiment analysis to the identification of story plotlines and it is also closely linked to the psychological concept of situation model building. Abstractly, a story can be represented as a partially specified trajectory in situation-state space: a temporally ordered sequence of events. Story comprehension then can be seen as the problem of inferring the most probable missing features of this trajectory, a cognitive process which is driven by affective-aesthetic processes of suspense or surprise. If the incoming information from the text is consistent with the situation model currently under construction (e.g. shares characters and locations), it is mapped onto the current model. If it does not overlap with the current model, a reader will shift the focus of attention to begin building a new structure that satisfies the constraints of the current information.

As outlined in Chapter 2, readers' brains code these in the form of situation models with the dimensions:

- *Time.* One event relative to another, and to the time of narration.
- *Space.* The spatial relations between events or protagonists in the situation model.
- *People* and *objects.* The animate or inanimate objects that are a part of the situation.
- *Goals and causation.* The protagonists' goals which shape their actions and the causal relationships between events or states.

Changes along these dimensions determine how and when information across events is integrated and updated into the situation model. Neuroimaging research has indeed shown that readers spontaneously segment the narrated activity into series of events, thus creating new situation models, accompanied by transient increases in neural activity at the points readers explicitly identified as boundaries between events.[164] This segmentation or event coding process, based on changes in the narrated situation, is revealed by neural responses to these event boundaries. These are mediated by cues such as changes in characters, their locations and their goals, that is, changes in one or more of the situation model dimensions.

In narratology, the plot of prototypical stories (third-person narratives) is viewed as a telic structure that includes an agent, a goal and a causal sequence connecting the agent's various actions with the achievement or nonachievement of the goal. Moreover, 'good storytelling' has been considered to be about compelling human plights that are accessible to readers, typically in the form of obstacles that have to be overcome to reach the goals. As mentioned in Chapter 3, what Roman Jakobson was for the analysis of poetry, Vladimir Propp was for the analysis of stories. In his 'Morphology of the Folktale', he invented a 'plot grammar', which described the types and order of abstracted plot pieces (called functions) that may occur in the folktales in his corpus. Propp's theory additionally described a level of tale organization (the 'move' structure), a set of long-distance dependencies between plot pieces (function subtypes), a number of exceptions and additional complications (order inversions and trebling) and common character types (the 'dramatis personae').

Following up on Propp's early 'plot grammar', reading psychology of the 1980s developed many competing 'story plot' or 'story grammar' models[165] that depended too heavily on the subjective judgement of a few annotators, could not be applied to voluminous bodies of literature such as entire books, and, most importantly, badly lacked broader empirical testing and support. This is why Anderson and McMaster, who were unsatisfied with the models of storytelling cognitive psychology offered at the time, invented their alternative method (see Figure 3.2 in Chapter 3). It was based on the idea that engaging narrative is an ebb and flow of emotional tension, traditionally expected to build towards a gratifying release near the end of well-crafted stories: computer-assisted modelling of affective tone, or, as it is called nowadays, sentiment analysis. This much simpler method was applied in 2016 by Archer and Jockers to crack the 'bestseller code',[i] helped them discover seven magic plotlines, and could explain the success of works like E. L. James' *Fifty Shades of Grey* or Salman Rushdie's *The Satanic Verses.* If readers structure narrative texts into a series of events in order to understand and remember them, a computational text analysis of stories must specify these events, and their cues, that is: time, locations and characters together with their relations and goals. Within *NLP,* this task is usually called *event detection,* and there are a number of tools that help manage this rather challenging task. Next, I will show some examples of how to extract cues for situation model building from text.

Who does What to Whom, Where, When and Why?

Table 6.1 specifies the elements that must be extracted from a sentence or paragraph to build a full-blown situation model. One of my students in the newly founded Data Science M.Sc. programme of FU Berlin, Anastasiia Todoshchuk, used this scheme to successfully identify events potentially supporting situation model building from literary texts of different complexities (fairy tales from the Dolphin Books' *Classic Tales Collection* vs. high literary

---

i Early and more recent theoretical and computational approaches to plot differ with regard to answering the question to what extent the emotional roller coaster revealed by sentiment analysis time series correspond with the narratological notions of *fabula* – the thematic content of a narrative – vs. *syuzhet* – the chronological structure of the events – or is something relatively independent. Here, I adhere to Matt Jocker's computationally and empirically validated position that it best estimates *syuzhet,* a position that is also supported by the above analyses.

stories from the *LitBank* dataset[166]). She employed a novel multilevel approach that consisted of extracting the events from both sentences and subordinate sentences (clauses).[167] Her algorithm for event detection reached accuracy scores of over 60 per cent when applied to fairy tales and of around 50 per cent for the *LitBank* dataset. I know of no current study that would achieve better results, suggesting that the task is not computationally trivial. The example below will give you an idea of the complexities.

Locations and agents/persons can be detected computationally via Named Entity Recognition (NER) tools. Consider the following six sentences of the first paragraph of Lyman Frank Baum's *The Wonderful Wizard of Oz*.

> Dorothy lived in the midst of the great Kansas prairies, with Uncle Henry, who was a farmer, and Aunt Em, who was the farmer's wife. Their house was small, for the lumber to build it had to be carried by wagon many miles. There were four walls, a floor and a roof, which made one room; and this room contained a rusty looking cookstove, a cupboard for the dishes, a table, three or four chairs, and the beds. Uncle Henry and Aunt Em had a big bed in one corner, and Dorothy a little bed in another corner. There was no garret at all, and no cellar – except a small hole dug in the ground, called a cyclone cellar, where the family could go in case one of those great whirlwinds arose, mighty enough to crush any building in its path. It was reached by a trap door in the middle of the floor, from which a ladder led down into the small, dark hole.

Table 6.1 Event elements that signal the potential building of situation models in texts as used to extract events.

Element of Event	*Description*
Action	Verb or verb phrase
Agent	Subject of Doer of action
Purpose	Purpose of the action
Cause	Cause of the action
Direct Object	Direct Object
Indirect Object	Indirect Object
Complement	Subjective/Objective complement
Location	Where the event took place
Time	When the event took place
Sentence ID	Reference to the original story text
Coref	Referent of the agent if it is a pronoun

Source: Adapted from Adolfo et al., 2017.[168]

When readers have to process more than a single line or sentence in chapters or poems, this is a game changer! Now the brain's big cognitive bottleneck, *verbal working memory*, kicks in. Its capacity lying somewhere between four and seven units, integrating say five words into a sentence Gestalt to decipher its meaning is no big challenge to most of us. But what about the eight lines of two quatrains in a sonnet or the above six sentences. In Baum's text, the brain would have to keep track of 165 words, but we know that while reading the second sentence ('Their house was small, for the lumber to build it had to be carried by wagon many miles.'), the mnestic echoes of the words of the first ('Dorothy lived in the midst of the great Kansas prairies, with Uncle Henry, who was a farmer, and Aunt Em, who was the farmer's wife.') already have faded. The brain keeps neither a visual-orthographic nor an auditory-phonological trace of them. Because such traces would clog the limited space in working memory and prevent new information about the next words read from being visually and phonologically (pre-)processed to create the text's surface form. However, the writer deftly helps young readers' brains to lift this form to the next levels that facilitate comprehension: the textbase and the situation model. The first paragraph of Baum's *The Wonderful Wizard of Oz* thus is a good example for a backgrounded text which nicely sets the stage by offering (young) readers an easy-to-grasp scene or situation with clear location cues (great Kansas prairies, small house), clear characters (Dorothy, Uncle Henry, Aunt Em) and elements of suspense that can raise 'what happens next' questions (cyclone cellar, dark hole). This paragraph tells the beginning of a story of both great comprehensibility and likeability that readers want to know more about.

We can apply publicly available NLP tools to the local or micro-analysis of situation model building at the sentence or passage level. The aforementioned *spacy* library is very practical for that purpose. Taking the first sentence from Baum's text, *spacy*'s NER tool would give the following output, identifying Kansas as a geopolitical entity (GPE) locating the event, together with three persons:

Dorothy PERSON
Kansas GPE
Uncle Henry PERSON.
Aunt Em PERSON

Once we have persons and locations, *time* comes next. Like location, the time dimension typically has macro- and microfeatures. The epoch in which a story develops (Middle Ages, eighteenth century, etc.) is a macrofeature just as could be the foreign or fantasy land in which a novel takes place. Local temporal microfeatures can be detected via noun-phrase temporal tags marking words like 'today', as provided by the *Stanford Core NLP* library.[169] Alternatively, one can use a simple look-up table (word list) containing all possible temporal cue words and phrases like ['yesterday', 'next week' and so on].

Regarding the identification of agents, actions and patients, next come a simple and a more complicated example using *spacy* on the last sentences of the following passage of Austen's *Emma*

> Emma turned away her head, divided between tears and smiles. 'It is impossible that Emma should not miss such a companion,' said Mr. Knightley. 'We should not like her so well as we do, sir, if we could suppose it; but she knows how much the marriage is to Miss Taylor's advantage; she knows how very acceptable it must be, at Miss Taylor's time of life, to be settled in a home of her own, and how important to her to be secure of a comfortable provision, and therefore cannot allow herself to feel so much pain as pleasure. Every friend of Miss Taylor must be glad to have her so happily married.'
> 'And you have forgotten one matter of joy to me,' said Emma, 'and a very considerable one – that I made the match myself. I made the match, you know, four years ago; and to have it take place, and be proved in the right, when so many people said Mr. Weston would never marry again, may comfort me for anything.'
> *Mr. Knightley shook his head at her. Her father fondly replied, 'Ah! my dear, I wish you would not make matches and foretell things, for whatever you say always comes to pass. Pray do not make any more matches.*

In *dependency grammar* notation, example (A) below reveals the subject (agent), action (verb) and object (patient) of the depicted event. Example (B) just illustrates how complicated such analyses can become with longer events.

A)
Mr. --> compound --> PROPN --> NNP
Knightley --> nsubj --> PROPN --> NNP
shook --> ROOT --> VERB --> VBD
his --> poss --> PRON --> PRP$
head --> dobj --> NOUN --> NN
at --> prep --> ADP --> IN
her --> pobj --> PRON --> PRP
. --> punct --> PUNCT --> .

B)
Her --> poss --> PRON --> PRP$
father --> nsubj --> NOUN --> NN
fondly --> advmod --> ADV --> RB
replied --> ROOT --> VERB --> VBD
Ah --> intj --> INTJ --> UH
--> dobj --> SPACE --> _SP
my --> poss --> PRON --> PRP$
dear --> npadvmod --> NOUN --> NN
I --> nsubj --> PRON --> PRP
wish --> parataxis --> VERB --> VBP
you --> nsubj --> PRON --> PRP
would --> aux --> AUX --> MD
not --> neg --> PART --> RB
make --> ccomp --> VERB --> VB
matches --> dobj --> NOUN --> NNS
and --> cc --> CCONJ --> CC
foretell --> conj --> VERB --> VB
things --> dobj --> NOUN --> NNS
for --> prep --> ADP --> IN
--> pobj --> SPACE --> _SP
whatever --> dobj --> DET --> WDT
you --> nsubj --> PRON --> PRP
say --> relcl --> VERB --> VBP
always --> advmod --> ADV --> RB
comes --> advcl --> VERB --> VBZ
to --> aux --> PART --> TO
pass --> xcomp --> VERB --> VB
. --> punct --> PUNCT --> .

Applying these tools, you could now summarize all of a protagonist's actions and their patients together with the corresponding times and locations to learn about what she did to whom, when and where. With a similar method, Archer and Jockers predicted whether a novel in their corpus was a bestseller with an accuracy of around 70 per cent.

But what about the *why question*? Automatically identifying the cause or purpose of an event's action to answer the why question is indeed trickier than answering the other 'Wh-questions'. One method makes use of sentences that fit the following scheme: Noun-phrase head (agent, subject), verb phrase (event) and verb phrase complement (purpose). Such patterns can be used to identify the adverb or prepositional phrase for time/place after a verb phrase in simple sentences like 'He was here for dinner'. A simple rule that can be implemented in *spacy* and trained on some annotated corpus would state that: 'any prepositional phrase appearing after another adverb or prepositional phrase is extracted as the value for the *purpose* field of the coded event'. Another simpler technique uses sentence pattern templates with causative verbs like 'have', 'get' or 'make' and causal conjunctions like 'because' or 'due to'. However, current tools for event detection still have their limits, although some work with up to 50 rules or sentence templates. Combining such tools with machine learning algorithms, one can achieve event detection accuracies of up to 75 per cent (as compared with human annotations), depending on the text and the dimensions of the event. Even so, many challenges remain, for instance when figurative language or an extended metaphor is used to represent an event as in: 'He had broken a thickness of ice, the formation of many a winter; had had his reasons for a long silence.' (Henry James, *The Turn of the Screw*). In this case, one of the currently best algorithms[170] failed to detect 'broken' as a cue for an event.

Moreover, some elements of Table 6.1 above are better to extract than others. Thus, in the study on fairy tales mentioned earlier, *actions* and *agents* achieved high accuracies (>90 per cent). *Locations* (~55 per cent) were harder to detect than *times* (~80 per cent), and – as could be expected – causes (35 per cent) and *purposes* (0 per cent) still need a lot of improvement. To summarize, state-of-the-art NLP tools like the 'Natural Language ToolKit'/*NLTK*,[171] *Stanford Core Nlp* or *spacy* allow automatic story analyses at both macro- and microanalytic levels, although not error-free. Hence, a time- and person-intensive middle reading approach is called for if one is unhappy with incomplete or error-prone analyses. Such an approach also seems called for to detect causes and purposes at the mesoanalytic level, when, for instance, a protagonist decides on an action that takes place many pages later. While complete computational answers to the six 'Wh-questions' are 'work in progress', the technique of identifying plot via sentiment analysis, initiated by Anderson and McMaster in the 1980s, is close to maturity.

Prototypical Plots

Theoretical and computational approaches to plot differ with regard to the prototypical number of plots. The simplest one distinguishes only between three plots at the macrostructural level: happy and unhappy ending, and tragedy.[172] These three plots are closely linked with the nature and fate of a central character: virtuous, selfish or struck by destiny, respectively. Other approaches share the idea of seven basic plots or plotlines, while at least two others propose even more (20 or 36), and one proposes the notion of six 'core emotional arcs' conceived as being relatively independent of the plots of stories. The following Figure 6.1 (upper panel) perhaps best represents the state of the art, since it can be derived from both a qualitative close reading account and Archer and Jockers' macrostructural distant reading account based on *univariate* (using a single predictor variable) sentiment analysis.

Briefly, these seven basic plots can be characterized as follows:

A) Comedy (*A Midsummer Night's Dream*, *The Client*). A gradual increase from an emotional low to a high comparable to a three-act structure with a relatively negative midpoint (the valley) and an end which is clearly more positive than the beginning. The trend here is upwards.
B) Tragedy (*Anna Karenina*, *The Metamorphosis*, *The Bonfire of the Vanities*). This is the mirror image of comedy with a steady downwards trend.
C) Rags to riches (*Cinderella*, *Jane Eyre*). A kind of three-act structure with a negative midpoint and an end which is more negative than the beginning; an up-down-up dynamics. Kurt Vonnegut called this the 'boy meets girl' plot in which the protagonist comes across something wonderful, gets it, loses it, then wins it for good. Archer and Jockers call it the 'coming of age' plotline with a central movement between success and failure.
D) Rebirth (*Beauty and the Beast*, *Fifty Shades of Grey*, *Wolf Hall*). The mirror image of (D) has a down-up-down dynamics where the protagonists experience some sort of transformation.
E) Voyage and return (*The Time Machine*, *Alice in Wonderland*, *Gulliver's Travels*). A sign-wave or 'W-shape' dynamics (down-up-down-up) with a midpoint peak or pivot around the middle of the story dear to many romance novelists (the peak often being the first love scene). Typically, the protagonists are confronted with whole other worlds that they become attracted to, but – after some dark turn – they return to a kind of happy normalcy.
F) The quest (*King Solomon's Mines*, *The Satanic Verses*, *The Corrections*). The mirror image of (E) with an up-down-up-down dynamics and a midpoint low. This is the typical adventure story where the main characters seek and find, explore unknown territories, experience dashed hopes, fight enemies and complete a quest in the end.
G) Overcoming the monster (*Beowulf*, *The Runaway Jury*). Basically, a typical good-bad-good-again dynamics that Vonnegut called 'man in the hole', where the protagonist gets into trouble, then gets out of it and ends up better off. This is the only plot in this set which has no mirror image, perhaps because people do not like to read stories in which things start badly, then go to really good and back to quite bad.

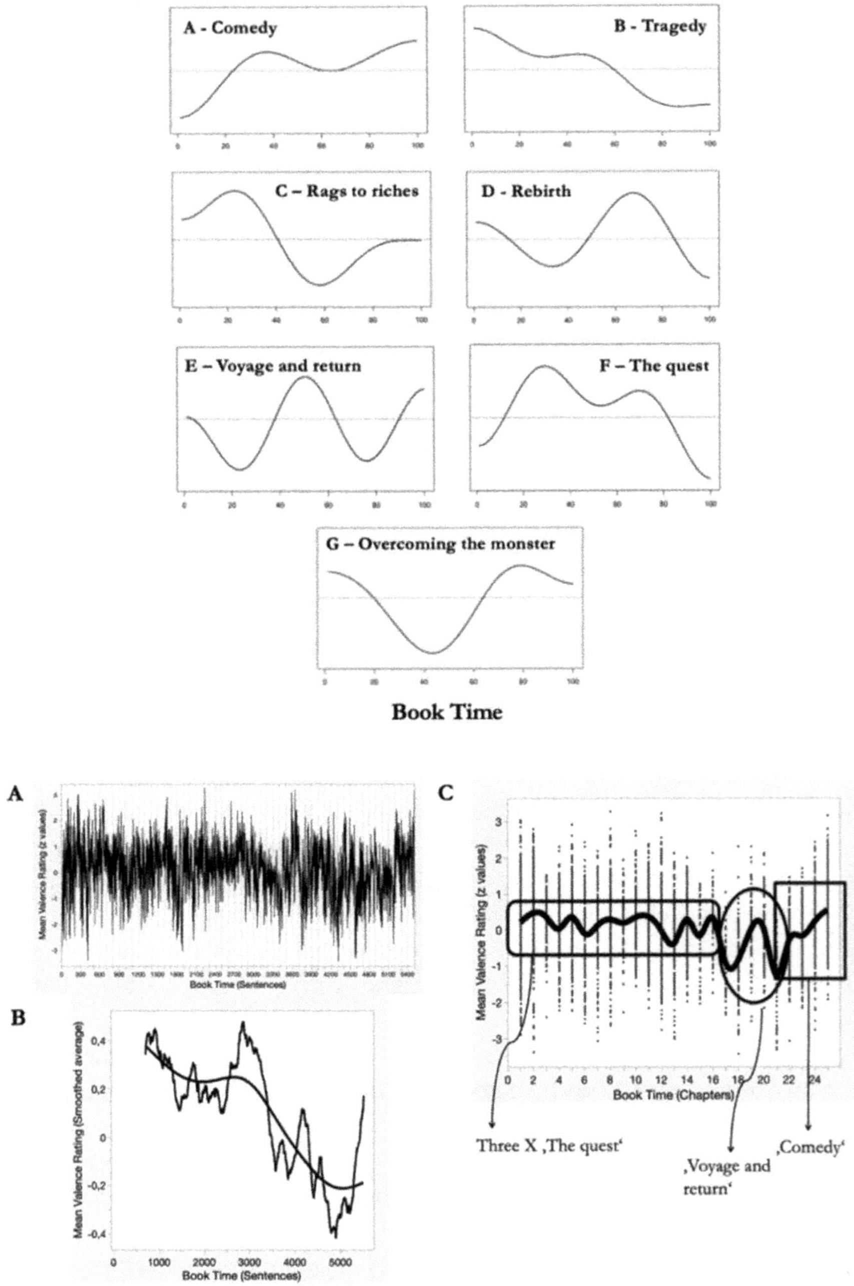

Figure 6.1 Upper panel. Seven prototypical plotlines. Source: Adapted from Archer and Jockers, 2016. **Lower panel.** Sentence-wise and chapter-wise sentiment (A,C), and plotline (B) computed via *SentiArt* for the German version of John Green's *The Fault in Our Stars.*

Theory vs. Human Data: Micro-, Meso-, and Macroanalysis

All the above accounts lack a central ingredient from a Neurocomputational Poetics perspective: solid empirical human data with which to compare the theoretical predictions.[ii] In a recent unpublished study, we had 20 readers rate the emotional valence of each sentence of entire children and youth books, a task which was well remunerated and took several weeks.[173] One of the four books we studied was the German version of John Green's *The Fault in Our Stars*, a story known to really take readers on an emotional roller coaster and literally make them laugh, cry and smile. It is about Hazel, a young teenage girl who has been diagnosed with lung cancer.

Figure 6.1 (lower panel) shows the results. What distinguishes Figures 6.1A–C (lower panel) is the level of detail. In Figure 6.1A (lower panel), I plotted the mean valence rating (average of 20 readers) against book time (in sentences, from 1 to 5,508). These *microanalytic* raw data reflecting the local sentence-to-sentence variation in ratings are very noisy and thus hard to predict and interpret. The interpretation is difficult because the big psychological question of *how a reader integrates the affective information aggregated across the individual words of a sentence into a rating about the valence of the entire sentence* is yet unanswered. I will return to this issue in a minute. Meanwhile, let us have a look at the other diagrams of Figure 6.1 (lower panel).

As a remedy to the noise problem, in Figure 6.1B (lower panel), I smoothed the microanalytic raw data from Figure 6.1A (lower panel) using a standard statistical procedure called *spline smoothing*[174] thus making the *macrostructure* visible to allow comparison with the seven prototypical plotlines from Figure 6.1 upper panel. It is not hard to see that John Green's novel best fits the tragedy pattern. Finally, the data in Figure 6.1C (lower panel) visualize the highs and lows of the emotional roller coaster, potentially revealing something about the story plot at the *mesoanalytic* level of the 25 chapters. The dots represent the mean data for each sentence of a chapter, the curved line represents the smoothed average (N = 700 sentences). The absolute low is reached in chapter 21, where Augustus Waters, the witty and charming friend of Hazel, dies of osteosarcoma, a rare form of bone cancer. The last chapter is the most positive one, in which Hazel and her parents first going for a family picnic in Holliday Park on Bastille Day (14th of July) and then visit Augustus's grave.

ii Matt Jockers' work published on his homepage (https://www.matthewjockers.net/2016/08/11/more-syuzhet-validation/) is an exception, but the sample sizes appear to be very small (N = 3). The predictive accuracy of his *Syuzhet* sentiment analysis tool is very impressive for a univariate approach, though, ranging from $R^2 = .38$ for 'Where'd You Go Bernadette' to $R^2 = .69$ for 'Alex Cross Run'.

At this mesoanalytic level, one can recognize a mix of the macroanalytic plotlines. Thus, chapters 1–17 appear to adhere to three 'The quest' patterns, followed by a 'Voyage and return' pattern across chapters 18 to 21, and a final rise which characterizes a 'Comedy' plotline.

To sum up: the above macro-, meso- and microanalytical data indicate that the most promising approach to a 'plot by sentiment analysis' of entire books uses a combination of strongly smoothed sentence-wise and moderately smoothed chapter-wise rating data to identify underlying prototypical plotlines like those proposed by Archer and Jockers. Such empirical data can inform close reading approaches to plot analysis by literary critics or *middle reading* approaches based on a combination of computational sentiment analysis and expert close reading, but lacking human rating data[175].

Predicting Human Rating Data with SentiArt: *Three Empirical Validation Studies*

In the preceding section, I have shown, for the first time, that the theoretical plotlines of literary theory and NLP can actually correspond with human behaviour, as represented by a relatively large sample of 20 readers and many thousands of data points per reader and book. This probably largest current data set for emotional book evaluation worldwide complements earlier sets we had collected on the reading and emotional evaluation of stories and book chapters in both German and English. It is now time to put the *SentiArt* tool to a critical empirical test: How well can human valence rating data on entire chapters and books be predicted by *advanced multivariate sentiment analysis*? The answer to this question, central to Neurocomputational Poetics, is given by the data of a series of empirical studies, which were analyzed in a predictive modelling approach summarized next.

Study 1. Harry Potter, Batman and Pippi Longstocking

In this study, a sample of readers read and rated the sentence valence of short excerpts from three books in German:

- Batman: Der Nebel des Grauens (Batman: *The Fog of Fear*) by M. Powell. 225 sentences, 21 readers.
- *Harry Potter und die Heiligtümer des Todes* (*Harry Potter and the Deathly Hallows*) by J. K. Rowling. 122 sentences, 29 readers.
- *Pippi Langstrumpf* (*Pippi Longstocking*) by A. Lindgren. 136 sentences, 38 readers.

Here are two example sentences from the Harry Potter excerpt together with their ratings:

- 'Sie brachten Voldemorts Leiche weg und legten sie in eine Kammer neben der Halle, abseits der Leichen von Fred, Tonks, Lupin, Colin Creevey und fünfzig anderen, die im Kampf gegen ihn gestorben waren.' (*They moved Voldemort's body and laid it in a chamber off the Hall, away from the bodies of Fred, Tonks, Lupin, Colin Creevey, and fifty others who had died fighting him.*); Rating = 2.4 (1 = very negative, 7 = very positive).
- 'Die Sonne ging stetig über Hogwarts auf, und die Große Halle glühte vor Leben und Licht'. (*The sun rose steadily over Hogwarts, and the Great Hall blazed with life and light.*); Rating = 6.3.

Study 2. The Sandman

In this study, 30 readers read and rated the valence of E. T. A. Hoffmann's famous uncanny story *The Sandman* (in German), which had been slightly shortened and segmented into 65 segments by literary experts so as to form about equivalent narrative units.

Here is the segment that obtained the most negative rating (1.8, scale from 1 to 7):

- Vor dem dampfenden Herde auf dem Boden lag mein Vater tot mit schwarzverbranntem, grässlich verzerrtem Gesicht, um ihn herum heulten und winselten die Schwestern – die Mutter ohnmächtig daneben! – 'Coppelius, verruchter Satan, du hast den Vater erschlagen!' – So schrie ich auf; mir vergingen die Sinne. Als man zwei Tage darauf meinen Vater in den Sarg legte, waren seine Gesichtszüge wieder mild und sanft geworden, wie sie im Leben waren. Die Explosion hatte die Nachbarn geweckt, der Vorfall wurde gemeldet und kam vor die Obrigkeit, welche den Coppelius zur Verantwortung vorladen wollte. Der war aber spurlos vom Orte verschwunden. (*On the floor of the smoking hearth lay my father dead, with his face burned and blackened, and hideously distorted, – my sisters were shrieking and moaning around him, – and my mother had fainted. 'Coppelius! – cursed Satan, thou hast slain my father!' I cried, and lost my senses. When, two days afterwards, my father was laid in his coffin, his features were again as mild and gentle as they had been in his life. My soul was comforted by the thought that his compact with the devilish Coppelius could not have plunged him into eternal perdition. The explosion had awakened the neighbours, the occurrence had become the common talk, and had reached the ears of the magistracy, who wished to make Coppelius answerable. He had, however, vanished from the spot, without leaving a trace.*)

Study 3. The Fault in Our Stars and Harry Potter and the Half-blood Prince

In this study, a sample of 20 readers read and rated the sentence valence of four entire children's and youth books in German, two of which are considered here:

- 'Schicksal Mieser Verräter' (*The Fault in Our Stars*) by John Green. 5,508 sentences.
- 'Harry Potter und der Halbblutprinz' (*Harry Potter and the Half-blood Prince*) by J. K. Rowling. 11,155 sentences.

Here are two example sentences together with their ratings:

- 'Ich hasse mich, ich hasse mich, ich hasse das, ich hasse das, ich ekel mich vor mir, ich hasse es, ich hasse es so, lass mich einfach endlich sterben, verdammte scheiße' (*'I hate myself I hate myself I hate this I hate this I disgust myself I hate it I hate it I hate it just let me fucking die.'*); Rating = 1.1.
- 'Wir haben gewonnen! Harry sah sich um; da kam Ginny auf ihn zugerannt; mit hartem, glühendem Gesicht warf sie die Arme um ihn. Und ohne nachzudenken, ohne es zu planen, ohne sich um die Tatsache zu kümmern, dass fünfzig Leute zusahen, küsste Harry sie.' ('*We won!' Harry looked around; there was Ginny running toward him; she had a hard, blazing look in her face as she threw her arms around him. And without thinking, without planning it, without worrying about the fact that fifty people were watching, Harry kissed her.*); Rating = 6.1.

To strengthen the signal (reduce noise), the sentences rated as neutral were excluded from the predictive modelling analysis[176] and the data from all three excerpts in study 1 were pooled to gain greater statistical power required for the supervised machine learning method using a neural net. Figure 6.2 summarizes some main results of these studies in the format of overlay plots, where the grey circles correspond to the actual human rating values and the black crosses to the predicted values. Both the actual and the predicted ratings – based on a set of 13 predictors[iii] – were smoothed as in Figure 6.1

iii The 13 features computed by *SentiArt* serving as predictors were (in order of importance): AAP, the minimum and maximum positive values of AAP in a sentence (posmnv, posmxv), the ratio of words with a positive AAP to those with a negative one (positive-negative ratio/pnrs):, the shift in the average AAP value from one sentence to the next (aapsh), the difference/span between the minimum and maximum valence value in a sentence (valspan), the difference/span between the minimum and

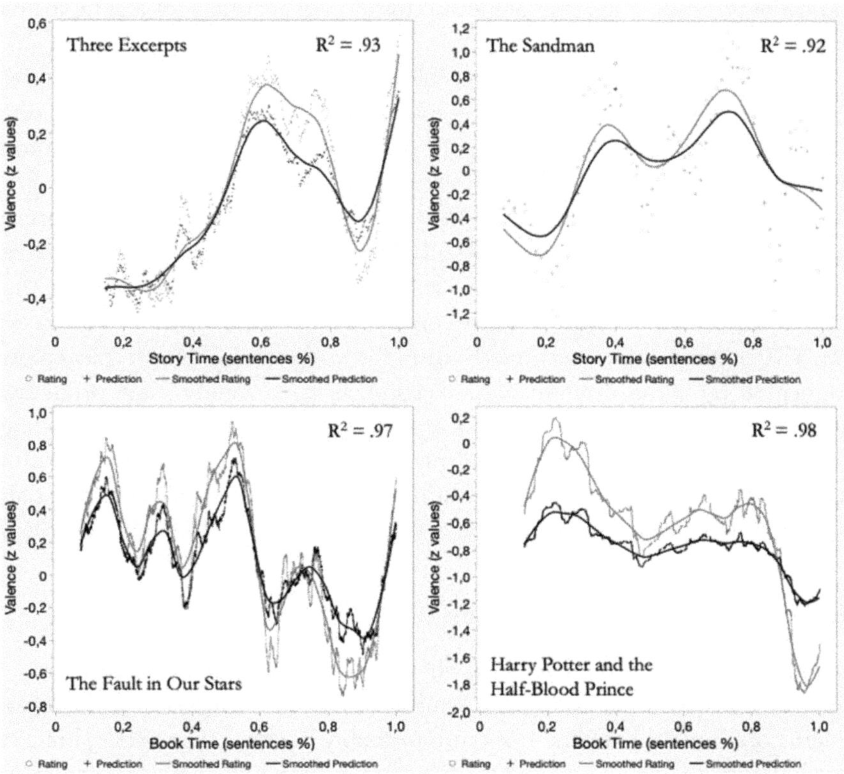

Figure 6.2 Predicted and actual valence ratings of sentences for different texts.

above (grey curve = human data, black curve = predicted data). The naked eye recognizes a good correspondence between the two time-series curves in all four cases. This is confirmed by the very high R^2 values of 0.92 to 0.98, meaning that the models in each case were able to predict the human data with an accuracy of over 90 per cent. This is quite an outstanding result, and

maximum arousal value in a sentence (arospan), the semantic similarity of a sentence with the preceding one (ssim), the shift in the average arousal value from one sentence to the next (arosh), the number of syllables (nsyl), the sentence syllable index: product of number words * average number of syllables in a sentence, a simple readability measure (ssi), log word frequency, the shift in the average surprise value from one sentence to the next (surpsh): surprise is a feature computed by *SentiArt* as the mean semantic similarity between the words in a line with the label 'surprise'. It is assumed to reflect to what extent a line's words can evoke associations with the basic emotion surprise.

I know of no other study that achieved this level of accuracy for a comparable data set.

With regard to the seven prototypical plots shown in Figure 6.1 (upper panel), the smoothed curves representing both human and computational data for *The Sandman* seem to resemble most the 'Rags to riches' pattern, those for *The Fault in Our Stars* match best with two consecutive 'Voyage and return' W-shaped patterns, and those of *Harry Potter and the Half-blood Prince* pretty much fit with *The Quest* (since the data of the three excerpts were pooled, no interpretation is given here). In sum, first the above analyses demonstrate that 'plot by sentiment analysis' of entire books as computed by *SentiArt* produces data that can nicely be interpreted within the framework of prototypical plots, confirmed by actual human data. Second, using a multivariate predictive modelling approach based on text features computed by *SentiArt* it is possible to predict human ratings of the valence of sentences or text segments with a very high precision (when both the human and the computer-generated data are smoothed for noise reduction).

Story Analysis II. Characters

Narrative theorists still are at strife whether the plot structure of a story is best described as events that happen to characters, or as the ways in which characters make events happen. The truth probably lies near the middle, but as a psychologist, I have a penchant for the second approach, which incorporates the psychology and experientiality of characters, such as their emotional or personality profiles. Popular computational story generators[177] also start with a protagonist or hero. The preceding 'plot by sentiment' analyses focused on emotional events developing over book time without any explicit reference to characters. In the next sections, I discuss (i) computational story analyses that extract the protagonists, their preferred places, actions and interactions, as well as (ii) their emotional and personality profiles.

Characters, Places and Actions

To identify protagonists and their places and (inter)actions, a story is first split up into sentences and their tokens (words) by help of tools like the *NLTK* library. The five diagrams in Figure 6.3 from a study published in 2021 show some examples from the German *Luther Bible.* The descriptive data in these diagrams serve as estimates of what a reader who has read the Bible carefully and repeatedly may have integrated into her *apperceptive mass*, for instance the names of at least the 20 most frequently mentioned persons (of ~2,000) and places in the Bible (Figure 6.3A), or the typical actions *Jesus* is most often

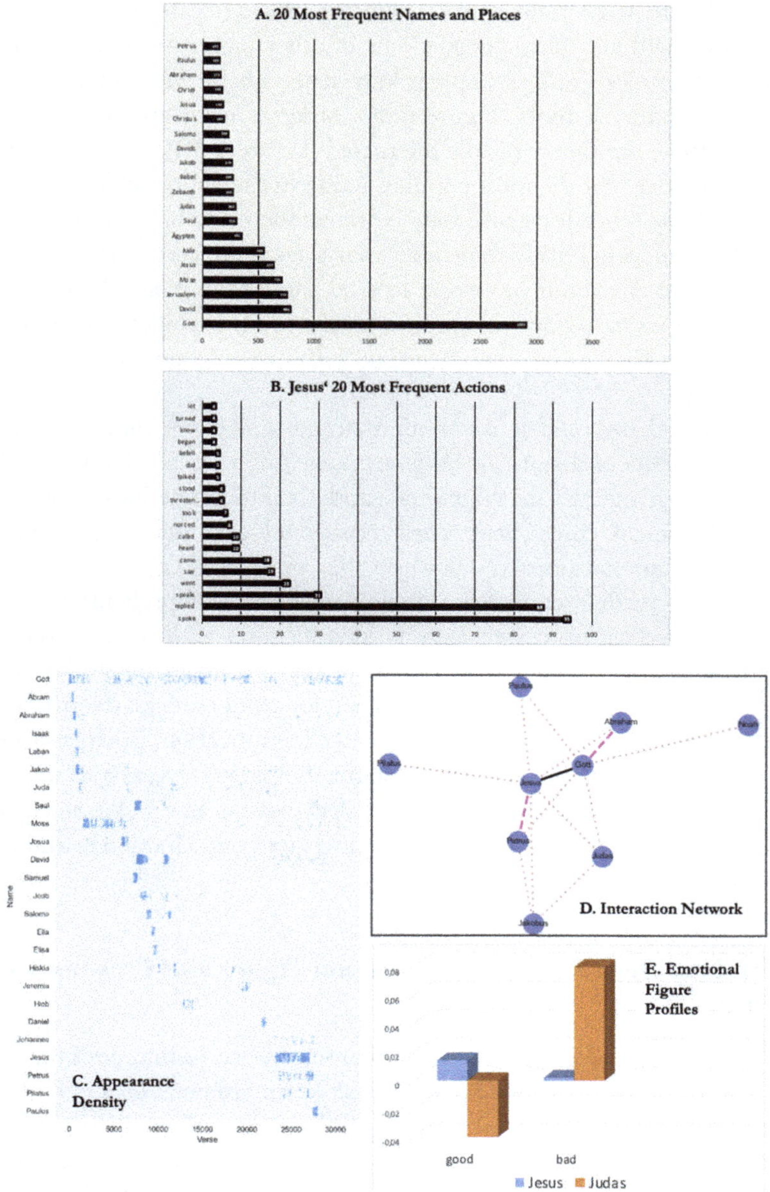

Figure 6.3 A. Twenty most frequent names and places in the German Luther Bible. **(B)** Twenty most frequent actions of Jesus in the Bible. **(C)** Appearance density of 25 major characters in the Bible ordered according to verse number.[178]. **(D)** Interaction network of nine major characters in the Bible (interaction frequency is represented by line width: bold >dashed>dotted). **(E)** Emotional figure profiles for Jesus and Judas computed with *SentiArt*; Source: Adapted from Jacobs & Kinder, 2022.[179]

associated with (e.g. 'Jesus spoke', Figure 6.3B). The associative networks of her brain will also have encoded lots of other pieces of information that can constitute more or less implicit knowledge about when major characters appeared in the Bible (Figure 6.3C; ordered according to verse number), or with whom they typically interacted (Figure 6.3D). Thus, this reader could remember that the most popular action in the entire Bible is *speaking* – including Jesus – but Jesus also may be remembered to have *threatened* a few times. Also, he would likely remember that Jesus was closer to Petrus than to Paulus, or that Abraham was closer to God (Gott) than Noah (Figure 6.3D). Finally, she may also have an opinion on the main protagonists' emotional figure profiles, such as whether Jesus and Judas were 'good' or 'bad' persons (Figure 6.3E).

Data like these inform us about macro-features relevant for predicting main aspects of a story or book a reader might recall. However, these computational analyses of characters and their (inter)actions lack a central psychological component: their emotional and personality profiles. Neurocomputational research, however, has produced ample evidence that the emotions readers experience during narrative comprehension depend upon psychological processes such as identification with a protagonist, or empathy and sympathy for story characters. The *likeability* of stories greatly depends on this, as has already been shown for child readers: the overall liking of a story indeed increases with greater identification, greater suspense and greater liking of outcome. While younger children (7 years) seem to prefer positive outcomes regardless of the valence of the main character, older children (10–12) appear to like happy endings for good characters and negative endings for bad characters.[180]

The Hybrid Hero Potential: Emotional Figure and Personality Profiles

Such results motivated me to include character features into *SentiArt*, allowing me to compute their *hybrid hero potential*. From Homer's *Iliad* to Gilligan's *Breaking Bad* fiction protagonists have been depicted with conflicting features or traits to make them more interesting or attractive to readers, listeners or viewers. Adding such features should improve both sentiment and plot analyses. For example, the perceived sentiment of a sentence or paragraph can very well depend on whether something bad happens to a good or to a bad character. So, we need a measure of character 'goodness' just as the ones for Jesus and Judas in Figure 6.3E above. We also know that readers often empathize more with characters who share personality traits with them. Thus, figure personality profiles may be useful to predict readers' empathy, identification and likeability responses. Finally, plot analyses can also can benefit from having a valid measure of a protagonist's emotional or personality features and their development across narrative time, such as Saul turning into Paul, Dr. Jekyll into Mr. Hyde or Daenerys Targaryen taking a turn from good to evil in *Game of Thrones*.

Figure 6.4A and B show two examples of *figure personality profiles* from the Harry Potter books based on an adapted version of the '*big5*' personality scale introduced in Chapter 4. Arguably, this scale, widely used in psychology, reduces human personalities to values on the five dimensions, sometimes called the *OCEAN* model. The exemplary data in Figure 6.4A – based on a special language model in German I trained on the Harry Potter books series – show the semantic relatedness scores computed for the words 'Harry' and 'Voldemort' with six labels representing the negative and positive poles of the 'Agreeableness' dimension. The labels 'affectionate', 'caring' and 'friendly' hypothetically represent the positive pole of the dimension, the other three the negative one. The final score for each dimension is computed by subtracting the averaged values for the negative labels from that for the positive ones. To the extent that my 'pseudo-big5' model for fictive characters is of any heuristic value, the data in Figure 6.4A suggest that the 'Harry' character is more closely associated with the semantic concepts 'affectionate', 'caring',

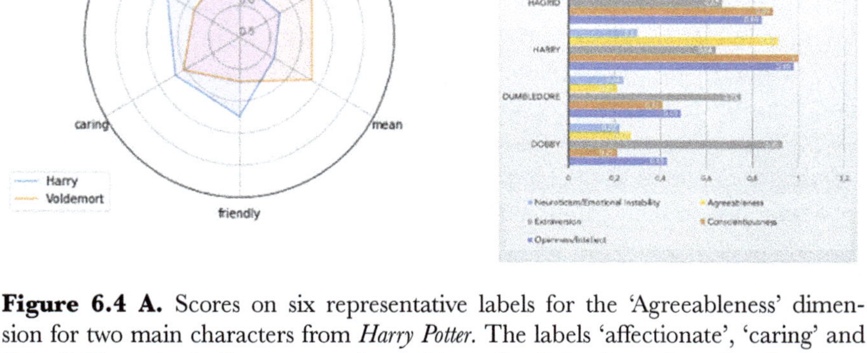

Figure 6.4 A. Scores on six representative labels for the 'Agreeableness' dimension for two main characters from *Harry Potter*. The labels 'affectionate', 'caring' and 'friendly' hypothetically represent the positive pole of the dimension, the other three the negative one. **B**. Pseudo-*big5* scores for seven main characters from *Harry Potter*. The scores are percentiles based on a sample of 100 characters appearing in the book series. Source: Adapted from Jacobs, 2019.[181]

and 'friendly', while 'Voldemort' is more related than 'Harry' to the negative concepts of 'deadhearted', 'hostile' and 'mean'. Still, the data also show the inherent ambiguity and complexity ('hybrid hero potential') resulting from this method: thus, Voldemort, although more deadhearted than Harry, also scores > 0 on the 'affectionate' dimension, while Harry, although being more friendly than Voldemort, also scores a 0.68 value for 'hostile'. And indeed, Voldemort can appear affectionate in certain contexts, such as when in the presence of Bellatrix, just as Harry can become hostile when confronting bad characters like Voldemort.

The data in Figure 6.4B are based on the same method showing the values for all five dimensions for a selective set of seven characters. The top scorer on the Openness, Conscientiousness and Agreeableness dimensions is 'Harry', while 'Voldemort' takes the lead on the Neuroticism dimension. Interestingly, 'Dobby' is the winner on the Extraversion dimension. In the absence of empirical data, I leave it up to readers of this book to judge the face validity of these tentative results. Their heuristic value is clear, though, and can readily be tested, for example, by an experiment with human readers who are invited to judge these seven (or more) characters on scales borrowed from the '*big5*' personality inventory.

A final quantification and empirical test of the *hybrid hero potential* must await future studies investigating its influence on affective-aesthetic reader responses. Such studies should examine which of the *big5* dimensions matters most for the perceived character ambiguity of a protagonist and its attractiveness and identification potential. Fanzine and other internet pages[182] offer lists of the most liked characters that could make use of data such as those in Figure 6.4 by adopting simpler opposite categories only, such as 'risky-cautious', 'good-bad' or 'nice-nasty'.

To summarize, the sophisticated application examples in the preceding sections have shown how one can compute textual features important for situation model building and coherence, how sentiment analysis can be used to identify prototypical plots and that multivariate nonlinear predictive modelling of human valence ratings for entire stories and books based on *SentiArt* can achieve very good predictive accuracies. Furthermore, the computational analysis of characters, places and actions, as well as *SentiArt*'s capacities to compute emotional figure and personality profiles as indices of the hybrid hero potential, was demonstrated using the Luther Bible and the Harry Potter books series.

Lyrics and Poetry Analysis – In Search of the Ideal Line

As assumed by the NCPM, prose and poetry texts typically differ on many feature dimensions, afford different processing routines by readers, and they usually are the object of different aspirations or reader motivations. So far, the analyses in this chapter have concerned prose texts, and it would not be complete without a computational analysis of lyrics and poetry introducing new features that have not been used in the above prose analyses, such as *assonance*, or *sonority score*. In the next sections of this chapter, I present unpublished work in progress: the computational text analysis and multivariate prediction of human ratings for a selection of song lyrics by Bob Dylan and for all 154 sonnets by Shakespeare.

Dylanology: Predicting the Most Likeable Lines in Songs by Bob Dylan

Oh God said to Abraham, 'Kill me a son.'
Abe says, 'Man, you must be puttin' me on.'
God say, 'No.' Abe say, 'What?'
God say, 'You can do what you want, Abe, but The next time you see me comin', you better run.'

'How does it feel
To be on your own
With no direction home Like a complete unknown
Like a rolling stone?'

Are these lines pieces of literature? If you hesitate, listen to what the author of these famous lines of song lyrics said when he won the Nobel Prize for literature in 2016. Actually, in his letter to the members of the Swedish academy, he said: *Not once have I ever had the time to ask myself, 'Are my songs literature?'*. And by what he said in his previous text he made clear that '*Just like Homer or Shakespeare*' would be a valid extension of this statement. While many a critic has raised arguments against the Nobel committee's decision, scientific studies of literature like those by Gerard Steen, a pioneer in metaphor theory, leave little doubt about the poetic quality of some of Bob Dylan's lyrics. As an example, the metaphoricity of 'Hurricane' a song from the album *Desire* (CBS, 1975) that has about 60 metaphorically used words (~1,000 words in total) offers linguistic, conceptual and communicative functions that can absolutely be considered poetic in Jakobson's sense.[183]

I have been a fan of Bob Dylan's art since the days I first learnt to play the few chords of 'Blowin' in the Wind' on my guitar, while trying to decipher the meaning of the American-English lyrics. I also became interested in empirically investigating what makes these songs special long before he received the Nobel Prize in 2016. During the last 10 years, in several empirical seminars I have run studies in which students have rated the likeability of selected songs and their lines, either simultaneously to listening to the music or focusing on the texts without any musical accompaniment. Since I never really found an effect of listening to the music on the ratings, the data I report here are from studies without music. I was interested mainly in what makes readers like the lyrics of a song or line more than others. Evidently, saying *that* you like a line of poetry or lyrics is a lot easier than explaining *why*. As expressed by Jakobson's poetic function, the liking not only depends on the content alone but also on the way this content is created and conveyed: sometimes it is the formal qualities of the lyrics that attract most of the attention. Bob Dylan's lyrics work exactly in this way to produce their literary effects. So, I used the *SentiArt* tool to generate predictions about the why on the basis of the lyrics' form and content features.

Predictive Modelling of Song Likeability

In one series of studies, I had several groups of undergraduate psychology students (overall N ~ 50) rate how much they liked the lyrics of 11 songs, eight of which had been classified as either of higher or lower literary quality by a group of experts from the humanities, among which my colleague from Mainz University Pascal Nicklas,[184] another fan of Bob Dylan, who participated in parts of these studies together with my colleagues from Glasgow and Belfast, Nigel Fabb and Liz Finnigan. The 11 songs were (in alphabetical order):

1. 'Abandoned Love', originally recorded in 1975 for inclusion on the 1976 album *Desire*.
2. The famous protest song 'Blowin' in the Wind' from the 1963 album *The Freewheelin' Bob Dylan'*.
3. The bluesy ballad 'Going, Going, Gone' from the 1974 album *Planet Waves*.
4. 'Highway 61 Revisited' from the 1965 album of the same name.
5. 'If Dogs Run Free' from the 1970 album *New Morning*.
6. The popular ballad 'I Threw It All Away' from the 1969 album *Nashville Skyline*.
7. 'I Want You' from the 1969 album *Blonde On Blonde*.
8. The top 10 hit 'Knocking on Heaven's Door' written for the soundtrack of the 1973 film *Pat Garrett and Billy the Kid*.
9. The country ballad 'Lay Lady Lay' released in 1969 on his *Nashville Skyline* album.
10. 'Like a Rolling Stone' from the 1965 album *Highway 61 Revisited*.
11. 'Love Minus Zero' from the 1965 album *Bringing It All Back Home*.

Among those, the song by far most liked by our students was 'Lay Lady Lay', followed by 'Going, Going, Gone' and 'I threw it all away'. The three least liked lyrics were from 'Highway 61 revisited', followed by 'Knocking on Heaven's Door' and 'I Want You'. Using *SentiArt* I computed four features[iv] for each line of the 11 songs and then averaged them for each song: the lexical affective semantic feature *AAP*, the sublexical phonological feature *alliteration*, the interlexical affective semantic feature *arousal span* and the supralexical surface feature *number of words*. With this simple four-feature model I could predict the liking ratings for the 11 songs with a 99 per cent accuracy. The *AAP* and *arousal span* features were the most important ones (both FIs = 0.28), followed by *alliteration* (FI = 0.25) and *number of words* (FI = 0.18). The main effects of the first three features were positively related to liking ratings, while the last one had a negative effect, that is, the fewer words a song had, the higher the likelihood of liking. Thus, our sample of readers liked song lyrics with not too many words ('Lay lady Lay') evoking associations with beautiful concepts ('I long to see you in the morning light'), drawing attention to their initial sounds by alliteration ('Lay Lady Lay') and by a contrast between positive and negative arousal ('His clothes are dirty but his hands are clean'). In this respect, 'Lay Lady Lay' seems perfect, doesn't it? Just taking the very short and very alliterative title and chorus line, which associations does it elicit? Rather beautiful or ugly ones? And how does your felt arousal level change when you read 'his clothes are dirty but his hands are clean'? Doesn't the original contrast 'dirty clothes' and 'clean hands' raise it? At any rate, even if this four-feature model interpretation of why our readers liked the 'Lay Lady Lay' lyrics best among the 11 songs were badly reductionist, undercomplex or even bluntly faulty, who can propose a better (with 100 per cent accuracy for a sample of ~50 readers), simpler (less than four reasons) and more plausible one?

Predictive Modelling of Line Likeability

Having successfully predicted which song lyrics were liked best as a whole, I then looked at individual lines. The marking of the most striking or beautiful word, phrase or line is a typical response measure in empirical studies of literature,[185] but so far no one has tried to *predict* this direct online measure

iv These four features were selected among the 85 that *SentiArt* usually computes for any text on the basis of a predictor screening procedure provided by the *jmp 16 pro* software (https://www.jmp.com/en_in/events/mastering/topics/new-in-jmp16-and-jmp-pro16.html).

quantitatively (or qualitatively), if I am correct. The top and flop five lines from this sample of 11 songs are shown next (song in brackets):

Top 5

- 'And you're the best thing that he's ever seen' (Lady).
- 'And you'll be fine at the end of the line' (Going).
- 'I long to see you in the morning light' (Lady).
- 'Grandma said, "boy, go and follow your heart"' (Going).
- 'I'll show them to you and you'll see them shine' (Lady).

Flop 5

- I threw it all away (I threw).
- He's always off somewhere when I need him most (Abandoned).
- I treated her like a fool (I threw).
- But I was cruel (I threw).
- How long must I suffer such abuse (Abandoned).

As could be expected from the previous analysis, 'Lay Lady Lay' takes the lead of the top 5 with three lines, followed by 'Going, Going, Gone' with two, while, interestingly, the third most-liked song, 'I threw it all away' leads the flop 5 with three lines, followed by 'Abandoned Love' with two. Thus, much-liked songs can still have some unliked lines, much as sad songs can be well-liked, too. Still, at least in our sample, positive lines like 'And you're the best thing that he's ever seen' win the race, leaving lines like 'How long must I suffer such abuse' as losers.

To try to explain why this is so, I trained a neural net model on the overall 285 lines (original: 337 minus duplicates in chorus) of the 11 songs – ach line transformed into a vector of 15 features again selected by the predictor screening procedure mentioned earlier – and obtained a maximum predictive accuracy of about 85 per cent. Just as for song likeability, two features stood out crossing the 0.1 FI criterion for main effects: alliteration and *AAP*. The effect of alliteration showed that lines with at least one alliteration were liked better than those with none. The *AAP* effect was a monotonic one with lines having positive *AAP* values clearly being liked better than those with negative ones. Other features being important regarding their total effect in interaction with the others were arousal span, surprise and word length. Lines with a positive arousal span received higher liking ratings, as did lines with positive surprise values and those with shorter (monosyllabic) words.

In sum, a prototypical likeable line by Bob Dylan has short, alliterating, surprising and beautiful words that differ notably in arousal like 'Lay lady lay, lay across my big brass bed'. Of course, now that you read it you would have predicted just that, or not? Perhaps, and, of course, to what extent these results are specific to this sample of 11 songs or can be generalized to the other hundreds of songs Bob Dylan wrote is a question for future research. Are they representative of Bob Dylan's art? I personally think so, but I would prefer having the means of testing this hypothesis empirically.

Shakespearology: Predicting the Most Striking Lines in Shakespeare's Sonnets

> *Our task is not to search for a unique paraphrase of the text, nor to find out how many meanings can be attributed to it, but to search for grounds that will constrain the basis of interpretations to a plausible set of alternatives.*
>
> –Reuven Tsur (2008, p. 147).[186]

The data from the 'Dylanology' studies demonstrate that the multivariate *SentiArt* tool can be successfully applied to lyrics to predict line and song likeability using sets of four to 15 features. These results encouraged me to tackle a perhaps even greater challenge: predicting the most striking lines in the 154 Shakespeare sonnets. Imagine you ask a theoretical linguist, a teacher of modern English, an expert on Shakespeare sonnets, an experimental psycholinguist, a poet and a neuroscientist to carry out this task: carefully read all 154 sonnets, then read them again and mark the most striking line of each. Once you have mastered this task on the altogether 2,155 lines, try to explain why you chose that particular line in each sonnet to the other five persons and to predict which line would be chosen by another reader. Although feasible, this task would require weeks and a symposium which surely will unveil many useful insights –albeit with some fair amount of academic quarrel. But how many testable quantitative predictions will emerge from it? There is another, less time- and money-consuming way, though, to shed some light on the issue.

My final example for a computational poetics study is from work in progress with only six participants in the empirical part so far, all of whom were trained in literature studies and well familiar with Shakespeare sonnets. The research question was to what extent the methods discussed in this chapter can be applied to predict the most striking lines in the 154 Shakespeare sonnets. Assuming readers are able to make such a decision – and indeed our participants can testify to that effect – the question is which of the many textual features we have talked about could be key in predicting the outcome of that decision. In this study, the participants read all 154 Shakespeare sonnets at home and at a self-chosen pace over several weeks and marked the most striking line in each. As far as I am aware, such a study has not been published before.

Descriptive Statistics

Using *SentiArt,* the first step in our study was to compute all possible features provided by this tool in its current version 2.0 (N = 85) for each of the altogether 2,155 lines of the 154 sonnets for which we collected reader choice data (two sonnets have 15 and 12 lines, respectively). This yielded a 2155 × N+1 dimensional table with the N columns representing *SentiArt* feature values and one column the reader response values (choice likelihood). So now we have N predictors for one response variable, and can use statistical software to do the multivariate nonlinear predictive modelling work you are already familiar with from the empirical validation studies presented in preceding sections.

I start with some descriptive statistics looking at line choice likelihood: the lion's share of 1,473 lines were never chosen as the most striking, that is 2/3 (~68 per cent). 482 were chosen at least by one reader (~22 per cent), 155 twice (~7 per cent), 37 three times (~2 per cent), six four times, and only two by five readers. No single line was chosen by all six readers, somewhat saving Richards' inkling that 'poetry is too subjective for scientific predictions'. Notwithstanding, 682 lines were chosen once or more and thus they must have something the other 1,473 do not: a higher foregrounding potential due to some unknown features according to the NCPM. Perhaps this something is a context effect rather than one due to single line features: thus, lines belonging to a popular piece like sonnet 18 may have a higher chance of being chosen. I checked this with a so-called *Analysis of Variance*[187] comparing the effects of poem number (identity) on line choice, and found no such context effect at all. But I also checked the possibility of a smaller context effect at the level of quatrains and couplets, and found something: a type of couplet bias.

The Couplet Bias

The couplet bias is a tendency in our data for choosing the last line: thus, line 14 was chosen as the most striking one in 80/154 sonnets by at least one reader. Examples are 'In sleep a king, but waking no such matter' from sonnet 87 ('Farewell! thou art too dear for my possessing'), which was chosen by 4/6 readers. Or, 'You had a father: let your son say so' from sonnet 13 ('O, that you were yourself! but, love, you are'), which was chosen by three readers. This is no coincidence. Of course, it may not be the end position in itself that gives line 14 a choice bias, but the fact that sonnets can be said to have a step-by-step movement towards the definite semantic closure provided by the couplet. A sonnet is *a system in motion*: Its four parts can be set in a number of logical relations such as successive and equal, hierarchical, contrastive or contradictory, successively louder or softer. They also play with changes of agency or speech act, rhetorical address, grammatical form or discursive texture, each producing its own emotional dynamic moves – within the speaker's mind and heart – and poetic effects in readers' mind-brains. According to sonnet expert Helen Vendler,[188] the dynamic can be assimilated to a narrowing down, funnel-shape movement from quatrain 1 (wide epistemological field) to quatrain 2 (queries, contradicts, subverts position in quatrain 1) to quatrain 3 (subtlest, most comprehensive/truthful position and solution) to the final couplet (summarizing, ironic or expansive coda – restating semantically the body of the sonnet from quatrain 1 to 3 – with a crucial tonal difference and an often a self-ironizing turn to the proverbial or idiomatic). The so-called *couplet tie* are the significant, usually thematically central words from the body (quatrain 1–3) repeated in the couplet. Actually, in another study on Shakespeare sonnets, my team found evidence for Vendler's funnel-shape movement hypothesis: the number of new text world referents decrease towards the end of a sonnet.[189] While quatrains 1 feature 87 per cent new words on average, this value drops to 76 per cent for quatrains 2 and 68 per cent for quatrains 3, reaching a plateau for couplets with 59 per cent (all $p<.0001$). This finding, supporting the view of a progressive narrowing down of the reader's text world, also strengthens the hypothesis that style figures like metaphors should be easier to recognize towards the end of lyrics or poems.[190] All of that may explain the overall 11 per cent choice likelihood for the last line of sonnets.

In general, striking lines were more often chosen from the final parts of the poem – the couplets and quatrain three – than for the initial two quatrains: couplet (0.85%) > quatrain 3 (0.81%) > quatrain 2 (0.74%) > quatrain 1 (0.55%). The difference between the couplet and the first quatrain was statistically significant ($p<.0007$) despite the tiny sample we have here. This was also the case for the comparison of quatrain 3 vs. quatrain 1 and quatrain 2 vs. quatrain 1. This clearly suggests that being part of the 1st quatrain did not really help a line to become the chosen one (~5% probability). Anyway, by doing some simple analyses, we have detected a context feature that matters. It will be excluded, though, from the following predictive modelling analyses because it is a constant: it is shared by all sonnets and thus cannot explain why certain lines in a couplet or quatrain were chosen while others were not.

Predictive Modelling of Individual Reader Responses

Since we had only six participants, working with average data made no sense. Instead, I ran the predictive neural net model on individual data. This also allowed me to look at personal sensitivities to particular poetry features. Indeed, poetry reception can be something very private and it would thus not be surprising if different features had different effects on different readers. In pilot studies, I followed the 4x4 matrix of Table 2.1 in Chapter 2 and selected a manageable batch of 20 features from the altogether 85 computed by *SentiArt* based on the aforementioned *predictor screening*. Two of them are sound features, within-line rime quotient (in short: rime) and sonority score, that are metrical and phonological, one is a simple surface feature (word length), and the remaining 17 are meaning features, that are morphosyntactic and semantic features, at all four levels from sub- to supralexical. In poetry reception, sound features like the within-line rime quotient or the sonority score are assumed to primarily shape the likeability of poetic lines – theoretically via the *NCPM*'s lower route's affective and aesthetic processing. Meaning features should shape both the lines' comprehensibility and likeability via both routes. Each line of each sonnet was first transformed into a vector of 20 numbers representing the feature values computed by *SentiArt* as illustrated earlier in Table 5.3. Table 6.2 summarizes the results indicating the ranks of the most important features for each of the six readers.

The results in Table 6.2 reveal the following. First of all, the predictive accuracy was excellent (≥ .94) for each of the six readers, so that I can have confidence in my interpretation of the *FI* values and ranks. Second, 18/20 analyzed features became important in at least one reader. The two that were not important were: topic 3 ('day, night, death') and topic 10 ('praise, heaven, muse'). Third, of the two sound features, the within-line rime quotient appeared three times at rank 1, making it a salient feature interesting for future studies. The sonority score appeared twice (ranks 3 and 7) and thus also deserves further consideration. Among the other features, all of which can be characterized as semantic, except for word length, *AAP* appeared 5/6 times as important. Venturing a generalization here, my bet is that also in future studies using more readers, a majority of them will be sensitive to the affective-aesthetic potential of words when having to decide which line of a poem is most striking. None of the other features was important for over 50 per cent of our tiny sample, so I will refrain from trying a generalization. What these data suggest at any rate is an impressive differential sensitivity of readers to both sound and meaning features in Shakespeare sonnets.

Among the 10 topics computed here, topics number one, two, four, five and six appeared to be most predictive in readers 2, 3 and 6, reflecting the

Table 6.2 Rank of most important line features for six readers (predictive accuracies in brackets).

Feature/Feature explanation/Reader/ (Accuracy)		*1 (.94)*	*2 (.94)*	*3 (.96)*	*4 (.97)*	*5 (.95)*	*6 (.95)*
AAP lexico-semantic	affective-aesthetic potential (cf. Chapter 5)	5	10	–	5	1	9
Eigensimilarity supralexico-semantic	semantic similarity with all other lines in sonnet	6	5	–	3	–	–
Nouns	Number of nouns	–	2	–	2	–	–
POS Entropy supralexico-morphosyntactic	the Shannon entropy representing variation in word types (POS)[v]	–	3	–	–	2	1
Pos-Neg Ratio	ratio of positive and negative words	–	12	–	–	–	7
Rime Quotient	ratio of within-line rimes and number of syllables	1	1	–	1	–	–

(*Continued*)

v The Shannon entropy represents variation in word types (POS) in a line. It is computed as:

$$H(X) = -\sum_{i=0}^{n} P(x_i) \log P(x_i)$$

where X is a binary variable representing two possible word orders like 'Adjective + Noun' and 'Noun + Adjective'. $P(x_i)$ is the probability of one of the orders, which equals its relative frequency in a given corpus. Without variation – the proportion is 1 for one word order and 0 for the reverse or vice versa – H(X) equals 0. If the proportion is 0.5, H(X) equals 1, representing maximum disorder. If one order is more frequent than another, H(X) varies between 0 and 1. When there are more categories than two – as is the case here with many POS labels (NOUN, VERB, DET, PART, etc.) – then H(X) can take on values > 1. Examples are line 6 from sonnet 106 ('*of hand, of foot, of lip, of eye, of brow,*') for which H(X) is 1.2 and ('*He pays the whole, and yet I am not free*') with an H(X) of 2.3.

Table 6.2 (Continued)

Feature/Feature explanation/Reader/ (Accuracy)		*1 (.94)*	*2 (.94)*	*3 (.96)*	*4 (.97)*	*5 (.95)*	*6 (.95)*
Semantic Neighbourhood Density	mean of semantic similarities between target word and its 50 nearest neighbours (cf. Table 6)	4	4	–	–	–	8
Sonority Score	(cf. Chapter 5)	3	7	–	–	–	–
Surprisal	probability[vi] of a word in a language model[191]	9	6	–	4	–	–
Topic 1. 'dear, friend, heart, love, true'	Topics and topic probabilities were computed via LDAMallet (cf. Chapter 3)	8	–	5	–	–	6
Topic 2. 'eyes, thine, heart'		–	–	4	–	–	3
Topic 4. 'old, new, waste, time'		–	13	2	–	–	4
Topic 5. 'tell, tongue, true, truth'		–	–	3	–	–	2
Topic 6. 'sweet, thyself, self, grow, friend, give'		–	9	6	–	–	5
Topic 7. 'life, love, decay, bear'		7	–	8	–	–	–
Topic 8. 'ill, thing, show, name'		–	11	7	–	–	–
Topic 9. 'desire, show, heart, bear, keep, change'		2	14	1	–	–	–
Word Length		–	8	–	6	–	10

vi $-\log_2(p(w_n|\text{context}))$ as computed on the basis of a trigram language model.

power of the eternal love and nature themes. Third, one reader (#5) seemed particularly sensitive to a combination of single-word beauty (*AAP*) and word order (*POS entropy*). Based on these results, in future studies I would look again at possible contributions of the *AAP* and POS entropy features which affected 5/6 and 3/6 readers' performance, respectively, as well as number of nouns, surprisal, semantic neighbourhood density and eigensimilarity.

Let me consider the data for at least one reader in greater detail. Thus, according to the data in Table 6.2, for reader 1, a striking, aesthetically appealing or pleasing line would be one that first of all has some within-line rimes like the last line from sonnet 57 ('Being your slave, what should I do but tend'): 'Though you do any thing, he thinks no ill'. Using the phonetic transcription of the line provided by *prosodic* [<ðoʊ > <ju: > <'du: > <'ɛ.ni: > <'θɪŋ > <'hi: > <'θɪŋks> <'noʊ > <'ɪl>] *SentiArt* computes a rime quotient of 0.6 (6 rimes divided by 10 syllables) with the phonemes [o, ʊ], [u:] and [i:] appearing twice each. Interestingly, the rime quotient feature also is a useful index of word repetitions within a line and thus a potential *chiasm* detector. Indeed, the lines with the highest rime quotient in the data of reader 1 all had word repetitions and chiasms and all were chosen as 'striking':

- Line 8 from sonnet 64 ('When I have seen by Time's fell hand defac'd'): 'Increasing store with loss and loss with store'.
- Line 3 from sonnet 119 ('What potions have I drunk of Siren tears'): *'Applying fears to hopes and hopes to fears'.*
- Line 4 from sonnet 28 ('How can I then return in happy plight'): 'But day by night, and night by day, oppressed?'

Apart from apparently liking within-line rimes and chiasms, reader 1 also – implicitly or explicitly – was sensitive to the sonority score in his most striking line choices. Indeed, lines with higher sonority scores were more likely to be chosen by him, such as line 1 from sonnet 113 'Since I left you, mine eye is in my mind' with a top sonority score of 7. Regarding semantic features, if a line was associated with topic 9 and its classic poetry buzz words 'desire', 'heart' or 'change', then its likelihood of being chosen increased for reader 1. Examples are:

- line 11 from sonnet 93 ('So shall I live, supposing thou art true'): 'Whatever thy thoughts or thy heart workings be', or
- line 9 from sonnet 10 ('For shame deny that thou bear'st love to any'): 'O, change thy thought, that I may change my mind!'.

Furthermore, if a line had a higher semantic neighbourhood density – meaning that it contains words with many close associates or a big 'fringe' as illustrated in Figure 5.1 – it also was more likely to be judged as striking. An example is line 2 from sonnet 62 ('Sin of self-love possesseth all mine eye'): 'And all my soul and all my every part', in which the word 'soul' has a high semantic neighbourhood density (0.39) with the nearest neighbours 'heart', 'spirit', 'conscience', 'mind' and 'brain'. The fifth most important feature for reader 1's line choice was *AAP*, so he was more likely to choose lines with more theoretically beautiful words than those with rather 'ugly' ones. An example is the last line of sonnet 23 ('As an unperfect actor upon the stage'): 'To hear with eyes belongs to love's fine wit', in which practically all words have high positive *AAP* values being associated with many other affectively or aesthetically pleasing words. The metaphoricity ('hear with eyes' 'love's [...] wit') surely emphasized the effect. The feature ranked number six in that reader was *eigensimilarity*: I coined this term in analogy to the *eigenvectors* in linear algebra[192] – also called 'characteristic vectors' – to refer to lines which semantically are most similar to the other lines in the sonnet, that is their semantic vectors are 'characteristic' of a text. Thus, line 2 from sonnet 138 ('When my love swears that she is made of truth') presenting one of the many antitheses: 'I do believe her, though I know she lies' was the top eigensimilarity line in reader 1's data. Next in rank comes the feature topic 7 with the buzz words 'life', 'love' or 'decay'. Lines associated with this topic also increased choice likelihood. Indeed, 20 of the 154 lines chosen by reader 1 (~13%) had the words 'love' or 'loves' in them, such as the above last line of sonnet 23. The related topic 1 ('dear', 'friend', 'heart', 'love', 'true') is the next most important feature followed by the last one 'surprisal'. The line with the highest surprisal value in reader 1's data was the last line from the last sonnet 154 ('The little Love-god lying once asleep'): 'Love fire heats water, water cools not love', a truly surprising one.

These detailed predictive analyses at the level of individual readers are a novelty, also in my own team's work, and they clearly suggest both diversity and commonality. Some readers appear sensitive to only 'a hand full' of features (#1, 3, 4, and 5), others to 10 or more. Some are more sensitive to form, others to content. Some pay attention to the beauty of individual words (*AAP*) and word order (POS entropy), others do less so. Still, with a mix of 20 features from practically all types and levels described in Table 3.1 of Chapter 3 (phonological to semantic, and sub- to supralexical), each reader's line choice performance could be predicted with great accuracy.

To sum up, the results of this exploratory study on *Shakespearology* strongly encourage further predictive analyses with the same and other materials of verbal art and larger samples of readers. Taking all data into account, what is it then that characterizes the ideal sonnet line for an average reader? According to Table 6.2, this line would have a mix of the following features:

- within-line rimes and several sonorous words (rime quotient and sonority score);
- short nouns that are positive, beautiful, surprising and that have a large fringe (*AAP*, nouns, pos-neg ratio, word length, semantic neighbourhood density, surprisal);
- a more complex syntactic pattern with greater variation in word type order (*POS entropy*); and
- a touch of universal poetic topics that speak of love and friendship, time and truth or heart and desires.

In closing this chapter, I must remind you that computational poetics is not an exact science. So even in an empirical study with a much larger sample than ours and an even larger set of textual features – including non-computational ones selected on the basis of a middle reading approach such as metaphor quality or density – we cannot expect perfect predictive accuracy. What is more, in the present analyses I have favoured simplicity and transparency over computational complexity. This is because I would like many people not familiar with computer programming to apply such simpler heuristic methods and measures that still can advance our knowledge on how literature, and poetry in particular, achieve their effects on our bodies and mind-brains. Furthermore, like those above, the present predictive modelling study is basically exploratory in nature. Although it arguably offers predictive causality (see Chapter 3), it does not provide definitive answers to the question about which feature caused exactly which effect on reader responses in concert with the others. However, it offers plausible sophisticated hypotheses that require further experimental testing to obtain causal scientific explanations. More sophisticated applications will no doubt follow once more researchers in disciplines less interested in data science use the present ones and weigh their pros and cons. The point is that the present application generates ideas, testable hypotheses and quantitative predictions for empirical studies like those discussed in the next two chapters, which really need them.

Summary

In this extensive chapter on sophisticated applications of computational poetics, I started with methods for analyzing two aspects of story analysis, plot and character, and ended with demonstrating the power of multivariate nonlinear predictive modelling for accurately foretelling which lines in lyrics by Bob Dylan and sonnets by Shakespeare readers find most likeable or striking. More particularly, in the first two parts, I discussed the possibilities and limits of current methods for event detection, the detection of prototypical plotlines via uni-and multivariate sentiment analysis and a novel technique for computing the hybrid hero potential of characters. In the final lyrics and poetry analysis part, I identified a number of text features that co-determine the likeability of lines as operationalized by readers' line choices. For Dylan's lyrics, the most important were alliteration, surprise, *AAP* and arousal. For Shakespeare sonnets, they were: within-line rime quotient, sonority score, *AAP*, number of nouns, positive-negative ratio, word length, semantic neighbourhood density, surprisal, POS entropy, and topics that speak of love and friendship, time and truth or heart and desires.

Chapter 7

NEUROCOMPUTATIONAL POETICS I: UPPER ROUTE STUDIES

Having dedicated two chapters to the discussion of methods of *computational poetics* able to predict behavioural aspects of the reading act such as liking ratings or line choice, I now turn to *Neurocomputational Poetics* studies. In these, I combine computational with experiential, behavioural and neuronal analyses that inform about the validity of the NCPM 's hypotheses and predictions regarding reading acts for diverse materials from single words to multiword expressions, stories and poems.

The central hypothesis of the NCPM mesomodel discussed in Chapter 2 with regard to the upper route is this: texts that have clearly more background than foreground elements likely trigger immersive experiences through activation of the brain's automatic reading network and implicit processing leading to a fluent reading mode. In contrast, those with a low background/foreground elements ratio tend to evoke an aesthetic trajectory associated with the operation of larger neural network including more right-hemispheric regions and explicit processing resulting in a dysfluent reading mode, that is, they activate the lower route. Empirical studies can test this hypothesis by finding traces of the operation of the upper and lower routes assumed by the NCPM at the three levels of observation: the neuronal, experiential and behavioural. Chapters 7 and 8 discuss key studies that examined the NCPM's central and other key hypotheses over the last decade. The upper route studies of Chapter 7 deal with the reading of prose and mainly examine the first boon of reading, immersive processes. The lower route studies presented in the next chapter focus on the second boon, aesthetic processes, mostly examined in poetry reception.

A short recap concerning the other main assumptions of the NCPM seems in order here before we consider the empirical evidence. In the introductory Chapter 1, I discussed the likely neuronal bases of immersion expressed in the *symbol grounding* and *neuronal recycling* hypotheses. In short, the first hypothesis claims that the neuronal processes evoked by words and sentences are similar to those evoked by the objects they refer to. The second postulates that 'exapted' structures in the brain, like the visual word form area, enabled efficient reading and the countless fast inferential and figurative processes 'running' in other brain regions that underlie it. The neuronal recycling hypothesis is tightly linked with what I called the *Panksepp–Jakobson* hypothesis in honour of these two pioneers whose work inspired mine so much. It states that feelings experienced during reading are based on the ancient circuits of affect that we share with all other mammals, mainly in the so-called limbic system. At the time when I was building the NCPM (~15 years ago), such a hypothesis was needed to bridge the *language-emotion gap* and allow the fourth key assumption of the model: the *fiction feeling hypothesis*. This was inspired by an early study of the *Languages of Emotion* project, which indicated that children's processing of stories eliciting affective and cognitive empathy is associated with medial and bilateral orbitofrontal cortex activation. The hypothesis submits that narratives with emotional contents invite readers more to be empathic with the protagonists and immerse in the text world than do stories with neutral contents, because in such narratives readers more likely engage the affective empathy network of the brain discussed earlier. The hypothesis is based on the notion of fiction emotions[193] when, for instance, readers experience vicarious or real fear as a consequence of events in the text world. All these hypotheses together help explain the sensual and intellectual experiences during verbal art reception.

The 'Do Words Stink?' Studies

Before I turn to the upper and lower route studies carried out in our *D.I.N.E.* labs at FU Berlin, I need to discuss a series of neurocomputational studies performed together with a large team of researchers from my old Institute of Cognitive Neuroscience in Marseilles founded in 1992. These studies were led by my friend and former Ph.D. student Johannes Ziegler, now the director of the successor institute in Marseilles. Even though these experiments were not particularly designed to test the *NCPM*, they nevertheless provided key results that fostered my confidence in the model because they produced the perhaps most striking evidence for the symbol-grounding and Panksepp–Jakobson hypotheses.[194]

The experiments dealt with the arguably truest or purest of all six basic emotions Charles Darwin believed to be common to all mammals: disgust. This emotion is scientifically of special interest because, on the one hand, it is innate and can be conditioned in a single trial. On the other hand, it is clear that it also can be culturally shaped. According to Darwin, disgust evolved to protect animals against noxious substances endangering life by signalling the threat of contamination, encouraging actions of withdrawal. Feelings of disgust helped humans during evolution to identify rotten smells that hint at toxins and thus to avoid infection and disease. It is also believed to prevent incest.

The results of many previous neuroimaging studies, clinical neuropsychological case studies involving patients with brain lesions and intracranial recording studies using electrodes directly applied to the open brain in humans all identified a specific brain region as being central for the experience of disgust: the *anterior insula*. It is part of the ancient neuronal circuits of affect central to the Panksepp–Jakobson hypothesis. The idea of our experiments carried out over many years simultaneously in the Marseilles and our labs was that the reading of single words like 'stink', 'shit' or 'vomit' not only evokes neuronal activation in the brain's left-hemispheric 'reading system', but – in contrast to control words like 'table' or 'statue' – also produce deeper neuronal traces in the insular cortex that is in charge of processing disgust in other sensory modalities like odours. To test this hypothesis, in one condition we showed participants short video clips of the type illustrated in Figure 7.1A with either 'neutral' or 'disgusted' facial expressions. In previous studies these clips had already been shown to reliably produce insular activation. In the other condition sketched in Figure 7.1B, we had them read either neutral

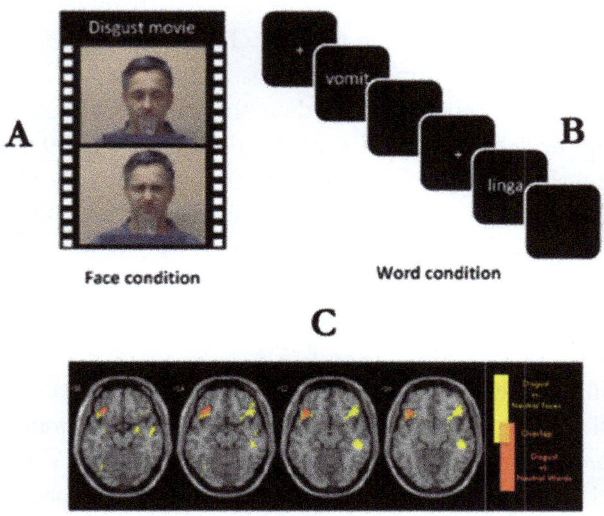

Figure 7.1 Stimulus conditions and results of the 'Do words stink?' study. **A.** Example of a disgust movie clip. **B.** Example sequence for the verbal disgust stimulus sequence. **C.** Brain activity overlap in the anterior insula region between the conditions exemplified in A. ('faces', yellow) and B. ('words', red). Source: Adapted from Ziegler et al., 2018.[195]

or potentially disgusting words. If we could demonstrate that both types of stimuli produce overlapping brain activity in the anterior insula that would be strong evidence for our hypothesis. And indeed, as shown in Figure 7.1C, this was what we found. However, standard neuroimaging studies can only reveal *neural correlates* of thoughts or feelings. This is no proof that the brain activity correlated with, say, the experience of disgust also caused that experience, even so it does not exclude the possibility.

In another experiment, we therefore used a sophisticated method called *repetitive Transcranial Magnetic Stimulation (rTMS)*. Through the application of strong magnetic fields, the rTMS apparatus – positioned closely to the head of a participant – can either stimulate or inhibit the normal functioning of targeted brain regions. In our case, we wanted to produce a kind of artificial, 'transient boosting' of the anterior insula to see whether that could modulate the size of the disgust effect compared with the stimulation of a control site (the vertex). We predicted that *rTMS* should modulate the size of the disgust effect in the reading task as compared with the control stimulation. The results showed that the size of the effect indeed varied as a function of stimulation site: It was largest after stimulation of the left insula, intermediate after stimulation of the right insula, and smallest in the control condition.

Together, these results suggested that the left anterior insula is not only an 'innocent bystander' but is causally involved in processing emotional content related to disgust during reading. The results of yet another study we ran using both intracranial recordings and *surface* EEG, corroborated this inference. The brain-electrical data showed an activation of the left insula during the processing of disgust words as early as 200 msec after the onset of the written word, that is, during the initial stages of visual word recognition. We interpreted this as evidence that the neural representation of disgust words necessarily includes the coactivation of the insula as part of the neural assembly that 'constructs' the meaning of these words. And this is just what the symbol grounding and Panksepp–Jakobson hypotheses would predict.

As we will see later in this chapter, my team also produced ample experimental evidence for the involvement of other ancient 'emotion structures' such as the *amygdala* or parts of the *ventral striatum* – the brain's reward or 'lust' centre – in the processing of verbal materials. But having shown that 'words can stink' has a very special place in the history of studies sustaining my Neurocomputational Poetics perspective.

The next studies were mainly carried out by former Ph.D. students supported by the Languages of Emotion grant, who all feature as first authors in the corresponding publications.

The Fact vs. Fiction Study

Let us play a little game. You read the following short text and decide whether it's fact or fiction.

> A man was a professional diver investigating an illegal wastewater discharge from a well-known chemical plant at great depth. When he suddenly became afraid that the toxins could be dangerous to him, he panicked, ascended too quickly and died a short time later of diver's sickness.

The text tells a story like those we consume every day in newspapers and magazines, in biographies and novels, via videotext or on the internet. Curiously, although the story's valence is clearly negative – and I don't need *SentiArt* to quantify this here – many individuals not only understand, but also appreciate or enjoy texts like this.[i] That is a variant of what is called the *sadness paradox* known at least since Aristotle's theory of tragedy: people indeed can enjoy sad plays, literature or music.[196] If the fiction feeling hypothesis is correct, at least for story reading, this is because they facilitate activation of the brain's affective empathy network. For most people, experiencing an emotion, even if negative or mixed, is a self-rewarding process – better than no emotion at all. And stories like the one above do evoke an emotional roller coaster, providing a bag of potential feelings like fear and hope, suspense and curiosity or empathy, sadness and being moved. The one below – which was part of the neutral control stories in our study – presumably does not.

> A diver was an employee on an oil rig where his job was to detect and remove debris from the feet of the rig underwater. His shifts lasted a few hours, which he also needed to keep the rig in good condition.

Now back to our game. Are these stories fact or fiction? If your answer is 'well, could be both', then this is what we wanted for our study run by my former Ph.D. student Ulrike Altmann.[197] We wanted stories with no clues as to whether they are real or invented. The reason was that when we invited participants to read those stories in our scanner that recorded their brain activity, we told half of them that they would be reading true stories. The other half was told they would read fictive stories. So, we had four conditions

i The text is the free translation of a text in German chosen from the card game *black stories*, a narrative-based game (©moses Verlag GmbH, 47906 Kempen, www.moses-verlag.de).

in this experiment, 40 negative and 40 neutral stories, either labelled as fact or fiction. We also had our readers complete the *Interpersonal Reactivity Index* mentioned in Chapter 4, but here we used the 'empathic concern' subscale that assesses the individual tendency to feel concern and compassion for other people. Since empathic concern has been associated with increased interest in tragic television news or the perception of a liked partner being in pain, we wanted to see whether our readers varied enough on the scores of that scale to find differential brain activity. Finally, we had a second group of participants rate the materials on valence ('How do you perceive the text?', scale from −3 'very negative' to 3-'very positive') and liking 'Do you like the text?,' scale from 1–'I do not like it at all' to 7–'I like it very much'. This allowed us, first, to check whether our readers really found the theoretically neutral stories less negative and less enjoyable, and, second, to analyze the brain data parametrically: that is, we could test the potential of increasing negative valence of story contents to activate the brain's 'empathy network' (see Figure 2.3 lower panel in Chapter 2), and uncover the neural substrate of liking negative narratives. With regard to the four methodological approaches discussed in Chapter 4, in the present study we thus combined a direct offline with an indirect online measure: ratings and brain activity.

The results of this innovative study supported our assumptions. First, they indeed revealed a stronger engagement of empathy-related brain areas with increasingly negative story valence, suggesting the validity of the fiction-feeling hypothesis. Second, the medial prefrontal cortex was identified as playing a special role: the more it became engaged during the reading of negatively valenced stories, the more coactivation we observed in other brain areas related to the neural processing of affective empathy. It seems to play the role of a hub for empathic processing of narratives. Third, positive coactivation between the medial prefrontal cortex and the anterior insula while reading negative stories compared to neutral ones correlated positively with the individual tendency to feel concern for other people, as assessed by the 'empathic concern' subscale. In other words, this particular brain co-activation was greater in readers who scored higher on this empathy scale than in those who had a lower score. This finding also corroborated the validity of the personality scale.

All this is very fine, you may reckon. But what about the fact vs. fiction manipulation? Did it show a difference in the brain? Indeed, it did, and how! For the first time, this study showed that our brains process identical textual information very differently depending on the paratextual information given, that is, 'reading fact vs. fiction'. Indeed, reading in a factual mode triggered a brain activation pattern known from previous studies on the mirror neuron system involved in action observation. This suggests that our readers were engaged in an action-based and possibly past-oriented reconstruction of what happened when the events depicted in a text are supposed to be real. In contrast, the pattern of brain activity during the fiction reading mode was in line with neuroimaging data from studies on the imagination of possible past or future events and thus seemed to reflect a constructive simulation of what might have happened.

In summary, 'reading facts' basically seems to evoke mental simulation processes about actions and their outcomes, involving, for example, increased activity in the premotor cortex and the cerebellum. In this reading condition, the left posterior cingulate/retrosplenial cortex was found to be especially activated and it is known to be responsive to the realness and self-relevance of recalled events or when answering questions concerning real persons as compared to fictional characters. In contrast, 'reading fiction' appears to elicit simulation processes especially concerning the motives behind an action and what is going on in the protagonist's mind. It invites more for perspective taking, relational inferences and even mind-wandering – as indicated by coactivation of the brain's 'affective empathy network' – than reading about facts. Thus, the mere labelling of a text as fictional seems to invite readers to enter a game of pretence and simulation associated with similar neuronal patterns as have been observed in studies on mental imagery or simulation of self versus others. Inducing fiction feelings via strongly emotional narratives such as the 'black stories' facilitates immersive processes. The same should apply to passages from the famous Harry Potter book series.

The Harry Potter Studies

This series of studies – led by my former Ph.D. student Chun-Ting Hsu – is based on different analyses of the same data set collected during one experiment in which participants read a special selection of short passages extracted from the Harry Potter book series in our brain scanner.

The Neuronal Correlates of Fiction Feelings and Immersion

A cloaked figure that towered to the ceiling. Its face was completely hidden beneath its hood. Harry's eyes darted downwards, and what he saw made his stomach contract. There was a hand protruding from the cloak and it was glistening, greyish, slimy-looking and scabbed, like something dead that had decayed in water [...]

New students at Hogwarts were sorted into houses by trying on the Sorting Hat. Professor McGonagall strode off towards her empty seat at the staff table, and Harry and Hermione set off in the other direction, as quietly as possible, towards the Gryffindor table.

When asked to describe your feelings during the reading of the above two passages, did you experience something like (vicarious) fear in the first? Did you momentarily forget the world around you more strongly in this than in the next passage? Were you more empathic with Harry in the first passage than in the second passage? Did you read the first faster than the second? According to the NCPM, the answer is four times 'yes', if applied to a sufficiently big number of similar passages and readers. In this first study of the series published in 2014, we analyzed reader responses to 40 theoretically 'fearful' and 40 theoretically 'neutral' passages, including the above ones. If the *NCPM* and the fiction feeling hypothesis were correct, especially the fearful, arousing and suspenseful passages – of which Harry Potter books have plenty – should facilitate immersion, for example, by inducing (vicarious) emotions and/or inviting readers to be more empathic with the protagonist. At the experiential-behavioural levels of observation, this should produce greater mean immersion ratings for the fearful than for the neutral passages. At the neural level, in the fearful passages, this should more likely engage the affective empathy network, which includes the mid-cingulate cortex, the amygdala, the anterior insula, the secondary somatosensory cortex and the IFG.

In this study, we investigated a specific version of the fiction feeling hypothesis. In particular, we assumed that readers more likely immerse in texts that reach the sensory-motor grounded affective resonance and autobiographical emotional memories of their readers through meta representations of global emotional moments (e.g. pain, fear), as reflected in selective anterior insula and mid-cingulate cortex activation. To test this hypothesis, we presented 80 text passages that – prior to the experiment – had been carefully selected by us and rated by an independent set of participants as either fearful or neutral. Pain, fear and personal distress are the focus of affective empathy that is essential for altruistic, prosocial behaviour in the social context. Furthermore, self–other matching for autonomic/emotional states of pain and fear has been evident across species such as rodents and monkeys. Therefore, as mentioned above, we expected not only higher immersion ratings for fear-inducing passages, which often describe pain or personal distress, as compared with neutral passages, but also a significant correlation of immersion ratings with activity in the affective empathy network, particularly mid-cingulate cortex and anterior insula, for fear-inducing, but not for neutral passages. Thus, in the present study, again combining a direct offline with an indirect online measure (ratings and brain activity), we tried to directly relate them via correlation analysis.

In support of our hypothesis, we found one cluster in the middle cingulate gyrus shown in Figure 7.2, for which the correlation between immersion

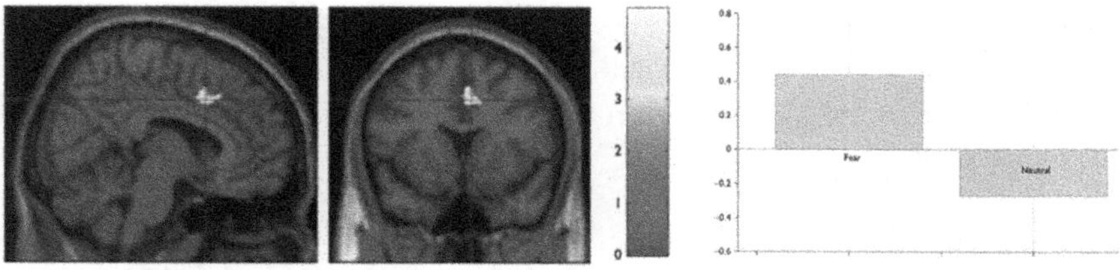

A B

Figure 7.2 **A**. The mid cingulate gyrus showing a significant correlation difference between passage immersion ratings and brain activity in the 'fear' vs. 'neutral' conditions. **B**. The estimated response strength in this brain region for both conditions. Source: Adapted from Hsu et al., 2014.[198]

ratings and brain activity was significantly more positive when reading fear-inducing passages than when reading neutral passages. We did not find any increased activity in the anterior insula, though. The middle cingulate gyrus has been considered to be the 'limbic motor cortex' and the site of emotional behavioural initiation, and the anterior insula its sensory counterpart.[199] In our passages from the Harry Potter series, behavioural aspects of emotion are particularly vividly described ('Harry's eyes darted downwards, and what he saw made his stomach contract'). We therefore assumed that the motor component of affective empathy might have predominated over the sensory one during emotional involvement. This assumption is in line with the claim that descriptions of behavioural components of emotions, as opposed to the labelling of emotions per se, are better markers of readers' mental representations of the protagonists' affective status.[200] And this might explain why our effects were restricted to the middle cingulate gyrus and did not extend to the anterior insula. Of course, this was speculative and required further empirical testing. Regrettably, the unexpected discontinuation of the Languages of Emotion grant prevented my Ph.D. students from continuing their work – they had to move on to post-doc jobs abroad – and, to my knowledge no other group has examined this issue further ever since.

In sum, together with the 'do words stink?' and 'fact vs. fiction' studies, this first Harry Potter study provided allied support for the main hypotheses of the *NCPM*. In all three studies, parts of the affective empathy network were selectively activated. 'Stinking words' especially activated the anterior insula, negatively valenced 'black stories' co-activated the medial prefrontal cortex and the anterior insula, and fearful passages from Harry Potter particularly activated the middle cingulate gyrus. All these studies used 'negative' texts supposed to induce negative emotions, but the emotion potential of texts also includes positive ones, such as joy, and also the arousal level induced by either positive or negative emotions. The next study examined whether positive texts also can elicit immersive processes. More particularly, it tested to what extent both lexical and interlexical affective features such as word valence and arousal span can predict brain activity in emotion-related areas such as the limbic system.

The Neuronal Correlates of the Emotion Potential of Texts

In agreement with dimensional emotion theories of psychology, the emotion potential of texts relates the valence of its words to their arousal as shown in Figure 7.3 (upper panel). Any word or text can thus be located in this 2d *Emotion Potential Space* diagram visualizing its emotion potential at a glance. The data in this diagram can serve as a reference space for many future studies. The green cloud illustrates the emotion potential of the over 2 million words contained in the *wiki.en.vec* language model[201] as computed by *SentiArt*. First, it shows that on average negative words like 'death' are more arousing than positive ones like 'mother', since, overall, arousal values decrease with increasing valence values, that is, the two features are negatively correlated. The highlighted blue crosses and red dots show the emotion potential of the words (as also computed by *SentiArt*) from two of our 120 Harry Potter passages (blue crosses = fearful, red dots = joyful). Even though – as can be expected – not all words of the fearful passage have a negative valence, if we compute the means for the entire passage, it is clearly more negative and arousing than the joyful one.

Frege's Axiom and the Question of Affective Meaning Integration

An intriguing question hidden in Figure 7.3 is to what extent word-based, lexical features can predict the emotion potential of larger text units, that is, entire sentences, passages or paragraphs. My *SentiArt* tool used to produce the data in this figure currently implements what I call *Frege's Axiom*: It computes the sentiment value of a sentence or larger unit of text as the average of the values of the (content) words appearing in it. The axiom is derived from the logico-philosophical tradition since Gottlob Frege, according to which the literal meaning of a sentence is considered to be determined by the meanings of its parts and their syntactical combination in a sentence. Applied to the task of sentiment analysis, it follows that the affective meaning of a sentence is a linear function of the affective meanings of its words, such as the arithmetic or geometric mean. Theoretically, the emotion potential of a phrase or text segment composed of mainly negative words could, of course, still be positive as a whole depending on its degree of figurativity and on context variables. Also, a single negation in the form of words like 'not', 'hardly' or 'without' in

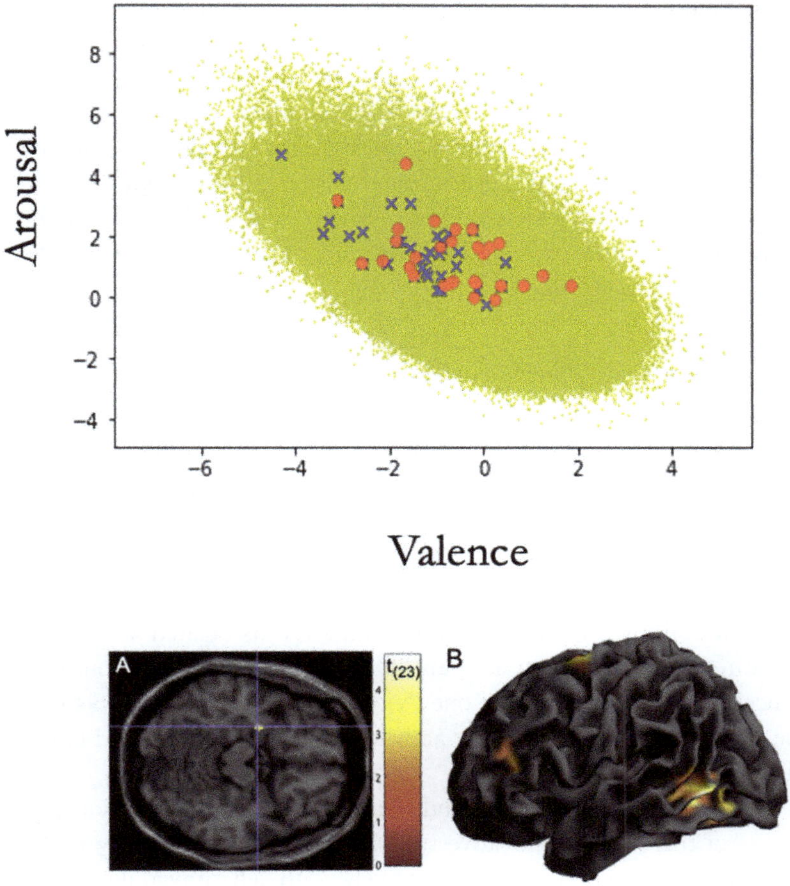

Figure 7.3 Upper panel. Emotion Potential Space showing the distribution of valence and arousal values for the >2 million words of the *wiki.en.vec* corpus (green cloud) and those from two sample segments of the Harry Potter stimuli: a 'fearful' segment (blue crosses) and a 'joyful' segment (red dots), both increased in size for better visibility. **Lower panel**. **A**: Transversal section of the brain showing a significant correlation between activation of the left amygdala and the lexical feature *valence*. **B**: Render of the left hemisphere showing significant positive correlations between the interlexical feature *arousal span* in the *LIFG* (including insula), as well as premotor area and *TPJ*. Source: Adapted from Jacobs, 2015, and Hsu et al., 2015.[202]

an otherwise positive sentence can change a lot. Finally, an empirical study I published with Jana Lüdtke in 2015 seemed to falsify this axiom. Using very simple sentences of the type: 'The grandpa is clever' (positive noun–positive adjective) or 'The burglar is lonely' (negative noun–negative adjective) in all six combinations, it showed that negative adjectives dominated supralexical evaluation, contributing more to the overall valence rating of the sentence than the noun. However, to what extent this observed negativity bias in sentence evaluation can be generalized to more complex sentences is an open question, and, alas, our earlier results did not reveal the true function relating the affective meaning of a sentence to that of its words. At any rate, the seminal empirical studies in *emotional stylometry* by Yves Bestgen and Cynthia Whissell[203] both suggested that the rated valence of supralexical units (sentences, lyrics, stories, poems) could be predicted to a considerable extent (30–60 per cent, depending on text length and content) as a function of the valence of their component words.

Lexical and Interlexical Affective Features

Going beyond Frege's axiom, in addition to lexical valence and arousal, in this study we also tested, for the first time, the potential influence of the interlexical affective feature arousal span: the range or spread of values across a passage reflecting the emotional dynamics and contrasts. The most positive passage of our sample of 120 had buzz words like 'laughed', 'mother', 'kiss' or 'hug' all associated with joy. Key words of the most negative segment like 'disgusting', 'filthy', 'blood' or 'traitor' all were associated with fear. The one with the greatest arousal span (2.83) contrasted a low-arousing word ('silence') with a high-arousing one ('viciously'). The question was which of these features would significantly activate which emotion-related brain area and which had the biggest effects.

I cannot report all the details and results of the complicated model-guided analyses of this highly innovative study, but will focus on a few highlights. First, lexical valence correlated positively with left amygdala activity, as shown in Figure 7.3A (lower panel). While amygdala activation has most often been associated with the processing of negative or high-arousing stimuli, this result together with those of an EEG study on the emotion potential of single words suggested that positive words are more salient attractors of attention early in word processing than negative ones, if the influence of arousal is held constant.[204] Second, as illustrated in Figure 7.3B (lower panel), the interlexical feature arousal span also correlated positively with activity in emotion-related areas, in particular, the amygdala, left anterior insula and the thalamus. These three areas belong to the core affect regions in main neuroscientific and psychological theories of emotion, and the brain's salience network. This was the first time that this original feature 'invented' in our book *Brain and Poetry* only four years before this study was empirically validated. It captures aspects of the dynamics and conflicts of emotional text processing not reflected in lexical features and presents a case in point of successful feature engineering in Neurocomputational Poetics.

To recap, on the one hand, the present results show that the emotion potential of the words averaged across a passage not only can very well predict whether the whole passage is rated as fearful or joyful, but also correlates significantly with brain activity in emotion-related areas. These lexical effects reflect the special power of emotion-laden words. Whether presented in isolation or in the context of sentences and passages, they have the potential to capture attention and bias the affective meaning integration of the larger unit. In addition, when we read a text, specific buzzwords reverberate in our minds beyond the more complex message conveyed by the entire text. Moreover, the art of choosing the right words with the appropriate affective impact is part of what defines the skill of good writers or speakers. And finally, single words also have a meaning beyond the specific context we find them embedded in: we have encountered these words in many other contexts before, and our semantic representation of these words potentially contains traces of all these different contexts, giving them complex emotional connotations. Superficially, these may not have much to do with the specific text we read. Rather, the automatic activation of complex emotional connotations in our memory may add the lexical grain of affective salt that flavours text processing, therefore enabling us to joyfully read between the lines.

But, on the other hand, our data also revealed the obvious limitations of Frege's axiom by providing evidence for the importance of dynamic shifts concerning emotional content of words across a text for affective reading experience: These shifts and their relevance cannot be captured via lexical means, because increasing shifts would always make means drift towards the neutral mean of the respective scale. Accordingly, after keeping the influence of alternative predictors including lexical valence constant via appropriate statistical procedures, the span of lexical arousal values of words encountered in a text passage proved to be the most fruitful predictor of activation in emotion-related brain areas in our study. I will close this chapter with a series of studies devoted to a phenomenon that is related to arousal span: suspense, perhaps the biggest force pulling readers into immersive states.

The Sandman Studies

This series of studies used the German narrative 'Der Sandmann' ("*The Sandman*') by E. T. A. Hoffmann as stimulus material. It is a prominent example of a romantic narrative devoted to the darker sides of emotional life. The story relates events in the life of the student Nathaniel who – traumatized by the early death of his father – is haunted since childhood by the mysterious Sandman. The story was chosen because of its suspenseful character and uncanny atmosphere famously discussed in Sigmund Freud's essay 'The

Uncanny', as judged by experts from both literary studies and psychology of the Languages of Emotion project. They also appreciated that the story features enough text passages inducing high as well as low suspense (as tested in a preceding pilot rating study). This ensured sufficient variability in the suspense ratings to use them as a parametric regressor in the neuroimaging data analysis. The story was presented in German. Special care was taken to ensure that the shortening of the text did not modify the plot or make the story less comprehensible. For the presentation in the scanner, the story was partitioned into 65 segments of approximately 100 words per segment. Segmentation was done by our experts in such a way that the theoretical level of suspense varied across text segments but remained relatively constant within one text segment.

According to the NCPM, feelings of suspense and immersion are closely related. More particularly, the fiction feeling hypothesis predicts that the core affect systems 'FEAR', 'ANGER' or 'CARE' described in Panksepp's emotion theory are likely to be involved in the suspense-building process mediated by feelings of empathy and sympathy, such as when a reader experiences suspense through vicarious fear, because a protagonist is in danger (especially when this danger is only known to the reader), which is

Predicting Human Suspense Ratings

In a series of behavioural studies, overall 50 participants read the story and after each of the 65 segments rated what they had just read on a set of nine scales: valence, arousal, suspense, immersion, imageability, fear (How scary was the text segment for you?), event/action (How eventful was the text segment for you?), emotion (The text segment triggered/produced real feelings within me) and concentration. Among the eight remaining ratings, the three most important predictors of suspense – as established via a standard predictive modelling analysis using a neural net that achieved an accuracy of 99 per cent––were:

- arousal (FI_{main} = 0.154)
- immersion (FI_{main} = 0.153)
- event/action (FI_{main} = 0.151)

Thus, at this subjective level of ratings, whenever readers feel aroused and immersed by an eventful piece of text, they also very likely experience suspense. To find out which text features are likely are behind these suspenseful reading experiences, I analyzed the story with *SentiArt* and ran another predictive modelling analysis.

The results of this second predictive modelling analysis which achieved an accuracy of 93 per cent with eight features, were clearcut, four features being most important for feelings of suspense:

- *AAP* (FI_{main} = 0.17)
- fear (FI_{main} = 0.16)
- minimum *AAP* value (FI_{main} = 0.133)
- shift in the mean *AAP* (aapsh, FI_{main} = 0.131)

The results suggest that segments with a negative *AAP* generally increase the likelihood of felt suspense, as do segments whose words are associated with fear, have a minimum *AAP* value of around −1, and whose mean *AAP* value shifts from positive to negative. Among these four features, the last one (aapsh) is particularly interesting. I included this feature reflecting a change in a segment's mean *AAP* from positive to negative (or vice versa) because a so-far untested hypothesis derived from media psychology is that suspense increases at inflection points when the sentiment – as estimated by *AAP* – turns. The data of this study support the hypothesis. Having shed light on how certain text features of a suspenseful story are associated with feelings of suspense, arousal and immersion, in the next section I look at how the brain of a reader responds to such text features and their accompanying subjective feelings.

The Neuronal Correlates of Suspense

In this neuroimaging study run by our former Ph.D. student Moritz Lehne, 23 participants read and rated the 'Sandman' story in our scanner.[205] Based on the suspense ratings, the analyses of the fMRI data looked at brain regions whose activity correlated significantly with the ratings. Figure 7.4 summarizes the results. It shows activation positively correlated with (rated) feelings of suspense in medial frontal cortex/*MFC*, superior temporal and TPJ. As hypothesized in the NCPM, and supported by the results of the above Harry Potter neuroimaging studies, selective activation of these medial frontal and temporo-parietal areas in our readers' brains could be due to the fact that they support adopting the perspective and inferring the mental states of the main characters of the story during emotionally engaging and suspenseful text segments. Suspenseful parts of a narrative plot (in particular the suspenseful text segments of the current experiment) often involve situations in which a main character of the story is facing situations of potential danger or threat. If the experience of suspense in dramatic presentations derives from the respondent's acute, fearful apprehension about deplorable events that

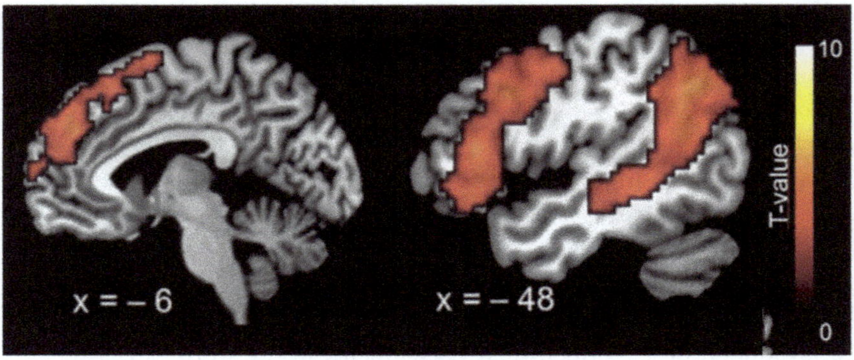

Figure 7.4 Three regions identified as main neural correlates of feelings of suspense: medial frontal cortex, superior temporal sulcus and temporo-parietal junction. Source: Adapted from Lehne et al., 2015.

threaten liked protagonists,[206] activation of the TPJ and MFC may reflect these fearful anticipations of upcoming events that depend on the ability to infer the mental states, goals and actions of characters of the story.

Summary

Four series of neuroimaging studies reported in this chapter all provided evidence for the main assumptions justifying the upper route of the NCPM. The 'do words stink' study showed that the neural representation of disgusting words activates the insula as part of the neural assembly that 'constructs' the meaning of these words. This finding supported the symbol grounding and Panksepp–Jakobson hypotheses. The 'fact vs. fiction' studies revealed a stronger engagement of empathy-related brain areas with increasingly negative story valence and thus supported the fiction-feeling hypothesis. The results of the 'Harry Potter' studies suggested that readers more likely to immerse in texts that reach the sensory-motor grounded affective resonance and autobiographical emotional memories of their readers through meta representations of global emotional moments like pain and fear, as reflected in selective anterior insula and mid-cingulate cortex activation. The latter brain region was singled out as a likely neural correlate of immersive experiences. Finally, the 'Sandman' studies established that suspense and immersion are big brothers in reading fiction and identified the TPJ and MFC as possible neuronal correlates of suspense as evoked by identification and empathy with a protagonist who faces threatening events. An additional computational poetics study using predictive modelling suggested that when the *AAP* of larger text segments that form a semantic unit shifts from positive to negative – so-called inflection points – suspense increases.

Chapter 8

NEUROCOMPUTATIONAL POETICS II: LOWER ROUTE STUDIES

In this section, my focus is on studies that informed us about the workings of the lower route of the NCPM and the second boon of reading: affective-aesthetic processes. For the sake of clarity and simplicity, I divided the section into studies dealing mainly with effects of sound and those investigating effects of semantics, knowing all too well that sound and meaning are not as independent as has been assumed. The first study serves as an introduction on the role of syllables, shedding light on the internal structure of syllables. The remaining 'sound' studies then directly speak to affective-aesthetic processes. The first three semantic studies concern the affective-aesthetic processing of single words, followed by two studies looking at cognitive-affective effects in meaning making for multiword expressions (literal and metaphoric compounds and idioms). The last study examines affective-aesthetic effects in proverbs and anti-proverbs.

The Sound Studies

Music and language can be seen as forms of sound that are meaningful within a society and can express a certain degree of intentionality, that is, they can represent or stand for things or states of affairs. As a hobby musician and great fan of both the music and lyrics of jazz standards like 'As Time Goes By' or 'Autumn Leaves' – whose original text was written by one of my favourite French poets, Jaques Prévert – I was always interested in how the two play together to create stronger emotions than each on its own. In both media, the sound material is split up into two sections, *pitch* and *rhythm*, its continuum being divided into notes on the one side and syllables on the other. Music combines its tones to chords to arrange them into a syntagma of time units such as rhythm, tempo and beat. Similarly, language combines syllables into words to arrange them into a syntax with its own time units: stress or accents, lengths, shortenings and breaks. So, if the syllables are so important, where do they come from? The next paragraph gives us a tentative answer to that question.

Phonemic Jargon Aphasia or Why Mr. Tan Had a Secret Preferred Syllable

Imagine you wake up in the morning, see your wife and want to say some nice words to her. But then, only the monosyllable 'tan' comes out of your mouth. Something similar happened to one of the most famous patients in the history of neurology, called 'Monsieur TAN' by his physician Paul Broca. The reason was simple: this otherwise healthy and intelligent patient could utter only a single syllable, T-A-N, a two-segment pseudoword with a nasalized vowel. Since Broca lacked the neuroimaging methods we have today, he patiently waited until Mr. *Leborgne-TAN* had changed into another mode of energy and dissected his brain. What he found constitutes the beginnings of modern cognitive neuroscience: the discovery of the 'speech centre' in what is still called Broca's Area, situated at the borders of the left frontal and temporal lobes of the brain. Broca inferred that this part of the brain, destroyed by a stroke, was responsible for speech production. He did not explain, though, why Mr. Leborgne could only produce TAN instead of, say, STRYK or MLUT.

During my time at France's first Centre for Cognitive Neuroscience in Marseilles, which I co-founded in 1992, and also later when I was a professor at a small private university near Munich, my team had already been working with neurological patients having language disorders. But only after we moved to FU Berlin in 2003 did a speech pathologist from my team, Prisca Stenneken, drew my attention to data she still had on her computer, and as it turned out, they would help crack the secret of Mr. TAN's preferred syllable. The data were from a so-called jargon aphasic,[i] a patient whose speech production after a stroke was like that in the transcript of a dialogue between the examiner (E) and him (KP) below (translation from German into English). Neologisms shown in brackets are transcribed from the patient's original utterance according to the *International Phonetic Alphabet*; pauses are marked by dots and intonational phrases by slashes.

---

i Phonemic jargon refers to aphasia with fluent speech production, in which the phonological structure of the utterances is impaired to the extent that lexical content is no longer identifiable.

> E: Did you enjoy your holiday?
> KP: yes, it was very [ʻkvɔɐnas] yes/and before we were then with the. with the [faxt] on the [ʻflɔʏɛs]/on the [ʻflʊtses]/
> E: Have you been there many times?
> KP: / no .. no not so much/well [ˌɪmə'fɛɐ] uhm till [ʻfɛntsiç] / because we five [ʻkɪmbas]. [gə'kan] had / [ʻfɛndən] can that before .. / and than had we than my little things. / that was my [ʻlaɪtzaɪn]

Several intelligible passages in KP's spontaneous speech suggest that rather complex syntactic frames for the utterances are established. One observation, also illustrated by the above example, is that neologisms are sometimes produced in slots, in which content words would be expected. Together with neurolinguists from the universities of Aachen and Groningen, we performed extensive analyses of KP's speech.[207] Since it did not show any phonetic or articulatory distortions, all of his utterances presenting phonemic deviations from standard German were categorized as either phonemic paraphasias – the substitution of a word with a nonword that preserves at least half of the segments and/or number of syllables of the intended word – or neologisms. Our aim was to find evidence for the hypothesis of a preferred syllable structure which theoretically is hard-wired in our brains. The prototype of this structure is the simple, open consonant–vowel syllable, usually noted as CV-. It is regarded as the least complex syllable type to be produced by the brain's motoric speech centre. And, as argued in the Introduction, when it combines phonotactically optimal phoneme contrasts with pleasurable images from semantic memory like in 'mama', it can acquire a micropoetic quality.

In any case, we found the evidence we were looking for. The main finding was the predominance of the CV syllable in KP's utterances, and especially the combination of obstruent and vowel (OV) as in 'p-a'. This was marked by both a high frequency of obstruents and vowels in syllable-initial position (OV-, 49.73 per cent, $n = 82{,}231$ observations), and by vowels in syllable-final position (-V, 31.62 per cent, $n = 52{,}282$). Thus, a tendency towards a maximum sonority contrast was observed in the onset position and towards a minimum contrast in the offset position. In sum, the results supported Clements' sonority theory and showed that the sublexical phonological feature sonority score introduced in Chapter 2 for poetry analyses also plays a role in daily speech, presumably from the first days of babbling. In summary, we cannot explain why Mr. Leborgne's preferred and only syllable was TAN, and not say TAK. However, we can explain why it was not STRYK or MLUT. Some secret meaning associated with the sound of TAN may be the cause, but Broca could not extract that from the dissected brain. The next two studies show how we can compute the affective meaning associated with the sound of syllables and words and how implicit sound-meaning processing affects the aesthetic evaluation of entire poems.

The 'Why PISS Is Ruder than PEE' Study

In Chapters 2 and 4 I mentioned the 'piss' vs. 'pee' phenomenon as an example of how the affective meaning of words can be influenced by their sound. Here I briefly present the original study led by my former Ph.D. student Arash Aryani that established this and, for the first time, quantified the phonological affective potential (PAP) of words.[208] The PAP is similar to the emotion potential of words. Without going into the details of the computational model underlying its computation, you can think of the PAP as the location of the *phonological form* of a word in the 2d emotion potential space illustrated in Figure 7.3 (upper panel) of the preceding chapter, but providing the valence and arousal values for its sound, not its meaning. Thus, in contrast to the data of this figure, which are based on the computation of the words' AAP via *SentiArt* – a semantic feature – the PAP is a phonological feature based on the affective values of a word's phonemes. These depend on a set of acoustic features, the most important being:

- Vowel length (duration). According to a hypothesis proposed in biology, calls produced by mammals in aggressive circumstances, termed 'barks' or 'grunts', are generally of shorter duration than those produced in appeasement contexts. With regard to human affective perception, long vowels are produced through a release of air from the mouth for an extended period of time. This is a behaviour similar to slow (vs. rapid) breathing that, in turn, is associated with decreasing (vs. increasing) emotional arousal; in other words, longer vowels have a calming effect.
- Voicing. Voiceless consonants sound on average more arousing and negative than voiced consonants, which, in turn, appear to make words sound softer and more pleasing.
- Plosive consonants. While plosives generally reduce sound energy, they also play a significant role in making the sound more negative and arousing.
- Hissing sibilants. A larger high-frequency energy and raising of the first formant – the broad spectral maximum that results from an acoustic resonance of the human vocal tract – are typical characteristics of hissing sibilants (alveolar fricatives and affricates like /s/, /z/, /ʃ/). These are strongly stressed consonants produced by a high-velocity jet of air against the teeth, which results in a literally high-arousing hissing sound. This may account for the cross- and paralinguistic use of these sounds for

attracting the attention of others (e.g. 'psst!') as well as for their prominent deployment in literature as a stylistic device for cacophony.

If these features come together, they provide an answer to the question in the title of this section. Indeed, it is the presence of a hissing sound following a short vowel that makes the small, but striking difference at the phoneme level between two words referring to one and the same concept from a very basic domain of physical human experience, out of which one is considered rather vulgar and rude, while the other seems more childish and polite: 'piss' vs. 'pee'.

The results of this extensive study with two experiments using 272 and 169 participants, respectively, confirmed the theoretical predictions of the psychoacoustic PAP model. Together with those of a series of other studies from my team,[209] they substantiate the psychological reality of iconicity in everyday language and, to borrow the term used earlier, they debunk de Saussure (see Tenet 3 in Chapter 2). In a follow-up neuroimaging study, we could show that affective iconic words like 'piss', for which the arousal values of meaning (lexical) and sound (sublexical) are congruent (both high), elicited increased brain activity in the left amygdala known for its role in multimodal representation of emotions.[210] This is illustrated in Figure 8.1 below. We also could identify two neural hubs (not shown in Figure 8.1), one in the left superior temporal gyrus/STG representative of processing sound and one in the LIFG for processing the meaning of words. These results provide a neural

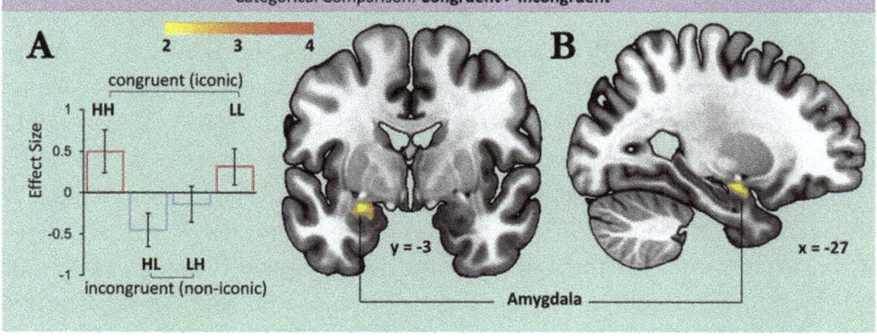

Figure 8.1 Iconic words as defined by the congruence between sublexical and lexical arousal elicited activation in the left amygdala. **A.** Parameter estimates of brain responses in left amygdala for all conditions of the experiment. In the HH (high lexical and sublexical arousal) and LL (low lexical and sublexical arousal) conditions meaning and sound are congruent; in the HL and LH conditions they are incongruent **B.** Increased activation of left amygdala for the contrasts between the HH vs. HL and LL vs. LH conditions, respectively. Source: Adapted from Aryani et al., 2019.

explanation for the facilitative role of iconicity in language processing and indicate that language users are sensitive to the interaction between sound and meaning aspect of words.

What is valid for everyday language should also apply, perhaps even more so, to poetic language. After all, poems are often 'read with the ear' and, as proposed in the initial quote of this chapter, iconicity is a major trait of poetry. This is nicely demonstrated by the next behavioural study.

Defence of the Wolves or the Basic Affective Tone of Poems

Along with metre, rhyme and rhythm, poets also make use of onomatopoeia, which to a greater or lesser extent plays with the phonological iconicity of words. This influences the affective basic tone and determines the overall emotional mood, or *global affective meaning*, of how a poem is received. This study was motivated by the existence of the EMOPHON tool: a probabilistic model for the prediction of the exceeding of a confidence interval for specific sublexical units concerning their frequency of occurrence within a given text, as contrasted with a reference corpus for the German language. Put simply, this tool can tell you how salient a given phoneme is in a text via computation of its relative frequency. We used it, for example, to test foregrounding theory's prediction of deviations in poetic language (compared to norms characterizing ordinary language) regarding the phonological level of analysis. And, indeed, comparing the salience of phonemes in 20 German poems with that of 20 newspaper articles, we found clear evidence for the prediction that poems featuring significantly more salient phonemes – deviating from the norms – than the prose texts.

In this study, EMOPHON was combined with the BAWL to compute the basic affective tone of poems and predict human ratings of valence, arousal, as well as the 'friendliness', 'spitefulness' and sadness of poems. The idea for our study arose because the dean of modern German Poetry, Hans Magnus Enzensberger, had himself attempted an intuitive classification of the 57 poems from his 1957 collection 'Verteidigung der Wölfe' ('Defense of the Wolves Against the Lambs') into the categories friendly, nasty and sad. He did this explicitly on the basis of lexical and supralexical features like the meaning of key words, lines and stanzas. Motivated by the iconicity assumption of the NCMP (Tenet 3), we were interested to see whether these poems also *sounded* friendly, spitefully or sadly, that is, whether their implicit sound or *basic affective tone* matched their *global affective meaning*.

Here's an example poem from the collection that the poet classified as 'nasty':

The wolves defended against the lambs

Should the vultures eat forget-me-nots?
What do you want the jackal to do,
cut loose from his skin, or the wolf?
Should he pull his own teeth out of his head? /
[…] there are plenty of victims, very few thieves:
You lambs, why crows would be
nuns stacked up against you:
all of you hoodwink each other /
Fraternity's the rule among wolves:
they travel in packs /
Blessed are the thieves:
you ask them up for a rape, then
throw yourself down on the moldy bed
of submission. /
Moaning you stick to your lies. /
You'd love to be torn limb from limb. /
You won't change the world. /

Naturally, the sound of this English translation does not match with the original German version, but its global affective meaning (spiteful) should.

First, we computed the EMOPHON values for each word of each of the 57 poems, thus quantifying the basic affective tone for each poem. Second, we had 252 native German speakers read and rate the poems – on average, each poem was read by at least 17 participants – using psychometric rating scales for:

- Valence, as measured on a 7-point rating scale ranging from −3 (*very negative*) to +3 (*very positive*).
- Arousal. 5-point scale from 1 (*very calming*) to 5 (*very arousing*).
- Friendliness. 5-point scale from 1 (*not friendly at all*) to 5 (*very friendly*).
- Sadness. 5-point scale from 1 (*not sad at all*) to 5 (*very sad*).
- Spitefulness. 5-point scale from 1 (*not spiteful at all*) to 5 (*very spiteful*).

We hypothesized, first, that our readers generally agree with the poet's own classification, that is, for example, the mean of their spitefulness ratings should be higher for the 17 poems pre-classified as spiteful than for the other two categories, and vice versa. Indeed, the differences in the rating scores were almost always consistent with the intended categorization by the author: the friendly poems were rated significantly friendlier than the sad and the spiteful poems, respectively. The sad poems were rated as significantly sadder than the friendly poems, but not than the spiteful poems; and the rating scores for spitefulness were significantly higher for the spiteful poems than for the friendly ones.

The fact that our readers did not as well discriminate spiteful vs. sad poems as they did for friendly vs. both sad and spiteful ones, respectively, is not really surprising. First of all, sadness and spitefulness both have a negative valence. Although the valence of spiteful poems was rated as more negative (mean = −1.39) than that for sad ones (−1.13), the difference was not statistically significant. In terms of dimensional emotion theories, they thus can best be discriminated on grounds of the second dimension, that is, by their arousal values. And indeed, the arousal ratings were significantly different (spiteful = 3.7; sad = 3.4). Discriminating between emotions based on a single rather than on two dimensions is more difficult than when they differ on both, as is the case for joy vs. sadness, which are opposed by a positive vs. a negative valence. If we apply Darwin's discrete emotion theory as an alternative to the dimensional one, the result is not surprising either. If we take anger as being the closest of the six basic emotions (anger, disgust, fear, joy, sadness, surprise) to spitefulness, the data from the biggest database for discrete emotion values of German words, the so-called *DENN-BAWL*,[211] indicate that the (significant) correlation between sadness and anger ratings is quite high (r = 0.56). Hence, many words rated as sad also have been rated as being associated with anger. Examples are: 'Krieg' ('war') with a mean sadness rating of 3.5 and an anger rating of 3.8 (scale from 1 to 5), or 'Drama' ('drama') with a sadness rating of 2.7 and an anger rating of 2.7.

In any case, if already single isolated words can be associated with more than a single of Darwin's six basic emotions, it is no wonder that entire poems can. People have a lot of mixed emotions and therefore strict categories such as those used by Enzensberger are an oversimplification. There is a certain amount of overlap between the words of the spiteful and sad poems and also between their topics: in general, the sad poems mourn the loss of nature and the ideal, the spiteful poems reject and ridicule nature and the ideal (drawing here on the two categories of elegy and satire of Schiller's poetic tripartite).

Second, and more importantly for the NCPM's validity, we hypothesized that to a certain extent the sound or basic affective tone of the poems corresponded with their global affective meaning. The results confirmed this hypothesis. The sublexical measure of arousal, based on salient phonological units computed by EMOPHON, accounted for 9.5 per cent of the variance in human sadness ratings, 17 per cent for friendliness ratings, and 22 per cent for spitefulness. All correlations between the computational predictor, phonological arousal and the human ratings were statistically significant ($.3 < r <$

.48, 0.001 $< p <$ .05). The highest arousal value was obtained for the spiteful poems (mean = 3.96), followed by the sad (3.68), and the friendly ones (2.1). We interpret these data as clear evidence that the iconic associations of foregrounded phonological units contribute significantly to a poem's emotional and aesthetic perception by the reader and the author, as assumed by the NCPM.

At the time of this study, published in 2015, we did not have the psychoacoustic model developed in the 'piss vs. pee' study, published three years later. Perhaps, augmenting the EMOPHON-based estimates of the basic affective tone by the features of this complex model would have produced even higher correlations between the computational phonological predictors and the human ratings. Nonetheless, it is clear that these pre-attentive, and probably unconscious, effects of implicit sound cannot be as strong as those of the explicit meaning of the words and lines of the poems for rating their global affective meaning. Whether the poet himself was aware of these sound effects, we do not know. When interviewed by one of the co-authors of this publication, he said that they certainly were not deliberately intended. To summarize, together with many other studies from my and other labs, not reported here, and in line with Tenet 3 of the NCPM, the results of the preceding two studies strongly suggest the existence of iconicity as a general property of human language (with apologies to de Saussure).

Although the NCPM is silent with respect to this special kind of affective-aesthetic response in humans, I would like to finish this section on sound effects with a study that examined it: humour. This response requires high-end linguistic skills, as anyone trying hard to be witty and humorous in a second language can witness. The majority of theories of humour and empirical studies deal with semantics, considering puzzling incongruities between levels of meaning as pivotal for humour processing. Thus, puns exploit random phonological similarities (homonymies) between semantically unrelated words for activating a funny interaction at the level of their meaning, while many jokes play with double meanings, such as the literal and the figurative meaning of an idiomatic expression. In contrast, non-semantic features such as rhyme and metre have been neglected by mainstream research on humour. In the next study, we tried to change this.

Prosody in Humorous Poetry and Proverbs – The Bergson Hypothesis

Es ist ein Brauch von alters her:/ Wer Sorgen hat, hat auch Likör!

(*From ancient times it has been true, He who has cares, has liquor, too.*)

The above quote is the translation of a couplet from the poem 'Die fromme Helene' (The Pious Helene) by the popular German humoristic poet Wilhelm Busch, whose rhymed and metered narratives have been published in several languages, including English. As we have shown in an empirical study using 60 such two-lined couplets, their special rhyme and metre features evoke humour and positive affective responses.[212] They also facilitate understanding and are better memorized than *de-rhetoricized* control stimuli, in which either rhyme and/or metre are destroyed while keeping overall meaning constant. Thus, for example, in the control 'Für alle Zeiten ist es wahr:/Wer Sorgen hat, hat auch Alkohol' ('For all times it has been true, he who has cares has also alcohol') both the original iambic metre and the salient rhyme ('her/Likör'; very infrequent and surprising in German) were destroyed.

To account for the effects of funniness that are based on the processing of formal incongruities between the historically predominant prototype of 'good' verse making and Busch's humoristic verses, we advanced the *Bergson hypothesis*: establishing an analogy between the metrical pattern of verses and dance movements, it states that 'mechanically' degrading the phonological and *prosodic gestalt* of prototypical poetic verses, that is, Busch's technique of deliberate attacks on a reader's aesthetic expectations shaped by the canonical art of poetry, has similar effects as body movements, which appear to degrade a living organism into a mere mechanically moving object, namely laughter, regardless of whether such movements are performed unintentionally or as a deliberate clownish performance.

Empirical observations showing that sensorimotor networks of the brain can be associated with rhythmic patterns and are responsive to poetic stimuli lend support to embodied theories of literary reading suggesting that it reaches deep into neural circuits. Thus, it has been shown that like music or movie scenes (spoken) poetry not only can cause goosebumps, but the rhythm of poetry can also synchronize heart rate and respiration: hexameter verse indeed exerts a strong influence on respiratory sinus arrhythmia by a prominent low-frequency component in the breathing pattern, generating a strong cardiorespiratory synchronization.[213]

The Semantics Studies

The above studies clearly demonstrate that meaning-making during language processing and especially reading verbal art already starts before the end product of lexical access becomes fully aware in our mind. The implicit, subconscious processing of the affective sound of words in brain regions like the left amygdala is a case in point. Meaning-making is a multi-phase process whose temporal distribution can last from milliseconds to minutes or more.

Thus, the average gaze duration on words during reading lasts only one-fourth of a second. It is prolonged at the end of sentences, sometimes even doubled, reflecting the meaning integration process including all words of the sentence. Deciding whether a sentence is logically correct or not, as in the *SLS-Berlin* test discussed in Chapter 4, takes 2–5 seconds, as measured by manual response times (button presses). Making meaning out of the roughly 220 words of the 6th paragraph from Jane Austen's 'Emma' shown below would take about one minute, considering average reading rates of 200–250 wpm as applying here.

> 'The event had every promise of happiness for her friend. Mr. Weston was a man of unexceptionable character, easy fortune, suitable age, and pleasant manners; and there was some satisfaction in considering with what self-denying, generous friendship she had always wished and promoted the match; but it was a black morning's work for her. The want of Miss Taylor would be felt every hour of every day. She recalled her past kindness – the kindness, the affection of sixteen years – how she had taught and how she had played with her from five years old – how she had devoted all her powers to attach and amuse her in health – and how nursed her through the various illnesses of childhood. A large debt of gratitude was owing here; but the intercourse of the last seven years, the equal footing and perfect unreserve which had soon followed Isabella's marriage, on their being left to each other, was yet a dearer, tenderer recollection. She had been a friend and companion such as few possessed: intelligent, well-informed, useful, gentle, knowing all the ways of the family, interested in all its concerns, and peculiarly interested in herself, in every pleasure, every scheme of hers – one to whom she could speak every thought as it arose, and who had such an affection for her as could never find fault.'

Continuing this time game and reckoning a wpm of 200 for this novel as adequate, reading the entire last chapter from *The Great Gatsby* (~5,400 words) would take around half an hour (5,400/200 = 27). Finally, if you read this book about Neurocomputational Poetics at a single blow without breaks and without spending time inspecting the many tables and figures, it would still take you about a day (roughly 8 hours). How many layers of meaning you would peel off (or not) of the words and sentences during this reading marathon, no one could ever tell, not even yourself. So let us start simple again and consider meaning-making for single isolated words.

As we have seen in Chapter 3, single words already have most of the basic features characterizing entire texts. These lexical features constitute the pivot of computational text analyses. It is thus of central importance that the text analysis tool you want to use produces valid and accurate predictions of lexical features such as those determining a word's euphony and eusemy. Long before I started developing the *SentiArt* tool, my team had developed a number of word lists for use in text analyses, called *BAWL, DENN-BAWL* and *kidBAWL*. All these provided human ratings for the likeability based on the affective meaning of German words (valence, arousal and also imageability), offering valuable information about why people like or dislike words. A first crucial test of *SentiArt*'s validity, before applying it to entire poems and books, was therefore to see how well it predicted these lexical ratings. This is what I discuss in the next paragraphs.

Predicting the Likeability and Beauty of Single Words

Following the long-familiar predictive modelling procedure, I first computed a set of (sub)lexical features with *SentiArt* for each of the words in the biggest publicly available English database – here called the *WKB database* – providing valence ratings for a large number of words.[214] After a predictor screening, I selected a candidate set from those features as predictors for the modelling studies and ended up with the following 10 features: *AAP, word length* and *frequency* (familiarity), *arousal, anger, disgust, sadness, concreteness, consonant-vowel quotient* (cvq) and *sonority score*. The predictive accuracy was good (0.88, a value so far not achieved in any other study I know), as can be seen in Figure 8.2. The three most important features were: *AAP* (FI_{main} = 0.31),

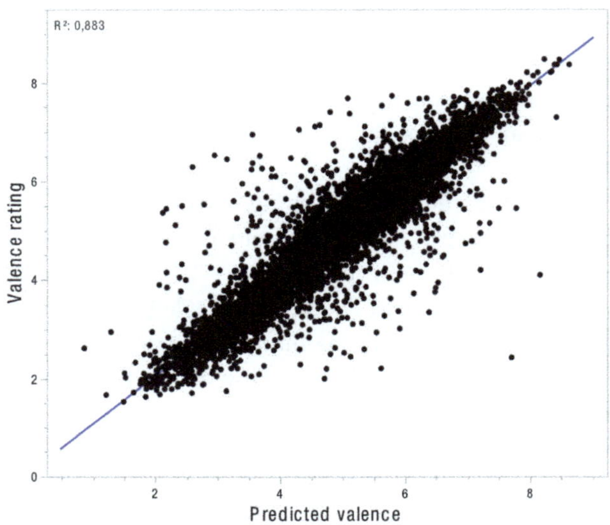

Figure 8.2 Rated and model-predicted valence of the ~12,000 words in the WKB database.

anger (FI_{main} = 0.11) and disgust (FI_{main} = 0.11). Their main effects on valence ratings were opposite: the higher *AAP* and the lower anger and disgust, the higher the rated valence. All features reached the importance criterion of >0.1 regarding their total, interactive effects and thus should be considered in future studies of word likeability. In sum, the outcome of this first series of modelling studies suggested a simple three-feature model for the likeability of words: to be likeable, a word should have a high *AAP* value, and be associated with anger and disgust as little as possible.

While there are many studies providing valence ratings for single words, as far as I know the only empirical study on the perceived beauty of words – worldwide – was run in my lab. In this study, published in 2017 in *Frontiers in Human Neuroscience*, I predicted the binary classification of human beauty ratings into either 'ugly' or 'beautiful' for 130 words like 'vomit' or 'rape' vs. 'rainbow' or 'moonshine' with an accuracy of >95 per cent[215] These words had been carefully chosen by psychology students from one of my courses on the basis of their subjective feelings. The most beautiful word was 'Libelle' (dragonfly) with a mean rating of 6.1/7, followed by 'Morgenröte' (aurora, 5.9) and 'Mittsommernacht' (midsummernight, 5.8). A hierarchical cluster analysis[216] – a statistical method which groups stimuli according to their similarity on a number of features – suggested that the most beautiful words described nine phenomena from nature (animals, flowers, stars etc.) and four states/objects of wellness (e.g. coziness), all rated high on beauty, valence and imageability, and low on arousal. In contrast, the overall 24 ugliest words were almost all swear words often associated with genitalia. The prediction was based on eight *SentiArt* features, of which *AAP* and *word length* were the most important ones, followed by *sonority score,* and *surprisal*, a context-sensitive estimate of word familiarity (predictability). According to this model, words were rated as more beautiful when they had higher AAP values and were relatively short, sonorous and unfamiliar.

Together, the likeability and perceived beauty studies suggest that the *AAP* feature of *SentiArt* is generally valid, being the most important of several features for successfully predicting word likeability and beauty ratings in two languages (English and German). They also show what has already been found in several other studies, including one on the perceived beauty of German romantic poems[217]: asking people whether they like something or whether they find it beautiful can be predicted by pretty much the same features, most importantly by their AAP value. This demonstrates the power of association: words that reside in a semantic neighbourhood with concepts like 'art', 'joy' or 'love' are found pleasant, as opposed to those which are surrounded in semantic space by neighbours like 'anger', 'gloom' or 'disgust'.

Sound and Meaning Beauty

However, somewhat surprised by the fact that the sublexical feature sonority score, a potential indicator of euphony, played no important role in the above studies, I ran two other studies (one in 2018 and another in 2021, so far unpublished) on word beauty with another set of 400 carefully selected words. The four groups of words were chosen from a large pool of the *SDEWAC corpus*[218] with help of *SentiArt*: based on the tool's two features for estimating euphony and eusemy (see Chapter 5):

A) HiHi. 100 words with a high theoretical sound and meaning beauty potential. German examples are: *Libelle* (dragon fly) or *Ballerina* (ballerina).
B) LoLo. 100 with both low sound and meaning beauty potential. Examples are: *Krebs* (cancer) or *Zecke* (tick).
C) LoHi. 100 with a low sound but a high meaning beauty. Examples are: *Antlitz* (visage) or *Nixe* (mermaid).
D) HiLo. 100 with a high sound and a low meaning beauty. Examples are: *Amöbe* (ameba) or *einsam* (lonely).

In these studies, we asked participants explicitly to rate either the sound beauty *or* the meaning beauty of each word by trying to mentally filter out – not paying attention to – the other dimension in each case. The hypothesis tested was that participants' ratings would follow the pattern predicted by *SentiArt*. Although the majority of participants reported that it is not easy to mentally focus on either sound or meaning separately, the data indicate that they managed to do relatively well: the correlations between the sound and meaning beauty ratings in the two studies were: $r = 0.47$ and $r = 0.52$, respectively. Taking the squared values (R^2), this means that in each case only about 25 per cent of the variance in the second rating was accounted for by the first. The other result, which is astonishing, is that with a totally different set of participants three years later, the ratings for both sound and meaning beauty correlated very highly: $r = 0.8$ for sound, and $r = 0.97$ for meaning beauty. Thus, these ratings are very reliable and can be generalized at least within this sample of German psychology students. The pattern of results indeed offered several insights.

First, I compared the mean values for explicit meaning beauty with sound beauty ratings for identical words. As can be seen in the violin plots of Figure 8.3 based on the most recent data of 2021, when meaning beauty was rated (blue dots), on average the ratings were higher for word groups A (both beautiful) and C (beautiful meaning only) and lower for the two groups with sound beauty only (B and D). The mean values (M_m for the

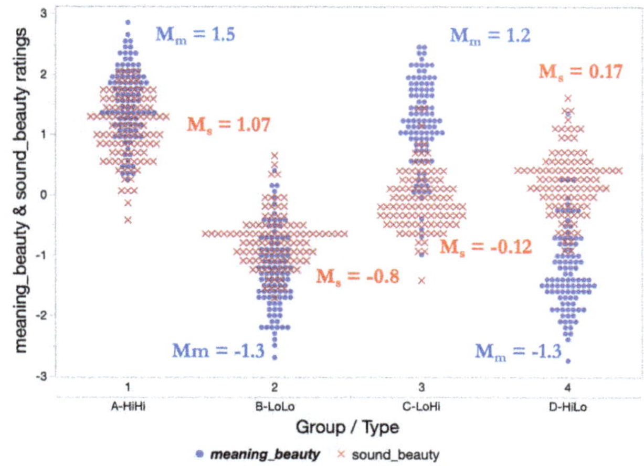

Figure 8.3 Violin plots showing the rating data for all words (averaged across readers) in the four conditions of the sound and meaning beauty study from 2021. Blue dots: meaning beauty rating task; red crosses: sound beauty rating task. M_m and M_s = mean values for meaning and sound beauty ratings.

meaning rating task, M_s for the sound rating task) for the meaning rating task (blue dots) reveal the following rank order: A > C > D ≥ B. When sound beauty was rated (red crosses), the pattern clearly changed to: A > D > C > B. That shows a clear influence of the instruction and that participants can – to a certain extent – abstract from one of the two dimensions. On the other hand, the data in Figure 8.3 reveal what we would have expected in this task of context-free single word ratings: 'meaning tops sound'. Readers can more easily abstract from the sound of a word than from its meaning.

Predictive Modelling of Meaning and Sound Beauty Ratings

Second, I used the ten features from the above 'liking study' in a predictive modelling analysis to see how well this model fared with the data of these two studies. The results confirmed the validity and generality of this simple six-feature model for predicting human liking and word beauty ratings impressively: for meaning beauty ratings, the accuracies were 0.91 and 0.92, respectively; for sound beauty ratings, they were 0.70 and 0.55, respectively. However, this time the FIs varied: *AAP* and *anger* again were the most important predictors of meaning beauty ratings (FI_{main} = 0.48 in both studies), followed by *word length* (0.18 and 0.13, respectively). However, for sound beauty ratings, *sonority score* came second in the 2021 study (0.28), and third in the 2018 one (0.25), after *word length* (0.26).

To summarize our findings on the likeability and beauty of single words, the 'average reader' finds words likeable and beautiful that

- are associated with pleasant concepts like art and love, or speak of nature and states of well-being;
- sounds well;
- are not too lengthy; and
- are not overly familiar.

Poets and authors of song lyrics know this, of course, as evidenced by their extensive use of such words for which we have seen plenty of examples in Chapters 5 and 6. The 10-feature model appears to capture the gist of this phenomenon and thus seems generally valid. So let us now have a look at neuroimaging data that can tell us which brain networks are involved in evaluating the likeability of words and responding to the beauty of multiword expressions. As argued in Chapter 5, these are much harder to computationally predict than those of single words because they involve computing higher-level interlexical and supralexical features and bringing figurativeness into play. I focus on four types of multiword expressions my team has extensively studied in the last decade: compounds, metaphors, idioms and proverbs.

Bivalent Compounds or Do You Like 'Fablelove' Better than 'Bombsex'?

In one neuroimaging study led by my former Ph.D. student Michael Kuhlmann, my team investigated the processing of a special form of two-word constructions: noun–noun compounds (NNCs) such as 'bedroom' or 'sexbomb'. These examples obviously vary in terms of a number of quantifiable features, such as degree of figurativeness, novelty, arousal, valence or semantic similarity. For example, while 'bed' and 'room' have a high semantic similarity as computed by *SentiArt* (0.53), that between 'sex' and 'bomb' is comparatively low (0.15). Now, computational metrics of semantic similarity usually fulfil the *symmetry axiom* of *Euclidean geometry* like our simple heuristic for predicting metaphor aptness from Chapter 5 [$s(t,v) = s(v,t)$]. So, this feature alone cannot explain why participants in this study found 'bombsex' stranger, more arousing, and more figurative than 'sexbomb'. Let us dwell a little on these combinations of nouns (or adjectives and nouns) that belong to a special linguistic realm.

'Bedroom', 'six-pack' or 'tennis shoe' are examples of close, hyphenated and open NNCs, which are more complex than single words, governed by morphology, but simpler than phrases or sentences, governed by syntax. Their morphological complexity does not stem from pre- or suffixes, but from their constituents' internal hierarchical structure. In German (and in English), NNCs are right-headed, that is, the second constituent or *head* determines the semantic category and the morphosyntactic features of the whole compound, while its meaning is altered by the first noun, the *modifier*. Compounds contain the information of a minimal sentence of the structure 'modifier has head', such as in 'fingerprint', or 'head is for modifier', like in 'raincoat'. They are an important mechanism for the creation of new words (e.g., internet), especially in German, where one can create an infinity of new compound words by just writing them together. The meaning of a compound may result from the combination of the meaning of the constituents (blueberry, snowball), thus being transparent or *endocentric*. More interesting for poetry are opaque *exocentric* compounds with no head, where the meaning does not emerge as the result of a simple semantic combination, as in 'humbug', which is not a kind of bug, or strawberry. In any case, compounds and similar bigrams often engage effortful semantic integration processes, which is especially true for novel compounds. Since compounds are processed slower when separated by a space, they likely are represented as whole lexical units or meaning gestalts in the brain. Most important for our two neuroimaging studies reported in this section was the fact that NNCs can be literal ('bedroom') or metaphorical ('sexbomb'), and their constituents can have the same affective semantic value (valence) or opposite ones. Thus, according to the aforementioned *WKB database*, both 'bed' and 'room' have a positive valence (bed: 1.64; room: 0.4; scale from −3 to +3), while 'sex' is positive (1.3), but 'bomb' is clearly negative (−2.03).

Like the familiar German 'Sexbombe', 'Abschaumknospe' (scum bud) is an example of an affectively *bivalent NNC*, one whose first constituent has a negative valence, while its second has a positive one. This raises interesting questions regarding their affective status and processing in the brain, such as: What is the likeability of a bivalent compound? Or, are compounds in which both nouns have a congruent valence, such as 'Fabelliebe' ('fablelove'; both positive) or 'Waisenleichnam' ('orphan corpse'; both negative), generally liked better than those with a conflicting valence, such as 'Bombensex' ('bomb-sex', negative–positive) or 'Hobbyhenker' ('hobby henchman')? Or, where is the affective conflict for meaning integration greater, for negative–positive or positive–negative compounds?

Using all four combinations of such NNCs (e.g., negative-positive, negative-negative, etc.), we had 24 participants reading overall 120 such compounds in our scanner, recording their brain activity. The verbal stimulus material had been created in pilot studies over several years with the help of students from my seminars, to whom I am grateful for their creative participation. Using a

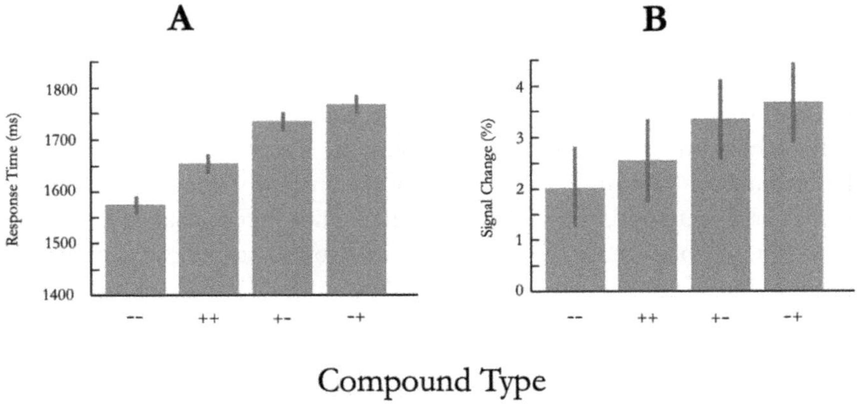

Figure 8.4 **A**. Response Times (ms) and **B**. Hemodynamic signal change (%) in the LIFG for the four compound type conditions; the vertical bars represent confidence intervals. Source: Adapted from Kuhlmann et al., 2017.[219]

speeded valence decision task, our participants had to explicitly decide as quickly as possible whether they liked or not the stimulus presented on the computer screen. Apart from their response type (Yes, No) and brain activity, we also recorded their response times, as shown in Figure 8.4A. The behavioural measures answer some of our questions: first, even if the within-group differences between the two congruent and incongruent conditions seen in Figure 8.3A were not statistically significant, there is a significant effect of congruency with affectively congruent (univalent) compounds (noted − − and ++, respectively) being responded to faster than incongruent, bivalent ones (+ −, − +). Thus, as was hypothesized, resolving an affective meaning conflict takes time.

The neuroimaging data summarized in Figure 8.4B show the change in brain activity in the repeatedly aforementioned LIFG, which is known to be involved in interactive and concurrent integration of phonology, syntax and semantics into a complex *meaning gestalt*.[220] The present study demonstrated that the basal affective meaning represented by uni- or bivalence is an integral part of this process. The neuronal data mirror the behavioural ones nicely. Again, the differences were statistically significant only between, but not within the congruent vs. incongruent conditions, but the descriptive rank order suggests that disliking decisions (−−) may be easier than liking ones (++), and that the affective conflict might be easier to resolve for compounds whose *head* is negative (+ −) than for those with a positive head (−+). Of course, this statement requires further empirical testing. With regard to the question posed in the title of this section, the answer for our participants is 'yes' and they took longer to decide that they dislike 'bombsex' than for affirming that they like 'fablelove'.

In the present study, we did not investigate whether the more or less apparent figurativeness of our NNCs had effects on readers' response times or brain activity. In the next study, however, we manipulated this feature systematically in German NNCs.

'The Brain Is the Prisoner of Thought' – The Novelty, Figurativeness and Aptness of Metaphors

Even though it might be a sleeping or dead one due to its frequent usage, the NNC 'sexbomb' still is a metaphor. But, like other things, the colours of figurative language can fade away. As we will also see for proverbs and idioms later in this section, the big equalizer feature, familiarity (or frequency of use/occurrence), can modulate the affective-aesthetic effects of figurativeness.

Novelty and Figurativeness

Novelty, familiarity's antagonist, is one of art's magic tricks. At least in unthreatening or, more specifically, artful contexts, being relatively unfamiliar or 'strange' helps opening the aesthetic trajectory, a central process of the NCPM's lower route. The brain's vital automatic object recognition process is then slowed down or perturbed, curiosity, surprise or interest is stimulated – accompanied by a certain tension and arousal – and, in the case of successful art, a feeling of goodness of fit or harmony results. Read for the first time, 'Juliet is the sun' can surprise and please, but after 1,000 encounters, its original aptness as a metaphor has worn off. With frequent use, original, novel metaphors lose their novelty, and as eventually they become conventionalized, fixed and familiar expressions, their perception changes from an effortful and often joyful to an automatic process, typically less emotionally arousing or aesthetically pleasing. No wonder that such conventional metaphors are sometimes called 'frozen'.

In the preceding study, we systematically varied the (bi)valence of German NNCs. In this neuroimaging study, led by my colleague from Budapest, Balint Forgacs, we manipulated their novelty (conventionality) and figurativeness (metaphoricity). Twenty participants silently read 200 NNCs in our scanner, recording their brain activity and judging their familiarity. We had 50 items in each of four groups. Examples are:

A) 'Alarmsignal' (alarm signal): conventional literal/CL.
B) 'Augapfel' (apple of the eye): conventional metaphoric/CM.
C) 'Holzflasche' (wood-bottle): novel literal/NL.
D) 'Duftgesang' (perfume chant): novel metaphoric/NM.

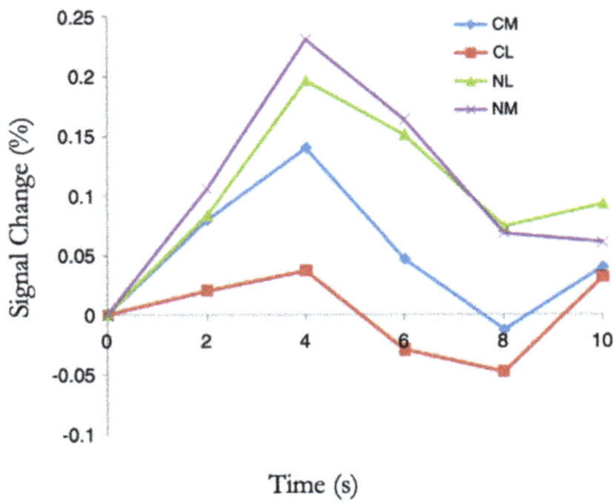

Figure 8.5 Hemodynamic signal change (%) in the LIFG for the four stimulus type conditions: NM = novel metaphoric, NL = novel literal, CL = conventional literal, CM = conventional metaphoric. Source: Adapted from Forgacs et al., 2012.[221]

According to the NCPM, the likelihood of lower route activation by these NNCs should increase from (A) to (D), that is with increasing defamiliarization, as should processing effort and time. The results were clear-cut and confirmed this prediction: together with the other 49 words of its group, NM items like 'Duftgesang' triggered much more brain activity in the LIFG than words like 'Holzflasche', 'Augapfel' or 'Alarmsignal', as shown in Figure 8.5. Moreover, increased activation in the left amygdala for groups (B) and (D) in contrast to (A) and (C) suggested that processing of metaphorical NNC*s* is coupled with stronger involvement at the emotional level. Apart from this 'affective' brain activity, we found no evidence for aesthetic processes signalled by an involvement of the brain's reward centre in processing metaphorical NNCs. This comes as no surprise, though, since in this study we were not interested in aesthetics and thus the large majority of our metaphoric stimuli like 'Frauenheld' ('womanizer'), 'Pechvogel' ('jinx'), 'Fantasiepapst' ('fantasy pope') or 'Ärgerberg' ('troube mountain') rather lack poetic potential, much as the NNCs of the preceding study. This is definitely not the case for the verbal stimuli used in the next study, which is computational 'only', that is without neuroimaging data.

When readers' brains process the information contained in lines like Lord Byron's 'The brain is the prisoner of thought' or 'Time is a bird' many neural circuits work together to enable meaning-making and there are elaborated accounts of how this could, theoretically, be achieved by our brains.[222] A key issue of considerable debate concerns the aptness (beauty or poeticity) of metaphors, introduced in Chapter 5. Nominally, 'aptness' refers to the extent to which the vehicle of a metaphor (its source or ground) captures important or crucial aspects of its tenor (topic or target), but the term is often used as a proxy for the literary or poetic quality of a metaphor.

Aptness

Luckily, there is one extensive empirical study led by Albert Katz that provides ample human rating data about the goodness or aptness of over 450 metaphors selected from earlier and later poetry collections featuring authors from Keats or Shakespeare to Cummings or Dylan Thomas.[223] For the three examples from Dylan Thomas given in Chapter 5, a simple heuristic based on the computation of *s(t,v)* sufficed to predict which of the three obtained the highest aptness ratings. In our paper published in 2017, we used this simple univariate heuristic and achieved an overall predictive accuracy for all 464 metaphors of 0.48 (0.44 for metaphors from earlier collections and 0.52 for later ones).[224] While at the time this result looked very promising to us, the progress made since, and especially the development of *SentiArt* which was not around then, lets it look rather unsatisfactory. To see if we can do notably better now with a multivariate *SentiArt* model, and encouraged by the success of the four-feature model applied to the *Cardillo database* (see Table 5.3 in Chapter 5), here I reanalyzed the data using predictive modelling based on a *SentiArt* analysis of all metaphors.

After having run a predictor screening, I trained a 10-feature model on a training subset of the 464 metaphors and obtained an excellent predictive accuracy for the remaining test set of 98 per cent. The most important feature – and the only one crossing the 0.1 criterion for main effects – was the number of common neighbours/CN (FI_{main} = 0.15). It had a nonlinear effect on metaphor aptness ratings illustrated in Figure 8.6: until an optimum value of about 75 neighbours, aptness increases with CN and then reaches a stable plateau with a slight final decrease beyond values of 110. However, five other features had important total (interactive) effects, the three most important being the semantic neighbourhood density of the vehicle/SND_{veh} (FI_{tot} = 0.5) which had an inversely U-shaped effect with an optimum value around 0.7, *s(t,v)* (FI_{tot} = 0.49) again showing an inversely U-shaped effect with an optimum value around 0.28, and the semantic neighbourhood density of the tenor/SND_{ten} (FI_{tot} = 0.48), also with a clear inversely U-shaped effect with an optimum value around 0.5. Other features with important interactive effects were the imageability of the vehicle (FI_{tot} = 0.32) – that was estimated using the *BV12 database*[225] – showing an optimum at a value of 0.35, and the similarity between the non-common neighbours (an estimate of the difference set in Table 5.3, Chapter 5) (FI_{tot} = 0.22). Aptness ratings increased with this feature until a value of 0.7 and then remained pretty much constant.

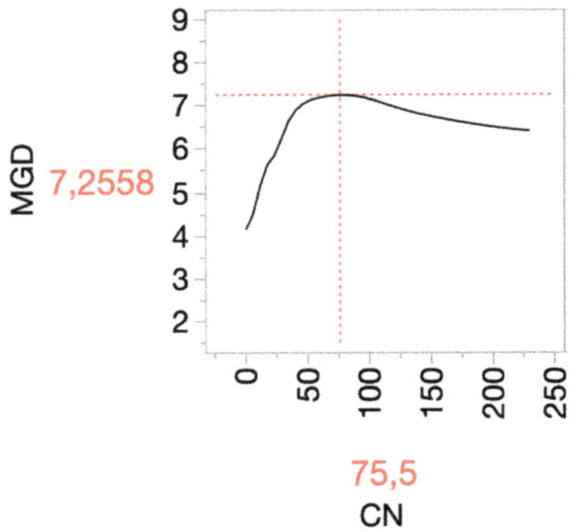

Figure 8.6 Metaphor aptness (MGD) as a function of the number of common neighbours (CN), as predicted by a neural net. A maximum mean aptness rating of 7.25 is achieved with an optimum value of 75.5 common neighbours between tenor and vehicle for this database.

To sum up, for the first time the human aptness ratings of the Katz metaphor database could be predicted with near-perfect accuracy using a multivariate *SentiArt* model. According to this model, a metaphor is judged of high aptness when its tenor and vehicle share an optimum value of common semantic neighbours. Apart from this most important feature, perceived aptness also increases when a metaphor's vehicle and a tenor both have an optimum neighbourhood density, and an optimum *s(t,v)* value, neither too low nor too high. These results are in line with the simple metaphor aptness heuristic and the more sophisticated model successfully applied to the Cardillo database in Chapter 5; and they provide additional support for the validity and generality of the semantic features computed by *SentiArt*.

Although, making meaning out of novel or ambiguous verbal stimuli like our NNCs is part and parcel of the wonders of literary reading and poetry reception in particular, we are only at the beginning of understanding its neuronal and cognitive-affective bases, and the longer the verbal stimuli under investigation become, the less we know. The next section spotlights the processing of verbal stimulus sequences with an average length of four to five words that arguably are considered the least creative part of figurative language, *idioms*. This is a good starting point for testing the assumption integrated in the NCPM – as sketched in Figure 2.3C (lower panel) of Chapter 2 – that the LIFG plays a part in the lower route's figurative meaning computation. Another prediction of the NCPM tested in the next study is that figurativeness positively affects likeability.

'To Have Pepper in the Ass' – The Likeability and Figurativeness of Idioms

Idioms like the German 'Pfeffer im Hintern haben' ('To have pepper in the ass' meaning to be lively, to be full of energy, not to be able to sit still) or the English 'Kick the bucket' are multiword expressions whose global meaning cannot generally be inferred merely on the basis of the meaning of the constituent words. They thus lack semantic transparency and their meaning has to be retrieved directly from semantic memory, as a popular psychological hypothesis assumes.[226] This stands in contrast to *proverbs* such as 'Too humble is half proud' which are considered to be literally and figuratively 'true' statements signalled by specific grammatical, phonetic and/or rhetorical patterns, or by a binary structure (theme/comment). Although some idioms can diachronically come from metaphors, they also differ from them, since metaphors – even the most frozen or dead ones – do not possess a unique standardized meaning and can convey more than one meaning depending on context.

'Jemandem sein Herz ausschütten' ('To pour out one's heart to someone') is a German idiom from the 'Psycholinguistic and Affective Norms of Idioms for German'/*PANIG corpus*.[227] It means 'to openly talk about one's problems with someone' and was part of a study in which we wanted to learn more about the role of figurative language in conveying affect. In a first behavioural study, we collected extensive rating data about the liking (valence), arousal, familiarity, concreteness, semantic transparency and figurativeness of these overall 619 idioms. The three most liked idioms in PANIG were: 'Vor Freude strahlen' ('To beam of joy', meaning to be happy), 'Im siebten Himmel sein' ('To be in seventh heaven', meaning to be extremely happy) and 'auf Wolke sieben schweben' ('To float on cloud seven', meaning to lighten up because of a positive event). The three least liked were: 'Jemandem die Seele aus dem Leib prügeln' ('To beat the soul out of someone's body', meaning to beat someone excessively), 'Eine Ausgeburt der Hölle sein' ('To be the spawn of hell', meaning to be a terrible person), and 'Die Fresse polieren' ('To polish someone's puss', meaning to beat someone up).

The data of this study allowed us to examine to what extent rated figurativeness contributes to the likeability (rated valence) of multiword expressions. To illustrate contrasting degrees of figurativeness of German idioms, consider the following examples for lower figurativeness: 'Das ist keine Kunst' (literal translation: this is no art; meaning this is not difficult), or 'keinen Pfennig mehr haben' (literal translation: to have no more cent;

meaning: to be broke/out of money). In contrast, idioms exposing higher figurativeness ratings are: 'Einen Kater haben' (literal translation: to have a tomcat; meaning to be hung-over), or 'Grün hinter den Ohren sein' (literal translation: to be green behind the ears; meaning to be immature or inexperienced).

Similarly to my re-analyses of the data from the 'Sandman' studies in the previous chapter, here I re-analyzed the data from the PANIG study using a predictive modelling approach to see which experiential–behavioural variables (other ratings) best predicted the likeability of idioms. Among the six other ratings, the most important predictor of idiom likeability (valence) – as established via a neural net predictive model that achieved only a moderate accuracy of ~55 per cent – was arousal ($FI_{main} = 0.21$). The effect was bipartite, split at a valence value of 0: that is, for about 50 per cent of the idioms, the direction (sign) of the correlation with arousal is reversed ($r = 0.3$ if valence < 0; $r = 0.14$ if valence > 0). This reflects a well-known tendency observed with both pictorial and verbal stimuli: dislikeable stimuli (valence < 0) become even more dislikeable when they are more arousing, enjoyable stimuli (valence > 0) become even more so when they are more arousing. Familiarity and figurativeness had FI_{main} values <0.1 ($FI_{main} = 0.08$; $FI_{main} = 0.07$, respectively), but had an important impact when considering their total effects ($FI_{total} = 0.42$; $FI_{total} = 0.36$, respectively). Familiarity had a linear positive effect, figurativeness a nonlinear, inversely U-shaped one with an optimum around a value of 4.8 (scale of 1–7). Since arousal and figurativeness were significantly correlated ($r_{part} = 0.31$), we can interpret the results as showing that at this subjective level of ratings, whenever readers find an idiom familiar and not too little or too much figurative, then they also like it and find it more arousing. Less familiar, and too little or too much figurative idioms are the more disliked the more they are arousing. Note that these are 'correlational' data though that do not establish causalities.

In sum, the likeability of idiomatic expressions is related to their perceived level of figurativeness, although not linearly; and it is modulated by their familiarity. For the NCPM, this means that interactions between key features of the upper route (familiarity) and the lower route (figurativeness) must be possible, some kind of cross-talk. Many idioms, however, can also be read 'literally', whatever their level of figurativeness. 'Kicking a bucket', or 'having a tomcat', after all, are literally not hard-to-understand expressions, at least when read out of context. 'It's raining cats and dogs' may pose more difficulties for a literal understanding, though. But a general question we were interested in is whether idioms, much like metaphors, also engage readers more strongly at the emotional level than literal expressions, as suggested by the correlational data regarding arousal ratings. The next study tried to shed more light on this issue.

Neuroimaging of the Processing of Idioms and Literal Control Sentences

In a study led by my former colleague from FU Berlin Francesca Citron, now at Lancaster University, we recently compared the processing of idiomatic and literal sentences read by 24 participants in an fMRI study to test the above hypothesis that idioms more likely evoke affective processes than literal expressions. Example items are: 'He does not leave any good hair at it.' (German idiom 'Kein gutes Haar daran lassen', meaning 'He has nothing good to say about it'.) or 'He can no longer tolerate that' (German literal control sentence: 'Er kann dies nicht länger tolerieren'). Idioms and literal sentences were unrelated but matched on a number of features like syntactic complexity, valence or arousal.

And indeed, we found that idioms elicited significantly enhanced activation of the left amygdala, and bilateral inferior frontal gyrus/IFG, the right temporal cortex and the right precentral gyrus. Thus, the comprehension of even highly conventionalized and familiar figurative expressions, namely idioms, recruits regions involved in emotional processing. Furthermore, we found a positive interaction between activation of the bilateral IFG and activation in the amygdala, suggesting that the stronger cognitive engagement for idioms (compared to literal sentences) is coupled with stronger involvement at the emotional level. The fact that we found no evidence for an activation of parts of the brain's reward system indicates that, as a whole our sample of idioms did not trigger the aesthetic trajectory. This can be due to the fact that the idioms and the literal controls were matched for valence and arousal. Also, the idiomatic meanings were very well known, with a mean rating of 6.5/7, making it unlikely that readers experienced artefact emotions like interest or fascination. Finally, we did not really expect this least creative class of figurative language to evoke notable aesthetic experiences. For the verbal stimuli used in the next study, this was a different matter.

Little Pearls of Wisdom – The Beauty of Proverbs

People love expressions like 'Speech is silver, but silence is golden', short sentences based on long experience, as Cervantes rightly remarked. This one not only juxtaposes two metaphors of the nominal type, it also features the stylistic devices of alliteration and syntactic parallelism (noun auxiliary adjective). Such 'little pearls of wisdom' called proverbs indeed typically are short, pithy statements contracting common experience into a memorable and often micropoetic form featuring metre, rhyme or metaphor) and believed to reflect a general reality or truth. As orally spreading memes of a special protoliterary genre, proverbs are characterized by the duality of written texts: a long-lasting verbal stability coupled with a context-dependent mutable cultural significance. They offer a mixture of prosodic, syntactic, semantic and pragmatic features that make them easy to pronounce – an enjoyable economical vocal production – and easy to remember. Their frequent and stable use in everyday life facilitates encoding, while their form properties help store and retrieve them. Moreover, apart from some individuals' use of them for bragging about their language skills or personal wisdom, for example by citing a Latin proverb, their parsimonious persuasiveness makes them a useful communication tool allowing to coordinate and manipulate speakers and harmonize or unite social groups. At any rate, they fulfil Jakobson's poetic function in speech acts and thus form a subcategory of poetics.

They also have an impact on our development and social life. Effectively using proverbs and figurative communication in general can promote personal and professional success, and proverb comprehension is both an important aspect of later language development and critical for acquiring cultural literacy, particularly difficult but helpful in a second language, as I can tell. The 'semantic energy and pragmatic potential – the notions and emotions riding in them – make proverbs' mental reception enjoyably invigorating'. Proverbs have a special integrative potential that 'reaches into the very structure of human awareness where cognition, emotion and volition often lose touch with each other to the detriment of all three.'[228] As either assertive or directive speech acts, they do not just describe situations or prescribe actions but tend to make simultaneous appeals to our elementary beliefs, feelings and desires from which our more complex worldviews, attitudes and projects originate. In sum, proverbs are useful 'memos' for social orientation and problem solving. The often-reported pleasures of proverb reception and re-production can be explicated with early psychological theories, for example, the *law of economic use* or *smallest measure of force*, or the principle of 'Ersparungslust' (*economy of expenditure*).[229] However, modern psychologists have long cherished the notion that understanding proverbs and figurative language processing in general requires abstract higher-order cognitive abilities (categorization and reasoning processes), for example, cause-effect reasoning ('He who lies down with dogs rises with fleas.'), dialectical vs. non-dialectical thought ('A man is stronger than iron and weaker than a fly' vs. 'What we speak of by day we dream of by night') or reasoning from a specific instance to a more general conclusion, as in 'One swallow does not make a summer'. Take the proverb 'A rolling stone gathers no moss': How much abstract thought is required to unpack this rather opaque 8-syllable meme to reveal the (hidden) general idea that someone who moves too much does not form many attachments rather than just referring to the situation of some physical interaction between a rolling stone and moss? What pleasurable 'aha moment' awaits the person discovering this hidden truth once the interplay of enough neurons and synapses has converged on a single attractor solving the riddle?[230]

Anti-proverbs

In terms of neuro-cognitive processing of literary adaptations, proverbs become particularly relevant when their 'poetic' and oftentimes anarchic offspring comes into focus: anti-proverbs. They represent a special case of linguistic adaptation – more or less artful alternations of original proverbs like 'A rolling stone gathers momentum'. As 'parodied, twisted, or fractured proverbs that reveal humorous or satirical speech play with traditional proverbial wisdom', anti-proverbs play with the recognition of the original proverb, giving pleasure to Freud's 'Id' by subverting the canonical meaning, but also requiring a successful completion of the memory task necessary for reading an adaptation as adaptation.[231]

We tested the latter conjecture in a neurocognitive study on German proverbs and their artfully defamiliarized adaptations (anti-proverbs) such as 'All roads lead to Rome' vs. 'All *sins* lead to Rome'. Thus, 'Wer wagt, gewinnt' (Who dares, wins) is a familiar German proverb, while 'Wer klagt, gewinnt' (Who laments, wins) is a defamiliarized, artful variation of this proverb: it keeps the rhyme and rhythm of the original, but changes the meaning by way of substituting only two letters. Anti-proverbs present a nice example of how background and foreground features can be combined in a single sentence and why the foregrounding construct should be treated as a complex, continuous multidimensional variable. On the one hand, due to their multiple rhetoric features, all proverbs can be considered foregrounded elements of language if seen against a background of non-rhetorical, non-figurative control sentences. On the other hand, anti-proverbs are foregrounded with regard to their originals. While the memory of the original proverb ('All roads lead to Rome') provides familiar background information, the one-word change ('sins') of the altered variant creates a foregrounding effect, a tension that should evoke affective and aesthetic reactions according to the NCPM.

However, when we tested this hypothesis, the first result was a positive correlation between explicit beauty judgements and stimulus familiarity: when participants rated groups of familiar proverbs together with the corresponding anti-proverbs (and other control conditions), overall they preferred the former over their artful adaptations. This confirmed the standard finding from empirical and theoretical aesthetics that familiarity is one feature affecting perceived beauty and aesthetic liking called *preference for familiarity*.[232] However, the correlation accounted for only about 30 per cent of variance in the beauty judgements, leaving two-third of variance to be explained by other factors. In addition, the observed correlation might also be explained with regard to the historical evolution of the material: A familiar proverb may be familiar precisely because specific aesthetic qualities account for its cultural success.

The crucial result of this study concerned the way our readers' brains responded to these anti-proverbs. When correlating the individual beauty ratings with functional neuroimaging data, we discovered that some spontaneous aesthetic evaluation takes place during reading, even if not required by the task (silent reading). Positive correlations were found in the dorsal striatum of the basal ganglia: the caudate nucleus. This is known to be a key structure of the dopaminergic system whose selective activation likely reflected the rewarding nature of our aesthetically pleasing anti-proverbs. This interpretation is supported by a study on sentences containing the aforementioned functional shifts that also found increased caudate nucleus activity in such sentences.[233]

To summarize, the main result of this innovative neuroimaging study on proverbs and their defamiliarized sisters, the anti-proverbs, supported both the *Panksepp–Jakobson hypothesis* and the hypothesis of an aesthetic trajectory – a key part of the lower route of the NCPM. Our finding of increased hemodynamic responses of two brain regions associated with reward and beauty to our anti-proverbs, the caudate nucleus and a part of the anterior cingulate cortex/ACC, provided first neuroimaging evidence for processes of spontaneous aesthetic evaluation during sentence reading. Thus, while our NNCs and idioms triggered affective but not aesthetic processes, our anti-proverbs evoked both. In the preceding 'semantics studies', I dealt with materials of varying length and verbal creativity. I shall close this chapter with an extensive study that took more than five years on some beloved materials by one of the most creative authors of all time.

Qualitative–Quantitative Analysis of Three Shakespeare Sonnets: An Eye-Tracking Study

Not marble, nor the gilded monuments
Of princes, shall outlive this powerful rhyme;

—William Shakespeare, Sonnets 55 (ll. 1–2)

The last and highlighted section of this chapter is special. It presents the work of a large interdisciplinary, international team of scholars from half a dozen countries, all fascinated by verbal art and willing to collaborate for many years to bridge the gaps between neuroscience and literary studies, psychology and education, and between qualitative and quantitative methods. In 2014, my nowadays favourite, and really tiny (~100 members only), scientific society, IGEL, organized a conference in Torino, Italy, which was the beginning of this formidable cross-disciplinary adventure I was lucky to become a part of thanks to the Norwegian reading expert Anne Mangen. She indeed convinced me there to join a group preparing the European grant 'Evolution of Reading in the Age of Digitisation (*E-READ*[234])' which started only a year later and laid the ground for this study on Shakespeare sonnets. Much like the final study of Chapter 6, this study aimed at examining the effects of the verbal art of Shakespeare sonnets on readers. However, this time we followed my earlier recommendation and used a multi-methodological approach that included all four methods discussed in Chapter 4, collecting not only direct and indirect offline data from questionnaires, ratings and memory tests, but also direct and indirect online data from line marking and eye tracking experiments. The data were collected by different teams in different countries (Germany, Italy, Hungary) and published in several articles.[235] Together, such an augmented data set puts greater constraints on the hypotheses and predictions based on the NCPM and the computational text analyses. After intensive discussions, three Sonnets from the Shakespeare corpus integrated in GLEC were chosen by an interdisciplinary team of experts. They took into account the considerable poetic quality of the poems and the representativeness of their motifs – not only within the corpus but also within European poetry in general – as well as their potential for evoking affective-aesthetic responses, as assessed by our computational analysis of all 154 sonnets[236]: Sonnets 27 ('Weary with toil [...] '), 60 ('Like as the waves [...] ') and 66 ('Tired with all these [...] '). Their universal motifs are: *love* as tension between body and soul (sonnet 27), *death* as related to time and soul (sonnet 60) and *social evils* during Shakespeare's life time (sonnet 66).

Sonnet 27

Weary with toil, I haste me to my bed,
The dear repose for limbs with travel tired,
But then begins a journey in my head
To work my mind, when body's works expired.
For then my thoughts from far where I abide
Intend a zealous pilgrimage to thee,
And keep my drooping eyelids open wide,
Looking on darkness which the blind do see.

Save that my soul's imaginary sight
Presents thy shadow to my sightless view,
Which like a jewel hung in ghastly night
Makes black night beauteous, and her old face new.
Lo thus by day my limbs, by night my mind,
For thee, and for my self, no quiet find.

Within the 'young man' or 'fair youth' group sonnets (1–126), sonnet 27 is the first of the rather quiet and meditative 'travel sonnets' where the poet writes about the agony of being separated from his friend on a journey. According to the earlier-cited work by Helen Vendler, its scenic rather than narrative drama about night, restlessness and jealousy offers few events but 'an inexhaustible supply of fresh scenes'. In our readers, sonnet 27 mainly evoked feelings of longing (love, passion, dependency), tiredness (exhaustion) and anxiety (discomfort, frustration, distress). Regarding categories of mental imagery reported by our participants after the act of reading, we found several that were mentioned repeatedly (at least eight times):

- HUMAN ACTION. The description contains an activity carried out by a human being such as 'Trying to see something but having your view obstructed'. (23 mentions)
- MENTAL ACTIVITY. A character doing mind-work like in 'Of a tired man lying in bed, unable to sleep as his thoughts wander'. (22 mentions)
- DARKNESS. The description refers to the lack of light in the image's scenery as in 'dark long nights'. (19 mentions)
- LOCATION. Localization of the characters/activity as in 'Trying to sleep on a hot night in a Spanish hotel'. (18 mentions)
- INABILITY. A character trying in vain to do something such as 'lying awake in bed at night; very tired, but unable to turn off your brain and fall asleep'. (16 mentions)
- TIREDNESS. The bodily feeling of exhaustion as in 'I thought of my own experiences with manual labour being physically exhausted after a day's work but mentally awake'. (13 mentions)
- TIME. Reference to an exact part of the day, such as 'The jewel in the night conjures up stars, but a shadow in the night conjures up almost the opposite'. (12 mentions)
- PERSON. Reference to a person. (9 mentions)
- FEELING. Reference to feelings. (8 mentions)

These nine examples shall suffice to give an idea about the frequency and diversity of mental images elicited by sonnet 27 in our readers. One can recognize elements of the dimensions of situation models (time, location, agent, action) generalizable across both prose and poetry texts, mixed with more specific poem-induced images (darkness, tiredness).

The Symbolic Imagery Index (SII) is a feature we had computed in our earlier computational analysis for all 154 Shakespeare sonnets. It refers to the occurrence of words associated with archetypal symbols such as sun, water or time.[237] A perfect example is one of the two lines with the highest choice likelihood of 83 per cent in the study reported in Chapter 6, line 9 of sonnet 135 ('Whoever hath her wish, thou hast thy will'): 'The sea all water, yet receives rain still'. This line has a high symbolic imagery index of 3 with the archetypal images of sea, water and rain. Applying the SII computation to sonnet 27, we find an even higher value of 4 as indicated by the following key words: 'night' (solar or nocturnal symbols), 'soul' (immortal/eternal/spiritual symbols), 'body' (body symbols) and 'black' (colour symbols). Of the three sonnets analyzed here, this is the highest, and indeed, only for sonnet 27, nine different imagery categories were mentioned. Thus, sonnet 27 prompted the most diverse array of mental images. A possible explanation for this is the presence of a person in the poem, to which readers can relate and project their own human conditions. Unlike the diversity of descriptions of the mental images, most of them told a story about a man or a couple, which reflected the high level of comprehension of the sonnet with a detailed, coherent situation model.

Sonnet 60

Like as the waves make towards the pebbled shore,
So do our minutes hasten to their end,
Each changing place with that which goes before,
In sequent toil all forwards do contend.
Nativity once in the main of light,
Crawls to maturity, wherewith being crowned,
Crooked eclipses 'gainst his glory fight,
And Time that gave, doth now his gift confound.
Time doth transfix the flourish set on youth,
And delves the parallels in beauty's brow,
Feeds on the rarities of nature's truth,
And nothing stands but for his scythe to mow.
And yet to times in hope, my verse shall stand
Praising thy worth, despite his cruel hand.

Sonnet 60, with its thematic triad 'waves', 'light' and 'nature' as models for life and their enemy, time, has an SII of 3 represented by: 'minutes' or 'time'

(time symbols), 'waves' or 'shore' (water symbols) and 'nature' (nature symbols). Quatrain 1 has a 'ritual and repetitive narrative' for which sections of Book XV of Ovid's *Metamorphoses* served as the template, while quatrain 2's tragic narrative is supposed to remind of the rise and fall of princes, as cued by the alliterative word chain 'crawls /crowned/ crooked / confound'. Its personified hero, time, is hybrid: first it gives, then it confounds and in quatrain 3 it becomes definitely the malign reaper. Sonnet 60 stands out for its prosody. It features a large number of *trochees*. These feet, with a metrically strong followed by a metrically weak syllabic position (/ ×) with regard to the *iambic* pattern (× /) typical for most lines of the sonnets, foreground the corresponding lines. As an example, the first two lines (LIKE as, SO do) beginning with trochees (but ending with a calm, iambic metre) draw readers' attention to and thus may evoke the image of the hastening of waves, as well as the attacks by eclipses and by time. Other reversed initial feet, according to Vendler, are CRAWLS to, CROOKèd, TIME doth, FEEDS on and PRAIsing.

In our readers, sonnet 60 mainly evoked feelings of hopelessness (25 mentions) and regret (14 mentions), but also of hope (13 mentions) and calmness (12 mentions). This just underlines what has been said before: Personal resonances evoked by a text are especially pronounced in poetry and indeed can lead to opposite emotional or aesthetic effects of the same poem. This favours a reader-specific approach like the one presented in Table 6.2 of Chapter 6. The mental images readers reported fell into six categories: 'nature' (34 mentions), 'person' (14 mentions), 'death' (12 mentions, as in 'It made me think of things slowing dying and becoming weaker'), 'human action' (11 mentions), 'change' (10 mentions of something becoming different like 'Wrinkles on a forehead as you age') and sound (8 mentions; auditory experiences like 'waves crashing on the shore'). Thus, sonnet 60 would have a slightly lower overall imagery diversity than sonnet 27, if these data can be generalized to other reader groups. Sonnet 60 also evoked the most topically focused images, that is, the images could be categorized around the lowest number of topics. Perhaps somewhat surprisingly, the same sonnet also generated the highest number of images; readers might have needed to search for an image to frame the abstract content. Moreover, only sonnet 60 featured sensory modality imagery among the most frequent categories: the images are rather picture-like impressions (like a kaleidoscope) with the hint of philosophical thoughts without coherent situations.

Table 8.1 summarizes the results of a qualitative–quantitative analysis carried out with the help of the 'Foregrounding Assessment Matrix' (FAM). This tool, inspired by the 4x4 matrix of Table 1.1, was developed during years of close collaboration with my literary scholar friends from the University of Catania, Grazia Pulvirenti and Renata Gambino. It provides a mapping of

Table 8.1 Foreground Assessment Matrix (FAM) as applied to sonnet 60.

	Phonological Foregrounding	*Morpho-syntactic Foregrounding*	*Rhetorical/Semantic Foregrounding*
Sub-Lexical Level	**Alliteration:** /th/ line 3; /ch/ line 3; /cr/ lines 6–7; /b/ line 10; /-and/ lines 12–13 **Assonance**: /waves/make/ line 1; /shall/stand/ line 13	**Prep./suffix denoting spacial direction:** -wards towards/to/forwards) lines 1,4.	
Lexical Level	**Anaphors:** And, lines 8–10–12–13 **Ploce:** time, lines 8,9,13; doth, lines 8–9; stand, lines 12–13		**Symbol**: Time = life, line 8; scythe = death, line 12
Inter-Lexical Level		**Syntactic Parallelism:** **noun+verb+prep (direction)** (waves make towards/minutes hasten to) lines 1–2. **Comparative clause (equivalence):** (Like as /so do) lines 1–2.	**Sinecdoche:** waves/ minutes, lines 1-2. **Metaphors:** main of light, line 5; maturity, line 6; glory, line 7; crooked eclipses, line 7; his gift, line 8; flourish set on youth, lines 9; delves the parallels in beauty's brow, line 10; nature's truth, line 11 **Metonimy:** my verse, line 13; his cruel hand, line 14. **Personification:** waves make, line 1; minutes hasten, line 2; minutes contend line 2, 4; nativity crawls to maturity, line 6; maturity crowned, line 6; crooked eclipses, line 7; eclipses fight, line 7; Time gave, line 8; Time confound, line 8; Time transfix, line 9, Time delves, lines 9, 10; Time feeds, lines 9, 11; nothing stands, line 12; scythe to mow, line 12; verse shall stand, line 13; verse praising, line 14.
Supra-Lexical Level		**Parenthetical clause:** once in the main of light/wherewith being crown'd, lines 5–6 **Enjambement:** Nativity/crawls, lines 6–7; Time/Feeds, lines 9–11; my verse/ praising, lines 13–14	**Simile**: Like as /So do, lines 1–2.

the multiple-layered foregrounded features to the lines of a sonnet, specifically pointing out their overlapping. In this study, we had asked our readers to mark the most striking line of each sonnet, and at least one line was chosen at least twice by our readers for each sonnet. The first line from sonnet 60 ('Like as the waves make towards the pebbled shore') is such a case. The FAM data for sonnet 60 summarized in Table 8.1 indicate that this line has the features: assonance, syntactic parallelism, comparative clause, synecdoche, personification and simile. These six features form what is called a 'foregrounded density field'.[238] According to the authors, a density field is a 'complex, continuous multidimensional variable structuring the tension and the trajectories of the reading act through the whole text, thus eliciting different kind of affective and aesthetic responses to the text'. Density fields can be interpreted as macro-attractors of the 'poetic function', their strength depending on the value (foregrounding at more or less levels) and distribution (evenly or with foci/hotspots) in the text. Of the three sonnets analyzed in our study, density fields are particularly visible for sonnet 60, as can be seen in the spatial clustering of foregrounding elements related to the key notion of 'time' in the poem.

Figure 8.7 illustrates this. Stretched across lines 2, 6–8, and 10, the main topic of time is linked to other semantic foregrounding elements in the text, effectively building the main meaning-making chain. In particular, the word 'time' as the centre of gravity of the semantic foregrounding is being related to:

- Two similes: Like as [...] / So do [...] (lines 1–2).
- One synecdoche: waves / minutes (lines 1–2).
- Seven metaphors: main of light (line 5); maturity (line 6); glory and crooked.

Eclipses (line 7); his gift (line 8); flourish set on youth (line 9); delves the parallels in beauty's brow (line 10); nature's truth (line 11).

- Two metonymies: my verse (line 13); his cruel hand (line 14).
- 13 personifications: waves make (line 1); minutes hasten (line 2); minutes hasten/contend (lines 2, 4); nativity crawls (lines 5, 6); maturity [...] crowned (line 6); crooked eclipses, eclipses fight (line 7); Time gave [...] confound (line 8); Time transfix (line 9), Time delves ... feeds (lines 9, 10); nothing stands and scythe to mow (line 12); verse shall stand (line 13); verse praising (line 14).

This example illustrates how complex and time-consuming close and middle reading stylistic analyses of literature can be. Now imagine we, as an interdisciplinary team of six or so persons, would do this for all 154 Shakespeare

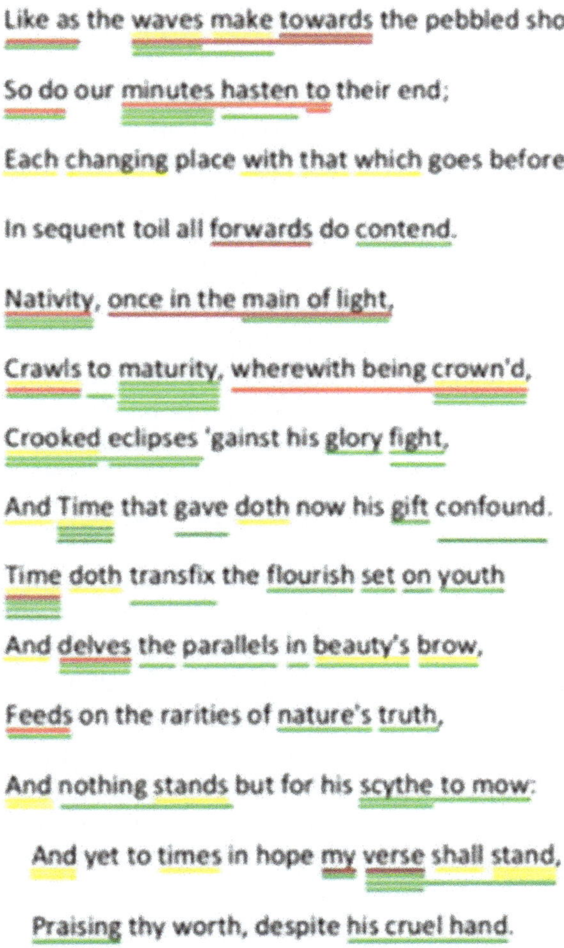

Figure 8.7 Density fields as a result of phonological (underlined in yellow), morphosyntactic (underlined in red), and semantic-rhetoric (underlined in green) figures identified in sonnet 60.

sonnets; it might take years. The task is not impossible for a single scholar, though, as evidenced, for instance, by Vendler's book on Shakespeare sonnets; an author who presumably spent a good deal of her professional career with the 154 sonnets. But imagine we would like to repeat such an analysis for thousands of poems by other authors, or entire novels like *The Great Gatsby*. Hard to imagine, if not impossible. This is why computational analyses have added value. They cannot provide the in-depth insights of close or middle reading; but they can provide very useful 'good enough' approximations of the affective-aesthetic qualities of thousands of texts from large literary corpora in comparatively little time.

Sonnet 66

Tired with all these for restful death I cry,
As to behold desert a beggar born,
And needy nothing trimmed in jollity,
And purest faith unhappily forsworn,
And gilded honour shamefully misplaced,
And maiden virtue rudely strumpeted,
And right perfection wrongfully disgraced,
And strength by limping sway disabled
And art made tongue-tied by authority,
And folly (doctor-like) controlling skill,
And simple truth miscalled simplicity,
And captive good attending captain ill.
Tired with all these, from these would I be gone,
Save that to die, I leave my love alone.

Vendler proposes the following couplet-summary of sonnet 66: 'Tired with all these (i.e., lines 2–12) from these would I be gone, Save that to die, I leave my love alone'. It features a world-weary, despairing list or procession of grievances of the state of the poet's society, the first half being only lament, the second adding an aspect of 'J'accuse', that is determination to name the causes for lament, as marked by the word 'by'. Thus, 'authority' made art tongue-tied, while 'Captain ill' is responsible for 'limping sway', or 'doctor-like folly'. Unlike most sonnets that feature a shift of thought or mood after the second quatrain at line 9, sonnet 66's mood only changes in the last line where the speaker proclaims his lover as the only thing that helps him survive. Accordingly, in our readers, sonnet 66 mainly evoked the negative feelings of despair (39 mentions), dissatisfaction (20 mentions), anger (14 mentions) and exhaustion (12 mentions), but also of love (13 mentions). The mental images readers reported could be subsumed under five categories: 'person' (11 mentions), 'feeling' (11 mentions), 'human action' (9 mentions), 'location' (9 mentions) and 'constrained by social issues' (societal restrictions/constraints as in 'A person tired of the wrongs going on in a society'). Sonnet 66 was the only one in our threesome that prompted 'feeling' as a frequent imagery category. This sonnet also evoked the highest number of perceived feelings. However, given that sonnet 66 evoked the lowest number of images of the three sonnets, this prominence of perceived feelings did not seem to support imagery development. The images related to sonnet 66 also have some story-like structure but compared to sonnet 27 the temporal setting and the main character are less concrete.

Methods

The procedure of one experiment run in our labs at FU Berlin used a mix of offline paper-pencil tasks with an online eye-tracking task. The paper-pencil tasks of the study included:

- *Demographic questions* (gender, age, handedness, field of academic studies, etc.)
- A *mood questionnaire* administered before reading the first of the three sonnets and after having read the last one. It assesses three bipolar dimensions of subjective feeling (depressed vs. elevated, calmness vs. restlessness, sleepiness vs. wakefulness) on a 7-point rating scale. The results suggested that our participants were in a neutral mood of calmness and slight sleepiness and that reading the sonnets did not induce longer-lasting changes in the global dimensions assessed by this scale.
- A *memory test* to assess whether readers paid attention to and tried to understand the poems. It asked readers to recognize rhyme-pairs and to indicate the topic(s) of the poem. Out of the overall 45 participants, two had to be excluded on the basis of their low memory test results.
- Valence and arousal scales to assess the global affective evaluation of the poem.
- A questionnaire assessing the readers' cognitive, affective and aesthetic responses.
- *Open questions* about emotions and mental imagery during reading, such as 'Please write down in your own words which feelings are described in the poem'.
- Two *marking tasks* in which the participants marked both the striking keywords and the most beautiful line for each sonnet.

The eye movements were recorded with a high-speed tracker that had a sampling rate of 1000 Hz (SR Research EyeLink 1000; SR Research Ltd., Mississauga, Ontario, Canada). Stimulus presentation was controlled by Eyelink Experiment Builder software (version 1.10.1630, https://www.sr-research.com/experiment-builder). Stimuli were presented on a 19-inch LCD monitor with a refresh rate of 60 Hz and a resolution of 1024 × 768 pixels. A chin-and-head rest was used to minimize head movements. The distance from the participant's eyes to the stimulus monitor was approximately 50 cm. We only tracked the right eye. Each tracking session was initialized by a standard 9-point calibration and validation procedure to ensure a spatial resolution error of less than 0.5° of visual angle. The 15 participants of this experiment read the sonnets at their own reading speed. They could go back and forth as often as they wanted within a maximum time window of two minutes (13/15 participants stopped reading before this deadline).

Prediction of the Most Beautiful Lines

In the earlier successful predictive modelling analysis of the choice of the most striking lines in the 154 sonnets, I had used 20 line features (see Chapter 6, Table 6.2). The question here was whether this 20-feature model could also predict line choice for this much larger sample of readers. This time, I took the mean data averaged across all 45 readers; discussing individual analyses simply would have filled too many pages. The answer to the question is: yes. The predictive accuracy of 95 per cent was as high as that of the other study with only six readers. This astonishing level of precision was mainly driven by two features with the highest main effect values, which both yielded clear monotonic relations with reader responses: choice likelihood increased with shorter *word length* ($FI_{tmain} = 0.17$), and higher *POS entropy* ($FI_{main} = 0.14$). Three other features came close to the 0.1 criterion: *semantic neighbourhood density*, *surprisal*, and *rime quotient*, while *sonority score*, *eigensimilarity* and *AAP* were of importance in combination with the others only (total effect >0.1). Thus, in this study, the 'average reader' most appreciated lines that have within-line rimes, a variable syntax with rather short, beautiful, surprising and nice-sounding words with fewer semantic associates. In sum, the 20-feature model appears robust (replicable) and valid. If it can be generalized from a sample of six readers to another independent sample of 45 readers, it is safe to assume that it will stand further empirical tests. The FI values may vary from reader to reader and sample to sample, as we have seen, but these 20 features appear to offer the right mix for successful applications to poetry reception, and I take this as a case of promising *feature engineering* for verbal art studies.

Prediction of Eye Movement Data

I now examine very different, indirect online response measures dear to many reading psychologists: gaze durations and mean total reading time (here: the sum of the gaze durations per line). Figure 8.8 shows a summary of the eye movement recordings of all readers of sonnet 60 carried out in the labs of the University of Catania by Daniela Giordano's team in the form of a heat map: the blobs indicate where the gaze has fixated most often, and the colour scheme codes gaze duration (dark blue to indigo > 400 ms, light green to red < 150 ms). There seems to be an evolution towards longer fixations from quatrain 1 to the couplet nicely reflecting the funnel-shaped movement and couplet bias discussed in Chapter 6.

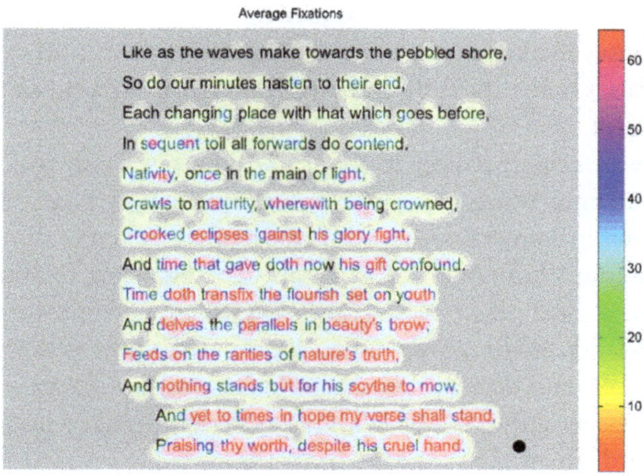

Figure 8.8 Fixations (gaze positions) of readers of sonnet 60. Average gaze duration is indicated by the colour bar.

Regressions

Figure 8.8 does not show the movements of the gaze that were illustrated in Figure 4.4 of Chapter 4. As a matter of fact, though, a major difference in the eye's behaviour between prose and poetry reading concerns the high number of backward saccades (regressions) both within- and across lines. Regressions are particularly informative because they often signal second attempts at meaning making, that is, another go after a failed or unsatisfying one. A typical value for prose reading is 10–15 per cent. In our eye-tracking study on Baudelaire's 'The Cats' mentioned earlier, the overall probability of regressions was 32 per cent, for the present three sonnets it was 45 per cent at the word level and 53 per cent at the line level. Thus, as predicted by the NCPM, reading via the lower route increases regression probability by a factor of 3 to 5, suggesting greater efforts at meaning-making together with processes of aesthetic evaluation or deeper (self-)reflection.

Keyword and Line Analysis

A first key question that can be answered by the data collected in this extensive multimethod study is whether there is any relationship between fixation probability or gaze duration and word-marking probability, on the one hand, and total reading time per line and line choice likelihood on the other. Do the readers in this study more often fixate – and/or spend more time on – those words that have been singled out as keywords? And do they spend more time on those lines that have been chosen as the most beautiful ones than on the other lines? In other words, is there any relation between implicit indirect online responses readers are not aware of (gaze duration) and explicit direct offline responses under the full control of readers? As far as I can tell, such an analysis is novel.

At the level of single words, in sonnet 27 'journey', 'toil' and 'jewel' were most frequently marked as keywords; in sonnet 60 it was 'time', 'nativity' and 'maturity', and in sonnet 66, the words most often picked in our experiment were: 'shamefully', 'unhappily' and 'disabled'. Regarding fixation probability, there was a clear effect of word type (POS): all content word categories (nouns, verbs, adjectives, adverbs) had high probabilities of $p > .9$; function words were split into determiners and prepositions ($p \sim .75$) vs. conjunctions ($p = .65$) and pronouns ($p = .59$). With respect to our initial question, I indeed found keyword effects on:

- Fixation probability: Keywords had a significantly higher mean probability of fixation ($p = .89$) than the other words ($p = .75$).
- Gaze duration: The mean gaze duration on keywords was significantly longer (910 ms) than that on the other words (670 ms).

Having found these keyword effects, would the same hold for lines marked as most beautiful? It does: 'beautiful' lines attracted longer total reading times than the non-marked lines, as shown in Figure 8.9. Line reading times increase in a monotonic and statistically significant fashion, albeit slightly nonlinearly, with the number of markings ($R^2 = 0.19$; $p < .02$). The lines most often marked were: 'Lo! thus, by day my limbs, by night my mind' from

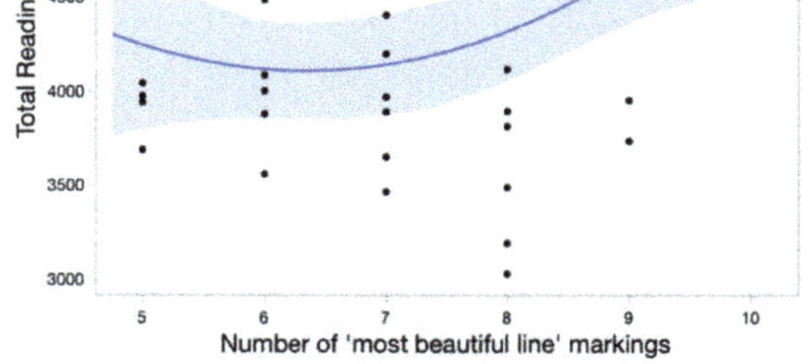

Figure 8.9 Total reading time for lines as a function of the number of 'most beautiful line' markings for sonnets 27, 60 and 66.

sonnet 27, 'And yet to times in hope my verse shall stand', from sonnet 60, and 'Tired with all these, from these would I be gone', from sonnet 66. Altogether, these results suggest that direct offline measures such as post-hoc (after the reading act) keyword and line markings can be used to predict indirect online measures (or vice versa) such as fixation probability, gaze duration and line reading time.

Of course, a Neurocomputational Poetics analysis must go further and ask which textual features contributed most to lines being marked and attracting longer reading times. As shown in Chapter 6, line choice can accurately be predicted by the 20-feature model already well-tried for all 154 sonnets. But can it also predict line reading times? If it can, it will be interesting to compare the features that most influenced eye-movement parameters with those that most influenced line choice: the first is an implicit measure, the second an explicit one, and it could very well be that they are shaped by different salient features. The results of this additional predictive modelling analysis revealed an almost perfect accuracy ($R^2 = 0.99$) with two features standing out by their FI_{main} values (0.12 and 0.11, respectively): number of nouns and rime quotient: lines with more nouns and within-line rimes attracted longer reading times. Surprisal ($FI_{tot} = 0.19$), sonority score ($FI_{tot} = 0.12$) and eigensimilarity ($FI_{tot} = 0.11$) only had important total effects in combination with the other features. In sum, although not identical in FI rank order, the big overlap between the features predicting line markings in the study of Chapter 6 and those predicting line reading times suggests that lines with a greater foregrounding potential or poeticity also take longer to read, which is in line with a central assumption of the NCPM: readers' affective-aesthetic appreciation requires more time. Future experiments manipulating these features in a controlled fashion will allow causal hypothesis testing for this finding.

Summary

In this extensive penultimate chapter, divided into a sound and a semantics section, I reported studies that shed light on the workings of the lower route of the NCPM. The first study provided background on the functioning of basal sublexical processes, demonstrating that syllables are uttered according to a preferred structure predicted by sonority theory, which is used in poetry and is presumably hard-wired in our brains. The next two sound studies provided both behavioural and neuroimaging evidence for the phonological iconicity assumption of Tenet 3 of the NCPM. Focussing on the prosody of entire poems, the last sound study produced data that can be interpreted by the *Bergson hypothesis* of humour that establishes an analogy between the metrical pattern of verses and dance movements. Degrading the phonological and prosodic *gestalt* of prototypical poetic verses has similar effects as body movements, which appear to degrade a living organism into a mere mechanically moving object, namely laughter. The semantics section presented a number of studies that improved our understanding of the features driving likeability and beauty experiences and their likely neuronal correlates, from single words to multiword expressions and entire poems. In the exemplary interdisciplinary study on three Shakespeare sonnets, finishing this chapter, I showed how a team of researchers can successfully apply a multimethod middle reading approach to learn about the text features and processes that determine how people come to understand and like poetry.

Chapter 9

CONCLUSIONS

This book started with the central claim of the NCPM that typically prose and poetry texts are processed by partially separable neuronal circuits that underlie different mental operations of implicit vs. explicit processing and lead to distinct experiences of immersion vs. aesthetic feelings, as well as different observable behaviours, such as shorter vs. longer gaze durations. In reality, there can be cases where this necessary simplification that enormously facilitates formal modelling and empirical investigation does not apply, but the majority of empirical data discussed in this book suggest its validity. Let me recap how verbal art reception functions according to the NCPM and point out its limitations.

Literary Reading According to the NCPM

To sum up the large model section of Chapter 2 in a nutshell, an individual act of literary reading could proceed like this: Influenced by the significative network, cultural norms (the codes in the metamodel) will bias the reader's inclination to start the reading act, as will multiple previous reading episodes that left their traces in the readers' semantic memory, her momentary mood and time budget, more permanent personality traits or the availability and richness of appropriate reading materials (an analogue or digital library). All this might contribute to creating (or not) a longing for the pleasures of ludic reading which can be biased in two directions. Either in favour of immersing oneself for longer periods of time (typically hours to days, with breaks in between) in enthralling text worlds inhabited by interesting characters entangled in suspenseful plots that activate the brain's affect and empathy networks and evoke emotions like joy, fear, hope, sympathy or anger. Although a minority, some personalities also might long for diving into conflicting inner monologues and rich inner life descriptions of his/her favourite character. Still others may favor more artful texts where suspenseful events are mingled with the occasional rhetorical device, most likely metaphor, hyperbole and idioms (cf. Chapter 5). Alternatively, the reader may be biased in the other direction and fancy some shorter 'reading through the ear' episodes (typically minutes to hours) due to a longing for rhythm and rhyme, amazing metaphors and puzzling figurative meaning in general, crazy syntax, multi-layered polysemy, feelings of interest, fascination, being moved, concernedness or extended (self-)reflective moments.

If the reader 'takes the immersion route', most likely associated with certain kinds of prose, his gaze will adopt a swift pace driven by 'what's next' moments and cliff-hangers, or, more generally, by a text full of familiar words of high imageability, strongly varying in emotional arousal and of high action density. Very likely, the reader longs for an emotional roller-coaster as those described in Chapter 6, no matter if it runs through a romance, adventure, mystery or science-fiction loop. If, in contrast, the reader engages in a formalist contract with author and text – thus 'taking the lower route' – this will cause a reading perspective characterized by a generally slower reading tempo, due to increased interest in and attention to surface or formal foreground features: whether for highly literary prose or for poetry texts, this reader is ready to fulfil Jakobson's 'poetic function', becoming open and sensitive to literary figure-ground constellations.

However, as you may guess, this is not an all-or-none decision. The contract with a poem by, say, Celan must and cannot be the same as the one with a novel by Tolstoy. Perhaps a pure or dominant 'poetic reading mode' can be maintained throughout an entire sonnet, but less so throughout a longer ballad like Coleridge's 'The Rime of the Ancient Mariner' and hardly during an entire novel. In the extreme, perhaps our brains cannot even maintain such a mode during the reading of a single line that presents a mix of simple and complex words. Take Celan's 'Black milk of daybreak we drink you evenings' from his 'Death Fugue'. The simple word 'of' in this line, as much as 'we' or 'drink', cannot 'not be read' – unless one closes one's eyes. Once reading has been learnt, one is 'doomed' to do it automatically. But not every word is read in an equally fluent or dysfluent way and some are even skipped: Familiarity, pronounceability, predictability, word type, case role, number and opacity of morphemes, imageability, associative density, semantic cohesion and a wealth of other quantifiable features addressed in Chapter 3 determine single word recognition, phrase comprehension and the general reading tempo. For instance, at the lexical level, the *spheric fragrance* of words, mentioned earlier, will play a role since words and the corresponding embodied thoughts and feelings are substance-controlled. This means that each word likely activates different functional brain networks, perhaps even never exactly the same twice, and surely 'black milk' will generate a different neural and oculomotor activity than 'of'. Just as 'milk' preceded by 'black' will not be processed as in the bigram 'sweet milk'. The (re)constructive mental processes will be different, and it is likely that 'of' will not be fixated by the strolling gaze at all, its meaning being inferred from context. In contrast, the gaze, after having jumped to and dwelled a while on the word 'daybreak', might well hop back to the word 'black', to gather more sensory information for the brain to close the meaning gestalt offered by this famous oxymoron. As mentioned earlier, whether a reader appreciates this line as poetry, babble or a disgust-arousing oxymoron depends on a wealth of factors and features, the Neurocomputational Poetics perspective attempts to specify as well as possible.

To what extent a reader is concerned by Celan's nine words, finds them beautiful or ugly, becomes interested in reading the rest of the poem – and possibly more of that writer – after this first line or the whole poem, and engages in a self-altering reading act depends as much on his apperceptive mass and many other factors as on the poeticity of the line. The same holds for the feeling of epiphany at the end of a line, poem or novel and the after-effects of the reading act described in the metamodel. The NCPM as a comprehensive general model abstracts from such micro-aspects of a complex act of verbal art reception which likely involve dynamic oscillations between its two routes that at present cannot be measured. We can only continue to learn as much as we can about the factors and features determining those aspects by improving our (neurocomputational) models and methods.

Future Developments

As evidenced by the studies in this book, computers are very good at discovering regularities in large databases and using the extracted knowledge for predicting types or other properties of texts (genres, authorship, valence, literariness, [...]), as well as human responses to those (neuronal, experiential, behavioural). They are not (yet as) good (as us) at constructing deeper meanings out of literature. What future developments of *chatGPT4* or similar AI tools will be able to do remains to be seen. Meanwhile, reading researchers from many different fields, like those who contributed the 19 chapters to the *Handbook of Empirical Literary Studies* Don Kuiken and I edited last year, should strive to extend and intensify cross-disciplinary collaborations, bringing together those sceptical of distant reading with those who appreciate its returns. In the foreword of our book, we wrote: 'There is still no theoretical model with sufficient breadth and precision to predict, for example, how specific experiential constructs are related to specific behavioural or physiological measures'. With the model and methods introduced in the present book, I hope to have opened doors leading to the falsification of this statement.

Even so, although the revised version of the NCPM introduced in Chapter 2 is both more specific and general than earlier versions,[239] it still may offer both too much and too little for some readers. Too much, because it addresses so many different aspects of the reading act – some of which are not yet sufficiently understood for computational modelling – that it is difficult to choose those one or two that most urgently deserve the investment of a doctoral thesis. And, as I can tell, there are only a handful of such theses in our field coming out each year. What is needed here is a concerted action by acolytes and scholars of the scientific study of literature, perhaps in the form of a special issue, for identifying the 'hot spots' that represent the biggest lacunae hindering theoretical progress. If the NCPM helps pushing this, I will not regret having spent so much time with it. On the other hand, the NCPM offers 'too little' because it could be more specific and computational in many respects. My grand goal is to develop a fully computational version of both the upper and lower route, but I do not know how many years it will take to implement a suspense mechanism in the upper route, for instance, or an efficient metaphor detection mechanism in the lower route.

Apart from model development, future work should aspire to the development of an open-access multilingual database that contains both an adequate number of literary texts (novels, poems) and of multi-method reader response data recorded during the reading of those texts. The *Algonauts project*[240] of my friend and successor at FU Berlin, Radek Cichy, is a neuroscientific model for what I have in mind for scientific studies of literature: a homepage offering open competitions (and rewards) for predicting open-access brain data using cutting-edge neurocomputational models. Thus, I would like to help create a similar homepage offering reading act data (ratings, eye tracking, neuroimaging) and challenging researchers to predict them as accurately as possible with computational models like those I have used in this book. Dealing with issues regarding copyright is not the least of the many challenges to tackle in this project. So, if some of you readers of this book want to join me in the *LitAlgonauts project*, do not hesitate to contact me via *sentiart0@gmail.com*.

REFERENCES

1. DFG Cluster of Excellence 302/1: 'Languages of Emotion' (2008–2014); DFG, FOR 778 TP4, JA 823/4-2 (Model-guided neurocognitive analysis of lexico-semantic and orthographic-phonological conflicts in implicit and explicit, 2009–2016); DFG-ANR (Emotions in time and space: the functional role of basic emotions in reading, 2011–2013); EU-COST Action IS1404 (Evolution of reading in the age of digitization [(-READ], 2015–2018); EU-ITN 'ELIT' (Empirical study of Literature Training Network, 2020–2024); DFG JA 823/14-1 'AFFDEC' (Neuronal representations as basis of affective and preference-guided decisions, 2021–2024); DFG SPP 2207 JA 823/12-1/2 Computational Literary Studies CHYLSA (Advanced sentiment analysis for understanding affective-aesthetic responses to literary texts: A computational and experimental psychology approach to children's literature, 2020–2026).
2. Willems, R., and Jacobs, A. M. (2016). Caring about Dostoyevsky: The untapped potential of studying literature. *Trends Cogn. Sci.*, 20, 243–245. doi: 10.1016/j.tics.2015.12.009
3. Schrott, R., and Jacobs, A. M. (2011). *Gehirn und Gedicht: Wie wir unsere Wirklichkeiten konstruieren (Brain and Poetry: How We Construct Our Realities)*. München: Hanser.
4. Van Peer, W. and Chesnokova, A. (2022). *Experiencing Poetry*. London: Bloomsbury Academics.
5. Tsur, R., Glicksohn, J., and Goodblatt, C. (1991). Gestalt qualities in poetry and the reader's absorption style. *J. Pragmat.*, 16(5), 487–500. doi: 10.1016/0378-2166(91)90138-N
6. Leech, G. N. (1969). *A Linguistic Guide to English Poetry*. New York, NY: Longman; Van Peer, W., Sopcak, P., Castiglione, D., Fialho, O., Jacobs, A.M., and Hakemulder, F. (2022). Foregrounding. In: *Handbook of Empirical Literary Studies*, eds. D. Kuiken & A.M. Jacobs. Berlin: de Gruyter, 145–176.
7. Neuhäuser, R. (1991). Sound and meaning in romantic poetry: Preseren's Poeziie. *Russian Lit.*, XXX, 85–108.
8. Peirce, C. S. (1931). *The Collected Papers* (eds. C. Hartshorne, P. Weiss, and A. Burks). Cambridge: Harvard University Press.
9. Jakobson, R. (1960). Closing statement: Linguistics and poetics. In: *Style in Language*, ed. T. A. Sebeok. Cambridge, MA: MIT Press, 350–377.
10. Jakobson, R. (1944). *Kindersprache, Aphasie und allgemeine Lautgesetze*. Uppsala. (Nachdruck: 1969 Frankfurt/M.: Suhrkamp).
11. Köhler, W. (1929). Gestalt psychology: An introduction to new concepts in modern psychology. Liveright.
12. Koestler, A. (1964). *The Act of Creation*. New York, NY: Macmillan.

13. Sternberg, M. (2003). Universals of narrative and their cognitivist fortunes (I). *Poetics Today* 24, 297–395.
14. Iser, W. (1976). *Der Akt des Lesens: Theorie ästhetischer Wirkung* (The act of reading). München: Fink Verlag.
15. Speer, N. K., Reynolds, J. R., and Zacks, J. M. (2007). Human brain activity time-locked to narrative event boundaries. *Psychol. Sci* 18, 449–455. doi: 10.1111/j. 1467-9280.2007.01920.x
16. Ryan, M. L. (2001). *Narrative as Virtual Reality. Immersion and Interactivity in Literature and Electronic Media*. Baltimore/London: Johns Hopkins University Press.
17. Bühler, K. (1934). *Sprachtheorie (Theory of Language)*. Stuttgart: G. Fischer.
18. Harnad, S. (1990). The symbol grounding problem. *Phys. D*, 42, 335–346. doi: 10.1016/0167-2789(90)90087-6
19. Wernicke, C. (1874/1977). The aphasic symptom complex (G. E. Eggert, Trans.) *Reprinted in Wernicke's Works on Aphasia: A Source Book and Review* (pp. 91–144). The Hague, Netherlands: Mouton.
20. Dehaene, S. (2005). Evolution of human cortical circuits for reading and arithmetic: The "neuronal recycling" hypothesis. In *From Monkey Brain to Human Brain*, eds. S. Dehaene, J.R. Duhamel, M.D. Hauser, & G. Rizzolatti. Cambridge, MA: MIT Press, pp. 133–157.
21. Wolf, M. (2007). *Proust and the Squid: The Story and Science of the Reading Brain*. New York: Icon Books.
22. Leder, H., Belke, B., Oeberst, A., and Augustin, D. (2004). A model of aesthetic appreciation and aesthetic judgments. *Br. J. Psychol*, 95, 489–508. doi: 10. 1348/0007126042369811; Pelowski, M., Markey, P. S., Forster, M., Gerger, G., and Leder, H. (2017). Move me, astonish me … delight my eyes and brain: The Vienna Integrated Model of top-down and bottom-up processes in Art Perception (VIMAP). *Phys. Life Rev.*, 21, 80–125.
23. Martindale, C., and Dailey, A. (1995). I.A. Richards revisited: do people agree in their interpretations of literature? *Poetics*, 23, 299–314. doi: 10.1016/0304-422x(94)00025-2
24. Fitch, W. T., Graevenitz, A. V., and Nicolas, E. (2009). Bio-aesthetics and the aesthetic trajectory: A dynamic cognitive and cultural perspective. In *Neuroaesthetics*, eds. M. Skov and O. Vartanian. Amityville, NY: Baywood, 59–102.
25. Miall, D. S., and Dissanayake, E. (2003). The poetics of babytalk. *Human Nat.*, 14(4), 337–364. doi: 10.1007/s12110-003-1010-4
26. Panksepp, J. (1998). *Affective Neuroscience: The Foundations of Human and Animal Emotions*. New York, NY: Oxford University Press.
27. Berridge, K. C., and Kringelbach, M. L. (2015). Pleasure systems in the brain. *Neuron*, 86, 646–664.
28. Knoop, C. A., Wagner, V., Jacobsen, T., and Menninghaus, W. (2016). Mapping the aesthetic space of literature "from below." *Poetics* 56, 35–49. doi: 10.1016/j. poetic.2016.02.001
29. Rowling, J. K. (1997). *Harry Potter and the Philosopher's Stone*. London: Bloomsbury. Rowling, J. K. (1998). *Harry Potter and the Chamber of Secrets*. London: Bloomsbury. Rowling, J. K. (1999). *Harry Potter and the Prisoner of Azkaban*. London: Bloomsbury. Rowling, J. K. (2000). *Harry Potter and the Goblet of Fire*. London: Bloomsbury. Rowling, J. K. (2003). *Harry Potter and the Order of the Phoenix*. London: Bloomsbury. Rowling, J. K. (2005). *Harry Potter and the Half Blood Prince*. London: Bloomsbury. Rowling, J. K. (2007). *Harry Potter and the Deathly Hallows*. London: Bloomsbury.

30. Oatley, K. (1994). A taxonomy of the emotions of literary response and a theory of identification in fictional narrative. *Poetics*, 23, 53–74. doi: 10.1016/0304- 422x(94)p4296-s; Cupchik, G., and Laszlo, J. (1992). *Emerging Visions of the Aesthetic Process: Psychology, Semiology and Philosophy*. New York: Cambridge University Press.
31. Hakemulder, F. (2013). Travel experiences: a typology of transportation and other absorption states in relation to types of aesthetic responses. In: *Wie gebannt: Aesthetische Verfahren der Affektiven Bildung von Aufmerksamkeit*, ed. J. Luedke. Berlin: Freie Universität, 163–182.
32. Marr, D. (1982). *Vision*. Boston: MIT Press.
33. McClelland, J.L., and Rumelhart, D.E. (1981). An interactive activation model of context effects in letter perception: part 1. An account of basic findings. *Psychol. Rev.*, 5, 375–407.
34. Hutzler, F., Kronbichler, M., Jacobs, A.M., and Wimmer, H. (2006). Perhaps correlational but not causal: No effect of dyslexic readers' magnocellular system on their eye movements during reading. *Neuropsychologia*, 44, 637–648; Thaler, V., Urton, K., Heine, Hawelka, S., Engl, V., and Jacobs, A. M. (2009). Different behavioral and eye movement patterns of dyslexic readers with and without attentional deficits during single word reading. *Neuropsychologia*, 47, 2436–2445.
35. Miall, D. S., and Kuiken, D. (1995). Aspects of literary response: A new questionnaire. *Res. Teach. English*, 29, 37–58.
36. Carroll, J. (2011). *Reading Human Nature: Literary Darwinism in Theory and Practice*. Albany, NY: SUNY PRINT.
37. Brink, T. T., Urton, K., Held, D., Kirilina, E., Hofmann, M., Klann-Delius, G., et al. (2011). The role of orbitofrontal cortex in processing empathy stories in 4-to 8-year-old children. *Front. Psychol.*, 2, 80. doi: 10.3389/fpsyg.2011.00080
38. Altmann, U., Bohrn, I. C., Lubrich, O., Menninghaus, W., and Jacobs, A. M. (2014). Fact vs fiction—how paratextual information shapes our reading processes. *Soc. Cogn. Affect. Neurosci.*, 9, 22–29. doi: 10.1093/scan/nss098
39. O'Sullivan, N., Davis, P., Billington, J., Gonzalez-Diaz, V., and Corcoran, R. (2015). "Shall I compare thee": The neural basis of literary aware ness, and its benefits to cognition. *Cortex*, 73, 144–157. doi: 10.1016/j.cortex.2015.08.014
40. Sperber, D., and Wilson, D. (1995). *Relevance: Communication and Cognition*. Oxford: Blackwell.
41. Shen, Y. (1997). Cognitive constraints on poetic figures. *Cogn. Linguist.*, 8, 33–71.
42. Jacobs, A. M., and Kinder, A. (2017). The brain is the prisoner of thought: A machine-learning assisted quantitative narrative analysis of literary metaphors for use in Neurocognitive Poetics. *Metaphor Symbol*, 32(3), 139–160. doi: 10.1080/10926488.2017.1338015
43. Perniss, P., and Vigliocco, G. (2014). The bridge of iconicity: From a world of experience to the experience of language. *Philos. Trans. Royal Soc., B: Biol. Sci.*, 369(1654), 20140179–20140179. doi: 10.1098/rstb.2014.0179 ; Schmidtke, D. S., Conrad, M., and Jacobs, A. M. (2014). Phonological iconicity. *Front. Psychol.*, 5, 1–6. doi: 10.3389/fpsyg. 2014.00080
44. Braun, M., Hutzler, F., Ziegler J.C., Dambacher, M., and Jacobs, A.M. (2009). Pseudohomophone effects provide evidence of early lexico-phonological processing in visual word recognition. *Human Brain Mapp.*, 30, 1977–1989.
45. Jacobs, A.M., and Kinder, A. (2022). Computational models of readers' apperceptive mass. *Front. Artif. Intell.*, 5, 718690. doi: 10.3389/frai.2022.718690

46. Jacobs, A. M. (2015). Neurocognitive poetics: Methods and models for investigating the neuronal and cognitive-affective bases of literature reception. *Front. Human Neurosci.*, 9, 186. doi: 10.3389/fnhum.2015.00186
47. Burke, M. (2011). *Literary Reading, Cognition and Emotion: An Exploration of the Oceanic Mind.* Philadelphia, PA: Taylor & Francis.
48. Pehrs, C., Deserno, L., Bakels, J. H., Schlochtermeier, L. H., Kappelhoff, H., Jacobs, A. M., Fritz, T., Koelsch, S., and Kuchinke, L. (2014). How music alters a kiss: superior temporal gyrus controls fusiform-amygdalar effective connectivity. *Soc. Cogn. Affect Neurosci.*, 9, 1770–1778.
49. Willems, R. M., Hagoort, P., and Casasanto, D. (2010). Body-specific representations of action verbs: Neural evidence from right- and left-handers. *Psychol. Sci.*, 21, 67–74. doi: 10.1177/ 0956797609354072
50. Jacobs, A. M., and Willems, R. (2019). The fictive brain: neurocognitive correlates of engagement in literature. *Rev. Gen. Psychol.*, 22, 147–160. doi: 10.1037/gpr0000106
51. Reisenzein, R. (2009). Emotions as metarepresentational states of mind: Naturalizing the belief–desire theory of emotion. *Cogn. Syst. Res.*, 10(1), 6–20.
52. Grainger, J., and Jacobs, A. M. (1996). Orthographic processing in visual word recognition: A multiple read-out model. *Psychol. Rev.*, 103, 518–565. doi: 10. 1037//0033- 295x.103.3.518
53. Miall, D. S., and Kuiken, D. (1998). The form of reading: empirical studies of literariness. *Poetics*, 87, 75–91.
54. Jacobs, A. M. (2015). Neurocognitive poetics: Methods and models for investigating the neuronal and cognitive-affective bases of literature reception. *Front. Human Neurosci.*, 9, 186. doi: 10.3389/fnhum.2015.00186
55. Richard L. W. *Clarke.* http://www.rlwclarke.net; LITS3303 Notes 10B.
56. Jacobs, A. M., and Willems, R. (2019). The fictive brain: neurocognitive correlates of engagement in literature. *Rev. Gen. Psychol.*, 22, 147–160. doi: 10.1037/gpr0000106; Liebig, J., Froehlich, E., Morawetz, C., Braun, M., Jacobs, A. M., Heekeren, H. R., and Ziegler, J. C. (2017). Neurofunctionally dissecting the reading system in children. *Dev. Cogn. Neurosci.*, 27, 45–57. doi: 10.1016/j.dcn.2017.07.002
57. Hsu, C.-T., Conrad, M., and Jacobs, A. M. (2014). Fiction feelings in Harry Potter: Haemodynamic response in the mid-cingulate cortex correlates with immersive reading experience. *Neuroreport*, 25, 1356–1361. doi: 10 .1097/WNR.0000000000000272
58. Hofmann, M. J., and Jacobs, A. M. (2014). Interactive activation and competition models and semantic context: From behavioral to brain data. *Neurosci. Biobehav. Rev.*, 46, 85–104. doi: 10.1016/j.neubiorev.2014.06.011
59. Lüdtke, J., Meyer-Sickendieck, B., and Jacobs, A. M. (2014). Immersing in the stillness of an early morning: Testing the mood empathy hypothesis of poetry reception. *Psychol. Aesth. Creativ. Arts*, 8, 363–377. doi: 10.1037/a0036826
60. Brewer, W. F., and Lichtenstein, E. H. (1982). Stories are to entertain: A structural-affect theory of stories. *J. Pragmat.*, 6, 473–486. doi: 10.1016/0378-2166(82) 90021-2
61. Lehne, M., Engel, P., Rohrmeier, M., Menninghaus, W., Jacobs, A. M., and Koelsch, S. (2015). Reading a suspenseful literary text activates brain areas related to social cognition and predictive inference. *Plos ONE*, 10(5). doi: 10.1371/journal .pone.0124550
62. Jacobs, A. M., & Lüdtke, J. (2017). Immersion into narrative and poetic worlds. In *Narrative Absorption*, eds. F. Hakemulder, M. M. Kuijpers, E. S. H. Tan, K. Bálint, & M. M. Doicaru. Benjamins, 69–96.

63. Tukachinsky Forster, R. (2022). Character engagement and identification. In: D. Kuiken & A.M. Jacobs (eds.), *Handbook of Empirical Literary Studies*. Berlin: de Gruyter, 251–278.
64. Batson, C. (2009). These things called empathy: Eight related but distinct phenomena. In *The Social Neuroscience of Empathy*, eds. J. Decety & W. Ickes. Cambridge: The MIT Press, 3–16.
65. Wispé, L. (1986). The distinction between sympathy and empathy: To call forth a concept, a word is needed. *J. Personal. Soc. Psychol.*, 50, 314–321.doi: 10.1037/0022-3514.50.2.314
66. Walter, H. (2012). Social cognitive neuroscience of empathy: Concepts, circuits, and genes. *Emot. Rev.*, 4(1), 9–17. doi: 10.1177/1754073911421379
67. Stockwell, P. (2002) *Cognitive Poetics*. London: Routledge.
68. Kutas, M., and Federmeier, K. D. (2011). Thirty years and counting: finding meaning in the N400 component of the event-related brain potential (ERP). *Annu. Rev. Psychol.*, 62, 621–647. doi: 10.1146/annurev.psych.093008. 131123
69. Bohrn, I. C., Altmann, U., Lubrich, O., Menninghaus, W., and Jacobs, A. M. (2012b). Old proverbs in new skins—An FMRI study on defamiliarization. *Front. Psychol.*, 3, 204. doi: 10.3389/fpsyg.2012.00204; Bohrn, I. C., Altmann, U., Lubrich, O., Menninghaus, W., and Jacobs, A. M. (2013). When we like what we know—A parametric fMRI analysis of beauty and familiarity. *Brain Lang.*, 124, 1–8. doi: 10.1016/j.bandl.2012.10.003
70. Keidel, J. L., Davis, P. M., Gonzalez-Diaz, V., Martin, C. D., and Thierry, G. (2013). How Shakespeare tempests the brain: Neuroimaging insights. *Cortex*, 49, 913–919. doi: 10.1016/j.cortex.2012.03.011
71. Fechino, M., Jacobs, A. M., and Lüdtke, J. (2020). Following in Jakobson and Lévi-Strauss' footsteps: A neurocognitive poetics investigation of eye movements during the reading of Baudelaire's 'Les Chats'. *J. Eye Move. Res.*, 13(3). doi: 10.16910/jemr.13.3.4
72. Jakobson, R., and Lévi-Strauss, C. (1962). 'Les Chats' de Charles Baudelaire. *L'Homme*, 2(1), 5–21. doi: 10.3406/hom.1962.366446
73. Schrott, R., and Jacobs, A. M. (2011). *Gehirn und Gedicht: Wie wir unsere Wirklichkeiten konstruieren (Brain and Poetry: How We Construct Our Realities)*. München: Hanser.
74. Turner, F., and Pöppel, E. (1983). The neural lyre: poetic meter, the brain and time. *Poet. Mag.*, 12, 277–309.
75. Hanauer, D. (1997). Poetic text processing. *J. Lit. Sci.*, 26, 157–172; Burke, M. (2011). *Literary Reading, Cognition and Emotion: An Exploration of the Oceanic Mind*. Philadelphia, PA: Taylor & Francis.
76. Jacobs, A. M., Lüdtke, J., Aryani, A., Meyer-Sickendiek, B., and Conrad, M. (2016). Mood-empathic and aesthetic responses in poetry reception: A model-guided, multilevel, multimethod approach. *Sci. Study Lit.*, 6(1), 87–130. doi:10.1075/ssol.6.1.06jac
77. Bransford, J. D., and Frank, J. J. (1976). Toward a framework for understanding learning. In *The Psychology of Learning and Motivation*, ed. G. H. Bower. New York, NY: Academic Press, 10.
78. Leder, H., Carbon, C. C., and Ripsas, A. (2006). Entitling art: Influence of different types of title information on understanding and appreciation of paintings. *Acta Psychol.*, 121, 176–198.
79. McQuarrie, E. F., and Mick, D. G. (1996). Figures of rhetoric in advertising language. *J. Consum. Res.*, 19, 424–438. doi: 10.1086/209459

80. Lausberg, H. (1990). *Handbuch der Literarischen Rhetorik. Eine Grundlegung der Literaturwissenschaft (Handbook of Literary Rhetoric)*. Stuttgart: Steiner.
81. Citron, F. M. M., and Goldberg, A. E. (2014). Metaphorical sentences are more emotionally engaging than their literal counterparts. *J. Cogn. Neurosci.*, 26, 2585–2595. doi: 10.1162/jocn_a_00654
82. Citron, F. M. M., Cacciari, C., Funcke, J. M., Hsu, C.-T., and Jacobs, A. M. Idiomatic expressions evoke stronger emotional responses in the brain than literal sentences, *Neuropsychologia* (2019). doi: 10.1016/j.neuropsychologia.2019.05.020.
83. Forgács, B., Bohrn, I. C., Baudewig, J., Hofmann, M. J., Pléh, C., and Jacobs, A. M. (2012). Neural correlates of combinatorial semantic processing of literal and figurative noun-noun compound words. *Neuroimage*, 63, 1432–1442. doi: 10.1016/j.neuroimage.2012.07.029
84. Hofmann, M. J., Kuchinke, L., Biemann, C., Tamm, S., and Jacobs, A. M. (2011). Remembering words in context as predicted by an associative read-out model. *Front. Psychol* 2, 252. doi: 10.3389/fpsyg.2011.00252
85. Hofmann, M. J., and Jacobs, A. M. (2014). Interactive activation and competition models and semantic context: from behavioral to brain data. *Neurosci. Biobehav. Rev.*, 46, 85–104. doi: 10.1016/j.neubiorev.2014.06.011
86. Leech, G. and Short, M. (2007). *Style in Fiction*. London: Pearson.
87. Vendler, H. (1997). *The Art of Shakespeare's Sonnets*. Cambridge, MA: Harvard University Press.
88. Moretti, F. (2000). Conjectures on world literature. *New Left Rev.*, 1, 54–68. https://newlef-treview.org/issues/II1/articles/franco-moretti-conjectures-on-world-literature
89. Höhle, B., Bijeljac-Babic, R., Herold, B., Weissenborn, J., and Nazzi, T. (2009). Language specific prosodic preferences during the first half year of life: Evidence from German and French infants. *Infant Behav. Dev.*, 32, 262–274.
90. Keidel, J. L., Davis, P. M., Gonzalez-Diaz, V., Martin, C. D., and Thierry, G. (2013). How Shakespeare tempests the brain: Neuroimaging insights. *Cortex*, 49, 913–919. doi: 10.1016/j.cortex.2012.03.011
91. Elman, J. L. (2004). An alternative view of the mental lexicon. *Trends Cogn. Sci.*, 8, 301–306.
92. https://radimrehurek.com/gensim/models/word2vec.html
93. https://huggingface.co/docs/transformers/model_doc/bert
94. Jacobs, A. M. (2018) The Gutenberg English Poetry Corpus: exemplary quantitative narrative analyses. *Front. Digit. Humanit.* 5, 5. doi: 10.3389/fdigh.2018.00005; Jacobs, A. M., and Kinder, A. (2022). Computational analyses of the topics, sentiments, literariness, creativity and beauty of texts in a large Corpus of English Literature. arXiv:2201.04356 [cs.CL], https://doi.org/10.48550/arXiv.2201.04356.
95. Van der Maaten, L. J. P., and Hinton, G. E. (2008). Visualizing data using t-SNE. *J. Mach. Learn. Res.*, 9, 2431–2456.
96. Jacobs, A. M., and Kinder, A. (2022) Computational models of readers' apperceptive mass. *Front. Artif. Intell.*, 5, 718690. doi: 10.3389/frai.2022.718690
97. https://wordnet.princeton.edu/
98. Kintsch, W. (2008). How the mind computes the meaning of metaphor: a simulation based on LSA. In *Handbook of Metaphor and Thought*, ed. R. Gibbs. New York, NY: Cambridge University Press, 129–142.
99. https://readable.com/readability/flesch-reading-ease-flesch-kincaid-grade-level/
100. http://cohmetrix.com/

101. Võ, M. L. H., Conrad, M., Kuchinke, L., Urton, K., Hofmann, M. J., and Jacobs, A. M. (2009). The Berlin affective word list reloaded (BAWL-R). *Behav. Res. Methods*, 41, 534–539. doi: 10.3758/BRM.41.2.534; Võ, M. L. H., Jacobs, A. M., and Conrad, M. (2006). Cross-validating the Berlin affective word list. *Behav. Res. Methods*, 38, 606–609. doi: 10.3758/bf03193892; Jacobs, A. M., Võ, M. L.-H., Briesemeister, B. B., Conrad, M., Hofmann, M. J., Kuchinke, L., Lüdtke, J., and Braun, M. (2015). 10 years of BAWLing into affective and aesthetic processes in reading: What are the echoes? *Front. Psychol.*, 6, 714. doi: 10.3389/fpsyg.2015.00714
102. Sylvester, T., Braun, M., Schmidtke, D., and Jacobs, A. M. (2016) The Berlin Affective Word List for Children (kidBAWL): Exploring processing of affective lexical semantics in the visual and auditory modalities. *Front. Psychol.*, 7, 969. doi: 10.3389/fpsyg.2016.00969; Sylvester, T., Liebig, J., and Jacobs, A. M. (2021). Neural correlates of affective contributions to lexical decisions in children and adults. *Sci. Rep.*, 11, 945. doi: 10.1038/s41598-020-80359-1;Sylvester, T., Liebig, J., and Jacobs, A. M. (2021). Neuroimaging of valence decisions in children and adults. *Dev. Cogn. Neurosci.*, 48, 100925. doi: 10.1016/j.dcn.2021.100925
103. Anderson, C. W., and McMaster, G. E. (1982). Computer assisted modeling of affective tone in written documents. *Comput. Hum.*, 16, 1–9. doi: 10.1007/BF02259727
104. Archer, J., and Jockers, M.L. (2017). *The Bestseller Code*. New York: St. Martin's Press.
105. https://github.com/thunlp/topical_word_embeddings/blob/master/TWE-1/gensim/models/ldamallet.py
106. http://www.forwardflow.org/
107. van Cranenburgh, A., van Dalen-Oskam, K., and van Zundert, J. (2019). Vector space explorations of literary language. *Lang. Resour. Eval.*, 53(4), 625–650. https://doi. org/10.1007/s10579-018-09442-4
108. Appel, M., Hanauer, D., Hoeken, H., van Krieken, K., Richter, T., and Sanders, J. (2021). The psychological and social effects of literariness: Formal features and paratextual information. In *Handbook of Empirical Literary Studies*, eds. D. Kuiken & A. M. Jacobs. De Gruyter, 177–202; Salgaro, M. (2018). Historical introduction to the special issue on literariness. *Sci. Study Lit.*, 8(1), 5–17. https://doi.org/10.1075/ssol.00005.sal; Herrmann, J.B., Jacobs, A.M., and Piper, A. (2022). Computational Stylistics. In: *Handbook of Empirical Literary Studies,* eds. D. Kuiken & A.M. Jacobs. Berlin: de Gruyter, 451-486.
109. Kintsch, W. (2012). Musing about beauty. *Cogn. Sci.* 36, 635–654. doi: 10.1111/j. 1551-6709.2011.01229.x
110. Schmidhuber, J. (1997). Low-complexity art. Leonardo. *J. Int. Soc. Arts Sci. Technol.*, 30, 97–103.
111. https://en.wikipedia.org/wiki/Hellinger_distance
112. Jacobs, A. M., and Kinder, A. (2022). Computational analyses of the topics, sentiments, literariness, creativity and beauty of texts in a large Corpus of English Literature. arXiv:2201.04356 [cs.CL], https://doi.org/10.48550/arXiv.2201.04356.
113. https://www.thereader.org.uk/about-us/
114. https://thegreatestbooks.org/authors/4737
115. Ng, A., Maarten, W. B., Leonid, S., and Boyang, L. (2018). Predicting personality from book preferences with user-generated content labels. *IEEE Trans. Affect. Comput.,* 1–12.
116. Davis, M. H. (1983). Measuring individual differences in empathy: Evidence for a multidimensional approach. *J. Personal. Soc. Psychol.*, 44(1), 113. doi: 10.1037/0022-3514.44.1.113

117. Appel, M., Hanauer, D., Hoeken, H., van Krieken, K., Richter, T., and Sanders, J. (2021). The psychological and social effects of literariness: Formal features and paratextual information. In *Handbook of Empirical Literary Studies*, eds. D. Kuiken & A. M. Jacobs. De Gruyter, 177–202.
118. Stanovich, K. E., and West, R. F. (1989). Exposure to print and orthographic processing. *Read. Res. Q.*, 24, 402–433. doi: 10.2307/747605
119. Tellegen, A., and Atkinson, G. (1974). Openness to absorbing and self-altering experiences ("absorption"), a trait related to hypnotic susceptibility. *Journal of Abnormal Psychology*, 83(3), 268–277. doi: 10.1037/h0036681
120. Kuijpers, M. M., Douglas, S., and Kuiken, D. (2018). Personality traits and reading habits that predict absorbed narrative fiction reading. *Psychol. Aesth. Creativity Arts.* 13(1), 74–88. doi: 10.1037/aca0000168
121. Hofmann, M. J., Jansen, M.T., Wigbels, C., and Jacobs, A. M. (2023). Individual internet search history predicts openness, interest, knowledge and intelligence. Talk given at the TeaP 2023, Trier, Germany.
122. Lüdtke, J., Froehlich, E., Jacobs, A. M., and Hutzler, F. (2019). The SLS-Berlin: Validation of a German computer-based screening test to measure reading proficiency in early and late adulthood. *Front. Psychol.*, 10:1682. doi: 10.3389/fpsyg.2019.01682
123. Jacobs, A. M. (2015). The scientific study of literary experience: Sampling the state of the art. *Sci. Stud. Lit.*, 5, 139–170. doi: 10.1075/ssol.5.2.01jac ; Jacobs, A. (2016). The scientific study of literary experience and neuro-behavioral responses to Literature: Reply to Commentaries. *Sci. Stud. Lit.*, 6, 164–174. doi: 10.1075/ssol.6.1.08jacissn2210-4372
124. https://scikit-learn.org/stable/
125. https://christophm.github.io/interpretable-ml-book/; https://en.wikipedia.org/wiki/Granger_causality
126. Jacobs, A. M., Schuster, S., Xue, S., and Lüdtke, J. (2017). What's in the brain that ink may character …: A quantitative narrative analysis of Shakespeare's 154 sonnets for use in neurocognitive poetics. *Sci. Stud. Lit.*, 7, 4–51. doi: 10.1075/ ssol.7.1.02jac
127. Cop, U., Dirix, N., Drieghe, D., and Duyck, W. (2017). Presenting GECO: An eye-tracking corpus of monolingual and bilingual sentence reading. *Behav. Res. Methods*, 49(2), 602–615.
128. Kaakinen, J. K., Werlen, E., Kammerer, Y., Acartürk, C., Aparicio, X., Baccino, T., et al. (2022). IDEST: International Database of Emotional Short Texts. *PLoS ONE*, 17(10), e0274480. doi: 10.1371/journal.pone.0274480
129. https://osf.io/9tga3/
129. https://en.wikipedia.org/wiki/Confidence_interval#:~:text=In%20frequentist%20statistics%2C%20a%20confidence,99%25%2C%20are%20sometimes%20used.
131. Green, M. C., and Brock, T. C. (2000). The role of transportation in the persuasiveness of public narratives. *J. Personal. Soc. Psychol.*, 79(5), 701–721. doi: 10.1037/0022-3514.79.5.701; Busselle, R., and Bilandzic, H. (2009). Measuring narrative engagement. *Media Psychol.*, 12, 321–347. doi: 10.1080/15213260903287259; Kuijpers, M. M., Hakemulder, F., Tan, E. S., and Doicaru, M. M. (2014). Exploring absorbing reading experiences: Developing and validating a self-report scale to measure story world absorption. *Sci. Stud. Lit.*, 4(1), 89–122. doi: 10.1075/ssol.4.1.05kui; Appel, M., Koch, E., Schreier, M., and Groeben, N. (2002). Aspekte

des Leseerlebens: Skalenentwicklung [Assessing experiential states during reading: Scale development]. *Zeitschrift für Medienpsychologie* [J. Media Psychol.], 14, 149–154 .doi: 10.1026//1617-6383.14.4.149 .

132. Kuiken, D., Campbell, P., and Sopcák, P. (2012). The experiencing questionnaire: Locating exceptional reading moments. *Sci. Stud. Lit.*, 2, 243–272. doi: 10.1075/ssol.2.2.04kui
133. Lüdtke, J., Meyer-Sickendieck, B., and Jacobs, A. M. (2014). Immersing in the stillness of an early morning: Testing the mood empathy hypothesis of poetry reception. *Psychol. Aesth. Creativity Arts,* 8, 363–377. doi: 10.1037/a0036826
134. Papp-Zipernovszky, O., Mangen, A., Jacobs, A.M., and Lüdtke, J. (2021). Shakespeare sonnets reading: an empirical study of emotional responses. *Lang. Lit.*, 0(0), 1–29. doi: 10.1177/09639470211054647
135. Magyari, L., Mangen, A., Kuzmičová. A., Jacobs, A. and Lüdtke, J. (2020). Eye movements and mental imagery during reading of literary texts with different narrative styles. *J. Eye Move. Res.*, 13(3), 3.
136. Wassiliwizky, E., Koelsch, S., Wagner, V., Jacobsen, T., and Menninghaus, W. (2017). The emotional power of poetry: Neural circuitry, psychophysiology and compositional principles. *Soc. Cogn. Affect. Neurosci.*, 12(8), 1229–1240. doi: 10.1093/scan/nsx069
137. Xue, S., Lüdtke,J., Sylvester, T., and Jacobs, A. M. (2019). Reading Shakespeare sonnets: Combining quantitative narrative analysis and predictive modelling: An eye tracking study. *J. Eye Move. Res.*, 12(5). doi: 10.16910/jemr.12.5.2 ; Xue, S., Jacobs, A. M., and Lüdtke, J. (2020). What is the difference? Rereading Shakespeare's sonnets: An eye tracking study. *Fron. Psychol.*, 11, 421. doi: 10.3389/ fpsyg.2020.00421
138. Jacobs, A.M., and Willems, R. (2019). The fictive brain: neurocognitive correlates of engagement in literature. *Rev. Gen. Psychol.*, 22, 147–160. doi: 10.1037/gpr0000106
139. Bohrn, I. C., Altmann, U., Lubrich, O., Menninghaus, W., and Jacobs, A. M. (2012). Old proverbs in new skins – an FMRI study on defamiliarization. *Front. Psychol.*, 3, 204. doi: 10.3389/fpsyg.2012.00204; Bohrn, I. C., Altmann, U., Lubrich, O., Menninghaus, W., and Jacobs, A. M. (2013). When we like what we know – a parametric fMRI analysis of beauty and familiarity. *Brain Lang.*, 124, 1–8. doi: 10.1016/j.bandl.2012.10.003; Menninghaus, W., Bohrn, I. C., Altmann, U., Lubrich, O., and Jacobs, A. M. (2014). Sounds funny? Humor effects of phonological and prosodic figures of speech. *Psychol. Aesth. Creativity Arts,* 8(1), 71–76. https://dx.doi.org/10.1037/a0035309
140. Jacobs, A. M. (2015). The scientific study of literary experience: Sampling the state of the art. *Sci. Stud. Lit.*, 5, 139–170. doi: 10.1075/ssol.5.2.01jac
141. Jakobson, R., and Waugh, L. R. (2002). *The Sound Shape of Language* (3rd ed.). Mouton de Gruyter.
142. Limbach, J. (2004). *Das Schönste Deutsche Wort (The most beautiful German Word).* Freiburg: Verlag Herder.
143. Whissell, C. (1996). Traditional and emotional stylometric analysis of the songs of Beatles Paul McCartney and John Lennon. *Comput. Hum.*, 30, 257–265. doi: 10.1007/bf00055109
144. Aryani, A., Conrad, M., Schmidtke, D., and Jacobs, A. (2018). Why'piss' is ruder than'pee'? The role of sound in affective meaning making. *PloS One*, 13(6), e0198430. doi: 10.1371/journal.pone.0198430; Aryani, A., Hsu, C. T., and Jacobs, A. M. (2018). The sound of words evokes affective brain responses. *Brain Sci.*, 8(6), 94; Aryani, A.,

Hsu, C.-T., Jacobs, A. M. (2019). Affective iconic words benefit from additional sound–meaning integration in the left amygdala. *Hum. Brain Mapp.*, 1–12; Aryani, A., and Jacobs, A. M. (2018). Affective congruence between sound and meaning of words facilitates semantic decision. *Behav. Sci. (Basel, Switzerland)*, 8(6).

145. Shapiro, M. (1998), Sound and Meaning in Shakespeare's Sonnets. *Language*, 74, 81–103.
146. Clements, G. N. (1990). The role of sonority in core syllabification. In *Papers in Laboratory Phonology I. Between the Grammar and Physics of Speech*, eds. J. Kingston & M. E. Beckman. Cambridge: CUP, 283–333.
147. https://github.com/jsfalk/prosodic1b
148. Epstein, R. (2004). Consciousness, art and the brain: lessons from Marcel Proust. *Conscious. Cogn.*, 13, 213–240. doi: 10.1016/s1053-8100(03)00006-0
149. Jacobs, A. M. (2017). Quantifying the beauty of words: A neurocognitive poetics perspective. *Front. Hum. Neurosci.*, 11, 622. doi: 10.3389/fnhum.2017.00622
150. https://github.com/matinho13/SentiArt
151. Katz, A., Paivio, A., Marschark, M., and Clark, J. (1988). Norms for 204 literary and 260 non-literary metaphors on psychological dimensions. *Metaphor Symb. Activ.*, 3(4), 191–214.
152. Jacobs, A. M., and Kinder, A. (2018). What makes a metaphor literary? Answers from two computational studies. *Metaphor Symb.*, 33(2), 85–100. doi: 10.1080/10926488.2018.1434943
153. Wainwright, J. (2011). *Poetry: The Basics.* London: Routledge.
154. Simonton, D. K. (1990). Lexical choices and aesthetic success: A computer content analysis of 154 Shakespeare sonnets. *Comput. Humanit.*, 24, 254–261. doi: 10. 1037/a0014632
155. Fodor, J. D. (2002, April). Psycholinguistics cannot escape prosody. Paper presented at the meeting of Speech Prosody, Aix-en-Provence, France.
156. Van Orden, G.C. (1987). A ROWS is a ROSE: Spelling, sound, and reading. *Memory Cogn.*, 15, 181–198; Ziegler, J., Van Orden, G.C., and Jacobs, A. M. (1997). Phonology can help or hurt the perception of print. *J. Exp. Psychol.: Human Percept. Perform.*, 23, 845–860; Braun, M., Hutzler, F., Ziegler J. C., Dambacher, M., and Jacobs, A. M. (2009). Pseudohomophone effects provide evidence of early lexico-phonological processing in visual word recognition. *Human Brain Mapp.*, 30, 1977–1989.
157. https://openai.com/blog/chatgpt/
158. Kreuz, Robert J., and Roberts, R. M. (1993). The empirical study of figurative language in literature. *Poetics*, 22 (September), 151.
159. Pragglejaz Group. (2007). MIP: A method for identifying metaphorically used words in discourse. *Metaphor Symb.*, 22, 1–39. doi: 10. 1207/s15327868ms2201_1
160. Gutierrez, E. D., Shuotva, E., Marghetis, T., et al. (2016). Literal and metaphorical senses in compositional distributional semantic models. Proceedings of the 54th Annual Meeting of the Association for Computational Linguistics. Berlin, 183–193.
161. Cardillo, E. R., Schmidt, G. L., Kranjec, A., and Chatterjee, A. (2010). Stimulus design is an obstacle course: 560 matched literal and metaphorical sentences for testing neural hypotheses about metaphor. *Behav. Res. Methods*, 42, 651–664. doi: 10.3758/BRM.42.3.651
162. Al-Azary, H., and Buchanan, L. (2017). Novel metaphor comprehension: Semantic neighbourhood density interacts with concreteness. *Memory Cogn.*, 45(2), 296–307. doi: 10.3758/s13421-016-0650-7; Al-Azary, H., McAuley, T., Buchanan, L., and

Katz, A. N. (2019). Semantic processing of metaphor: A case-study of deep dyslexia. *J. Neurolinguist.*, 51, 297–308. doi: 10.1016/j.jneuroling.2019.04.003
163. Kukkonen, K. *The Living Handbook of Narratology*. http://www.lhn.uni-hamburg.de.
164. Speer, N. K., Reynolds, J. R., and Zacks, J. M. (2007). Human brain activity time-locked to narrative event boundaries. *Psychol. Sci.*, 18, 449–455. doi: 10.1111/j.1467-9280.2007.01920.x
165. de Beaugrande, R. De., and Colby, B. N. (1979). Narrative models of action and interaction, *Cogn. Sci.*, 3, 43–66.
167. https://paperswithcode.com/dataset/litbank
168. Todoshchuk, A. (2022). *A Multilevel Approach to Extracting Events from Literary Texts*. Master's thesis, Data Science Master programme, FU Berlin.
166. Adolfo, Bianca Trish, Lao, Jerson, Rivera, Joanna Pauline, Talens, John Zem, and Ong, Ethel Chua Joy. (2017). Generating children's stories from character and event models. In: *International Workshop on Multidisciplinary Trends in Artificial Intelligence.* Springer, 266–280.
169. https://stanfordnlp.github.io/CoreNLP/
170. Sims, M., Park, J. H., and Bamman, D. (2019). Literary event detection. In *Proceedings of the 57th Annual Meeting of the Association for Computational Linguistics*, 3623–3634. doi: 10.18653/v1/P19-1353
171. https://www.nltk.org/
172. Harris, W.F. (1959). *The Basic Patterns of Plot.* Oklahoma: University of Oklahoma Press.
173. Lauer, G., Herrmann, B., Lüdtke, J., and Jacobs, A. M. (2019). Advanced sentiment analysis for understanding affective-aesthetic responses to literary texts: A computational and experimental psychology approach to children's literature. DFG Projekt, SPP2207 'Computational Literary Studies'.
174. https://en.wikipedia.org/wiki/Smoothing_spline
175. Elkins, K., and Chun, J. (2019). Can sentiment analysis reveal structure in a plotless novel. *arXiv preprint arXiv:1910.01441.*
176. Dodds, P. S., Clark, E. M., Desu, S., Frank, M. R., Reagan, A. J., Williams, J. R., et al. (2015). Human language reveals a universal positivity bias. *Proc. Natl. Acad. Sci. U.S.A.*, 112, 2389–2394.
177. https://michaelpaulukonis.github.io/malepropp/ or *https://www.plot-generator.org.uk/*
178. https:// pmbaumgartner.github.io/blogfholy- nlp/.
179. Jacobs, A. M., and Kinder, A. (2022). Computational models of readers' apperceptive mass. *Front. Artif. Intell.*, 5, 718690. doi: 10.3389/frai.2022.718690
180. Jose, P. E., and Brewer, W. F. (1984). Development of story liking: character identification, suspense, and outcome resolution. *Dev. Psychol.*, 20, 911–924. doi: 10.1037/0012-1649.20.5.911
181. Jacobs, A. M. (2019). Sentiment analysis for words and fiction characters from the perspective of computational (neuro-)poetics. *Front. Robot. AI,* 6, 53. doi: 10.3389/frobt.2019.00053
182. e.g., https://www.cbr.com/game-of-thrones-best-favorite-characters-hbo
183. Steen, G. J. (2004). Can discourse properties of metaphor affect metaphor recognition? *J. Pragmat., 36*(7), 1295–1313.; Steen, G. J. (2006). Discourse functions of metaphor: An experiment in affect. In *The Metaphors of Sixty: Papers Presented on the Occasion of the 60th Birthday of Zoltán Kövecses*, eds. R. Benczes & S. Csabi. Budapest: Eötvös Loránd University.

184. Nicklas, P., and Jacobs, A. M. (2017). Rhetorics, neurocognitive poetics and the aesthetics of adaptation. *Poetics Today*, 38, 393–412. doi: 10.1215/03335372-3869311.
185. Hoffstaedter, P. (1987). Poetic text processing and its empirical investigation. *Poetics*, 16, 75–91. doi: 10.1016/0304-422x(87)90037-4; van den Hoven, E., Hartung, F., Burke, M., and Willems, R. (2016). Individual differences in sensitivity to style during literary reading: Insights from eye-tracking. *Collabra: Psychol.*, 2(1), 1–16. doi: 10.1525/collabra.39 ; Kraxenberger, M., and Menninghaus, W. (2016). Emotional effects of poetic phonology, word positioning and dominant stress peaks in poetry reading. *Sci. Stud. Lit.*, 6, 298–313. doi: 10.1075/ssol.6.1.06kra
186. Tsur, R. (2008). Deixis in literature: What isn't cognitive poetics? *Pragmat. Cogn.*, 16(1), 119–150. doi: 10.1075/p&c.16.1.08tsu
187. https://en.wikipedia.org/wiki/Analysis_of_variance
188. Vendler, H. (1997). *The Art of Shakespeare's Sonnets.* Cambridge, MA: Harvard University Press.
189. Jacobs, A. M., Schuster, S., Xue, S., and Lüdtke, J. (2017). *What's in the brain that ink may character ...: A* quantitative narrative analysis of Shakespeare's 154 sonnets for use in neurocognitive poetics. *Sci. Stud. Lit.*, 7(1), 4–51. doi: 10.1075/ssol.7.1.02jac.
190. Steen, G. J. (2004). Can discourse properties of metaphor affect metaphor recognition? *J. Pragmat.*, 36(7), 1295–1313.
191. Jacobs, A. M. (2018). (Neuro-)cognitive poetics and computational stylistics. *Sci. Stud. Lit.*, 8(1), 165–208. doi: 10.1075/ssol.18002.jac
192. https://en.wikipedia.org/wiki/Eigenvalues_and_eigenvectors
193. Kneepkens, L. J., and Zwaan, R. A. (1994). Emotion and cognition in literary understanding. *Poetics*, 23, 125–138. doi: 10.1016/0304-422X(94)00021-W
194. Ponz, A., Montant, M., Liegeois-Chauvel, C., Silva, C., Braun, M., Jacobs, A. M., and Ziegler, J. C. (2014). Emotion processing in words: a test of the neural re-use hypothesis using surface and intracranial EEG. *Soc. Cogn. Affect. Neurosci.*, 9(5), 619–627.
195. Ziegler, J., Montant, M., Briesemeister, B., Brink, T., Wicker, B., Ponz, A., Bonnard, M., Jacobs, A. M., and Braun, M. (2018). Do words stink? Neural re-use as a principle for understanding emotions in reading. *J. Cogn. Neurosci.*, 30(7), 1023–1032. doi: 10.1162/jocn_a_01268
196. Menninghaus, W., Wagner, V., Hanich, J., Wassiliwizky, E., Jacobsen, T., and Koelsch, S. (2017). The distancing-embracing model of the enjoyment of negative emotions in art reception. *Behav. Brain Sci.*, 40, e347. doi: 10.1017/S0140525X17000309
197. Altmann, U., Bohrn, I. C., Lubrich, O., Menninghaus, W., and Jacobs, A. M. (2012). The power of emotional valence – from cognitive to affective processes in reading. *Front. Hum. Neurosci.*, 6, 192. doi: 10.3389/fnhum.2012. 00192

Altmann, U., Bohrn, I. C., Lubrich, O., Menninghaus, W., and Jacobs, A. M. (2014). Fact vs fiction – how paratextual information shapes our reading processes. *Soc. Cogn. Affect. Neurosci.*, 9, 22–29. doi: 10.1093/scan/nss098
198. Hsu, C.-T., Conrad, M., and Jacobs, A. M. (2014). Fiction feelings in Harry Potter: Haemodynamic response in the mid-cingulate cortex correlates with immersive reading experience. *Neuroreport*, 25, 1356–1361. doi: 10 .1097/WNR.0000000000000272
199. Craig, A. D. (2009). How do you feel – now? The anterior insula and human awareness. *Nat. Rev. Neurosci.*, 10, 59–70.
200. Gygax, P., Tapiero, I., and Carruzzo, E. (2007). Emotion inferences during reading comprehension: What evidence can the self-pace reading paradigm provide? *Discourse Process*, 44, 33–50.

201. https://fasttext.cc/docs/en/english-vectors.html
202. Hsu, C.-T., Jacobs, A. M., and Conrad, M. (2015a). Can Harry Potter still put a spell on us in a second language? An fMRI study on reading emotion-laden literature in late bilinguals. *Cortex*, 63, 282–295. doi: 10.1016/j.cortex.2014. 09.002
203. Bestgen, Y. (1994). Can emotional valence in stories be determined from words? *Cogn. Emot.*, 8(1), 21–36. doi: 10.1080/ 02699939408408926; Whissell, C. (1996). Traditional and emotional stylometric analysis of the songs of Beatles Paul McCartney and John Lennon. *Comput. Hum.*, 30, 257–265. doi: 10. 1007/bf00055109
204. Recio, G., Conrad, M., Hansen, L. B., and Jacobs, A. M. (2014). On pleasure and thrill: The interplay between arousal and valence during visual word recognition. *Brain Lang.*, 134, 34–43. doi: 10.1016/j.bandl .2014.03.009.
205. Lehne, M., Engel, P., Rohrmeier, M., Menninghaus, W., Jacobs, A. M., and Koelsch, S. (2015). Reading a suspenseful literary text activates brain areas related to social cognition and predictive inference. *PLoS ONE*, 10(5), e0124550. doi:10.1371/ journal .pone.0124550
206. Zillmann, D. (1980). Anatomy of suspense. In: *The Entertainment Functions of Television*, ed. P.H. Tannenbaum. Hillsdale, NJ: Lawrence Erlbaum Associates, 133–163.
207. Stenneken, P., Bastiaanse, R., Huber, W., and Jacobs, A. M. (2005). Syllable structure and sonority in language inventory and aphasic neologisms. *Brain Lang.*, 95, 280–292.
208. Aryani, A., Conrad, M., Schmidtke, D., and Jacobs, A. (2018). Why 'piss' is ruder than 'pee'? The role of sound in affective meaning making. *PloS ONE*, 13(6), e0198430.
209. Schmidtke, D. S., Conrad, M., and Jacobs, A. M. (2014). Phonological iconicity. *Front. Psychol.*, 5, 80. doi:10.3389/ fpsyg.2014.00080; Aryani, A., Jacobs, A. M., and Conrad, M. (2013). Extracting salient sublexical units from written texts: 'Emophon,' a corpus-based approach to phonological iconicity. *Front. Psychol.*, 4, 654. doi:10.3389/fpsyg.2013.00654; Aryani, A., Kraxenberger, M., Ullrich, S., Jacobs, A. M., and Conrad, M. (2016). Measuring the basic affective tone of poems via phonological saliency and iconicity. *Psychol. Aesth. Creativity Arts*, 10, 191–204. doi:10.1037/aca0000033
210. Aryani, A., Hsu, C.T., and Jacobs, A.M. (2019). Affective iconic words benefit from additional sound-meaning integration in the left amygdala. *Human Brain Mapp.*, 40(18), 5289–5300. doi: 10.1002/hbm.24772
211. Briesemeister, B. B., Kuchinke, L., and Jacobs, A. M. (2011a). Discrete emotion norms for nouns – Berlin affective word list (DENN-BAWL). *Behav. Res. Methods*, 43, 441–448. doi: 10.3758/s13428-011-0059-y
212. Menninghaus, W., Bohrn, I. C., Altmann, U., Lubrich, O., and Jacobs, A. M. (2014). Sounds funny? Humor effects of phonological and prosodic figures of speech. *Psychol. Aesthet. Creat. Arts*, 8, 71–76. doi: 10.1037/a0035309
213. Cysarz, D., Von Bonin, D., Lackner, H., Heusser, P., Moser, M., and Bettermann, H. (2004). Oscillations of heart rate and respiration synchronize during poetry recitation. *Am. J. Physiol. Heart Circ. Physiol.*, 287, H579–H587. doi: 10.1152/ajpheart. 01131.2003
214. Warriner, A. B., Kuperman, V., and Brysbaert, M. (2013). Norms of valence, arousal, and dominance for 13,915 English lemmas. *Behav. Res. Methods*, 45, 1191–1207. doi: 10.3758/s13428-012-0314-x
215. Jacobs, A. M. (2017). Quantifying the beauty of words: a neurocognitive poetics perspective. *Front. Hum. Neurosci.*, 11, 622. doi: 10.3389/fnhum.2017.00622

216. https://en.wikipedia.org/wiki/Hierarchical_clustering
217. Lüdtke, J., Meyer-Sickendiek, B., and Jacobs, A. M. (2014). Immersing in the stillness of an early morning: testing the mood empathy hypothesis in poems. *Psychol. Aesth., Creativity Arts*, 8, 363–377. doi: 10.1037/a0036826; Jacobs, A. M., Lüdtke, J., Aryani, A., Meyer-Sickendiek, B., and Conrad, M. (2016b). Mood-empathic and aesthetic responses in poetry reception: A model-guided, multilevel, multimethod approach. *Sci. Stud. Lit.*, 6, 87–130. doi: 10.1075/ssol.6.1.06jac
218. https://www.ims.uni-stuttgart.de/forschung/ressourcen/korpora/sdewac/
219. Kuhlmann, M., Hofmann, M. J., Briesemeister, B. B., and Jacobs, A. M. (2016). Mixing positive and negative valence: Affective-semantic integration of bivalent words. *Sci. Rep.*, 6(30718), 1–7. doi: 10.1038/srep30718
220. Hagoort, P., 2005. On Broca, brain, and binding: A new framework. *Trends Cogn. Sci.*, 9.
221. Forgács, B., Bohrn, I. C., Baudewig, J., Hofmann, M. J., Pléh, C., and Jacobs, A. M. (2012). Neural correlates of combinatorial semantic processing of literal and figurative noun-noun compound words. *Neuroimage*, 63, 1432–1442. doi: 10. 1016/j. neuroimage.2012.07.029
222. Bohrn, I. C., Altmann, U., and Jacobs, A. M. (2012). Looking at the brains behind figurative language—A quantitative meta-analysis of neuroimaging studies on metaphor, idiom and irony processing. *Neuropsychologia*, 50, 2669–2683. doi: 10.1016/j. neuropsychologia.2012.07.021; Gibbs, R. (Ed.). (2008). *The Cambridge Handbook of Metaphor and Thought*. New York, NY: Cambridge University Press; Lakoff, G. (2008). The neural theory of metaphor. In *Cambridge Handbook of Metaphor and Thought*, ed. R. Gibbs. New York, NY: Cambridge University Press, 17–38.
223. Katz, A., Paivio, A., Marschark, M., and Clark, J. (1988). Norms for 204 literary and 260 non-literary metaphors on psychological dimensions. *Metaphor Symb. Activ.*, 3(4), 191–214.
224. Jacobs, A. M., and Kinder, A. (2017). The brain is the prisoner of thought: A machine-learning assisted quantitative narrative analysis of literary metaphors for use in neurocognitive poetics. *Metaphor Symb.*, 32(3), 139–160. doi: 10.1080/10926488.2017.1338015
225. Bestgen, Y., and Vincze, N. (2012). Checking and bootstrapping lexical norms by means of word similarity indexes. *Behav. Res. Methods*, 44(4), 998–1006. doi:10.3758/s13428-012-0195-z
226. Cacciari, C. (2014). Processing multiword idiomatic strings: many words in one? *The Mental Lexicon*, 9, 267–293.
227. Citron, F. M. M., Cacciari, C., Kucharski, M., Beck, L., Conrad, M., and Jacobs, A. M. (2016). When emotions are expressed figuratively: Psycholinguistic and affective norms of 619 idioms for German (PANIG). *Behav. Res. Methods*, 48, 91–111. doi: 10.3758/s13428-015-0581-4
228. Hernadi, P., and Steen, F. (1999). The tropical landscapes of proverbia: A crossdisciplinary travelogue. *Style*, 33(1), 1–20.
229. Fechner, G. T. (1876). *Vorschule der Ästhetik. [Preschool of aesthetics]*. Hildesheim: Olms.
230. Gibbs, R. W., and Beitel, D. (1995). What proverb understanding reveals about how people think. *Psychol. Bull.*, 118, 133–154.
231. Mieder, W. (2004). *Proverbs: A Handbook*. Westport, CT: Greenwood Press; Hernadi, P., and Steen, F. (1999). The tropical landscapes of proverbia: A crossdisciplinary travelogue. *Style*, 33(1), 1–20; Jacobs, A. M. (2015). The scientific study of

literary experience: Sampling the state of the art. *Sci. Stud. Lit.*, 5(2), 139–170. doi: 10.1075/ssol.5.2.01jac ; Nicklas, P., and Jacobs, A. M. (2017). Rhetorics, neurocognitive poetics and the aesthetics of adaptation. *Poet. Today*, 38, 393–412. doi: 10.1215/03335372-3869311

232. Reber, R., Winkielman, P., and Schwarz, N. (1998). Effects of perceptual fluency on affective judgments. *Psychol. Sci.*, 9, 45–48; Kuchinke, L., Trapp, S., Jacobs, A. M., and Leder, H. (2009). Pupillary responses in art appreciation: effects of aesthetic emotions. *Psychol. Aesth. Creat. Arts*, 3, 156–163.
233. Keidel, J. L., Davis, P. M., Gonzalez-Diaz, V., Martin, C. D., and Thierry, G. (2013). How Shakespeare tempests the brain: Neuroimaging insights. *Cortex,* 49, 913–919. doi: 10.1016/j.cortex.2012.03.011
234. https://ereadcost.eu/
235. Gambino, R., Pulvirenti, G., Sylvester, T., Jacobs, A. M., and Lüdtke, J. (2020). The foregrounding assessment matrix: An interface for qualitative-quantitative interdisciplinary research. *Enthymema*, 26, 254–277. doi: 10.13130/2037-2426/14387; Magyari, L., Mangen, A., Kuzmičová, A., Jacobs, A., and Lüdtke, J. (2020). Eye movements and mental imagery during reading of literary texts with different narrative styles. *J. Eye Move. Res.*, 13(3), 3; Papp-Zipernovszky, O., Mangen, A., Jacobs, A.M., and Lüdtke, J. (2021). Shakespeare sonnets reading: An empirical study of emotional responses. *Lang. Lit.,* 0(0), 1–29. doi: 10.1177/09639470211054647; Xue, S., Lüdtke, J., Sylvester, T., and Jacobs, A. M. (2019). Reading Shakespeare sonnets: Combining quantitative narrative analysis and predictive modelling: An eye tracking study. *J. Eye Move. Res.*, 12(5). doi: 10.16910/jemr.12.5.2; Xue, S., Jacobs, A. M., and Lüdtke, J. (2020). What is the difference? Rereading Shakespeare's sonnets: An eye tracking study. *Front. Psychol.*, 11, 421. doi: 10.3389/ fpsyg.2020.00421
236. Jacobs, A. M., Schuster, S., Xue, S. and Lüdtke, J. (2017). Whats in the brain that ink may character …: A quantitative narrative analysis of Shakespeares 154 sonnets for use in neurocognitive poetics. *Sci. Stud. Lit.*, 7(1), 4–51. doi: 10.1075/ssol.7.1.02jac.
237. Meireles, R. C. (2005). The hermeneutics of symbolical imagery in Shakespeare's sonnets. Unpublished Dissertation, University. Porto Alegre, Bresil.
238. Gambino, R., Pulvirenti, G., Sylvester, T., Jacobs, A.M., and Lüdtke, J. (2020). The foregrounding assessment matrix: An interface for qualitative-quantitative interdisciplinary research. *Enthymema*, 26, 254–277. doi: 10.13130/2037-2426/14387
239. Jacobs, A. M. (2021). The neurocognitive poetics model of literary reading 10 years after. In: *Neuroaesthetics in Focus*, eds. A. Chatterjee & E. Cardillo. Oxford: Oxford University Press.
240. Cichy, R. M., Roig, G., and Oliva, A. (2019). The Algonauts project. *Nat. Mach. Intell.,* 1, 613–613; Cichy, R. M. et al. (2021). The Algonauts Project 2021 challenge: How the human brain makes sense of a world in motion. Preprint at https://doi.org/10.48550/arXiv.2104.13714; http://algonauts.csail.mit.edu/

INDEX

www.ingramcontent.com/pod-product-compliance
Ingram Content Group UK Ltd.
Pitfield, Milton Keynes, MK11 3LW, UK
UKHW021835100926
8556IPUK00004B/350

9 781839 987700